DISCARDED

SCIENCE AND SECRETS OF ENDING VIOLENT CRIME

Other Books by Irvin Waller

Less Law, More Order: The Truth about Reducing Crime

Rights for Victims of Crime: Rebalancing Justice

Smarter Crime Control: A Guide to a Safer Future for Citizens Communities, and Politicians

SCIENCE AND SECRETS OF ENDING VIOLENT CRIME

Irvin Waller

ROWMAN & LITTLEFIELD
Lanham • Boulder • New York • London

Published by Rowman & Littlefield
A wholly owned subsidary of The Rowman & Littlefield Publishing Group, Inc.
4501 Forbes Boulevard, Suite 200, Lanham, Maryland 20706
www.rowman.com

6 Tinworth Street, London SE11 5AL, United Kingdom

British Library Cataloguing in Publication Information Available

Library of Congress Cataloging-in-Publication Data
Names: Waller, Irvin, author.
Title: Science and secrets of ending violent crime / Irvin Waller.
Description: Lanham : Rowman & Littlefield, [2019] | Includes bibliographical
    references and index.
Identifiers: LCCN 2018048720 (print) | LCCN 2018053989 (ebook) | ISBN
    9781538118078 (Electronic) | ISBN 9781538118061 (cloth : alk. paper)
Subjects: LCSH: Crime prevention. | Crime—Government policy.
Classification: LCC HV7431 (ebook) | LCC HV7431 .W3264 2019 (print) | DDC
    364.4—dc23
LC record available at https://lccn.loc.gov/2018048720

Printed in the United States of America

For the next generations, who should be outraged by our failure to end the ravages of violent crime. This is your world. You must shape it or someone else will.

CONTENTS

PART IV   SECRETS TO GET BUY-IN

ACKNOWLEDGMENTS

This book is about sparing the lives of women, men, and children from violence and confronting the reality that more young people's lives are lost to violence because more young men's lives are lost behind bars, and not the reverse. I am dedicating the book to all those who work daily and effectively to stop such violence. I am particularly dedicating the book to those in the generations that follow mine, those who are rekindling the torch to light a smarter way forward and persuading politicians to reinvest smartly in the number one right of their constituents: to live in communities that are safe from violence.

This book builds on my fifty years of working around the world to prevent violent crime and implement rights for victims of crime, work that has taken me to over fifty countries, to advise a political leader, to present a keynote speech, to work as part of a special task force, or for a media interview and, sometimes, to do all or several of these things. From Buenos Aires to Beijing, Cape Town to London, or Chicago to Ottawa and many places in between, it has been an exciting ride.

Over those many years and miles, I have had the privilege of working with myriads of wonderful people who share my vision. They are colleagues in governments, academics, journalists, or advocates in nongovernmental organizations. For each encounter and relationship, I am humbly grateful. Not only did these individuals welcome me to their communities, but they also treated me as a trusted fellow traveler and became my friends. From them, I learned about compelling innovations and how the world could do better. Their ideas and passion infuse this book. I only wish I could mention each one by name. Their invitations around the globe truly enriched my life, and I hope I enriched theirs as well as their country or city.

In addition to wanting to thank those many colleagues and friends whose work and passion parallel mine, I also must acknowledge the titans who pioneered violence prevention science, the term I have adopted from John Carnochan, who along with Karyn McCluskey in Glasgow inspired the world with sustained use of this new science. In my previous books—*Less Law, More Order*; *Rights for Victims of Crime*; and *Smarter Crime Control*—I recognized those scientific titans for their remarkable contributions. Their rigorous studies and publication in leading journals and erudite books have made violence prevention science solid and provided so many of the endnotes to support the effectiveness of crime prevention solutions.

The tireless efforts of those working in organizations that make that science freely available also must be acknowledged. Special kudos go to the National Institute of Justice of the US Department of Justice, the Washington State Institute for Public Policy, the England and Wales College of Policing, the World Health Organization, and Public Safety Canada's new portal.

Unfortunately, science, and making it accessible, is not enough. The challenge at hand is how to tackle putting effective solutions into practice to end violent crime. To that end, I point to the high-level agreements by world governments at the UN General Assembly, particularly the remarkable consensus about the need for prevention of victimization and justice for victims of crime outlined in the 1985 Victim Magna Carta. Thirty years later, governments also agreed to achieve Sustainable Development Goals by 2030; a number of the SDGs directly call for reduction in violent crime. These decisions at the General Assembly are supported by important governmental resolutions at the UN Economic and Social Council, UN Office on Drugs and Crime, the World Health Assembly, and UN-Habitat. Most of the titans behind these resolutions have the satisfaction of government approval, not the publication of their name.

Yet even governmental consensus on the essentials for success has not been enough to get effective solutions implemented. What do we need to do to tip the scales in favor of victims, to end victimization and at least balance punishment with prevention? My effort with this book is to present a compelling argument for *investing in people* to make people safer! I am not alone in thinking this is the silver bullet to end violent crime. The March for Our Lives on March 24, 2018, is just one event confirming that many,

many women and men—voters—believe the same, even if politicians and law enforcement officials do not. Yet with this vocal groundswell, we are at a watershed moment. As Victor Hugo said, "Greater than the tread of armies is an idea whose time has come." The challenge now is to lead more and more decision-making leaders to the light and action.

Noting that, I want to extend a hearty thank-you to those few but enlightened power brokers who have started to use phrases such as "smart on crime," phrases I discuss at length in *Less Law, More Order* and use in the title of *Smarter Crime Control*. These forward-thinking individuals, who can lead the way for their colleagues, are exasperated by the failure of the war on drugs and mass incarceration. They admit they cannot arrest their way out of crime. Slowly, they are coming to see the value in balancing effective social prevention with smart enforcement. I now encourage these early adopters of smart violence prevention to be bold and keep marching forward.

Now, I must name names. My personal mission to make a contribution has benefited from a number of intimate collaborators, always supportive, always believing that we can and will make the difference. In alphabetical order by last name, they are Jack Calhoun in Washington, DC; Arturo Cervantes Trejo in Mexico City; Elizabeth Johnston in Paris; Lucie Léonard in Ottawa; Erich Marks in Heidelberg; Felix Munger in Waterloo, Canada; Claudio Stampalija in Buenos Aires; Jan van Dijk in Amsterdam; Claude Vezina in Montreal; Elmar Weitekamp in Tubingen; Nigel Whiskin in Bath, England; Marlene Young in Newberg, Oregon; and Sheri Young in Wilsonville, Oregon. Last, but very much not least, I owe a very special thank-you to Veronica Martinez and Oscar Aguilar in Mexico City for including me on their team.

Then, there is the gang of brilliant minds and careful researchers that make up the small group of graduate students who made my life at the University of Ottawa so rewarding. Jeff Bradley, Samantha Cima, Paula Hirschmann, and Audrey Monette, in particular, have contributed directly and indirectly to this book. Many of the ideas and sources were developed together, particularly in the context of efforts to get Canadian municipalities to harness evidence to prevent crime. This book also has benefited immeasurably from the editorial skills and support of Ruthie Matinko-Wald. The figures and tables are the labor of Machele Brass.

Truly, I hope the fruits of this clarion call to end violent crime through the use of science, essentials, and secrets will justify the sacrifices of those around me, particularly those of my patient and visionary wife and partner, Susan Tanner.

PREFACE

Science of violence prevention is solid. If governments do not apply it, they should be challenged. It's public money! It's public safety! It's science!

—John Carnochan, in a tweet in January 2018

In 2017 alone, 17,000 people lost their lives to homicide in the United States, and 29,000 people were killed in Mexico. More than 1,270,000 women were raped in the United States, as were likely at least a proportionately similar number of women in Mexico (see chapter 1, figure 1.1). Homicide and rape rates may be lower for countries such as England and Wales or Canada, but the number of violent crimes happening throughout the world—in rich as well as not rich countries—is still much too high.

These are just a sampling of the statistics that represent the tragedies occurring unnecessarily in countries across the globe. Behind the numbers are men and women who have lost their lives, families who have been devastated by loss and pain, individuals whose quality of life has been destroyed, and victimized children who suffer and then go through consequential chronic disease and emotional anguish. Violent crimes also affect the countries where the crimes occur, reducing the gross domestic product and threatening the rule of law in neighborhoods and regions.

Are we shocked by the statistics, by the ruin violent crime causes in homes and communities throughout the world? We should be. We also should be shocked that the policies and practices of criminal justice systems lag behind so many other domains. For example, medical advances are enabling us to live longer with a greater quality of life. Technological innovations never stop, offering us more and more gadgets with which to play and work. We are even conquering outer space and finding cures for cancer.

Yet the number of violent crimes in the world continue to increase and, in some places, skyrocket. Why isn't the current system of criminal justice making a dent in the slaughter and senseless destruction of human life taking place? The bottom line is that, in the thriving domains, decision makers have applied science in a way that criminal justice policy makers have not. To make matters worse, this means that everyday people continue to pay ever increasing taxes for a reactive criminal justice system that is neither the most effective nor cost-effective solution for dealing with violent crime.

That our criminal justice system is so inefficient and ineffective is sad but true, and especially sad because we know what will stop violence! In the past fifty years, criminology titans have been hard at work measuring the causes and risk factors for violent crime. We, thus, have solid empirical evidence about how adverse experiences in childhood correlate to criminal activity, and, through scientific research, we know what programs and practices can effectively mitigate those adverse experiences and make violent crime less likely. This knowledge, based on hundreds of experiments, is readily available in many scientific publications and on the websites of various prestigious agencies. For instance, there are now portals on the science of violence prevention maintained by the National Institute of Justice of the US Department of Justice; the nonpartisan research group of the Legislature of Washington State, known as the Washington State Institute for Public Policy; the College for Policing in England and Wales; and the violence prevention team of the World Health Organization.

Despite the free and ready availability of the research-based information about what will reduce violence, not many legislators with responsibility for public safety nor executives in the standard criminal justice system seem to know the many cures for violence. Even fewer have applied the science or adopted effective solutions for violence prevention. Granted, a few cities around the globe have "seen the light." Glasgow, Scotland, is one, thanks to the leadership of John Carnochan.

Carnochan, now retired, served as a senior police officer in that beautiful city. During his tenure, John collaborated with Karyn McCluskey, an epidemiologist, to reduce Glasgow's violent crime rates. Their plan was not just to make policing smarter but also to mobilize social services, schools, hospitals, and more in an effort to tackle the risk factors and causes of violence. They based their approach on an analysis of data about the why and where of violence as well as on the assessment of the outcomes of their programs and policies. It did not pit law enforcement against prevention but had them work smartly as partners. The result? A significant reduction in violent crimes. They also resolved to put in place a permanent violence reduction unit to sustain the trend, something not known in Canada, England and Wales, Mexico, or the United States. The inspired work of John and Karyn proved that applying carefully the science of violence prevention actually delivers fast results. But cities like Glasgow are the exception to the rule, and too many tragedies from violent crime are still taking place in every corner of the world.

In 2014, by writing *Smarter Crime Control*, I made an attempt to bridge the gap between the new science of violence prevention and decision makers who have the ability to influence policies and programs related to crime. That book spells out the scientific and affordable solutions that enhance public safety and the precise actions legislators need to take. In *Smarter Crime Control*, I also make the case that, if legislators in the US acted on the necessary reforms and invested in violence prevention programs the equivalent of a modest 10 percent of what they spend on law enforcement, courts, and corrections, they would spare innumerable victims a whopping $300 billion every year in loss of quality of life and save taxpayers' money.

But even just knowing what works and investing in the right programs and policies is not enough. Governments must create an infrastructure, like Glasgow did, at the city level to sustain their violence prevention programs and funding. Governments, when making resolutions through the UN, actually understand the importance of this focus because they have resolved that implementing effective violence prevention solutions requires particular "essentials," four of the most important being (1) a permanent authority, (2) adequate and sustained funding, (3) being informed by violence prevention science, and (4) being managed by skilled and capable people. Indeed, the few cities that have implemented these essentials of effective crime prevention have achieved positive results, whereas governments following only some of the essentials have had some short-term but unsustained success.

With the big picture of *sustainable* implementation of effective violence prevention in mind, I decided to write this current book for decision makers and the public. My goal with the book is to showcase the effective solutions, the essentials for implementation, and some of the secrets of getting buy-in. In it, I begin by exploring the outrageous extent and impact of violent crime, with the hope that the number of unnecessary painful tragedies would gain the interest of, and maybe shock, many more policy makers into action. Then, I highlight examples of successful violence prevention programs, with the dream that becoming aware of the effectiveness of these programs along with their cost benefits will ultimately encourage policy makers to take seriously the essential elements for operationalizing the programs and ensuring long-term support.

But the book is about much more. It shows that investing in effective violence prevention is much more affordable than policy makers understand. It is also much more achievable because the majority of voters actually want these solutions. Most voters want taxes spent better, particularly if the spending creates new jobs, and smart spending on violence prevention gives many such dividends. Granted, some governments are doing right by violence prevention some of the time, and some cities are achieving amazing success and even sustaining that success. The key is to get a majority of governments—national, regional, and local—engaged and proactive about violence prevention on a long-term basis.

The bottom line is that we can no longer accept the status quo of the criminal justice system. We need effective and cost-effective solutions to stop violent crime, to save the lives of our children, mothers and fathers, relatives and friends, neighbors, and brothers and sisters throughout the world. The answer lies with the solid science of violence prevention. I hope you will join me in spreading the word.

In addition, citizens, I challenge you to stand up and hold your governmental officials responsible for preventing violence rather than just reacting to it. If they don't, vote! And, policy makers, pay attention to the science and implement policies and programs that actually work in your community and region to end violence once and for all!

INTRODUCTION

From Effective Solutions to Ending Violent Crime

Denial is not a river in Egypt.

—Anonymous

Every day we read about another violent crime in the news. So many tragedies. So many lost or ruined lives. Our current system of criminal justice, largely invented in the nineteenth century, is not stopping the tragedies. Yet we have a solid violence prevention science whose application would end the violence. Governments have even reached consensus on how to use that science across cities and countries. But we continue to deny the problem, the solutions, the investments to the detriment of the safety and well-being of people everywhere. It is time for action.

In the United States, Edna Chavez experienced tragedy, and she acted. The seventeen-year-old from South Los Angeles was a youth leader and survivor of violence. At the March for Our Lives in Washington, DC, in 2018, Edna shared her story and her demands:

I have lost many loved ones to gun violence. . . . I learned to duck from bullets before I learned how to read. My brother, he was in high school when he passed away. It was a day like any other day. Sunset going down on South Central. You hear pops thinking they are fireworks. They weren't pops. You see the melanin on your brother's skin turn grey. Ricardo was his name. I lost more than my brother that day. I lost my hero. I also lost my mother, my sister, and myself to that trauma and that anxiety. If the bullet did not kill me, that anxiety and that trauma will. . . .

It is normal to see flowers honoring the lives of black and brown youth that have lost their lives to a bullet. How can we cope with it when our school district has its own police department? Instead of making black and brown students feel safe, they continue to profile and criminalize us. Instead, we should have a department specializing in restorative justice. We need to tackle the root causes of the issues we face and come to an understanding of how to resolve them. . . .

Policymakers, listen up! . . . [F]und mentorship programs, mental health resources, paid internship and job opportunities. . . . We need to focus on changing the conditions that foster violence and trauma![1]

In England and Wales, a young Temi Mwale also experienced tragedy, waking up one morning to her BlackBerry buzzing with the news of the senseless shooting and killing of her friend Marvin Henry. Rather than being paralyzed by pain, Temi decided to act and, starting at the age of sixteen, has made social change her life's work. Her youth-led social enterprise, 4Front Project (http://4frontproject.org/), strives to reduce youth violence and the systemic conditions that cause it by empowering young people and communities to improve their lives. In her TEDx talk, Temi ponders the impact of violence and potential remedies:

People do die every day, but people aren't killed every day. . . . Every killing is a tragedy, and what it does is it leaves a hole in the lives of that young person's community—their friends and their family. . . . Nothing could have prepared me for the morning I woke up and picked up the paper and my friend's face was on the front cover. Because the pain and grief that I felt can't be translated through the media.

We really have to ask ourselves what happens in the first thirteen years of a young person's life to make them feel like they have to arm themselves every day before they leave the house. . . . What if we are able to design long-term, holistic interventions that work with young people to rebuild their sense of security, of protection, and to increase their trust?[2]

An ocean away from Temi, Audette Shephard experienced tragedy in Toronto, and she acted as well. Audette lost her only child, Justin Garth Shephard, when he was shot dead at the age of nineteen. Justin had been one of Canada's most promising young basketball players, and he dreamed of joining his half brother in the NBA. Audette shared her pain when she stated, "He was a part of me—a part of me that I cherish so much. And now that he died there's a big part of me that's dead. . . . I don't want to see another mother go through something like this."[3]

Out of much sorrow came much resolve as Audette began working to help youth and to find solutions to end youth violence. She has become a well-known antigun activist and cofounded UMOVE (United Mothers Opposing Violence Everywhere), an advocacy group comprised of mothers who have lost children to senseless acts of violence. UMOVE members promote alternatives to violence, teach problem-solving skills, and support mothers who have lost their children to street bloodshed. They also offer a motivational example of a grassroots community effort that engages local politicians through their citywide UMOVE Day of Nonviolence.[4] Check out their Facebook page at https://www.facebook.com/UMOVEto/.

In Mexico, Javier Sicilia also experienced tragedy and acted. Javier's world was shattered by the killing of his son, Juan Francisco, a university student. Juan Francisco, twenty-four years of age, was an innocent in a drug-trafficking attack in the city of Cuernavaca. He was found bound and shot, along with six friends.

Devastated by his son's murder, poet Javier Sicilia said goodbye to poetry forever, reading in public his last poem, dedicated to his murdered son:

> The world is no longer worthy of words
> They suffocated them within
> As they suffocated you
> As they tore apart your lungs
> And the pain does not leave me
> Only a world remains
> By the silence of the righteous
> Only by your silence and my silence, Juanelo
> The world is no longer worthy of words
> This is my last poem
> I cannot write more poetry
> Poetry no longer exists in me.[5]

Juan Francisco's senseless death captivated his nation, a country reeling from drug cartel violence that left nearly 40,000 people dead in just four years.[6] Motivated to do something proactive in response to his son's slaying, Javier made the decision to renounce poetry in order to dedicate himself to giving voice to the voiceless so that the politics governing the fight might shift. Since then, he has led marches with the slogan, *Estamos Hasta la Madre!* (We've had enough!). He and his supporters have called for respect for the Mexican constitution, an end to the drug war, the withdrawal of military forces from the streets, the legalization of drugs, and the removal of the Mexican president. More than 200,000 people took part in one of the marches in Mexico City. Similar marches were held in thirty-one other Mexican cities and seventeen cities throughout the world as part of the Estamos Hasta la Madre movement.

In response to the attention and activism his son's death triggered, Javier Sicilia poignantly noted, "What my son did was give a name and face to the 40,000 dead. My pain gave a face to the pain of other families. I think a country is like a house, and the destruction of someone is the destruction of our families."[7]

TOO MANY TRAGEDIES

These vignettes underline the tragedy of violent crime. Just as importantly, they showcase how a horrific event can motivate survivors to act, to make a difference in their communities. Most notably, the priority of Edna Chavez, Temi Mwale, Audette Shepherd, and Javier Sicilia was neither punishment nor revenge. Instead, each survivor sought ways to prevent violence from happening again. The solutions they called for were local and low cost. More importantly, as this book showcases, the solutions they called for were likely to be extremely effective, according to our accumulated and solid violence prevention science.

This book is about sharing information about violence prevention science, which gives us effective solutions that could end much of violent crime. It is a science turning tragedies into useful statistics. By understanding the statistics, we can better understand the big picture and be more successful in countering crime in the first place.

Before digging into specifics, let's quickly review the numbers related to the countries of our vignette survivors (also, see figure 1.1 in chapter 1). In the United States, to begin with, the tragedy of Edna's brother is being lived at outrageous rates. US families are losing a loved one to homicide at a rate of 5 per 100,000 citizens in a year.[8] That translates to 17,000 families in 2017. Homicide is the country's third major cause of loss of life for young persons between the ages of fifteen and twenty-four and the leading cause for African Americans in that age range. The rates per capita for African American males are 48 per 100,000, a rate four times what the World Health Organization (WHO) labels an "epidemic" and twenty-four times that of White males in the United States.

Regarding disparity, Edna Chavez is spot on, but not just about the use of firearms in the United States, where 82 percent of all firearm homicides in the world occur.[9] Of the tragic number of Black men in America who are murdered, 86 percent meet their death by a firearm.[10] Furthermore, Wisconsin, the US state with the highest disparity between Black and White firearm homicide rates, has the second-highest gap of any state between Black and White unemployment rates.[11] As we will see in chapter 3, incarceration rates tend to follow rates of violent crime, so, not surprisingly, Wisconsin also has the second-highest gap with much higher rates of incarceration for Blacks than Whites.[12]

The tragedy of Temi Mwale's friend Marvin is a rarer event in England and Wales than in the United States. Also, England and Wales do not capture race in their national statistics. Nonetheless, an analysis of murders in London from May 2017 to May 2018 shows a gradual rise in the number of young men being killed with knives and guns.[13] Many of these men are Black. Overall, the rate at which families in England and Wales will lose a loved one to homicide is now slightly higher than 1 per 100,000 citizens. This translates into 700 homicides in a year. The City of London has a lower homicide rate at 1.6 per 100,000 than New York City at 3.4 and, indeed, every major US city.[14]

The tragedy of Audette's son is also a rarer event in Canada than in the United States. There are some 650 murders in Canada each year, and Canada has a population of 36 million. In comparison, there are some 650 murders each year in the US city of Chicago, where 2.7 million people reside. Also, although Canada does not break down its homicide statistics by race, one in four of all Canadian murder victims is an indigenous person, a rate seven times that for nonindigenous people. Overall, the rate at which families generally will lose a loved one to homicide in Canada is now 1.8 per 100,000 citizens.[15] The proportion of murder with a firearm is close to 33 percent.[16] It is also important to note that almost 50 percent of the guns used in these violent crimes originate in the United States.[17]

Finally, what's the statistics story of homicide in Mexico, where Javier's son, Juan Francisco, lost his life? Unfortunately, Mexico's murder rates are even worse than the sad US statistics. Mexico is the largest Spanish-speaking country in the Latin American and Caribbean region. Whereas Latin America comprises 9 percent of the world's population, it suffers 33 percent of the world's homicides. In Mexico itself, murder rates doubled between 2007 and 2011, when Juan Francisco was killed. But the tragedies have gotten even worse. In 2017 alone, close to 30,000 people were killed in the country, more than half of whom were murdered with a gun, and more than 70 percent of those guns originated in the United States.[18] Overall, the rate at which families will lose a loved one to homicide in Mexico is now 21 per 100,000 citizens, about average for Latin America and proportionate to a population the same as Chicago.[19]

But homicide is not the only violent crime. In this book, I also will address intimate partner and sexual violence, which is too often overlooked in policies to end violent crime. The tragedies caused by intimate partner and sexual violence may be different; the physical harm may not be so final as in homicide, but the pain and sense of loss that comes with such violence are devastating. In addition to the immediate suffering, the survivors of intimate partner and sexual violence often end up debilitated with headaches, chronic pain, and more. Many of the symptoms have long-term consequences and manifest as the likes of asthma, irritable bowel syndrome, and diabetes.[20]

Regarding statistics related to intimate partner and sexual violence, the US Centers for Disease Control and Prevention (CDC) has pioneered the gold standard for measuring the prevalence of these violent crimes with its National Survey on Intimate Partner and Sexual Violence. Because of the CDC, we know that in America today, one in three women and one in four men will experience physical injury in intimate partnerships.[21] Specifically, one in five women will be a victim of rape, 80 percent of them before twenty-five years of age. The total for rape translates into a staggering 1.3 million US women each year.[22]

Unfortunately, most of these rapes are not reported or recorded by the police. For instance, the FBI reports only 130,000.[23] Note that the CDC study does not include whether women who were raped reported it to police nor whether the police recorded the crime even if it were reported. However, the comparison between the number recorded by the FBI and that of the CDC shows that 90 percent are either not reporting or the police are not recording the complaint. This staggering reality is consistent with other major surveys done in the United States before the CDC survey, which confirmed that 82 percent of rape victims are not reporting.[24] This nonreporting limits the usefulness of FBI numbers, and so I will use the CDC survey data in this book.

Sadly, whereas statistics and information about effective crime prevention programs are freely available, they are too often ignored by politicians and other national decision makers across the world. For too many decades, those in power have been all too ready to pay for more and more police, courts, and incarceration in reaction to violence. They have not been proactive about investing upstream in what might actually prevent violent tragedies. Thus, this book also is not only about the numbers but, more importantly, about getting decision makers to stop violent crime. It's about transforming our world to get results.

THE STANDARD CRIMINAL JUSTICE SYSTEM

Across the world, most criminal justice systems cope with violent crimes by "picking up the pieces." This coping strategy, which I call the standard "criminal justice system" (CJS), does little to end the violence. The standard CJS usually looks like this:

- Police respond to 911 calls or their equivalent.
- If relevant, police then attempt to identify and arrest a suspected perpetrator.
- If they catch a suspect, that person is processed through a system of criminal courts by a government-sponsored lawyer, called a prosecutor.
- The prosecutor attempts to convince a judge and maybe a jury "beyond a reasonable doubt" that the suspect committed the crime.
- The suspect is defended by a defense lawyer.
- If the accused is convicted, a judge sentences the offender to a term of incarceration for more serious crimes or to some other penalty for lesser crimes, of which a fine is the most likely.
- If the crime is violent, the likelihood of the suspect being incarcerated is high, both before the trial and then to serve the sentence.

I will use the word *incarceration* to refer to jails, prisons, penitentiaries, and correctional facilities because countries use different words to refer to the same thing. In short, "incarceration" refers to a person being put behind bars by a government on suspicion or after being found guilty of a behavior defined as a crime.

In the four countries identified in our original vignettes, the CJS varies in terms of size and cost. In the United States, for example, taxpayers footed a CJS bill of $284 billion in 2015, the most recent year for which data was available. Of this, $135 billion went to policing, $87 billion to corrections, and $61 billion to courts.[25] This represents about 2.4 million jobs in the CJS and is about 1.5 percent of the $18.5 trillion of the US GDP.[26] The size of and expenditures for policing, incarceration, and courts have grown rapidly in the past forty years because the federal government has encouraged states and local governments to grow their capacity to incarcerate by building more prisons and hiring more police.[27]

The taxpayers in Canada, England and Wales, and Mexico still have significant bills to pay, as can be seen in figure 1.1. Relative to GDP, the numbers are 1.5 percent for the United States, 1.25 percent for Mexico and England and Wales, and 1 percent for Canada. The US percentage of its huge GDP is higher than any other country's.[28]

The big question is, are these expenditures the best way to end violent crime? Solid prevention science says no. We would be much better off spending those taxes on preventing the violent crimes in the first place—investing in people! We need to motivate and show politicians that the "art of the possible" holds the key to getting results that can heal our world.

DOES VIOLENCE REALLY REQUIRE MORE AND MORE POLICE?

If policing were the solution to crime, then more police should be associated with less crime. But the opposite is true. In 1991, there were slightly fewer police officers per capita in the United States than in 2017.[29] Yet crime rates have declined without any major change in police numbers.

Take Chicago, for instance, a city with more than 13,000 members in the police force, and growing.[30] In 1990, Chicago experienced 850 murders, whereas in 2017 there were 685 murders.[31] In comparison, the Canadian city of Toronto, which has a marginally larger population than Chicago, has relatively low homicide rates that have changed very little over the past few decades: there were 59 homicides in 1991 and 61 in 2017.[32] Yet Toronto has only 5,200 police officers.[33] Clearly, the size of the police force does not correlate with violent crime rates in this important instance. Hiring more police is not a silver bullet!

Unfortunately, media headlines reinforce the view that arrest and incarceration are the best solution to crime. They justify spending on policing and jails as the means to holding offenders accountable. In short, they proclaim, "If you do the crime, you must do the time!" But wild increases in the use of incarceration in the United States since 1970 have increased punishment without proving their overall effectiveness in ending violent crime.

Granted, policing is very important to a civil society. Every country needs police to respond to 911 calls and handle the many crises arising every day in a community. But the work of police officers is somewhat like firefight-

ing. Yet in the case of fire*fighting,* we know we need fire *prevention* just as much, if not more, and so we spend on prevention. Yet crime *fighting* is not yet accompanied with significant spending on effective crime *prevention!*

Nevertheless, the dominant way for governments around the globe to cope with crime is through the after-the-fact standard CJS. The media and political discourse on violent crime imply that this system is an adequate solution to the problem. But if the ultimate aim is to stop violent crime in cost-effective, humane ways—which it should be—nothing could be further from the truth.

THE WORLD'S LARGEST JAILER BUT NOT ITS SAFEST COUNTRY

Just as the size of the police force does not correlate with rates of violent crime, incarceration also does not correlate with violent crime reduction. If incarceration were the major contributor to safer communities, the United States, which incarcerates 20 percent of everyone in the world behind bars, would be the world's safest affluent country. It is not. Its incarceration rates are at least four times higher than those of the closest G7 country, England and Wales, so it's even higher than the other G7 countries, including Canada, France, Germany, Italy, and Japan, and six times higher than those of China.[34] But its homicide rate is close to three times that of any other G7 country.[35] In fact, overuse of jailing has little to do with declining crime rates. Rates of incarceration actually follow rates of violent crime and not the reverse.[36]

In New York City, for example, the homicide rate has plunged from 2,600 murders in 1990 to 300 in 2017 while the jail population also has plummeted, from 22,000 in 1992 to 8,500 in 2017.[37] Although this decline in the use of incarceration is exceptional in the United States, it shows that incarceration is also not a silver bullet. Similarly, the Netherlands has reduced its incarceration rate by 50 percent, from 126 prisoners to 60 per capita.[38] This reduction follows a decline in crime, particularly violent crime.[39] This inventive country has closed some prisons and is actually profiting from overuse of incarceration in Belgium and Norway by renting its other empty prisons to them!

If you visit Philadelphia, the City of Brotherly Love, you can visit a new museum housed in the remains of a famous, old penitentiary. Eastern Penitentiary's closure was thought to have coincided with the end of outdated punitive policies in reaction to crime, but it has not happened yet. Along with a variety of interesting artifacts, the museum boasts an impressive 35,000-pound, 16-foot-tall statue, known as The Big Graph. The statue highlights that the United States gets the gold medal for being the world's leading jailer, with 2.2 million incarcerated people, a staggering 655 inmates for every 100,000 people.[40] But The Big Graph also shows that the United States has not always been a gold-medal incarceration performer, though it has been a heavy user for many, many decades. Prior to 1970, the US incarceration rate was a more modest 215 per 100,000 people, far behind Stalin's communist Union of Soviet Socialist Republics.[41] However, this number was still more than twice that of any other developed democracy's, such as Canada or England and Wales.

From 1970 forward, however, the US rate started rising slowly and then exploded almost exponentially from 1980 to 2000, growing with significant financial encouragement from successive federal administrations. This is not news to anyone in the crime policy business. But it may be news to politicians. Today, the US incarceration rate of 665 per 100,000 is four times that of England and Wales and Mexico, six times that of Canada, and eight times that of Germany.[42]

Another major but sad "wow" of The Big Graph is that approximately 40 percent of US inmates are Black, a rate six times that for Whites. Some 20 percent are Hispanic, which is a more modest three times the rate for Whites. In simple terms, the more violent crimes recorded by the police, the higher the incarceration rate. The states of Louisiana and Mississippi would be the world champions, if they were countries, for their population of inmates in jails and state prisons on a per capita basis.

In 2010, legal scholar Michelle Alexander wrote a well-researched book on the subject of how rates of incarceration correlate with race. In *The New Jim Crow: Mass Incarceration in the Age of Colorblindness*, Alexander presents very disturbing facts and challenges politicians. What's pertinent here is that *The New Jim Crow* has reached *New York Times* best-seller status. In other words, these facts are no longer news to the many Americans who picked up her book.

Yet too many fail to see the ramifications of the numbers, if not the important humane ramifications, at least the pocketbook ones. For the United States to be the runaway winner of the gold medal for the most use of incarceration in the world is expensive to US taxpayers. The country spends $87 billion a year to house 2.2 million inmates for a per capita rate of 665 per 100,000. The truth is, US taxpayers are paying more per capita for their CJS than citizens of other countries because of these exceptionally high incarceration rates. This is significant to understanding whether taxes are effectively utilized. If the United States incarcerated at the Canadian rate, instead of spending $87 billion, the United States would spend only $15 billion; at the Mexican rate, $23 billion; and at the rate for England and Wales, $19 billion.[43] Such a shift could represent potential savings of $60 billion or much more, and those savings could be invested in effective crime prevention solutions or used for other noncrime-related purposes, such as health care, education, or job creation.

ENTER THE ERA OF SOLID VIOLENCE PREVENTION SCIENCE

In the past fifty years, the world has undergone a sea change in terms of knowing what stops violent crime. Thanks to many dedicated experts around the world, we now have accumulated significant, scientifically proven information that forms the basis of the solid violence prevention science. One mastermind of using violence prevention science is John Carnochan. As a senior detective, Carnochan applied violence prevention science in Glasgow, Scotland, and cut violent crime in that city by a whopping 50 percent within three years. His program is just one of the examples I use in chapter 9 to illustrate successful efforts based on violence prevention science.

Ironically, much of the information about such programs and the science behind them is readily available throughout the world via websites or what are called "portals" on the World Wide Web, but governments rarely use the information when considering solutions to violent crime. One reason for the lack of government use is that the information is often not provided in a user-friendly way. In 2014, I overcame this hurdle by writing *Smarter Crime Control: A Guide to a Safer Future for Citizens, Communities, and Politicians*. The book, which has been widely distributed across the United States and other countries and is translated into Spanish and Chinese, explains what can stop violent and property crime. It features information from a wealth of governmental and intergovernmental sources, including the WHO and the National Institute of Justice of the US Department of Justice, and highlights specific policy changes that could achieve significant reductions in violent and property crime.

In this current book, I have added to my already extensive list of sources and information, and I showcase successful model violence prevention projects, projects that have invested in young people and are tackling gender-based issues. As we will see in chapter 9, many of these model projects have been responsible for a 50 percent or more reduction in violent crime within just three years across the cities where they were initiated. The positive results of these prevention programs significantly outshine the standard CJS's rates for stopping crime. Returns on investment also have been more laudable for the model violence prevention programs, which, for instance, return an average of seven dollars for every one dollar invested, as we will see in chapter 4. For some projects, that return is even greater.

Imagine if the United States invested even just the equivalent of 10 percent of its current expenditures for policing, courts, and corrections on effective and proven crime preventive programs! As I will show in chapter 10, with a resulting 50 percent reduction in victimizations, as per the numbers noted, the magnitude of the benefits is impressive. For instance, US victims could save $272 billion in fewer homicide and rape tragedies and nearly $70 billion in taxes, after paying for the additional investment.[44] Specifically in the United States, there were 17,250 victims of homicides according to FBI statistics in 2016, and 1,270,000 rapes in 2010 according to the CDC. Considering these actual numbers, a 50 percent crime reduction would represent over 8,000 lives saved, nearly 600,000 rapes avoided, and a million fewer assaults involving injuries.[45] And investment in social prevention doesn't just stop violence! The myriads of downstream positive effects of social prevention projects include youth empowerment, improved parenting, and better jobs.

The United States is not the only country where a 50 percent reduction in violent crime is needed. Most Western democracies would also greatly benefit; they just do not have such high rates of victimization as does the United States, so the numbers do not look as alarming. In Canada and England and Wales, for instance, cutting the murder rate in half would save 350 lives each; in the European Union, 1,000 lives would be spared.

Mexico is a different story. In that country, thousands of young men are losing their lives and way too many women are being traumatized by intimate partner and sexual violence each year because politicians are not implementing effective solutions successfully. A 50 percent crime reduction there would save more than 14,000 lives and avoid millions of rapes annually. In the case of homicide, this reduction would return the victim numbers and crime rate to 2006 levels, before Mexico's skyrocketing of violent crime.

Unfortunately, awareness and interest are not enough. If they were, those holding a country's purse strings would decrease overreliance on general law enforcement or jails and prisons and increase funding for youth services, school curricula on life skills, family and parenting support, and so on. Indeed, a US government report in 2016 showed that the opposite was happening: state and local spending on prisons and jails has increased at triple the rate of funding for public education for preschool through grade 12 since the 1990s.[46]

GETTING POLITICIANS AND LAW ENFORCEMENT OFFICIALS ON BOARD TO STOP VIOLENT CRIME

What I share in this and my other books as well as in my lectures and talks around the globe is good news that can change the world. By embracing violence prevention science and acting on it, we can significantly reduce homicides and rapes for a lot less money than countries are spending on their current approaches to crime fighting. Interestingly, the governments of the world at the UN actually endorse the approach I'm recommending. In various official resolutions, they call for well-planned violence prevention programs that are based on violence prevention science.

In addition, in 2015, world leaders gathered at the UN and committed to achieve seventeen Sustainable Development Goals (SDGs) by 2030. In addition to protecting the planet, their goals include greater prosperity and well-being for all, and they plan to accomplish these goals through a focus on results and getting those results through significant transformations in how governments do business. Among the seventeen SDGs are two that specifically mandate violence reduction: SDG 5 and SDG 16. SDG 5's objective, to achieve gender equality and women's empowerment, can be met only if all forms of violence against women and girls are eliminated. On a broader level, SDG 16 is dedicated to promoting just, peaceful, and inclusive societies. To achieve this goal, one of the identified top targets is significantly reducing all forms of violence and related death rates everywhere, and another is improving access to justice for victims of crime.

Organizations such as the WHO, the UN Office on Drugs and Crime (UNODC), UN Children's Fund (UNICEF), UN Human Settlement Program (UN-Habitat), and UN Entity for Gender Equality and the Empowerment of Women (UN Women) are leading the charge on stopping violence worldwide. They partner with governments, other UN agencies, civic organizations, and other institutions to increase awareness of the causes and consequences of violence and work to prevent and respond to violence. All agree that investing in prevention is the most cost-effective, long-term means to getting results. They know that by tackling the causes and risk factors upstream, before violence happens, we can afford to deliver safer homes, schools, and lives to all.

Thankfully, several cities throughout the world, from Glasgow in Scotland to Ciudad Juaréz in Mexico as well as some medium-sized US cities, have embraced the philosophy and acted in a way consistent with UN guidelines. As a result, their homicide rates have plummeted within just a few years. Yes, with the right leadership, communities can reduce rates of violence in a relatively short time, and those who do it right sustain it!

You would think other local and national governments would be paying attention to and following the lead of those places seeing results from their investments in evidence-based violence prevention strategies and that there would be many success stories. Consider, for example, that there are nine Mexican cities as well as the US cities of Baltimore, Detroit, New Orleans, and St. Louis on the list of the fifty most violent cities in the world.[47] Chicago just missed the list.[48] Action is long overdue!

Granted, internationally, there have been a number of early adopters of innovation based on violence prevention research, but not all have sustained their efforts. England and Wales, for instance, embarked on a significant investment in effective solutions. Within a couple of years, however, their program had quietly disappeared. Similarly, the Canadian Province of Alberta put $1 billion over six years into effective solutions as part of a popular "tough-on-causes, tough-on-crime" campaign, but the small funding for the key agency concerned with masterminding their brilliant safe-communities program was mysteriously cut. Also, ironically, whereas the US Agency for International Development funds violence prevention in Latin America and the Caribbean—including a favorite model project, Cure Violence, which is among the ten most successful nongovernmental organizations in the world—violence prevention funding within the United States is insignificant and would not show on The Big Graph in Eastern Penitentiary. It is a drop in the bucket compared to the money that goes into policing and incarceration.

The radical solution the world needs from responsible and honest politicians is investing in what works to stop violent victimization. We need funding for effective prevention in sectors such as youth outreach, schools, social services, public involvement, and health as well as in problem-solving policing and courts. As will be explored later in the book, some specific ideas include the following:

- Hiring more street workers to outreach to young men
- Expanding school curricula to teach life skills

- Working with families
- Fostering better parenting
- Working with high-risk youth to stop them from carrying illegal handguns
- Creating jobs and sport experiences that include mentoring personal skills
- Proactive policing that solves problems

We need to advocate for change and stand up at the ballot boxes and elect forward-thinking leaders who want to stop the tragedies and have the wisdom to follow the evidence of violence prevention science. We need to get this knowledge across to those leaders. We need to help them know how to get these solutions implemented.

THE NEW SMART ON CRIME MOVEMENT

A new movement is gaining momentum using the phrase, "smart on crime." The Organization of American States calls it "smart security." No matter the terminology, smart on crime or smart security advocates want to curtail governments from misspending on what does not work to stop crime: much of reactive policing, the criminal courts, and incarceration. Instead, we promote using evidence-based research and smart investment to reduce violent crime rates. Note that we focus on how to reduce the number of victims of violence, not on the number of inmates.

I used the term "smart on crime" in 2006 in my book *Less Law, More Order* as a way to reduce crime. Kamala Harris, currently a US senator from California, wrote a book on the subject in 2009. In *Smart on Crime*, Harris, like me, warns that the old approaches to dealing with crime are not working. She spells out necessary changes that will increase public safety, reduce costs, and strengthen communities. She also says these improvements will not happen until politicians and law enforcement officials learn how to become "smart on crime." My 2014 book, *Smarter Crime Control*, furthers Harris's call to action by compiling the accumulated evidence on what really works to reduce crime and what specific actions politicians can take to stop violence.

A great example of the momentum we are seeing in the United States related to being smart on crime is the recently formed coalition, Mayors for Smart on Crime (https://www.smartoncrime.us/). The twelve mayors who initially joined the alliance included those of New York, Philadelphia, and

Los Angeles. On their website, this group offers numerous informational resources and captures well the crossroads our cities face related to crime-reduction policies. They write:

> Reforming the criminal justice system is a top priority across the country. But the momentum for reform is jeopardized by the return of dangerous and ineffective "tough on crime" rhetoric and policies. Cities, however, are ramping up efforts to drive comprehensive reform—from policing to reentry—because mayors understand that right-sizing the criminal justice system and making it fair and equitable for all involved increases public safety. In today's landscape, it is critical to support local leaders in the efforts to be smart on crime, and their voices must be heard.[49]

It is important to note that the smart on crime movement is very different from the "smart justice" movement, which is fighting for less mass incarceration in the United States, the top jailer in the world. The smart justice movement is led by an army of progressive US organizations, the most famous being the Sentencing Project and the American Civil Liberties Union. In their work to illuminate the issue of mass incarceration, the Pew Charitable Trusts has popularized the term "justice reinvestment" and emphasizes the role played in incarceration by a variety of important human rights violations, such as the lack of a right to vote, the overuse of solitary confinement, and overcrowding.

Yet despite these noble efforts, little headway has been made on the massive overuse of incarceration in the United States. But then the leaders of the smart justice movement have not embraced violence science and looked upstream at prevention for the solutions to the incarceration problem. The solutions to criminal justice lie outside the CJS. Consider that most inmates were arrested or convicted for some act of violence; a significant minority were jailed for a drug offense. Knowing the numbers, why wouldn't we shift the focus of policy reform from unfair and overuse of incarceration to the prevention of violence in the first place?

A CALL TO ACTION: HOW THIS BOOK CAN HELP

This book is about change and transformation—what actions will end violent crime and how to afford and implement those actions. My goal is to make violence prevention science accessible and crystal clear to policy makers and the general public. I also strive to share the essentials of what governments must do to get those effective solutions in the right place at the right time and sustained. In addition, this book is about convincing decision makers with compelling arguments and spiking their excuses for inaction. These are the secrets that will change knowledge in theory to science in practice. We must all work together to transform the way we deal with crime to avoid the loss of thousands of lives, millions of serious injuries, and billions of dollars.

Looking forward, I have divided the book into four parts. I begin with a review of the main types of criminal violence in our world, including urban violence, gender-based violence, and violence against young children. You will learn the frequency of violence and its tragic costs as I highlight the urgency to snuff it out once and for all.

The second part of the book takes a close look at the science of violence prevention, which proves that the most effective—and cost effective—way to end violence is prevention. To support the research, I share concrete examples of proactive, positive programs and investments that have had better results than the CJS in ending violent crime. Some of these programs include proactive policing, but most of them include parent coaching, youth outreach and mentoring, job creation, organized sport, and more.

Then, I delve into what governments must do to put their money where the science is. The essentials include mobilizing human talent, sustaining adequate funding, and establishing permanent crime reduction boards to ensure the efforts stay the course. Ultimately, to save young men, women, and children from the risk and ravages of violent crime, we need responsible and honest politicians and law enforcement officials to invest in the structures and strategies that will finally stop violent victimization.

In part IV, I show that money is available and can be budgeted in balance with reactive expenditures. In other words, we can reallocate funds for "picking up the pieces" to more positive investments. Basically, I will share the secrets of working for change. You will see the strong economic arguments for investing now in research-based effective solutions because they not only save lives but also generate economic development. You will also learn that prevention is much more popular than many think because organized marchers and mothers are sounding the alarm for crime prevention action as they did to tackle drunk driving deaths forty years ago.

Finally, in the epilogue, I leave you with seven priority actions to get effective solutions implemented successfully. We must do more to counter myths and overcome inertia to foster the positive transformations by decision makers. We must act on the local, state, and national levels to save lives, reduce trauma, restore our violence-plagued communities, and save money. The time is now!

I

THE CHALLENGE
OF VIOLENT CRIME

It always seems impossible until it's done.

—Nelson Mandela

1

TOO MANY TRAGEDIES

Trauma, Loss, and Misspent Lives

As the press headline more young men dying from gun shots in Chicago, "The weekend forecast calls for widespread apathy with a slight chance of selective outrage and some rain, too."

—HeyJackass.com

A World Health Organization (WHO) 2016 report provides a lay of the land of violent crime around the globe:

- Homicide has taken the lives of 475,000 people, 80 percent of whom are male.
- Thirty-eight percent of murders of women have been by an intimate partner or ex-partner.
- Globally, one in three women have experienced physical and/or sexual abuse by an intimate partner or sexual violence by a nonpartner.
- Globally, one billion children and youth have suffered physical, sexual, or psychological violence in the past year.
- Twenty-five percent of all children have experienced physical violence.
- Twenty percent of girls and 7 percent of boys have been affected by sexual abuse.

According to WHO's director general, "Such violence not only leads to deaths and injuries but also has consequences for mental health problems.

Women and girls in particular experience adverse sexual and reproductive health consequences of violence. . . . Behind these numbers are individual stories of untold and unimaginable suffering and pain."[1]

Yes, one homicide or rape is a tremendous tragedy. Such violent crimes end or shatter the life of the individual victim as well as those who care about the victim. But 10,000 homicides or one million rapes are statistics. Such statistics poignantly call out the need for governments to transform policy and to measure whether policy actually works to reduce the numbers and, eventually, end the harm.

In our Information Age, an understanding of the extent of the harm caused by violence is no longer just based on numbers of police arrests, court statistics about offenders, and hunch. Instead, we now have sophisticated surveys and research about violent crime and the victims. The disturbing trends these surveys and the research expose may not be well known to the public, politicians, or the media. But they need to be!

The stark numbers and horrific stories of violence should generate outrage. The world should be demanding that politicians around the globe seek and implement effective solutions to ending violence. Violence is preventable! As this book will show, the solid science of violence prevention is the key. Only by monitoring, evaluating, innovating, and improving public policies and practices will we be able to make violence a thing of the past. And governments will know what particular policies and programs are working only by counting the prevalence of occurrence and paying attention to what the numbers show.

UN GENERAL ASSEMBLY ADOPTS MAGNA CARTA FOR VICTIMS

One major shift that occurred in the late twentieth century was instrumental in making headway with smarter crime control. That shift involved finally considering the *victims* of crime. For centuries in the past, criminal justice systems (CJSs) throughout the world focused on having law enforcement officials and lawyers balance the interests of government with those of the accused. Government officials were not required to do anything more for the victims than use their testimony to make the case against the accused. In other words, they used victims as the reason to arrest and convict offenders.

In 1985, however, the UN General Assembly's Resolution 34, also known as the "Declaration of Basic Principles of Justice for Victims of Crime and Abuse of Power," included a "magna carta" for victims.[2] In it, the world's governments resolved to recognize, for the first time, that crime is not just an offense against the state but it also causes harm to victims. Before the Victim Magna Carta, it was rare for state officials to even listen to the needs of victims or attempt to support their recovery. Granted, those officials arrested and incarcerated offenders, but to what end? Even if the punishment were merited, were the victims healed or supported? Did violence stop happening? We all know the answers. (In chapter 6, I will explore exactly what has changed to support and provide justice for victims.)

In simple terms, governments across the world resolved to act on the Victim Magna Carta, which recognized the prevalence and harm done to victims, and to increase attention for actually stopping victimization. They noted at the UN General Assembly, "Millions of people throughout the world suffer harm as a result of crime and the abuse of power, and . . . the rights of these victims have not been adequately recognized."[3] In other words, all governments of the world participating in that international session of the august United Nations led the way to focus on the message that crime damages victims and their families. It is not just an offense against the state.

In 2006, the degree of that damage was well stated in a proposal for a cogent draft that all governments could sign. The goal of the proposal was to accelerate the shift in governmental policy toward preventing victimization and supporting victims: "Crimes are not just against the state but impact millions of people including many women and children, vulnerable groups, and indigenous populations. . . . [They suffer] loss, injury, and mental harm each year, and . . . may be victims more than once in that year. . . . [Yet] the rights of these victims still have not been adequately recognized, and . . . they may, in addition, suffer hardship when assisting in the prosecution of offenders."[4] Unfortunately, the outrageous numbers and impact of violent crime and the draft of solutions have not caught the attention of government decision makers, yet. Crime victims continue to be the orphans of our government policy, which is still obsessed with offenders.

It is one thing to set a goal, but implementing strategies to achieve that goal is another thing. The governments at the UN in 1985, thus, resolved to prevent victimization by attacking its myriads of causes. They called on all governments to implement particular social, health (including mental health), educational, economic, and crime prevention policies and to promote community efforts and public participation in crime prevention. Specifically, their proposal called for the following:

- Measures to reduce the risk of occurrence of crimes by tackling their multiple causes

- Strategies to reduce the opportunity for crime by improving protection for property and people
- Collaboration between civil society and relevant governmental institutions in areas such as schooling, social services, family, public health, and economic sectors
- Institutional frameworks to improve the planning, cost effectiveness, and sustainability of strategies
- Greater public participation in and engagement with strategies in both the short and long term
- International cooperation to exchange proven and promising practices and seek transnational solutions[5]

Again, governments have done little to implement these strategies, other than to agree on some detailed principles that will be discussed in chapter 7. The result? Too many victims and their families continue to have their lives affected and ruined by violent crime.

THE ERA OF VICTIMIZATION SURVEYS

One of the reasons for lack of action on preventing victimization is that governments have not focused on relevant indicators. Too many law enforcement officials and policy makers are still stuck measuring crime rates based on what victims report to police. Some discuss "clearance," which measures the proportion of crimes known to the police that result in an identified offender. Another reason we are not stopping crime is that politicians do not seem to be aware of the extent of the violence in their communities nor its impact on the people who vote them into office. They continue to focus on *reacting* to their city's or state's murders, shootings, and rapes rather than *acting* to prevent them. They are still fighting the alligators instead of draining the swamp!

To begin a proactive prevention strategy, we must shift policy from a focus on how many arrests and how long the prison sentence to how many homicides, rapes, robberies, or serious assaults *have been prevented*. The ability to measure what violent crime has been prevented has improved in leaps and bounds in the past fifty years because of the national and international victimology movement.[6]

Starting in the 1960s, researchers pioneered the first surveys of how many adults were crime victims and what the consequences were. In the late 1980s, governments launched their own versions of these surveys.

Such surveys are now commonplace in both rich and less rich countries. They provide specific data, which policy makers could be using as indicators for knowing whether their policies and practices are working. The surveys track, for example, the number of people who are victims of crime, their characteristics, and the consequences for them. They reveal the disappointing realities of whether victims reported to the police, whether support agencies helped them, what attitudes they have toward government criminal justice policies, and so on. Based on the surveys and subsequent research, we have a treasure trove of information that governments should be using to establish policy. The rest of this chapter highlights some of the key conclusions of the victimization surveys and advocates using those conclusions to spur effective action that will end violent crime.

THE PREVALENCE OF VIOLENT CRIME

Who are these victims? As noted earlier, according to a 2016 WHO report, nearly half a million people were murdered around the world that year, 80 percent being male; one in three women globally experienced physical and/ or sexual abuse by an intimate partner or sexual violence by a nonpartner; and one billion children and youth globally suffered physical, sexual, or psychological violence.[7] In the United States, specifically, we know from the 2016 National Crime Victimization Survey that residents aged twelve or older experienced 5.7 million violent victimizations.[8] For a city of 100,000 people, there were 120 rapes or sexual assaults, 180 robberies, 400 aggravated assaults, and 1,400 simple assaults upon its citizens ages twelve or older. This is a combined rate of 2,100 crimes of violence. Though offenders were primarily males, the rates of victimization involving "serious violence," as defined by the National Crime Victimization Survey, fell roughly equally on men and women.[9] These are outrageous numbers for a country spending $238 billion on the CJS!

There is also an International Crime Victim Survey that enables the public as well as policy makers to know how the chance of being a victim of crime varies between countries. These rates are based on small samples, so the survey should be used with caution. Nonetheless, the survey shows rates of robbery and assault in England and Wales to be higher than in Canada or the United States.[10] For Latin America, another survey shows rates of robbery and assault in Mexico to be roughly double those of Canada and the United States.[11]

According to the WHO 2015 *Global Status Report on Road Safety*, we also know that, overall, the traffic fatality rate for Mexico is at 12; for the United States, at 11; for Canada, at 6; and for the United Kingdom, at 3 (out of 100,000 people) annually. Close to 10,000 persons in the United States lose their lives in motor vehicle crashes specifically attributed to alcohol. In Canada, that number is 1,400, whereas it is 600 in England and Wales. In the United States alone, half a million victims of drunk drivers are injured.[12]

	CANADA	ENGLAND & WALES	MEXICO	USA
Number of Homicides to nearest 100	700	700	29,000	17,000
Rate of Homicides per 100,000 total population	1.8	1.2	23.4	5.2
Approximate **Number of Rape Victims** if rate per capita similar to USA	141,000	227,000	486,000	1,270,000
Number of Persons Incarcerated on an average day to nearest 1,000	41,000	83,000	218,000	2,121,000
Rate of Persons Incarcerated per 100,000 total population	114	141	176	655
Population to nearest million	36	58	124	324
Total Expenditures on police, courts, and prisons in billions of national currency	Can$22	£21	Mex$288	$284

See appendix for sources.

Figure I.I. Number of Victims of Homicide and Rape with Incarceration and CJS Expenditures

Homicide

When it comes to homicide specifically, police reports have been a particularly valuable source of statistics for the past few decades. They tell us, for example, that on a national scale, five families for every 100,000 persons lost a loved one to homicide in 2017 in the United States. In the 1970s and 1980s, the US rate was as high as 10 per 100,000. European countries generally have much lower rates than the United States, with England and Wales, for instance, close to 1.2 families for every 100,000 persons experiencing the pain of homicide. Canada is slightly higher at 1.8. And Mexico is at 23.4 families for every 100,000 persons, which is close to the average for Latin America as a whole. Note that Mexico's homicide rate declined to around 10 in the early 2000s, but then it doubled in the next six years and has oscillated around 20 for a number of years.[13]

To put these numbers in perspective, I present them with the rates per 100,000 for the four countries in figure 1.1. We will come back to other statistics in this figure later in this chapter. The US rates reflect 17,000 families who lost a person to murder in 2017. Mexico's rates indicate that 29,000 families were affected by homicide in the same year, and in Canada and the United Kingdom, some 700 families in each country will be mourning the death of a loved one. Of those killed, four out of five will be males, mostly in their twenties. In the United States, half the victims will be Black and between the ages of eighteen and thirty-four, with the homicide rate for Blacks being six times that for Whites.[14]

On a world scale, of those killed, 38 percent were gunned down. In Latin America and the United States, the proportion of homicide by firearm is close to 60 percent![15] In fact, in the United States, according to the US Department of Justice 2016 statistics, 7,000 persons were killed by handguns and another 3,000 by other guns, in relation to approximately 500,000 victimizations in which a gun was used.[16]

Intimate Partner and Sexual Violence

Thanks to very specific and relatively new victimization surveys, we also have prevalence numbers on intimate partner and sexual violence. In the past, little was known about gender-based violence because the data was not readily traceable via police administrative data because the victims of intimate partner and sexual violence most often do not report the crime. One major survey for the US Department of Justice shows only 18 percent of women who have been raped reporting the victimization to the police.[17]

Now, however, both men and women are surveyed about intimate partner and sexual violence. The world's gold standard in this arena is the US National Intimate Partner and Sexual Violence Survey, a joint venture of the National Institute of Justice of the US Department of Justice and the US Centers for Disease Control and Prevention.[18] These specialized, sophisticated surveys ask explicit questions about intimate partner violence and sexual assault and expose rates that are higher than in general victimization surveys and much higher than those recorded by policing agencies, such as the FBI.[19]

Nonetheless, the rates are disturbing. In 2010, some 1.3 million American women were victims of rape, some by an intimate partner. In addition, the report notes that in the lifetime of an American, one in three women and one in four men experience physical injury from intimate partner violence. Notably, one in five women are victims of rape before twenty-five years of age.[20] The lifetime numbers equate to 18 million women![21] That is 18 million women who have suffered the original pain and indignity and 18 million women whose lives are still marked by the original horror and devastation of sexual violence.

In figure 1.1, I have used the number of rapes from the National Intimate Partner and Sexual Violence Survey because it measures the number of victims, not the number who reported to the police. England and Wales have a sophisticated survey of their own. Mexico has its own survey, and Canada will have a survey in 2018. Nonetheless, the definitions of rape and sexual violence vary from country to country, so they cannot be used for comparison. Instead, for the countries other than the United States, I use an estimate for numbers of rapes relative to the population of each country based on this survey because it gives the most plausible estimate that is comparable. When we explore implementing effective solutions later in the book, these numbers provide a ballpark estimate of the number of women who will avoid being raped.

Researchers believe that the number of forcible rapes proportionate to the number of adult women has not been rising or falling significantly in recent decades; the numbers today are likely similar to the rate in 1982. If governments were being results oriented and doing what needs to be done, as will be discussed in chapters 7 and 10 to 12, they would be measuring such indicators regularly and assessing whether innovations have made any difference. They also would be asking themselves why current policies and programs are not putting a dent in the statistics. (Note that, as we will see in chapter 11, when individual countries develop indicators to measure success, they are expected to use their own surveys.)

Violence Against Children

When it comes to violence in the home, children are just as often the victims as partners.[22] In the United States, three quarters of a million children are officially victims of neglect and abuse.[23] This is a rate of 9 per 1,000 children. The economic consequences of these confirmed cases alone are estimated at $124 billion a year. Add to that the many incidents of sexual abuse outside the nuclear family by relatives, friends, and strangers that go undetected and unknown to authorities and researchers, and the impact in financial terms is massive, but nothing compared to the psychological, emotional, social, and even physical lifetime damage caused by the tragedies.

A side note to these unacceptable numbers is that early-life victimization predisposes boys to become—and stay—involved in crime. In addition, an examination of the data from studies that follow child development from birth to adulthood points to "inconsistent and uncaring parenting" as a key factor involved in the development of persistent offending abuse.[24] Parenting shortfalls may have many reasons. The parent may be

- in jail,
- suffering with addictions,
- working around the clock in minimum wage jobs, or
- never on the receiving end of good parenting skills when growing up.

Whatever the reason, children who are brought up without the love and care of a supportive parent have difficulty thriving and staying away from committing crime.

We could not discuss violence against children without an exploration of school shootings. Many of these start from bullying, which affects close to one in every three students[25] and causes half a million children to miss school each year in the United States.[26] About one in four bring weapons to school.[27] Media headlines about school shootings rightly raise the ire of the public, who demand solutions. School shootings, however, statistically represent a small proportion of the ways school children are killed in homicides. To state it bluntly, if we are rightly debating solutions to school shootings, we also should be giving as much, if not more, attention to shootings away from schools. Only 20 of the 1,168 homicides of school-aged youth (ages five to eighteen) in the year ending June 2015 in the United States occurred at school.[28] The numbers can vary from year to year, but we must pay attention to implementing effective solutions for both school and nonschool shootings. Any life lost to a gun is one too many, no matter where the shooting takes place!

Repeat Victimization

Before leaving our discussion of the prevalence of violent crime, we must discuss repeat victimization. It is in domestic violence situations that repeat victimization is not only the most frequent but also potentially the most dangerous. Wife battering tends to happen more than once to the same victim who continues to live with the same partner. This is also true of sexual incidents.

The British Crime Survey provides data annually about repeat victimization. According to that survey, 44 percent of all crime is concentrated on 4 percent of victims. Following are the proportions of victims who will be a victim of a similar offense within a year of the event:

- 41 percent for domestic violence
- 40 percent for a sexual incident
- 30 percent for assaults and robberies
- 24 percent for burglary
- 13 percent for car theft[29]

The rates are likely similar for Canada, Mexico, and the United States, although it is difficult to get specific statistics for other countries.

LOCATION: AN IMPORTANT CHARACTERISTIC OF VIOLENT CRIME

Now that we know the numbers, it is imperative to dissect other factors the victimization surveys uncover. First, the surveys and police administrative data indicate that crime is concentrated in particular places. The fact is, for most people, homicide is not part of their daily reality, unless they are living in a place of relative poverty, social breakdown, or exclusion.

Within countries, homicide rates can vary considerably depending on the region. Here are the statistics:

- In the United States, states with homicide rates at 8 per 100,000 or above are Alabama, Illinois, Louisiana, Maryland, Mississippi, and Missouri.
- In the United States, states with homicide rates at 3 per 100,000 or less are Connecticut, Hawaii, Idaho, Maine, Massachusetts, Minnesota, Nebraska, New Hampshire, North Dakota, Oregon, Rhode Island, Utah, Vermont, and Washington.[30]

- In Mexico, states with homicide rates at 30 per 100,000 are Chihuahua, Colima, Guerrero, and Sinaloa.
- In Mexico, the states with homicides rates at 3 per 100,000 or less are Campeche and Yucatan.[31]
- In Canada, all provinces have homicide rates of 3 or less per 100,000, except Manitoba and Saskatchewan, which have homicide rates of 4 per 100,000.
- In Canada, the territories (Northwest, Nunavut, and Yukon) have homicide rates at 8 per 100,000 or above.[32]

The prevalence of violence also varies between cities in each country. Every year, Mexico's Citizens' Council for Public Security ranks the world's 50 cities with a population of 300,000 or more with the highest rates of homicide.[33] In 2017, there were 4 in the United States; 12 in Mexico; 30 in other Latin American countries, including 17 in Brazil; and 5 in Venezuela. Three are in South Africa.

- In the United States, cities included are St. Louis, with a homicide rate of 66; Baltimore, 56; New Orleans, 40; and Detroit, 40. Chicago, with a rate of 25, does not make the list (which has a lowest rating of 35).
- In Mexico, cities included in the list range from Ciudad Juaréz at 56 to Tijuana at 100.

I am often asked for comparisons with other cities. Here are some selected cities with their homicide rate per 100,000 for 2017: New York, 3.4; Toronto, 2.4; Glasgow, 2.0; and London, 1.2.[34] For all the cities noted, the homicide rates will be low in many areas, with a few concentrated areas where the violent crime is very high. We will see in chapter 3 examples where 3 percent of addresses account for 50 percent or more of 911 calls and how the high-crime zip codes are "hot spots" and "problem places" for police.[35]

IMPACT OF INTERPERSONAL VIOLENCE

Following a violent crime, victims who survive may struggle with physical injuries and loss of productivity. Most will experience posttraumatic stress disorder (PTSD) and feelings of anger, depression, and worthlessness, and more will oscillate and reverberate for weeks, months, and possibly even years. Those who care about the victims also know the incredible toll of violent crime, as do first responders such as police personnel, paramedics, emergency surgeons, and nurses. Today, a growing number of advocates and social scientists also acknowledge the lifelong health consequences, pain, shock, humiliation, and loss of control crime victims may suffer for the rest of their lives. In addition, we recognize that, although many victims will not report the crime to the police, if they do, they also might experience the disillusionment of being a "witness" rather than a "client." (I will discuss this difficult dichotomy in chapter 6.)

Physical Consequences

In 2017, 17,000 people died as direct victims of homicide in the United States.[36] In addition, 1.6 million victims of crime are treated in hospital emergency rooms for nonfatal physical injuries.[37] Some may be bruised in a fight, some knifed, and some shot. Some will be sexually assaulted, which is calamitous enough, but the encounter may lead to pregnancy or a sexually communicated disease, such as AIDS. Many will be able to return home from the hospital the same day. Others will need to remain hospitalized. Many US victims of crime will worry about how their medical care will be paid because they do not have health insurance.

Beyond the Physical

Not only will the consequences be physical, but victims of violent crimes also are more often than not left with mental and emotional turmoil. They may be in a state of shock, anger, frustration, and fear, all of which can keep them from sleeping, working, or even leaving the house. For some, this will pass in a few days or weeks. But when the crime was experienced as life threatening, involved sexual assault, or inflicted serious injury, that victim may experience intrusive and traumatic recollections of the crime. These recollections may lead to persistent feelings of trauma; avoidance of even normal, everyday activities; sleeping difficulties; outbursts of anger; and an exaggerated startle response—symptoms of PTSD. For some, these reactions may endure for many years after the victimization. For a small but important proportion, the severe and enduring trauma and physical injury will never go away. They will never have closure. Their families also may suffer trauma not only in cases of murder but also in many less heinous incidents, such as burglary.

PTSD is now part of our everyday language. We are most familiar with the term because we know or hear about soldiers who have PTSD from having served in wars and battle situations, such as Vietnam, Iraq, or Afghanistan. The term, however, originated as a diagnosis for what was happening with mental health workers who helped rape victims, and it was first included in the *Diagnostic and Statistics Manual of Mental Disorders* (*DSM*) of the American Psychiatric Association in 1980. The definition is currently being refined for *DSM-5*. Whereas this revision may help a crime victim recover insurance or restitution from an offender, such recognition does not make the violent crime less painful or difficult to bear.

Most surveys do not focus on the range of other emotions lived by crime victims, but some resources offer insights into what the victims are experiencing. For instance, interviews with burglary victims document their upset, anger, and fear. The feelings of fear are most prevalent and persistent for women. Interviews with rape victims point to their concern about being believed as well as the difficulties they have with males in their entourage around their reaction to the rape. (For more details about the emotional and mental health consequences related to rape, refer to the CDC's *Intimate Partner and Sexual Violence Survey*[38] as well as various WHO publications.[39]) In addition, victims must cope with the practical problems of visits to doctors, support for children or elderly family members, and even repairs. In many cases, victims of crime have to clean up, change locks, and repair broken furniture. How does one manage such mundane activities in a time of such brokenness?

THE COST OF VICTIMIZATION

The pain and suffering to victims of violent crime and their families is tragic and appalling. From a government viewpoint, one wonders how this victimization translates into dollars. The seminal report on these total costs in the United States was published in 2000 and has received considerable attention. The total costs of victimization were estimated at US$450 billion or the equivalent of nearly $1,600 per American per year in 1994.[40] These costs were made up of accumulated medical costs at $18 billion; property loss, mental health, emergency, and productivity losses at $87 billion; and quality of life at $345 billion. On productivity alone, a World Bank study shows that one in five of the days lost from work by women in established market economies are due to gender-based violence.[41]

Cumulatively, the monetary harm to victims and the costs to the public are immense. It is interesting to note that, while rates of victimization for most common crimes in the United States came down by about 50 percent from 1994 to 2018, the costs of living in the United States increased by more than 50 percent. To arrive at more current numbers, I have recalculated the various costs using the exact figures from the National Crime Survey, so current estimates of the cost of victimization in the United States currently remain in the same dollar range.[42]

In fact, violent crime causes 14 percent of injury-related medical spending. In addition, violent crime is a significant factor in mental health usage. Sources indicate that as much as 10 to 20 percent of mental health expenditures in the United States can be attributed to crime, primarily for victims treated as a result of their victimization. About half of these mental health expenditures are for child abuse victims receiving treatment for abuse experienced years earlier.[43]

One of the most commonly used ways to measure the costs to victims is presented in figure 1.2.[44] Considering only tangible, out-of-pocket costs to the victim and the state, the average rape (or attempted rape) costs $8,000, which covers the medical and mental health costs to victims. However, if rape's effect on the victim's quality of life is quantified, the average rape costs $133,000, many times greater than the cost of one professional to run just one intensive program to reduce sexual assault. (In chapter 5, we will explore programs, such as Fourth R, that could help to prevent rapes and sexual assaults.)

Estimates calculated in a similar way for medical and tangible costs in Canada as well as England and Wales show costs in similar ranges for the crimes. Estimates point to costs to Canadian victims at Canadian $55 billion in 2017.[45] The cost estimate for England and Wales was £37 billion (US$50 billion) in 2005.[46] The tangible costs include medical expenses, loss of property, and loss of wages. The British Home Office and Public Safety Canada have used these numbers to calculate the costs of particular types of offenses. One of the main differences between calculating victimization costs for the United States, Canada, and England and Wales is that the United States has so many more homicides per capita. Another difference is that many crime victims in the United States do not have insurance to cover their medical costs. Whatever the numbers, the tragedy of homicide or rape is huge. The material losses are dwarfed by the intangible pain that often leads to the chronic problems highlighted by the WHO and CDC that are flagged in figure 1.2.

TYPE OF COST	HOMICIDE	RAPE	COST OF CRIME TO SOCIETY*	EXAMPLES OF BEHAVIORAL AND HEALTH CONSEQUENCES FOR VICTIMS**
Tangible to Victim	$1,285,000	$41,000	Medical expenses, lost earnings, and victimization costs	Injuries, disabilities, sexually transmitted disease, and pregnancy
Intangible to Victim	$8,442,000	$199,000	Pain and suffering, diminished quality of life	PTSD, depression, and chronic disease such as arthritis and diabetes
CJS Costs to Taxes	$392,000	$26,000	Cost of police protection, courts, and corrections	
Earnings Lost	$148,000	$9,000	Career criminal legal earnings for GDP foregone	
Subtotal of Costs	$10,267,000	$275,000		
Annual Number of Victims	17,000	1,270,000		
Annual Total of Costs	$174,539 million	$349,250 million		

*McCollister et al. **WHO, 2014.
See appendix for sources.

Figure 1.2. Tangible and Intangible Costs to Victims of Homicide and Rape

VICTIMIZATION'S THREAT TO ECONOMIC DEVELOPMENT AND EVEN DEMOCRACY

The most violent region in the world can be found in Latin America and the Caribbean. There, 24 people were killed per every 100,000 in 2015—four times the global average.[47] According to the World Bank, this violence results in a loss of 2 to 15 percent of the GDP of these low- and middle-income countries.[48] That is a significant blow to economic development. And crime is on the rise! Yet despite the seriousness of the problem, the costs of crime and violence in the region have only recently received systematic attention.

A seminal study by the Inter-American Development Bank of seventeen of the countries in this volatile region estimated their combined total for costs of crime at US$165 billion, with an average cost of approximately US$300 per capita! Of these costs, 42 percent is for public spending (mostly police services); 37 percent is for private spending; and 21 percent is for social costs of crime, mainly victimization.[49] In the higher violence countries in Central America, the costs per capita double. The tangible and intangible costs of these exorbitantly high crime rates are significant: people change their behavior to avoid crime or engage in criminal activity themselves, households spend what little money they have on attempting to protect themselves and their property, firms reduce their investment and incur productivity losses, and governments shift the allocation of resources.[50] With so much at stake in these ravaged countries, the potential benefits to their economy and for the well-being of their citizens from implementing effective solutions to ending violent crime can be massive.

Whereas it is tragic that victimization threatens the economic stability of some countries, what is even worse is that violent crime can affect democracy itself. Frighteningly, the World Bank has drawn attention to this monumental global dilemma. We cannot deny that the lack of effective strategies to curb violence has led to the destabilization of governments. This, in turn, can lead to further victimization through abuse of power that infringes on human rights as governments turn to military solutions.[51]

KEY TAKEAWAYS

- Governments recognized the extent to which violent crime affects victims in a major resolution at the UN General Assembly in 1985 and called for preventive action to reduce violence. Unfortunately, governments have taken too little action to implement the resolution.
- The ultimate violent crime of murder kills too many young, disadvantaged men, at rates much higher than the rest of the population, often with handguns.
- Victims of violent crime, if not killed, are too often victims more than once.
- As with most crime, violence is concentrated in limited areas in countries and in particular cities and even in a single zip code.
- Some high-violence cities in Mexico and the United States have homicide rates much above the levels identified by the WHO as "epidemic." Cities in Canada and England and Wales have rates below the epidemic threshold but likely have neighborhoods with epidemic levels.
- Though media and politicians have not caught up, national statistics agencies use their own surveys to measure violent crime. These surveys show violent crime to be much more frequent than police reports indicate. They also show that close to 50 percent of serious violent crime is not reported to the police in the United States.
- The CDC uses a remarkable survey to measure rates and impact of intimate partner and sexual violence. Intimate partner and sexual violence rates are at least nine times higher than what is reported through police. This survey highlights disturbing rates of trauma and chronic diseases.
- The costs of violent crime to governments come primarily from the costs of the standard CJS, but the costs to victims are much higher and less visible, unless we use surveys.
- Costs of violent crime to government also come from the loss of economic prosperity in cities and loss of GDP, particularly for low- and middle-income countries.
- High rates of violence can threaten democracy and the rule of law.

II

THE SCIENCE OF
EFFECTIVE SOLUTIONS

Violence is not inevitable. It is preventable.

—Nelson Mandela

2

VIOLENCE PREVENTION SCIENCE AT OUR FINGERTIPS

Solid Consensus on Effective Solutions

Better to drain the swamp than fight the alligators.

—Anonymous

After more than fifty years of research and development, the world now has access to an impressive accumulation of knowledge on the causes of and risk factors for violent crime as well as on effective crime prevention. This research and knowledge is available on websites and portals of various prestigious organizations, such as the World Health Organization (WHO), the College for Policing in England and Wales, Public Safety Canada, and the National Institute of Justice of the US Department of Justice. National academies in the United States and Canada and, recently, the Parliamentary Committee on Youth Violence in England and Wales have even developed consensus reports. Plus, each year, new portals open with more evidence-based information and more examples of violence prevention research to put into practice, all with the same conclusions.

CAUSES AND RISK FACTORS

Analyses comparable between countries and over time show that crime trends directly link to poverty, inequity, and a lack of social safety nets. Specifically, fewer resources related to preschool, education, welfare, job prospects, unemployment insurance, and health care correlate with higher rates of violent victimization. Furthermore, analyses of violent crime trends, particularly related to homicide, confirm the impact of access to guns and alcohol, poor parenting, lack of safety nets, and poverty.[1]

In England and Wales, the United States, and other countries, a number of longitudinal studies have followed cohorts of children raised in disadvantaged areas. The researchers have collected data for these children on various negative and positive life experiences as well as on whether the children ever get arrested. The studies show that those children arrested most often have more negative life experiences than those not arrested.[2] The most impactful negative life experiences that correlate with later delinquency identified by these longitudinal studies are now well known.[3] They include the following:

- Socioeconomic factors, such as low income and poor housing
- Family factors, such as poor parental supervision and harsh or erratic parental discipline
- High impulsiveness and low intelligence
- Peer factors, such as having friends who are delinquent
- School factors, such as attending a high delinquency–rate school
- Neighborhood or community factors, such as living in a high-crime neighborhood
- Arrest leads to more arrest[4]

Other studies pertinent to understanding the causes and risk factors of interpersonal violence are those related to "adverse childhood experience," often referenced by the acronym ACE. One major study identifies an ACE as "a traumatic experience in a person's life occurring before the age of eighteen that the person remembers as an adult."[5] The original ACE study, known as the CDC–Kaiser Permanente Adverse Childhood Experiences (ACE) Study, is one of the largest investigations of childhood abuse and neglect and later-life health and well-being.[6] It involved asking 17,000 adults in Southern California—in two waves, from 1995 to 1997—about their early childhood history and current health and behaviors. The results illumined how ACEs disrupt neurodevelopment and cause social, emotional, and cognitive impairment that could lead to risky behaviors. In a later study, the 2011 Minnesota telephone survey, individuals were asked if they had experienced any of nine types of ACEs. These nine ACEs include the following:

- Physical abuse
- Sexual abuse

- Emotional abuse
- Mental illness of a household member
- Problematic drinking or alcoholism of a household member
- Illegal street or prescription drug use by a household member
- Divorce or separation of a parent
- Domestic violence toward a parent
- Incarceration of a household member[7]

Over time, understanding ACEs has become an important component of violence prevention. The US Centers for Disease Control and Prevention (CDC) asserts that negative childhood experiences have a tremendous impact on future violence victimization and perpetration.[8] Specifically, one study cited by the CDC shows that "being abused or neglected as a child increased the likelihood of arrest as a juvenile by 59 percent. Abuse and neglect also increased the likelihood of adult criminal behavior by 28 percent and violent crime by 30 percent."[9] Another study compared offenders convicted of various intimate partner violence and sexual violence of adults and children with a normal population and showed that the "offender group reported nearly four times as many adverse events in childhood than an adult male normative sample."[10] Furthermore, the US Substance Abuse and Mental Health Services Administration (SAMHSA) contends that ACEs make mental illness and substance abuse more likely.[11]

Socio-Ecological Risk Factors

Experts from the WHO working on violence prevention often use a "socio-ecological model" to help decision makers understand their perspective on overlapping groups of risk factors. These risk factors include *individual* factors, such as age and gender or child abuse; *relationship* factors, such as poor parenting practices or witnessing family violence; *community* factors, such as schools or poverty; and *societal* factors, such as health and social policies. It is possible to show how effective solutions tackle one or more of these risk factors.[12] The WHO model stresses the importance of youth outreach, family and parenting, schools, and health services as solutions.

Geographic Concentration

Particularly important in understanding the causes and risk factors associated with violence is that violence is usually concentrated in limited areas of cities. The award-winning documentary *Milwaukee 53206* highlights this fact as it chronicles life in this US zip code where the homicide rate is 250 per 100,000 and 62 percent of its Black males have served time in jail.[13] We will come back to this in chapters 3 and 4, but for now, know that areas with high crime rates also often exhibit high rates of unemployment, family breakdown, and exclusion.

WHERE TO FIND THE INFORMATION ABOUT VIOLENCE PREVENTION

Using the knowledge about the negative life experiences that predispose some people to engage in criminal activity, numerous organizations and criminologists have studied and proven what works to tackle those risk factors. Some crime prevention programs focus on reforming and retooling the existing reactive systems of law enforcement, courts, and corrections to stop reoffending. Some studies make a compelling case for taking crime prevention programs—not police officers—into schools and the community with a goal of identifying and preventing at-risk individuals from starting a life of crime in the first place. I advocate for a combination of both.

By "program," I am referring to a systematically delivered service with clear strategies and goals. The most effective of these programs feature innovations that remedy the risk factors listed above. For instance, one good crime prevention program sends public health nurses into the homes of drug-addicted young moms weekly to help mitigate inconsistent and uncaring parenting. Another innovative crime prevention program teaches boys in high school about why and how to avoid perpetrating sexual violence, despite living in a culture rampant with sexual violence in their neighborhoods and on their media 24/7.

The body of evidence on crime prevention has been held to rigorous scientific standards. Many of the studies are based on randomized controlled trials, which compare the crime-reduction results achieved through an experimental program with the outcomes of the crime rates among similar groups of individuals who did not participate in the new program; this method is the same testing method used by the US Food and Drug Administration (FDA) before allowing pharmaceuticals on the market. Once the testing is completed and the results determined, then independent experts scrutinize the data before the study is published in scientific journals. With numerous peer-reviewed articles on violence prevention programs now available, experts can review the lessons learned from the most scientifically sound articles. These reviews are known as "meta-analyses," and they provide a compelling basis for the conclusion that preventive strategies are the most effective and cost-effective ways to reduce the number of and the harm to crime victims. This knowledge is remarkably strong and, thankfully, easily accessible at no cost through some respected and several government authorities.

PORTALS OF EFFECTIVE VIOLENCE PREVENTION SOLUTIONS

Name and approximate number of programs or practices examined as of 2018:

Blueprints for Healthy Youth Development, Center for the Study of Prevention of Violence, University of Colorado Boulder: 1,400 projects

Campbell Collaboration: 83 records

Center for Problem-Oriented Policing, University at Albany, State University of New York (originally funded by the US Department of Justice): number of files not known

*England and Wales, College of Policing: 60 entries

*Inter-American Development Bank (in process): 172 data sets

*Public Safety Canada, Crime Prevention Inventory: 193 records

*SAMHSA, US Department of Health and Human Services: number of files not known

*US Department of Justice, National Institute of Justice, Crime Solutions.gov: 118 effective, 353 promising, 152 not effective

What Works to Prevent Violence Against Women and Girls Program: 174 studies

*WHO, Violence Prevention Information System (Violence Info): 3,767 studies

* = *Governmental*

To illustrate the extent of this solid violence prevention science, read on for more detail about a select few of the leading portals.

WHO

The WHO (http://www.who.int) has developed a number of useful resources specifically on violence prevention. The easy-to-read, well-organized set of 2009 WHO briefings, titled *Violence Prevention: The Evidence*, are available

for download at http://www.who.int/violence_injury_prevention/violence/
the-evidence/en/. They provide detailed information on how to prevent violence by implementing evidence-based knowledge. This is my favorite portal. Other than my book *Smarter Crime Control*, it is the only publication
that is easy for a decision maker or member of the public to read. You do
not need to be a millennial with computer abilities or a doctoral candidate
in criminology or public health to understand this briefing. You just need to
be able to read in one of the many languages in which it is offered. Plus, the
proven and promising violence prevention actions the WHO recommended
in 2009 are just as relevant in 2019. They include the following:

- Promoting safe, stable, nurturing relationships between children and
  their parents and caregivers
- Developing life skills in children and adolescents
- Reducing the availability and harmful use of alcohol
- Reducing access to guns and knives
- Promoting gender equality to prevent violence against women
- Changing cultural and social norms that support violence
- Implementing victim identification, care, and support programs[14]

In 2014, the WHO offered a similar but expanded list of recommended
"best-buy" violence prevention strategies in its *Global Status Report on
Violence Prevention 2014*, available at http://www.who.int/violence_injury_
prevention/violence/status_report/2014/en/. The report, jointly published
by the WHO, the UN Office on Drugs and Crime, and the UN Development Program, calls for a scaling up of violence prevention programs, stronger legislation and enforcement of laws relevant to violence prevention,
and enhanced services for victims of violence. Unfortunately, the best-buy
strategies are written in such a way that they are not readily digestible for
a decision maker or a violence prevention advocate. They may need some
"interpretation."

Then, in 2017, the WHO produced yet another wonderful resource, the
Violence Prevention Information System (Violence Info), available at http://
apps.who.int/violence-info/. Violence Info draws on thousands of published
studies related to violence prevalence, consequences, risk factors, and prevention and response strategies. The portal also features what individual
countries have done to address violence and, for each area of violence,
various program examples. Unfortunately, the portal is not user friendly; it
is encyclopedic and probably best used by specialists preparing recommendations for decision makers.

US Department of Justice's Office of Justice Programs

In 1996, a group of criminologists at the University of Maryland completed a review of more than 500 evaluations of projects funded by the US federal government. It came to important conclusions about what works, what does not, and what is promising.[15] In 2011, the National Institute of Justice of the US Department of Justice released its own online version of what works and what doesn't. This website posts new profiles each year. To get a sense of the depth of its offerings, note that in 2017, CrimeSolutions.gov (https://www.crimesolutions.gov) showcased 539 programs in its database, of which 96 are confirmed as being "effective," 321 are certified as "promising," and 122 are evaluated as "ineffective." Sadly, few of the effective programs are being used. Even more sadly, many of the popular programs listed as having no or a negative effect on crime prevention, such as Scared Straight and Boot Camps, are still used extensively.

As figure 2.1 shows, about 65 percent of effective programs involve pre-crime prevention, rather than an action by the police, courts, or corrections. More than half of the ninety-six effective programs specifically tackle problems in families and schools, focus on improving life skills of youth through mentoring, attempt to deal with problematic substance use, or advocate for trauma treatment programs.

Note that CrimeSolutions.gov defines a *program* as a specific set of activities carried out according to guidelines to achieve a defined purpose. The website differentiates "programs" from "practices," in that CrimeSolutions.gov defines a *practice* as a general category of programs, strategies, or procedures that share similar characteristics with regard to the issues they address and how they address them. In other words, practice profiles demonstrate the average result across multiple evaluations of programs. With that differentiation in mind, CrimeSolutions.gov presents sixty-two practices that are proven effective by tackling a particular identified risk factor and ultimately reducing victimizations from violent as well as property crime.[16] Most of those practices point to a need to divert attention and resources from the old, unproven, and costly reactive approach to crime and, instead, invest in preventing it! Whereas this portal is indeed a great source of invaluable data, a person with a background in the science of violence prevention may be needed to interpret it.

College of Policing, England and Wales

The College of Policing (http://www.college.plice.uk/Pages/Home.aspx) was established in 2012 as the professional body for everyone working for

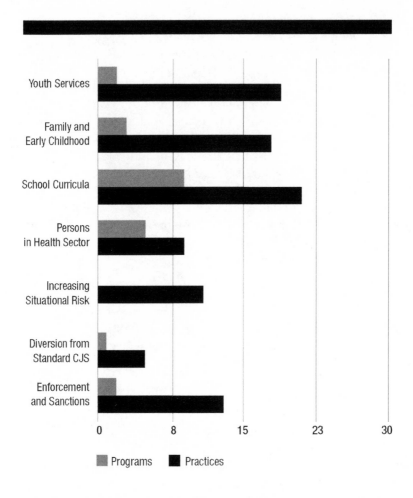

Figure 2.1   Sectors for No. of Effective Solutions on CrimeSolutions.gov

the police service in England and Wales. The purpose of the College is to provide those working in policing with the skills and knowledge necessary to prevent crime, protect the public, and secure public trust. One of the offerings of the College of Policing is a Crime Reduction Tool Kit, which includes a careful assessment of the science on more than sixty interventions. Each intervention is rated as effective, promising, or neither, in a manner similar to CrimeSolutions.gov. In addition, the tool kit explains how each intervention works, where it works, how to implement it, and whether there is evidence of cost effectiveness. Most of the twenty-eight programs rated as effective by the College of Policing can also be found on CrimeSolutions.gov.

It is particularly interesting to note the extent to which the use of the Crime Reduction Tool Kit is embedded in an agency tasked with training police in England and Wales. This, most likely, increases the chances that crime prevention interventions will be utilized. In addition, the organization is involved in research and development with many of the regional police services in England and Wales, including services related to contentious police practices, such as stop and frisk. The College potentially overcomes an important missing link in Canada, Mexico, and the United States: getting violence prevention utilized in law enforcement efforts.

Center for Problem-Oriented Policing

Another great resource on violence prevention is the website of the Center for Problem-Oriented Policing (http://www.popcenter.org). This nonprofit organization, established in 1999, strives to advance the practice of problem-oriented policing by bringing together police practitioners, researchers, and universities dedicated to criminal justice. The flagship of the Center is its deep website, which currently is supported by funding from the School of Criminal Justice, University at Albany, State University of New York. Prior to 2013, the Center was funded by the Office of Community-Oriented Policing Services of the US Department of Justice.

Its website compiles data concerning situational crime prevention and proactive policing techniques proven to be effective. It also provides guides to identify problems and solutions, information on effective models used in various initiatives, and educational tools. While not deeply science based, the portal provides examples of how others have tackled particular problems related to situational crime prevention. This is helpful, but it would be more beneficial if the Center's website would offer more results-based evaluations.

Washington State Institute for Public Policy

Not only is prevention the silver bullet for ending violence, but prevention is also the most *cost-effective* way to deal with crime. Much of how evaluations of effective programs and practices prove this benefit from the cost of implementation has been compiled by the Washington State Institute for Public Policy (http://www.wsipp.wa.gov). This nonpartisan research institute informs the US State of Washington legislature about issues involving education, criminal justice, social services, and health care. Its website is the go-to portal for benefit–cost analyses across the world, so it can be a valuable resource for policy makers worldwide who are looking for the cost–benefit of programs that tackle crime. The summaries of the organization's findings demonstrate clearly that investing in crime prevention programs not only reduces harm to victims but also reduces the cost of crime to the state. The organization shows how significant reductions in crime and victimization free up resources from "reaction" for positive investment, including savings to expenditures in the police and incarceration sectors.[17] Such a gold standard, the Washington State Institute for Public Policy has inspired my own approach to this work.

A Few Other Key Resources

- Center for the Study and Prevention of Violence, Institute of Behavioral Science, University of Colorado Boulder (http://www.colorado. edu/cspv/): vigorously reviewed over 1,000 programs that target risk factors before identifying its top 11 "Blueprints-certified" programs
- Public Safety Canada's Crime Prevention Inventory (https://www. publicsafety.gc.ca/cnt/cntrng-crm/crm-prvntn/nvntr/index-en.aspx): the first national database of evidence-based crime prevention programs in Canada, which provides resources to inform approaches to evidence-based crime prevention
- SAMHSA, US Department of Health and Human Services (http:// www.samhsa.gov): aims to alleviate the impact of problematic substance use and mental health issues by providing information on research and a variety of services
- CDC's VetoViolence program (https://vetoviolence.cdc.gov/): offers an interactive and user-friendly website on how to implement evidence-based research in policy making

OTHER EVIDENCE OF THE SOLIDITY OF VIOLENCE PREVENTION SCIENCE

So the science of crime and violence prevention is sound, and we are certain that many crime prevention programs have reduced violent crime more than the CJS. A lot of these proven programs are veritable road maps for stopping crime, and they are just waiting to be followed!

Yet another source of verification for the solid science of violence prevention is consensus reports from organizations, such as The National Academies of Sciences, Engineering, and Medicine. In short, these reports are the culmination of a comprehensive analysis of a particular topic by academic experts from various disciplines with different perspectives. A few pertinent consensus reports include the following:

- *Fairness and Effectiveness in Policing: The Evidence* (2004) by the US National Research Council[18]
- *The Growth of Incarceration in the United States: Exploring Causes and Consequences* (2014) by the US National Research Council[19]
- *Policing Canada in the 21st Century: New Policing for New Challenges* (2015) by the Council of Canadian Academies[20]
- *Proactive Policing: Effects on Crime and Communities* (2018) by The National Academies of Sciences, Engineering, and Medicine[21]
- *Interim Report* (2018) by the Youth Violence Commission[22]

Nongovernmental organizations and individual researchers also have made significant contributions to the research on violence prevention. Some particular work and publications that stand out follow:

- Campbell Collaboration (www.campbellcollaboration.org): An international research network that produces systematic reviews of the effects of social interventions of crime and justice, education, international development and social welfare. Through rigorous approaches to research synthesis, the network improves the knowledge base for decisions on policy and practice.
- *The Costs of Crime and Violence: New Evidence and Insights in Latin America and the Caribbean* (2017), prepared by Laura Jaitman and colleagues for the Inter-American Development Bank.[24]
- *Mapping of Homicide Prevention Programs in Latin America and the Caribbean* (2016), coordinated and researched by Ignacio Cano, Emiliano Rojido, and João Trajano Sento-Sé for the Laboratório de Análise da Violência, State University of Rio de Janeiro.[25]
- *Smart Spending on Citizen Security: Beyond Crime and Punishment* (2018), for Latin America and the Caribbean, prepared by Rodrigo Serrano-Berthet and colleagues for the Inter-American Development Bank.[23]
- *Smarter Crime Control: A Guide to a Safer Future for Citizens, Communities, and Politicians* (2013), my first comprehensive book on what

works for violence prevention. Translations in Spanish and Chinese available.

- *What Works in Reducing Community Violence: A Meta-Review and Field Study for the Northern Triangle* (2016), prepared by Thomas Abt and Christopher Winship for Democracy International, Inc., for review by the US Agency for International Development.[26]

KEY TAKEAWAYS

- Longitudinal studies of child development confirm that adverse childhood experiences (ACEs), such as child abuse, family violence, and poverty, are more common in violent offenders than in the general population.
- Scientific analyses of crime trends and randomized controlled trials (often in the United States or the United Kingdom) have shown that interventions tackling risk factors have prevented or reduced violence.
- In the past fifty years, solid science has shown what prevents violence. This information is available free from portals, such as those of the College of Policing in England and Wales, the US National Institute of Justice of the US Department of Justice, and the WHO.
- Information on various violence prevention portals may need to be interpreted by violence prevention experts to be understandable by decision makers and others interested in ending violent crime.
- More than 60 percent of solutions identified as "effective" on the US Department of Justice portal are geared toward youth services, family and early childhood, schooling, and health.
- Benefit–cost analyses by the Washington State Institute for Public Policy confirm that violence prevention strategies result in significant savings to victims and the CJS.
- CrimeSolutions.gov has shown some proactive policing projects and ways of protecting potential victims to be effective.
- Consensus reports by experts call out the costs and consequences of incarceration but confirm reductions in crime from social development, proactive policing, and diverting social problems away from the police.

3

SMARTER USE
OF POLICE AND PRISONS

Being Proactive and Lightening the Load

> Give the cops fewer things to do, and reallocate the money accordingly.
>
> —Alex Vitale, from *The End of Policing*

The standard criminal justice system is a significant industry today, employing nearly two million persons in the United States alone. It often makes the news because of some horrific event, the drama of a court case, or possibly the unfortunate death of a suspect at the hands of the police.

Most politicians react to crime, particularly when it is in headlines, by asking their police chief for solutions and, sometimes, by pumping more money into policing and incarceration. The science of violence prevention—with its solid evidence of what works and what does not work in policing and incarceration today—is rarely part of the political debate or the media stories. As Barry Friedman in a recent *Washington Post* article pointed out, "We spend $100 billion on policing. We have no idea what works. Police are more likely to adopt new technology because another department has it [rather] than because of reasoned cost–benefit analysis."[1] (I would add, whether it ends homicides or rapes.) Yet, as noted in chapter 2, solid violence prevention science on what works in policing and incarceration is readily available from various portals and national science reports, although, I must admit, some of those portals and reports are not very general-public or politician friendly. (We have work to do there, starting with this book.)

Nonetheless, one of the insights that violence prevention science offers is that numbers of police do not determine the rates of crime, unless you withdraw them completely. England and Wales, for example, decreased the number of police by 22 percent through attrition and retirement without any direct impact on crime rates. So reacting to crime by spending more on policing is plain just not smart. But a reverse variation of this may be true because some argue rightly that the decline in crime rates may justify fewer police.[2] In the introduction, I made the comparison between Chicago in the United States and Toronto in Canada because it reinforces this argument. Both cities have populations close to 2.8 million, Chicago slightly less and Toronto slightly more. Chicago has 13,000 police officers and encouragement to increase this number.[3] Toronto has 5,200 police officers and pressure to decrease that number.[4] Chicago had more than 650 homicides in 2017.[5] Toronto had fewer than 65 in 2017.[6] Yes, there are other explanations for the lower crime rate in Toronto, but these dramatically different statistics emphasize there is a lot more to ending violent crime than numbers of police.

The same goes for incarceration, particularly in the United States. That country spends $87 billion a year to incarcerate criminals, a rate per capita that is five times that of England and Wales and six times that of Canada—money spent without any evidence that jails and prisons reduce rates of violent crime in any significant way. They do not.

THE NUMBERS

To explore why being smart on crime means spending less on the standard criminal justice system (CJS), let's take a look at the numbers related to today's CJS in a few countries. In policing, the United States alone employs more than 700,000 sworn officers and 200,000 civilian staff at an annual cost of $135 billion.[7] Some 75 percent of this component of the US multi-billion-dollar CJS industry is paid for out of municipal taxes.[8] The number of police officers per capita in Canada, England and Wales, and the United States is 200, 250, and 230, respectively, per 100,000 population.[9] In Canada, police numbers have not grown significantly, though salaries have. In fact, Canadian policing expenditures from 2000 to 2010 doubled—representing a 43 percent growth over inflation.[10] In Mexico, one report pins the number of police officers at a rate of 450 per 100,0000 population, close to double the rate for the United States but with much lower income.[11] In Mexico, the expenditures grew 61 percent from 2008 to 2015.[12] But salaries are still very low in Mexico, and commentators question whether the salary is sufficient and the officers are adequately trained.[13]

Like policing, incarceration also is a significant industry, although the relative size varies from country to country. In the United States, jails and prisons employ 687,000 prison guards, cost over $87 billion annually, and incarcerate 2.2 million offenders on an average day. This is a rate close to 655 persons incarcerated per 100,000 people and accounts for about 20 percent of all people incarcerated in the world. As we saw in figure 1.1, this rate, proportionate to population, far exceeds the rates for Canada, Mexico, and England and Wales, which are closer to the world average of 150 per 100,000. Their rates are 114, 141, and 176, respectively.[14]

The sad irony is that spending more on law enforcement has not solved the problems. If it did, high crime cities in the United States would fare better than cities in Canada or England. However, as we will see in later chapters in part II, spending more on the standard CJS—police, security, incarceration, and courts—does not even come close to the effectiveness of investing in upstream social preventive programs to stop violence, particularly when combined with proactive or smart policing.

Granted, the CJS insidiously is too often the response to many problems for which it should not be. Brooklyn College professor Alex Vitale, in his book *The End of Policing*, stresses that policing has accepted many problems for which policing is not appropriate, societal issues that governments are not adequately funding. For example, too often, frontline police officers responding to 911 calls must deal with homelessness, mental illness, and addictions.[15] Police may be the go-to for a variety of reasons:

- They are available 24/7, whereas most mental health professionals and organizations are not.
- Politicians may have overlooked at budget time the need to tackle the roots and causes of violence by investing in the prevention of mental illness, homelessness, drug addiction, and more.
- The special interests of those working in criminal justice have been able to win more funds for their cause.
- Some politicians, unlike the opinion polls or the evidence, still believe that arrest and prison time is the solution to crime.[16]

In fact, the reason the CJS still seems mistakenly to many to be the silver bullet for violence in our communities may be a combination of all the above.

In addition to police, courts, and incarceration, people also protect themselves against potential offenders through various other strategies. One such strategy is using private security. Despite the increases in spending and numbers in the CJS, the number of persons working in private security has increased rapidly in the past decades.[17] Today, US Department of Labor Statistics identify 1.1 million persons in the private security business, which is more than the number of sworn police officers.[18] In fact, the number of private security guards is estimated to be expanding by 6 percent per year. This means that the private security industry doubles its size every ten years and will increase its importance much faster than public policing. Generally, private security is a service for the rich who want to pay for more security than can be provided by the public police.[19] However, many more people in Mexico than in Canada or England and Wales use private security to protect their homes and businesses.

Yet one more way people protect themselves today is called "situational crime prevention." The classic methods include spending money for installing locked fencing around a house or reinforcing the windows in homes. Other strategies include using cameras and technology that can lead to detection and potentially the arrest of an offender by the police. In general, situational crime prevention protects potential victims by making crime harder to commit, less rewarding, or more likely to lead to arrest.

STANDARD POLICING AND INCARCERATION: A COSTLY WAY TO STOP VIOLENT CRIME

The standard ways of policing and criminal justice do provide some protections from violent crime, at least until smarter ways have been put in place. In fact, when policing is absent, as occurs temporarily when police go on strike, property and violent crime increases in the short term.[20] Although police strikes are rare because governments have prohibited them, a recent police strike in a Brazilian city vividly reminded us what can possibly happen. During that strike, there was a sixfold increase in homicides and widespread looting of stores until the army and federal police moved in.[21]

Policing Reacting to 911

Policing itself has changed significantly over the past five decades. As we have just seen, because of increased governmental funding of police, the number of police officers has increased, some officers are better paid (and so less corruptible), and there has been money for improved training as well as modern equipment. Police are now equipped with new technologies, such as cell phones, computer analysis, DNA analysis, and tasers. Big data is leading to algorithms used to predict where and when offenders are likely to commit an offense, close to what we see in the action detective movie thriller *Minority Report*. The "war on drugs" and then terrorism has fostered even quasi-military technology, such as personnel carriers with SWAT teams and more. And cybercrime is creating a new set of challenges.

Much of the standard police budget today, however, goes to responding to 911 calls. In fact, the National Research Council in 2004 showed that, in the United States, two-thirds of police dollars go to patrols responding after a crime has occurred.[22] This reality can be traced to an influential experiment in the early 1970s. Prior to the experiment, preventive patrols throughout communities were standard practice. The experiment involved Kansas City police increasing preventive patrols in some areas and reducing them in others. The results confirmed no change in crime rates or public confidence in policing when preventive patrols were employed. In other words, preventive policing did nothing to deter crime in Kansas City.[23] It so happens that the timing of this experiment coincided with the increasingly widespread use of cars and the introduction and rapid spread of 911 as the North American emergency telephone number. Thus, after news of the Kansas City experiment spread, policing began ever so slowly to shift its resources from preventive policing to responding to 911 calls *after* a crime had taken place.

In turn, this significant shift in approach to policing has separated police from the communities where they enforce laws. So, despite the infusion of funds and technology, fewer victims of crime are reporting to police. Further, police today are making fewer arrests proportionate to the crimes brought to their attention, particularly for homicide.[24]

Policing Budgets and Crime

While policy makers debate the impact of adding or subtracting additional police officers, expert commissions generally conclude that numbers of police are not closely related to crime levels.[25] Comparing numbers of police per capita with crime rates between affluent countries also does not show any correlation. In addition, per capita expenditures on policing vary widely among cities. One study of twelve major US cities showed a variation from $772 in Baltimore and $537 in Chicago (which have high homicide rates) to $581 in New York and $381 in Los Angeles (which have moderate homicide rates).[26] These statistics show that more crime exists with more police and not the reverse.

If one looks at England and Wales, budgets for policing from local and national sources have declined by 18 percent since 2010, resulting in a 19 percent reduction in the number of police per capita and a 22 percent reduction in total staff per capita.[27] Most of these cuts happened in the first two years of a broad government austerity program to cut spending on all government services, not just the police.[28] It is difficult to see any significant impact of these police cuts on crime rates because recorded crime continued to decline in the years of the cuts and victimization survey data showed an even steadier decline. There has been, however, a slight rebound in crime in 2016 and 2017, although the rates fall short of those from around the peak in 2007. In the city of London, for example, knife crime increased in 2017 and 2018, but that is unlikely related to police staffing. Nonetheless, London continues to be a city with much lower homicide rates than cities such as New York City or even Toronto.[29]

Looking at Mexico, a 61 percent increase in expenditures since 2007 has done little to slow down inflation in homicide rates. While expenditures might have been better spent on targeted social development, one of the reasons for the high homicide rates is because police officers and courts are not reducing impunity, in major part because of inadequate wages, selection, and training.[30]

Incapacitation

The contribution of standard CJS—arrest and deter—to stopping violent crime is based on two logics. The first is called "incapacitation" and refers to the reduction in crime when an offender is incarcerated because he has been arrested by police, sentenced by the courts, and held behind bars by corrections. During the time of incarceration, the prisoner is unable to commit offenses and is, thus, "incapacitated." The second logic is called "deterrence," which I will explore after incapacitation.

The United States has provided an extraordinary test of the incapacitation effect. Up to 1965, approximately 200 persons were behind bars for every 100,000 in the total population.[31] This was already a much higher rate than that of other affluent democracies at the time. Even so, from 1965 to 1990, this rate increased to 700 per 100,000, or 2.2 million persons behind bars.[32] During those two and a half decades, most indicators of crime rates increased. Yet, in the period from 1990 to today, the rate of incarceration in the United States has stayed steady at this level of hyper- or mass incarceration while crime rates have generally declined. Note that crime rates also declined in other countries, such as Canada, which did not increase their rates of incarceration, and crime rates also declined in England and Wales, where incarceration rates increased but only to 145 per 100,000, about 20 percent of the US rate.[33]

In 2016, the National Academies of Sciences, Engineering, and Medicine completed a milestone report on the causes and consequences of the growth of incarceration in the United States.[34] The report suggests that incapacitation, or the number of offenders behind bars, has some effect on crime reduction, but it is small and mostly in the first few years of a young man's sentence. Typical persistent offenders are committing many offenses when they are in the fifteen- to twenty-five-year-age range; after that, their offending becomes less frequent. One study suggests that a 25 percent increase in the rate of incarceration accounts for a mere 2 percent decline in crime rates.[35]

This does not mean that incapacitation is the best choice for dealing with crime because a 25 percent increase in incarceration in the United States would cost more than $20 billion to taxpayers and do significant harm to the communities to which the prisoners return. We shall see in later chapters that there are alternative ways to stop violent crime that not only cost significantly less to taxpayers, but they also have fewer negative consequences and many positives—including financial ones—for the offenders and their families and communities.

More generally, US rates of incarceration show a tendency for incarceration use to follow crime rates rather than the opposite. For the United States overall, there were 5.5 homicides per 100,000 people in 2016, with an average rate of incarceration (excluding federal prisoners) of 580 per 100,000. Figure 3.1 shows the extent to which rates of incarceration are higher in US states with higher rates of homicide. But the higher the murder rate, the higher the rate of incarceration, not the reverse.

Deterrence

The contribution of the "deterrent effect" to crime reduction is real but much more nuanced than many realize. Many people not living disadvantaged lives think about deterrence through the lens of how the threat of punishment influences their driving behavior. Drivers change their behavior to avoid penalties that are typically annoying but affordable fines, so they do not speed if they think they are going to be caught. Social science research confirms this reality, but not just for driving. When looking at the deterrent effect of prison sentences on potential property or violent offenders,

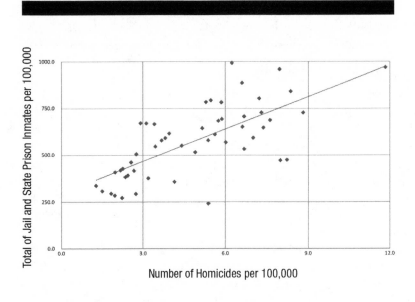

Number of Homicides per 100,000

See appendix for sources.

Figure 3.I.   Plot of Rates of Incarceration vs. Homicide for US States

it is the *perception of the certainty of apprehension or detection* that is the important deterrent, not the severity of the penalty.[36] Consistent with this, when many offenders are not getting arrested and many are acquitted in the courts—high levels of impunity—as in Mexico, violent crime rises seemingly uncontrollably.

Likewise, heavy and inhumane penalties have little perceivable impact on reducing violence. As noted earlier, in 2010, the England and Wales government began reducing spending across most departments, including prisons (so significantly cutting the number of prison staff).[37] By 2017, the budget for prisons had been reduced by 5 percent, but the flow of prisoners had not been cut.[38] The result, not surprisingly, has been severe overcrowding, cuts in positive programming, inhumane prison conditions, and riots in prisons in England and Wales.[39] With prison conditions at their worst, crime rates in London have been rising modestly from 2015 to 2017, indicating that severity of punishment is not a significant deterrent.

As further evidence of how little severe punishment has to do with curtailing violence, research shows no increase in crime rates in countries where prison populations have been significantly reduced. The Netherlands, for instance, has reduced its rate of incarceration per 100,000 from 125 in 2006 to 76 in 2016; at the same time, its crime rate went down, and more offenders were diverted from the system. As I mentioned in the introduction, their decline in incarceration is so great that the Dutch are closing prisons *for their prisoners*, but they are paying their corrections staff to guard prisoners from Belgium and Norway, thereby making money for Dutch taxpayers. A win-win!

Also consider New York City. In the 1990s, New York City had 22,000 prisoners in its city jails. Twenty years later, the mayor of New York plans to shut down Rikers Island, its main jail complex, and build a modern prison for only 5,000 inmates.[40] New York City is able to do this in part because its crime rate has plummeted, likely because of successful social and economic policies.[41] One additional reason for the decline in the jail population is because police have chosen to use misdemeanor charges or summary offenses, which have short maximum jail time, instead of felonies or indictable offenses, which have much longer prison time, thus stopping judges from overfilling the jails.[42]

Despite an accumulation of research and efforts to make corrections "correct," the best corrections projects have achieved little. The classic indicator of "failure" for a person released from a prison is whether he or she commits another offense. This relapse into criminal behavior is termed "recidivism" and is measured by whether the person gets rearrested. Some correctional programs achieve reductions in the likelihood of rearrest, but few do better than 25 percent.[43]

Interestingly, recidivism rates from state prisons have been declining in the United States with the decline in rates of crime.[44] However, one of the more extraordinary indictments of incarceration as a successful way to end violent crime is a US government study of what happens to men released from state prisons. This study followed a sample of 400,000 prisoners for nine years after their release from prisons in thirty states and showed that they accumulated two million new arrests. Some 44 percent of the prisoners were rearrested at least once in their first year, and 83 percent had been rearrested at least once by the end of nine years.[45] Two-thirds had been rearrested within three years. This was no surprise to me. My own research through Ford Foundation grants in the 1970s in Canada had shown the same pattern. Ultimately, the pattern can be explained mostly by the adverse experiences lived by these men before they were placed behind bars and by the challenges inherent in transitioning from prison to free society.

One new initiative intended "to cut spending and reinvest savings in practices that have been empirically shown to improve safety and [yet] hold offenders accountable"[46] is "justice reinvestment." In short, the idea of this data-driven approach is to substitute community programs for prison time to save the costs of incarceration. It is now being used in some way in thirty-five US states, where some reductions in prison use coincide with declining crime rates.[47] It is not yet clear whether it is the selection of inmates who are less likely to recidivate that contributes to the apparently lower arrest rates, but either way, justice reinvestment saves money and reduces the negative consequences on offenders' communities.

The bottom line is, for violence to end, both policing and incarceration must be treated like a scarce resource, and budgets must control how many prisoners can be held at any given time.

PROACTIVE POLICING AS A MEANS TO STOPPING VIOLENCE

Shifting law enforcement from reactive crime control to smart prevention is not easy. Police officers are constrained to respond to priority and urgent 911 calls and to a range of other problems outside the crime domain. That is, when decision makers choose not to address community issues such as mental illness, homelessness, and substance abuse, police become the last resort too often. With so much of police time spent *reacting* to crime, particularly to 911 calls, research shows that law enforcement resources are not going to *prevent* crime in the first place.

I do not intend to imply that police around the world have completely fallen short of smart innovations that help keep our communities and citizens safe. A number of police services and individual officers have undertaken their own programs and practices to overcome the limitations of standard policing and implement effective solutions, and some of these have been scientifically evaluated. These new approaches to policing are generally called "proactive" or "problem-oriented" policing because they strive to get upstream of crime before it occurs rather than react to it after it happens. Most of these proactive efforts focus on problem places, problem people, repeat offenders, and repeat victims and are grouped under headings such as "focused deterrence," "hot spot policing," and "stop and frisk" (when used carefully).[48] I will discuss these industry-specific strategies in the remainder of this section as well as cover what we know about whether the actions are, in reality, effective solutions to ending crime.

The state-of-the-art report on "proactive policing" comes from the US National Academies of Sciences, Engineering, and Medicine. Utilizing exceptional talent and solid violence prevention research, this 2017 report demonstrates that many proactive policing programs have been "somewhat effective," at least in the short term, though rarely sustained.[49]

NAME	EXAMPLE	RANGE OF REDUCTIONS*	COMMENT ON EVIDENCE
Reorient Policing to be Proactive and Problem Solving			
Focused Deterrence	Focusing on likely offenders to increase deterrence using call-in and prosecution, as in ending gun violence (Boston)	27 to 63%	Strong across cities for 3 years, enhanced by social services
Hot Spots Policing	Identifying hot spots of high crime rates and focusing police to suppress the problem, as in foot patrols (Philadelphia)	6 to 77%	Strong in hot spot for up to 1 year
Stop and Frisk	Stopping people in high crime areas with reasonable suspicion and frisking, as for weapons (New York City)	2 to 5%	Weak and mixed evidence in problem area for up to 1 year, controversial
Use Situational Crime Prevention and Avoid Overuse of Policing			
Situational Crime Prevention	Designing ways to make crime harder, riskier, or less attractive, as in burglary repeat victimization reduction (Kirkholt)	50 to 70%	Large city-wide reductions possible and $4 return when done well
Diversion	Diverting people of elevated risk to treatment for mental health issues or substance abuse, to schools for life-skills training, and more, as in a hub (Prince Albert)	15 to 37%	Promising across city for 5 years
Reducing Penalties	Using cautioning, fines, or decriminalization, as in legalizing drugs like cannabis for personal use (Colorado)	40 to 80%	Promising across state for 5 years

* It is not possible to identify one percentage from the national science reports or the portals, so a range is used to give a general idea of the %. Most of these actions achieve a reduction close to 33%, if implemented well.
See appendix for sources.

Figure 3.2. Effective Solutions Using Proactive or Reduced Policing

Before delving into the specifics of proactive and problem-solving policing, take a few minutes to review figure 3.2. This chart highlights examples of proactive policing and situational crime prevention. I have chosen to feature "focused deterrence," "hot spot policing," and "stop and frisk" as the three proactive policing strategies because they were showcased in the National Academies of Sciences, Engineering, and Medicine report, though there are other similar ones I could have used. My aim with that section of the chart is to help interested citizens or politicians identify some ways policing can be more proactive about reducing violent crime and to spark enough interest that readers will look deeper into the strategies. The second part of the chart, on situational crime prevention, diversion, and decriminalization, features effective ways to reduce the workload on police.

Focused Deterrence/Person-Focused Policing

In 2018, the US attorney general claimed that "focused deterrence" was a significant way of reducing violent crime.[50] The evidence supports this claim. The idea of focused deterrence is to concentrate police action on a group of people believed to be likely to commit crime. It is a proactive policing tactic that increases the perception that offending behavior will be met with certain and severe punishment.

Focused deterrence's best-known application is its use in relation to young men believed by the police to be carrying and using weapons. The young men on the police list are invited to attend a forum or "call in," usually to a central location, during which the police (and sometimes prosecutors) warn the men that police action is going to be focused on them, that there is going to be a crackdown. This is usually followed by police making more gun-related arrests and prosecutors arguing for longer sentences. The success of this strategy is impressive, with many focused deterrence projects demonstrating around 33 percent reduction in crime and a range from 27 to 63 percent reduction in gun violence specifically.[51]

We know the effectiveness of focused deterrence because it has been the subject of two meta-analyses—one published in 2012 and the second, more extensive one published in 2018.[52] What these meta-analyses show is that focused deterrence reduces gun violence, at least in the short term, and that reduction may last a few years. But we also learned from the meta-analyses that the effectiveness of focused deterrence projects is generally not sustained longer than the first few years.

The practice of focused deterrence became popular in the 1990s, after its use, in combination with spending on focused social services, was shown to reduce shootings and homicides by more than 60 percent in Boston. Since that time, its use has been encouraged by the National Network for Safe Communities as a way to stop urban gun violence.[53] The National Network proposes its use in combination with social services and is able to present a significant list of cities where large reductions have been achieved.[54]

But focused deterrence without social services or other efforts to change offending behavior has not always been easy sailing. The success in Boston inspired pilots in ten other cities under the banner of the Strategic Approaches to Community Safety Initiative (SACSI) around 2000. Before the results of the SACSI had come in—they were later shown to be mixed— the US government launched Project Safe Neighborhood as primarily a focused deterrence action, but *without* the social services. The result was a very disappointing overall reduction in crime of a mere 4 percent.[55] However, there was an exception, with a particularly successful project in one Chicago district that achieved a 33 percent reduction in crime. This outlier had supplemented the focused deterrence initiative with strategies to change offender attitudes.[56] Unfortunately, a subsequent assessment of the Chicago project shows that the effects did not last.[57] Even the Boston example from the 1990s did not last and had to be repeated almost ten years later.[58]

It is interesting to note, in returning for a minute to the meta-analyses on focused deterrence discussed earlier, those researchers did not identify the contribution of social services or the joint strategy to the effectiveness of the proactive policing efforts they studied. Because focused deterrence is often implemented in combination with new, targeted social programs, it is unclear how much of the reductions over the immediate years after the launching of focused deterrence projects is actually due to the social services. I will discuss such social services in more detail when I address citywide success stories in chapter 9. Undoubtedly, however, the combination of this proactive policing tactic with targeted social services managed by a permanent crime reduction unit, such as in Glasgow, is much more effective in ending violent crime than proactive policing on its own.

Problem-Oriented Policing

In problem-oriented policing, police services or officers begin each case with an analysis of the problem at hand. Their ultimate aim is to prevent crime. To accomplish their goals, they innovate proactive policing tactics and may also engage the courts or correction systems in targeting offenders and youth in a way that uses punishment as a deterrent.

Problem-oriented policing started in the 1970s but became a national program in the mid-1990s, when the US Department of Justice established the Center for Problem-Oriented Policing (POP Center). As noted in chapter 2, its website (http://www.popcenter.org) is the go-to portal on both problem-oriented policing and situational crime prevention. On the website, we can find ways to tackle different crime problems but not strong measures of outcomes. Problem-oriented policing is also featured on the portal of the College for Policing in England and Wales. That portal highlights some specific problem-oriented policing actions that have worked, which relate to property crime. On the other hand, CrimeSolutions.gov gives the practice of problem-oriented policing a lesser rating of only "promising."[59]

It is valuable that policing innovations focused on proactively tackling crime problems have been evaluated. Every bit of information takes us one step closer to knowing what effective solutions are for reducing and finally ending violence. Unfortunately, we still know very little about whether proactive or problem-oriented policing strategies have saved taxes. That would be helpful as we search for cost-effective ways to support the transformation of police from being reactive to preventive.

Hot Spot/Problem-Place Policing

Recall we discussed the 2017 report from the US National Academies of Sciences, Engineering, and Medicine on proactive policing. Another main contribution of that landmark report is that it confirms what many police executives have known for a long time and researchers have been exploring since the 1980s: that many of the most frequent crimes, most persistent offenders, and most often victimized people are concentrated in a limited number of areas. One analysis in Minneapolis showed that 3.5 percent of the addresses in the city accounted for 50 percent of their 911 calls.[60] It makes sense, therefore, to concentrate proactively on the "problem places" to reduce crime. In fact, there are now so many examples of the problem-place approach to policing that criminologists Anthony Braga and David Weisburd wrote a book on the subject, *Policing Problem Places: Crime Hot Spots and Effective Prevention*.

When the research about the impact of problem-place policing began to surface a few decades ago, police services began to target so-called hot spots with increased patrols. These efforts showed modest reductions in crime. As such experiments were taking place, police departments also began to adopt mapping technology—including CompStat, which adds police accountability—which made it easy to identify hot spots. Over the course of time, several problem-place policing projects have been evaluated and show some crime reduction. The evaluations, however, tend to focus on the short term and on projects in limited areas rather than on citywide efforts, for which the most important payoffs would occur.

Hot spot strategies typically commence with some type of analysis to determine the causes or risk factors for the high crime rates. For instance, one project in Jersey City involved efforts to reduce crime specifically in public housing projects. Following a rudimentary analysis, three strategies were identified to address the problem: stepping up arrests in public areas, enhancing situational crime prevention by installing better lighting in public areas and stopping public phones from receiving calls (for drug deals), and having social services reach out to families in difficulty.[61]

CrimeSolutions.gov identifies 34 problem-place practices as effective and 97 as promising.[62] In a well-known project in Lowell, Massachusetts, where those affected by a hot spot project were compared with those in similar areas without the project, an evaluation showed a 14 percent reduction in calls for service—fewer 911 calls—and an impressive 42 percent lower rate for robberies between the project and the comparison groups.[63] The 2017 report from the National Academies of Sciences, Engineering, and Medicine also confirms the statistical significance of reductions in many hot spot or problem-place projects, including many focused on prostitution and drug markets. The report, however, stresses that the effects are short term and do not displace crime. It is difficult, in fact, to get a reliable estimate of the range of reductions, so for figure 3.2, I used a wide range of 12 percent to 77 percent for hot spot policing, based on an example in the report.[64]

Interestingly, new applications for hot spot policing have coincided with new technologies. For example, CCTV, when used with dedicated patrols, has reduced violent crime by more than 40 percent.[65] ShotSpotter can use the same tactic to identify where a firearm has been discharged.[66] In Chicago, dedicated analysts using the new technology have seen some initial reductions, but scientific evidence of the long-term effectiveness of such efforts is still to come.[67]

Stop and Frisk/Person-Focused Policing

Stop and frisk is a tactic used by many large law enforcement agencies, generally in problem places identified through problem analysis. It involves officers targeting an individual or set of individuals deemed to be suspicious and then frisking them. For example, stop and frisk has been an important tool in combating the carrying of handguns by young men involved in gang lifestyles.

Stop and frisk is a person-focused policing strategy. CrimeSolutions. gov identifies 16 person-focused policing strategies as effective and 42 as promising.[68] For example, the Philadelphia Policing Tactics Experiment focused on repeat violent offenders operating in neighborhoods with high violent crime rates. The results of the experiment showed an impressive 42 percent reduction in violent crime.[69] In Kansas City, one person-focused law enforcement effort increased the number of guns seized by 65 percent and achieved a 49 percent decrease in gun crime rates.[70]

Nonetheless, major evaluations of the effectiveness of stop and frisk have been completed on a large scale. The results relating to its use in New York City were mixed.[71] After the strategy was cut back because of concerns about racial profiling, the New York City crime rate has continued to decline, providing strong evidence that stop and frisk is not a necessary tactic for crime reduction. In London, a similar tactic showed only marginally lower crime rates.[72] It seems person-focused policing stop and frisk is not necessarily any more effective than other proactive policing or social service strategies.

Not All Programs Are Created Equal

Be aware, though: labeling programs as "preventive" does not *prove* they stop violent crime. DARE is one of the most popular programs in schools across North America. Developed by the Los Angeles Police Department in collaboration with the city's school board, the program originally focused on emboldening kids to resist drugs. At one point, it was in 75 percent of US high schools. Unfortunately, evaluations of its efficacy showed that it did not stop drug abuse. Now, DARE's efforts focus on helping kids to make good decisions.[73] Several other programs have not been confirmed through evaluation to be successful at violence prevention. These include Scared Straight, School Resource Officers, and Neighborhood Watch.

Situational Crime Prevention

Situational crime prevention aims to lower the level of opportunity to commit crime, increase the risk of being arrested, or eliminate or reduce any benefits to the offender. The strategy fits under the category of being problem oriented but not only for policing. It often relies on environmental design, increased use of technology, or targeting specific criminal activity through housing design, architecture, engineering, surveillance, or lighting. Think locks, safer crosswalks, well-lit parking structures, visible alarms, and proper street lighting. Situational crime prevention also includes actions to help potential victims take more effective precautions.

One example of a successful implementation of situational crime prevention comes from the late 1980s. The city of Kirkholt in the United Kingdom removed opportunities and motivations to commit burglary by developing a program similar to Seattle's *original* community crime prevention program, which reduced burglary by 50 percent. Officials in Kirkholt, overwhelmed with home break-ins, analyzed what was going on—that many of the situations involved repeat victimization—and took action. Learning that cash was the most stolen, they focused efforts on potential victims and got them to take precautions, such as installing locks on windows and doors and engaging the watchful eyes of neighbors. They also focused attention on persistent offenders. The result was a program that worked (particularly with persistent offenders and repeat victims) to achieve a 75 percent reduction in break-ins over a four-year period. They demonstrated the equivalent of four dollars in savings in police time alone for each dollar spent on the program.[74]

Another example of situational crime prevention was an effort focused on restoring vacant lots in cities, such as removing trash and debris, grading the land, planting new grass and trees to create a parklike setting, and maintaining the renovated space. This intervention was shown to be highly cost effective, with initial costs averaging about five dollars per square meter and maintenance averaging fifty cents per square meter thereafter. Perhaps more importantly, in a scientific evaluation, participants living near the treated vacant lots reported a 58 percent reduction in safety concerns, a 76 percent increase in the use of outside spaces for relaxing and socializing, and a 29 percent decrease in gun violence in the area. With 15 percent of the land in US cities deemed vacant or abandoned, similar situational crime prevention efforts would reap significant rewards nationwide.[75]

POLICING: NOT A SOLUTION TO HOMELESSNESS, MENTAL ILLNESS, OR DRUG ADDICTION

Like the introduction of 911 changed policing, so too have many other events and developments changed what policing is today. One major contributor to what the institution of policing has become was the emptying of mental hospitals in the 1980s. Since then, many people with mental illness in our communities in our affluent democracies have become the subject of 911 calls and end up being arrested and incarcerated. Local jails have become the institutions housing the largest number of mentally ill persons. The three largest facilities holding the mentally ill in the United States are jails.[76]

In addition, homelessness and vagrancy are no longer status offenses but lead to people being charged with specific offenses. All too often, those vulnerable individuals are part of a revolving door of being released and then rearrested for similar offenses. This sad situation costs taxpayers small amounts for each occurrence; over a decade or more, the cost is huge. The English-born Canadian journalist and author Malcolm Gladwell highlighted this reality in his famous 2006 *New Yorker* article on "Million-Dollar Murray," a homeless alcoholic in Reno, Nevada, who cost the CJS over a million dollars.[77] The same story could be written about other homeless, mentally ill, alcoholic, and drug-addicted people.

Much of the problem is that calling 911 makes it easy for citizens to get emergency assistance, but because of their 24/7 availability, police are the main responders, no matter the degree or type of emergency. Without investment in other specific categories of response, police departments are overtaxed as they attempt to address issues related to mentally ill and homeless people. Despite valiant efforts, the evidence shows that police are largely ineffective in handling such situations. Plus, they are expensive. Worse still, politicians have continued to use policing, courts, and corrections to cope with other problems, including the sex trade, immigration, and illicit drugs.[78] In Canada, expenditures on policing doubled from 2000 to 2015, whereas there is no evidence of increasing expenditures on mental health and housing.

ARREST AND INCARCERATION HARMS OFFENDERS

At best, an arrest may do little harm. Rich and powerful people generally are not likely to be arrested for crimes. But poor people of color living in disadvantaged circumstances, oh, how they can be affected by standard police actions! Consider the close to 1,000 people who are killed by police in the United States each year.[79] In her book, *The New Jim Crow*, Michelle Alexander demonstrates the extent to which police killings are racially biased.[80] In addition, the National Academies of Sciences, Engineering, and Medicine[81] stresses that penal policies in the United States fall heavily on the poor, Blacks, and Hispanics. They are even offered fewer rehabilitative or positive programs. In addition, the families of incarcerated men have problems with keeping housing, and behavioral problems run rampant among their children, who, at 2.1 million, number as many as the inmates.[82]

Though the rhetoric of corrections talks about rehabilitation, in practice, corrections does very little to correct. Rather, arrest and incarceration usually make rehabilitation harder. For example, though prisoners may improve their school educational level, they rarely learn a skill that can be used after release to get a job or maintain a family relationship. They also leave jail without any useable work experience or references. Plus, having a criminal record makes getting a job extremely difficult. The rehabilitation rhetoric also may include cognitive behavioral therapy but, despite its affordability and effectiveness, is the exception not the rule.

In effect, upon release, prisoners have difficulty getting jobs, have lower incomes, and return to communities plagued by joblessness, family breakdown, neighborhood disadvantage, substance abuse, and continued violence. And this comes at a significant financial cost to taxpayers. In addition, the investment in a prisoner's arrest and incarceration takes potential funds away from the prevention agenda discussed in the previous chapter, with more about it to come. Consider that some law enforcement strategies target the possession and low-level trafficking of marijuana, whereby contributing both to taxpayer costs as well as to racial bias in the courts and correctional systems, without accomplishing much when it comes to reducing harm to victims. In sum, arrest and incarceration are not investments in the future of the young offenders. The takeaway point of "first, do no harm" is that, in certain cases, it may be better to do nothing rather than to intervene and potentially cause more harm than good.

Diversion from Police to Social Services

A solution to this difficult dilemma includes the implementation of projects that divert offenders from the police and CJS in order to avoid charges or arrest. Staff from such projects might follow along on a 911 call and divert the person in conflict with the law to a more appropriate service such as mental health counseling, restorative justice measures, or community-based sanctions. Police officers may also decide to use lesser charges. That is, law enforcement can choose more appropriate and humane restitution and reduce costs to taxpayers by using the least serious penalty that is still effective; in many cases, this will mean using misdemeanor charges, which are effective at stopping crime and are a lot more cost effective than felony convictions.[83]

A good example of responding in a new light to problems that come to the attention of the police can be found in Ontario, Canada. Police have pioneered hubs where the frontline workers from agencies dealing with such things as policing, mental health, alcoholism, and homelessness work together to triage cases to the appropriate agency, thereby reducing some of the unnecessary and ill-equipped work on police. This mindful approach to policing mitigates elevated risk situations, reduces identified risks, and promotes and maintains community safety and well-being.

Let's consider an example of dealing with elevated risk situations by the effective approach of diversion from policing to social and other services. Starting with pioneering innovations in Prince Albert, Saskatchewan, most Canadian provinces now have "hubs" in many municipalities. These hubs share information on individuals and on redirecting them, particularly from policing, to more appropriate social and other nonpolice services. Members of these hub services meet weekly to determine solutions to elevated risk situations and to coordinate a response, such as referring clients to appropriate services, such as mental health treatment, housing agencies, counseling services, or learning centers.

One evaluation of the Prince Albert model confirms some reduction in crime and savings to the CJS.[84] Of note is that the coordinating body of the Prince Albert project was more than a hub; its policy board, called a Center of Responsibility (COR), was made up of leaders from key sectors, similar to the boards in comprehensive community safety models, which foster better allocation of resources. Other evaluations of outcomes from similar diversion-from-police projects do not yet exist. We do know, though, that most do not have a COR, which has been shown to be extremely valuable in ensuring success of violence prevention efforts, as we will see in chapter 8.

Overpolicing

There are several ways to avoid overusing police and incarceration. I have already mentioned using misdemeanors instead of felonies as well as justice reinvestment. The British use "cautioning" when an offender admits the offense and is cautioned in a recorded warning by the police. Another strategy, restorative justice, will be discussed in chapter 6.

One controversial but important issue when it comes to avoiding overpolicing is the decriminalization of drugs, a policy recommended by the Global Commission on Drugs.[85] Studies of the impact of laws to allow medical use of marijuana in US states bordering on Mexico show reductions in violent crime, including a 40 percent reduction in homicides related to drug trade.[86] Early findings on legalization of marijuana in Colorado show a 50 percent reduction in marijuana possession arrests. Furthermore, since voters in several US states have legalized marijuana for adult use, millions of dollars have been saved. In addition, arrests for possession, cultivation, and distribution have plummeted, thus preventing the criminalization of thousands of people.[87]

KEY TAKEAWAYS

- Politicians, police departments, and correctional agencies need to take research-based knowledge into account and transform how policing and incarceration are used.
- The number of people employed in standard policing and incarceration can be reduced significantly without an increase in violent crime.
- Shifting police resources from standard to proven proactive policing, such as focused deterrence and hot spot policing, has the potential to reduce violent crime, at least in the short term. Focused deterrence *as part of sustained partnership with social services* will be shown in chapter 9 to be even more effective.
- Increased use of situational crime prevention and third-party policing are proven to be effective, cost effective, and sustained over time.
- Adequately funding agencies serving the mentally ill, homeless, drug addicted, and victims of sex trafficking would reduce the demand for policing as a service of last resort.
- Establishing a citywide or community-wide hub that diverts 911 calls (to which a police patrol is normally dispatched) to an agency appropriate to the problem would reduce demand for police services.
- Arrest and jail do significant harm to offenders and their communities, so these costs also must be weighed with reductions in harm to victims and costs to taxpayers when choosing ways to end violent crime.
- Alternatives to heavy penalties save money without increasing crime, such as greater use of misdemeanors in place of felonies, justice reinvestment, cautioning, restorative justice, and decriminalization.

4

HELPING YOUTH
FLOURISH UPSTREAM

Investing in At-Risk Young Men and Their Families

We must go beyond a response by our criminal justice system—police, courts, and corrections—if we are to prevent crime in our cities. Our response must be part of a long-range approach, yet be responsible to immediate needs. Crime prevention must bring together those responsible for housing, social services, recreation, schools, policing, and justice to tackle the situations that breed crime.

—*Agenda for Safer Cities*, Declaration by European Forum for Urban Safety, Federation of Canadian Municipalities, United States Conference of Mayors, Montreal, 1989

To paraphrase Nelson Mandela, "Violence is not inevitable, but it is preventable." Even shootings and homicides can be prevented. The renowned Prevention Institute in California has this to say about what's working today to prevent violent acts in our communities:

A growing research base demonstrates that it is possible to prevent shootings and killings through approaches such as hospital-based intervention programs, the Cure Violence model, and Advance Peace. A growing number of safety plans across the country include upstream strategies such as youth employment [and] neighborhood economic development.[1]

The work of the Prevention Institute on stopping violence was inspired by Dr. Deborah Prothrow-Stith,[2] the person responsible for the public health components in the strategy in Boston that cut homicides by 66 percent within a few months of being implemented in the 1990s. She was an emergency room doctor who became the first Black woman to have tenure in public health at Harvard University.

Other organizations, such as the Prevention Institute, also share the same message. The National Institute of Justice's CrimeSolutions.gov, in fact, endorses as effective 96 out of more than 546 crime prevention programs. Of these, no less than 67 involve investing in children and youth. Many of these 67 also are endorsed by other prevention-focused organizations, such as the Blueprints for Healthy Youth Development program.

As discussed in chapter 2, numerous portals and organizations provide access to a wealth of information about violence prevention science. But they do not make it easy for the politician or the general public to see the wood for the trees. For this chapter, I have selected some of the best-known examples of effective solutions from those portals and from other research and innovations. My goal is to illustrate the types of social policies and particularly targeted social programs that have been proven to stop crime. Given the paramount importance of tackling causes and risk factors of violence before crime happens, most of these programs provide upstream investment in the futures of young, disadvantaged and at-risk men. My selection also demonstrates the range of sectors that must be engaged if we are to end violent crime, avoid the tragedies from violence, and shift from misspending on the costly and ineffective standard criminal justice system (CJS).

As we will see, these stellar prevention projects individually have been proven to lower crime rates, sometimes by as much as 50 percent better than the CJS. Their cost advantages over the standard reactive systems of law enforcement, courts, and particularly corrections, vary in amount from $2 to $20 or more. Without a doubt, significant investments in these programs would be more effective at stopping crime than continuing to pay to react after the fact. Importantly, these programs prove that a 50 percent reduction in crime rates within a five-year period is not only possible but would be of cost savings to taxpayers—and of great benefit to victims. In fact, even if the programs did not stop violence or save taxpayers money, they would help young people flourish. The programs I present herein do all three.

WHAT SOCIAL STRUCTURE INVESTMENTS WORK

One of the many "truths" proven through violence prevention science is that the more a government improves long-term social protection for its citizens, the less violence there will be. That is, programs and policies that stimulate job growth, reduce poverty, ensure food and housing security, offer educational opportunities, provide a social safety net, and guarantee health care unequivocally reduce the numbers of violent crimes committed in a community.

Job growth is particularly important in mitigating risk factors related to violent crime. A recent review in the United Kingdom by the Rowntree Foundation concluded that the rise and fall of crime rates, before and after the 1990s, correlated with the decrease and then increase in the job prospects of young, unskilled men. (With technology predicted to replace many unskilled jobs, politicians and policy makers should take heed.) The report also highlighted that, if UK inequality were reduced to the median level seen in the developed OECD (Organization for Economic Co-operation and Development) countries, then there would be 33 percent fewer murders, and 37 percent fewer people would be incarcerated.[3] The solution? Inequality can be reduced if accessibility to the job market is more readily available for *all* people, especially disadvantaged young men. Sometimes, this is as easy as providing public transport from a poor area to a zone where hiring is taking place.[4] Providing a social safety net for young men who lose jobs is also important as a way to reduce homicide rates.[5]

Later in this chapter, I will stress the importance of job training and positive parenting as important protective elements. Programs focused on improving job skills and training can help young people increase their social capital, whereby enhancing their chances of employment. Positive parenting that reduces child abuse, known to be an adverse childhood experience, can break the cycle of crime. Just as prenatal classes have become a new norm and help mothers and babies thrive, so positive parenting classes would contribute to fewer adverse childhood experiences, help youth thrive, and give parents great satisfaction.[6]

New York City is a good example of how general upstream economic and social policies can reduce homicides. In 1990, when David Dinkins started as mayor, there were 2,605 murders (a rate of 37 per 100,000) in the city.[7] In 2017, with Bill de Blasio at the city's helm, there were only 290 murders (a rate of 3 per 100,000).[8] That impressive 90 percent decline in the homicide rate of New York City started during Mayor Dinkins's tenure, before Rudy Giuliani's time. Over the course of those nearly three decades, the decline in crime has been steady and prolonged, continuing even to today. Whereas the media have pointed to a hyped police computer system called CompStat, "broken windows policing,"[9] and Mayor Giuliani's CJS reforms in the 1990s as being the driving forces behind such significant improvement on the streets, crime experts disagree. The main and most careful scientific analysis of the possible explanations credits the following:

- Job creation
- Increased college enrollment (to have skills for the jobs)
- Alcohol taxes
- Maturing of the crack cocaine markets
- Incarceration, with a very minor reference to policing using misdemeanor charges[10]

Given this interesting list of contributing factors, Mayor Giuliani's ability to stimulate the economy probably was quite helpful, certainly more so than the small contributions from early proactive policing strategies.[11]

Other US cities, such as Philadelphia, and major cities in England and Wales and Canada have experienced similar declines in homicide rates as those occurring in New York City. Experts continue to debate the explanations, but the best evidence supports that what has made the most significant impact on violence prevention has been increased postsecondary school enrollment, more jobs, and new technologies that make it harder to steal cars and from homes.[12] But other areas, such as positive parenting and providing social safety nets, are also important for the future.

TARGETED SOCIAL PROGRAMS

Governments generally engage social programs and consider altruistic economic policies for the good of their constituents, not particularly with violence prevention in mind. Nevertheless, violence prevention is just one of the many by-products of upstream investment in people!

Whereas all citizens can benefit from such investment, the majority of the programs showcased by the Institute for Prevention and highlighted in this chapter specifically focus on helping children and young adults who are living in problem places; they are not general programs meant for everyone. They also are not very costly yet give significant and sustained reductions within just a few years. Of note is that researchers are right: crime is concentrated in problem places, but those places are problems because of social issues! And the evidence supports tackling those social issues. Doing so will mitigate the risk of young people becoming violent criminals and (mis)spending their lives behind bars, thus stopping the cycle of crime.

In figure 4.1, I have listed the main programs and project examples I am going to overview in this chapter, and I have grouped them under the social sector in which they operate, be it services for young men, parenting and early childhood, health, school, jobs, or sports. For each sector, I have identified one or more of the names of the best-known projects, with a short explanation of their essence. Then, I have presented the percentage reduction in offending compared to the CJS and, when available, the type of returns achieved in savings in harm to victims and costs to the CJS.

Several of the targeted violence prevention projects I feature herein and in figure 4.1 were shown in a scientific evaluation to have achieved reductions of 50 percent and a very high social return on investment. The reductions in crime are typically achieved within just a few years, though the HighScope preschool project focused on early childhood so reductions in violent crime did not occur until the children were adults. I also included a positive parenting program that reduces child abuse and, ultimately, violent crime at least a decade later in adolescence and early adulthood. Those programs show a return on investment further down the road because it will take longer before the children move into high-crime age groups and the efficacy of a program can be proven.

Whereas I discussed effective projects—including several of those listed in this chapter—in more detail in my book *Smarter Crime Control*, my aim herein is to offer a sampling using up-to-date data that showcases the breadth of projects that invest in young people that have impressive results. Again, I also want to stress the importance of mobilizing a number of sectors that are not part of the standard CJS. That said, some strategies that combine effective proactive policing and targeted social programs may do better in some cases than either the proactive policing or the social programs on their own, as we will see in chapter 8.

OUTREACH TO YOUTH AND YOUNG MEN

This violence prevention program category focuses on actions that target youth between the ages of six and twenty-four in a noneducational, nonfamilial, and noncarceral context. They emphasize improving life skills of youth to prevent challenging future behavior through approaches such as mentoring, youth development, tutoring, career education, counseling, and life-skills training.

SOCIAL SECTOR	NAME OF PROGRAM	WHAT IS PROGRAM	REDUCTION OF OFFENDING*	SAVINGS TO VICTIMS & CJS PER $1 INVESTED
Outreach Services to Young Males	Cure Violence	Street workers outreaching to young men to interrupt gang affiliations and mediate violent conflict	50%	N/A
	Youth Inclusion Programs (national)	Street workers outreaching to engage young men at risk into youth centers with sports, computers, and mentoring	65%	N/A
	Mentoring/ Mentoring Plus	Mentoring disaffected youth, plus focusing on education, training, and work	32%	$4
Parenting and Early Childhood	Multisystemic Therapy	Therapists work in home, school, community 24/7 to provide parents tools to transform lives of troubled youth	63%	$3
	Triple P (Positive Parenting Program)	Gives parents practical strategies to build strong, healthy relationships and prevent developmental problems	31%**	$9
	Highscope Preschool	An enriched preschool program based on participatory learning with support for parents	35%	$7
Health	Hospital-based violence intervention programs	Works with victims of violence in emergency wards to deal with trauma and abandon violence and revenge	80%	Positive

Figure 4.1. Effective Crime Prevention Solutions Using Targeted Social Development

SOCIAL SECTOR	NAME OF PROGRAM	WHAT IS PROGRAM	REDUCTION OF OFFENDING*	SAVINGS TO VICTIMS & CJS PER $1 INVESTED
School	Life Skills	Develops self-management skills such as decision-making, problem-solving, goal setting, and coping with anxiety	50%	$23
	Becoming a Man	Addresses impulsive responses causing violence in group sessions at schools using cognitive behavioral therapy	50%	$8
	Stop Now and Plan (SNAP)	Focuses on emotion regulation and problem-solving for children with behavioral problems, and their parents	52%	$32
Jobs	Job Corps (national)	Helps disadvantaged youth become productive with job placement, education, vocational training, and social skills	17%	Positive
	Jobs with Mentoring	Combines job experience with mentoring and cognitive behavioral training to increase self-regulation	40%	$4
Sports	Sports with Life Skills	Using power of sports and coaches trained in mentoring and life skills to help youth with decisions and problem-solving	N/A	N/A

*At least one scientific evaluation has shown a percentage reduction at this level.
**Reduction in child abuse by parents.
See appendix for sources.

Cure Violence

Through Cure Violence (http://cureviolence.org), ex-gang members, most of whom have served time, often long sentences, reach out to youth in high-risk neighborhoods and mediate vendettas and fights. Their goal is to stop the spread of violence in communities by detecting and inter-rupting conflicts, identifying and treating the highest-risk individuals, and changing social norms. To implement Cure Violence, program directors must determine the appropriateness of the neighborhood (a high level of violence); engage community leaders; identify appropriate community partners, including appropriate hospital-response partners; hire and train credible messengers; garner technical assistance; and examine the data. In fact, Cure Violence has become an important component of the ac-tions that have reduced gang and youth violence across the United States as well as in many high-violence countries in Latin America and South Africa.

The program was developed in Chicago, where evaluations showed a 16 percent to 28 percent reduction in gun violence due to Cure Violence in four of the project areas, in comparison with similar areas.[13] At one time, there were 14 Cure Violence projects in Chicago. When funding was cut in 2015, the 14 projects were reduced to 1, and the number of workers, from 71 to 10. The consequence of the cuts was an additional 810 deaths over the next 18 months, mostly in the areas where the program was dropped.[14] In New York City, 18 Cure Violence programs have been implemented and continue in 2018 throughout the city.

Outcome Several evaluations of Cure Violence and its predecessor, CeaseFire (not to be confused with Boston's Operation Ceasefire in the 1990s), have been carried out in Chicago as well as in Baltimore and New York City, with very promising results. The reduction of homicides in the Baltimore Cure Violence project was over 50 percent (and is the percent-age I use in figure 4.1).[15] New York City has seen an 18 percent reduction in homicides across 13 Cure Violence sites,[16] and shootings have gone down by 34 percent. The Cure Violence website uses a range from 41 percent to 73 percent for the drop in shootings and killings.[17]

Youth Inclusion Program

In England and Wales in 1998, the government instituted the Youth Justice Board and tasked it with preventing youth crime.[18] This permanent board is unique in the world and will be discussed as a model for other countries in chapter 9 because it embodies the essentials of what govern-ments must do to implement and sustain effective solutions.

The main and initial upstream action of the Youth Justice Board was to set up Youth Inclusion Programs in 72 high-problem neighborhoods across England and Wales to target first-time and persistent offenders. Team members reach out to each community's 50 most at-risk youth, build trust, and invite them to a neighborhood center where they learn new skills, par-ticipate in sports and other activities, and receive tutoring and mentoring by staff and volunteers. The aim is to change each adolescent's attitudes toward education and crime. Because of the proven success of the program with thirteen- through sixteen-year-olds, the program has been expanded to include ages eight to thirteen.[19] To this day, the program remains popular with experts but no longer receives central government funding.[20]

Outcome   Evaluation data has demonstrated a 65 percent reduction in rates of arrest for 50 participating youth, as used in figure 4.1, and a 16 percent reduction in crime in the neighborhood.[21]

Big Brothers Big Sisters of America

The Big Brothers Big Sisters of America (BBBS; http://www.bbbs.org) program pairs at-risk youth ages six to eighteen who are living with a single parent with an adult mentor who can develop a healthy relationship with the young person. The ultimate goal of this early-intervention program is to lower the likelihood that a child's future will involve violence and criminal-ity. Mentors are required to meet at least three times per month for four hours or more with the young person to be a steady influence and develop a strong bond.

Outcome   Research shows that BBBS relationships can lead to a 46 percent reduction in drug use. In addition, program participants are 33 percent less likely to engage in violence.[22]

Mentoring Plus

In England and Wales, a program called Mentoring Plus has been mak-ing the news. The "Plus" signifies helping young people with education, life-skills training, and work; levels of offending; drug use; and general psychological well-being.[23] Though an evaluation of Mentoring Plus was not able to show reductions in offending, the evaluation examined the is-sues of implementation and made several recommendations to increase the program's future likelihood of violence reduction effectiveness and success.

FAMILY SERVICES

Family services engage the family unit and aim to counter family violence, improve parenting skills, and offer preschool programs that provide both consistent child care and parent support. Such programs can be implemented in the community, family home, or preschool. Outstanding examples of such programs follow.

HighScope Perry Preschool Project

This renowned project has been studied and restudied because of its high success rate (https://highscope.org/perrypreschoolstudy). For the project, between 1962 and 1967, 123 low-income African American children identified as being at high risk of school failure were selected for a study. Half were chosen at random to attend a high-quality preschool experience. The other half who did not participate in the special preschool experience were the comparison group. The test group of three- and four-year-olds participated in daily 2.5-hour classes taught by certified public school teachers, with the average child–teacher ratio being 6:1. The curriculum emphasized active learning with support from adults. The teachers also visited the child's home weekly in an effort to engage the child's mother in the educational process and help implement the preschool curriculum at home.[24] One study found that adults at age forty who participated in the Perry Preschool Project had higher earnings, were more likely to hold a job, were more likely to have graduated from high school, and committed fewer crimes than adults who did not have a preschool education.

Outcome   Arrest rates were cut from 55 percent for the comparison group to 36 percent for the treatment group by the age of forty.[25] For every $1 invested, there was a return of almost $13.[26] The renowned economist James Heckman showed a return of $7 for every dollar invested in high-quality preschool.[27]

Triple P—Positive Parenting Program

The accumulation of evidence on the effectiveness of Triple P (https://www.triplep.net/glo-en/home/) relates to parents of children up to twelve years old. The program is included in figure 4.1 as the example for this age range. The outcome measure relates to reductions in child abuse and foster care placement, both of which are adverse childhood experiences (ACEs), which are found disproportionately in perpetrators of violent crime as teenagers and adults.[28] There is also a version for parents and teenagers.[29]

Triple P empowers parents with tools that enable them to parent more effectively and consistently. Ultimately, parents learn how to foster healthy relationships and how to prevent their children from developing behavior problems. Participation in Triple P decreases child abuse, thereby breaking down the intergenerational cycle of violence relevant to ACEs. Originally developed in Australia, Triple P is currently used in over twenty-five countries because it is one of the most effective programs for improving consistency and care in parenting. At a cost of $23 per family (as of July 2018), it is also one of the most affordable.

Outcome   Parents participating in Triple P showed a 31 percent reduction in substantiated cases of abuse.[30] Washington State Institute for Public Policy shows a $9 return for every dollar invested.[31] As an indication of its tremendous cost–benefit, Triple P was expected to save the Province of Alberta $10.2 million in other social services.[32]

Multisystemic Therapy

Multisystemic Therapy (MST; http://www.mstservices.com) is a scientifically proven intervention for at-risk youth. The way this therapy works is that specially trained MST counselors work in the home, school, and community and are on call 24/7 to provide caregivers with the tools they need to support troubled youth. MST specifically targets youth between the ages of twelve and seventeen who have serious problem and criminal behavior. Using a home-based model of service delivery, MST therapists strive to reduce barriers that keep families from accessing services.

MST therapists have small caseloads of four to six families, work as a team, are available around the clock, and provide services at times convenient to the family. The average treatment occurs over approximately four months. Therapists concentrate on empowering parents and improving their effectiveness by identifying strengths and developing natural support systems, such as extended family, neighbors, friends, and church members. They also work to remove barriers, such as parental substance abuse, high stress, and poor relationships between partners.[33]

Outcome   Research demonstrates that MST reduces criminal activity and other undesirable behavior. At the close of treatment, one study showed 87 percent of participating youth have no arrests.[34] Another showed 26 percent of MST participants compared to 71 percent of the comparison group participants were arrested at least once within four years, a reduction of 63 percent, as used in figure 4.1, with cost savings ranging from $3 for every dollar spent.[35]

Functional Family Therapy and Multidimensional Treatment Foster Care

I included MST in figure 4.1 as the example of an effective family therapy program focused on youth and their parents, but two other programs are also well known and effective. Functional Family Therapy is a systematic form of counseling of parents and youth to reduce problem behaviors.[36] It has been shown to reduce arrest rates from 41 percent to 9 percent and demonstrates a return for every dollar spent of $10 or better.[37] Multidimensional Treatment Foster Care uses clear, consistent limits and follow-through on consequences for problem behavior, combined with a caring relationship with a mentoring adult and separation from delinquent peers.[38] It has shown impressive results in the first three years following enrollment. One study demonstrates a reduction in violence from 41 percent for the nonparticipant control group to 0 percent.[39] It has achieved a $5 return on each dollar invested.[40]

Nurse-Family Partnership

Nurse-Family Partnership (http://www.nursefamilypartnership.org) is an evidence-based nurse home-visiting program that aims to prevent child maltreatment by improving the health, well-being, and self-sufficiency of vulnerable and/or first-time parents and their children. The way the program works is that Nurse-Family Partnership sends nurses to the homes of pregnant women who are predisposed to infant health and developmental problems.[41] It has had impressive results, although the long-term reductions in offending applied only to girls.[42]

SCHOOL-BASED PROGRAMS

Many school-based programs have been shown to be effective in reducing crime and violence. For instance, programs that prevent bullying, teach peaceful conflict resolution, and encourage respect are well known.[43] Ultimately, these programs and others like them improve the lives of the students by encouraging academic success and student involvement in prosocial behaviors to reduce the likelihood of criminal involvement. They can be implemented in any educational institution and are generally delivered by a teacher trained in a particular technique or program. Note that the popular DARE program was delivered by police officers and has had negative assessments.[44] The three school-related programs included in figure 4.1 illustrate a range of highly successful and effective programs.

LifeSkills Training

LifeSkills (https://www.lifeskillstraining.com) is a universal classroom-based prevention program geared toward children ages twelve to fourteen. The training is intended to reduce the risks of alcohol, tobacco, drug abuse, and violence by promoting healthy alternatives to risky behavior and targeting the major social and psychological factors that promote the initiation of substance use and other risky behaviors. Taught in the classroom by teachers over the course of three years, LifeSkills incorporates information as well as self-management, social, and resistance skills in relation to alcohol and other drugs. As the name suggests, the program teaches positive coping mechanisms youth can use in a variety of situations.

Studies testing LifeSkills have not only demonstrated short-term effects but also provided evidence of its long-term effectiveness, with several studies providing five- to six-year follow-up data and one study providing ten-year follow-up data.[45] So thoroughly researched and successful, LifeSkills has been endorsed by Blueprints for Healthy Youth Development, the Public Health Agency of Canada's Canadian Best Practices portal, the Public Safety website, Smarter Crime Control, UNICEF, Washington State Institute for Public Policy, and the US White House.

Outcome LifeSkills has achieved a 40 percent reduction in delinquency. It reduces use of alcohol by as much as 60 percent and marijuana use by 70 percent.[46] It also is affordable at $34 per individual student (as of July 2018), has a payoff of $251 in reduced reactive crime control (more than $7 saved), and a return of $785 in reduction of other costs that incorporate harm to victims.[47] This is a return of $23 saved for every $1 of cost.

Becoming a Man

Youth Guidance serves more than 8,000 students in Chicago's schools. More than 95 percent of their students are African American and Hispanic/Latino, and most of these youth reside in low-income communities. The highly trained Youth Guidance staff works directly with schools, parents, and families to meet kids where they are—physically within schools, socially, and emotionally. Their ultimate goals are to help youth break cycles of violence, overcome life and academic obstacles, make positive choices, and remain on the right path toward life success.[48]

One of Youth Guidance's counseling and prevention programs is Becoming a Man, or BAM (http://www.youth-guidance.org/bam/). Launched in 2001, BAM focuses on moderating the impulsive, automatic responses that can lead to violence by offering weekly group sessions during the school day and teaching youth through cognitive behavioral therapy how to slow down in high-stakes situations. BAM now reaches 7,000 students across Chicago schools. Youth Guidance piloted a similar program in a Boston school in 2017 and has plans to expand its offerings elsewhere.

Outcome In two randomized controlled trials, the Crime Lab found that BAM cuts violent crime arrests among youth in half and boosts the high school graduation rates of participants by nearly 20 percent.[49] The Crime Lab estimates benefits of $30 per dollar.[50] Washington State Institute for Public Policy estimates a cost–benefit ratio of $8 saved per dollar.[51]

Stop Now And Plan

Stop Now And Plan's Under-12 Outreach Project (SNAP-ORP; https:// childdevelop.ca/snap/) has received significant evaluation.[52] This award-winning program targets at-risk families by increasing their skills in dealing with emotions in social situations. It is one of the programs developed by the Child Development Center in Toronto, Canada, and uses cognitive behavioral skills training to teach boys self-control, thereby preventing later offending.

Outcome CrimeSolutions.gov reports a 52 percent reduction in crime for SNAP participants, as used in figure 4.1.[53] The benefit-to-cost ratio is $32 for every $1 spent on SNAP, when including unreported crime.[54] A SNAP cost–benefit study also found that SNAP reduced convictions for crime by 33 percent. It prevented 168 crimes per 100 boys and saved society $147,423 per boy.[55]

HOSPITAL-BASED VIOLENCE PREVENTION INTERVENTION PROGRAMS

Although this category might seem out of place in a chapter on investing upstream in youth, engaging the health sector in crime prevention is crucial to a systemic and sustainable end to violence. Physical consequences to violent crime, posttraumatic stress disorder, problematic substance use, and mental illness all demand the services of trained healthcare professionals.

When an offender or victim is under medical care, opportunities for social intervention may present themselves that keep an offender from returning to the emergency room with yet another gunshot wound, a mentally unstable person from being arrested, or an injured child from going back home to his or her abusive parent. That's where the following programs and ideas come in. Some of the programs collaborate with street outreach projects, such as Cure Violence.[56]

For a comprehensive overview of various programs in this sector, check out the website of the National Network of Hospital-Based Violence Intervention Programs at http://nnhvip.org.

Violence Intervention Program

This is one example of a hospital-based violence intervention program. Violence Intervention Program (http://www.violenceinterventionprogram. org) strives to break the cycle of young men entering an emergency room with a gun injury, getting discharged, and then being readmitted months later because of another, often more serious violent injury.[57] As yet, there are no multiple proven evaluations, but a program in Winnipeg, Canada, for victims of interpersonal violence in hospital emergency rooms has shown success in reducing returns to the emergency ward.[58] One study showed a reduction from 4 percent to 2.5 percent and associated savings.[59]

Outcome An overview of Violence Intervention Program studies shows reductions from 26 percent to 5 percent—an 80 percent reduction—for persons returning to emergency care and significant savings to hospital emergency room costs.[60] It is not yet possible to calculate a return on investment, but assuredly it is positive.

JOBS AND TRAINING

Lack of jobs is concentrated in areas that are "problem places," as discussed in chapter 3. Clearly, the root of the job problem is social, especially in America. As a *New York Times* op-ed notes, "Young Black men who live in segregated, hollowed-out areas of America's cities have long suffered disproportionately high rates of joblessness, which makes those communities especially vulnerable to family instability and acts of violence committed by young people who have no stake in society."[61]

As discussed earlier, research shows that the stark drop of crime rates in the 1990s correlated directly with job creation, particularly for unskilled workers. Given this fact, we could not explore upstream solutions to ending violent crime without examining programs that make meaningful work more attractive than crime and help young people, especially young men of color, find gainful employment.

Job Corps

This federally initiated US program was designed and implemented with the overall goal of helping disadvantaged youth between the ages of sixteen and twenty-four become responsible, employable, and productive (https://www.jobcorps.gov). Administered by the US Department of Labor through state-based Job Corps offices, participants are offered free-of-charge education and vocational training. Services also include job placement; personal and professional skills development; and social support services, such as counseling. Job Corps has been subjected to various evaluations, showing that high-risk youth get jobs from the program and that the program reduces some crime.

I have included Job Corps in figure 4.1 because it is much more than a small project; it is national. Given the overall benefits of Job Corps, it is undoubtedly an important program to consider when planning a strategy for crime reduction in a community.[62] In addition, the large number of youth passing through the program is important because political elites would be right to be cautious about projects with small sample sizes, even if the effect on crime is proportionately large.

Outcome Evaluation data demonstrates a 16 percent reduction in arrests and/or contact with law enforcement by Job Corps participants.[63] There is no precise cost benefit, though participants earned more than nonparticipants, so the benefit is positive.

Summer Jobs for Disadvantaged Kids[64]

Young males without jobs—and without hope—has been a particular problem in Chicago. In 2014, for example, extraordinarily high proportions of young Black males had no work and often were not in school. One commentator cites that nearly half of twenty- to twenty-four-year-old Chicago Black men were neither employed nor enrolled in school in 2014 and 89 percent of sixteen- to nineteen-year-olds also had no job.[65]

Chicago's One Summer Plus program stepped in to fill the gap. In addition to helping the men and boys find a summer job, either in government or a nonprofit organization, participation in the program included mentoring as well as cognitive behavioral training. The goal was to increase interpersonal, self-regulatory, and conflict-management skills, with the hopes that those life skills would be put to good use after the summer employment ceased. The evaluation of this Chicago program showed sustained reductions in violent crime.[66] Another study in Boston underscores the importance of combining jobs with life-skills training. Improvement in social and emotional skills, such as learning to manage one's emotions and resolve conflicts with a peer, was associated with larger declines in the number of arraignments for both violent and property crimes.[67]

Richmond, a city in California's Bay Area, is trying a different approach to tackling having so many young, disadvantaged youth of color engaged in violent crime. Through their Office for Neighborhood Safety (ONS), they identify the men and boys at risk for being the worst offenders and offer them a stipend rather than a job to turn their lives around. The amount, which ranged from $300 to $1,000 per month, depends upon the young man's progress following a "life map" of personal and professional goals, including staying out of trouble. Although the ONS program met with early success, that success may not be long lived, and evaluations of the program are yet to come.[68]

Outcome   The Chicago One Summer Plus program showed reduction in violent crime arrests by 33 percent for participants in the twelve months after random assignment, or by 7.9 fewer arrests per 100 participants.[69]

CRIME PREVENTION THROUGH SPORTS

The research on sports as crime prevention is limited.[70] However, some pioneer programs exist that may eventually bear fruit. For example, the UN Office on Drugs and Crime developed a Youth Crime Prevention component to enhance the resilience of youth against crime, violence, and drug use. In 2016, the organization launched a global youth initiative that utilizes the power of sports to support their goal. With coaches specially trained in mentoring and teaching life skills through its Line Up Live Up curriculum,[71] the program aims to sharpen the critical-thinking, decision-making, and problem-solving skills of youth, thereby teaching them to say no to substance use and criminal activities.

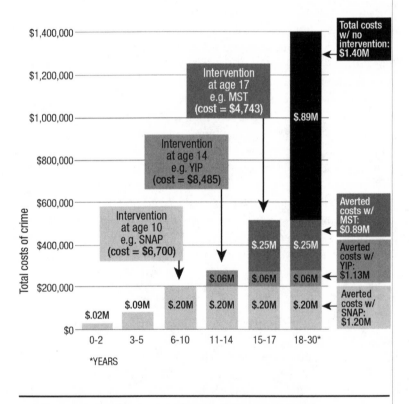

Who is Tyler?

A fictional character based on a prototypical chronic young offender in Canada. The story of Tyler is intended to demonstrate the risk factors of criminality, the cumulative costs associated with chronic offending, and how such costs can be avoided with proper and effective interventions.

The Story of Tyler
The High Costs of an Offending Pathway

Total costs w/ no intervention: $1.40M

Intervention at age 17 e.g. MST (cost = $4,743)

Intervention at age 14 e.g. YIP (cost = $8,485)

Intervention at age 10 e.g. SNAP (cost = $6,700)

$.89M

Averted costs w/ MST: $0.89M

Averted costs w/ YIP: $1.13M

Averted costs w/ SNAP: $1.20M

$.25M $.25M

$.06M $.06M $.06M

$.02M $.09M $.20M $.20M $.20M $.20M

Total costs of crime

$1,400,000 $1,200,000 $1,000,000 $800,000 $600,000 $400,000 $200,000 $0

0-2 3-5 6-10 11-14 15-17 18-30*

*YEARS

Community Safety and Countering Crime Branch, Research Division. *Tyler's Troubled Life*. Ottawa, ON: Public Safety Canada. 2016.

Figure 4.2. Illustration of Reduction to Cost of Standard CJS with the Intervention of a Combination of Three Upstream Effective Solutions

The program was first tested and piloted in Brazil in 2017 and is currently being implemented in other countries around the world, with the support of the State of Qatar. Given its newness, the Line Up Live Up curriculum has yet to have enough data to confirm its effectiveness. It is, however, based partly on the mentoring and life-skills programs already mentioned herein, and, I suspect, it will show similar results in preventing crime.

RETURN ON INVESTMENT

I would like to reiterate that the majority of the programs mentioned in this chapter are focused on people in problem places and are not general programs meant for everyone. It is in this capacity that the program must be multiplied. Instead of reacting with billions of dollars in an ineffective way after many people have already become victims, politicians and policy makers would be wise to invest in these problem places and give disadvantaged youth a chance to thrive and not merely struggle to survive, which can lead to a life of criminal behavior.

The Canadian government has produced figure 4.2 to summarize the savings from investing now in three of the programs mentioned. The idea is to engage a child in SNAP at age ten; the Youth Inclusion Program, at fourteen; and MST at seventeen.[72] The research report shows that "Tyler" would have cost the CJS $1.4 million by age thirty. It does not include intangible costs to victims, which normally far exceed tangible costs for violent crime. The infographic also shows that, if Tyler had participated in the three programs, half a million dollars of the total costs of $1.4 million would have been saved.

In chapters 7, 8, and 9, we will see that exposing a child to more than three projects is possible. The more exposure to upstream social programs, the more savings to the CJS and the less cost to victims. In chapter 10, we will see how these expected reductions in costs can accumulate to provide significant reductions in serious crime and so achieve even larger reductions in costs to the CJS and to victims. This evidence makes a strong and compelling case for being proactive about making such cost-effective investments. But the benefits are not just financial. An investment in any of the projects highlighted in this chapter offers myriads of benefits to young people as well because they are investments in helping them flourish.

KEY TAKEAWAYS

- General social policies that reduce poverty, provide a social safety net, create jobs, and improve parenting also end violent crime.
- Various programs that support at-risk young men and their families in problem places have achieved up to 50 percent reductions in violent crime within a year or two of engagement with the program.
- Social sectors that prove effective in reducing or stopping violent crime include services for youth; family; early childhood; school; hospital emergency; employment; and, likely, sports.
- Because social prevention programs reduce the number of victims, they also reduce the need for the standard CJS. For every one dollar spent on prevention, science has demonstrated potential savings in the CJS as multiples of the prevention cost.
- In addition to reducing violent crime, investments in social sectors help youth flourish in positive ways and eliminate the negative consequences that young men and their families and communities would experience if they entered the criminal justice system.

5

GENDERING SAFETY

How to Protect Women and Improve Men

Violence against women . . . it's a men's issue.

—Jackson Katz, TED Talk, 2012

In the introduction, we saw that, in the United States today, one in three women and one in four men will experience physical injury in intimate partnerships and one in five women will be a victim of rape, 80 percent before they are twenty-five years of age.[1] The total for rape translates into a staggering 1.3 million US women who are raped each year. The World Health Organization (WHO) confirms a similar disturbing number for countries that track statistics: one in three women will be physically or sexually assaulted in their lifetime.[2] Many more women will live in fear of male mistreatment and make significant life alterations to avoid the violence. Some of the assaults will be perpetrated by strangers, but more often, the men on whom the women depend and trust will be those inflicting the injury and pain.

Each occurrence of physical or sexual assault is a tragedy. As discussed in chapter 1, the agony; loss of quality of life; and, ultimately, the chronic illness each victim experiences is too often hidden from plain sight. Not only is the impact horrible and life altering for the women and girls being victimized, but children who witness the violence in their home or are the victims of such violence also bear the wounds. This, in turn, increases the likelihood of the children themselves growing up to commit violence because childhood abuse and violence against a parent are known adverse childhood experiences (ACEs) recognized as direct risk factors for perpetrating violence later in life.

Beyond the individual and the family, physical and sexual assault of women and girls reaches its ugly tentacles into the community and causes a loss of economic productivity. Although monetizing the impact may seem crude—as gender-based violence is no less than a gross violation of basic human rights—an accumulation of economic loss due to the violence amounts on a national scale to an average cost of 1.2 percent to 2 percent of GDP across countries.[3] The estimated rates of such violence in Latin America are worse: the World Bank recently identified the losses to victims of gender-based violence in Latin America to be equivalent to 3.7 percent of the GDP.[4]

Despite the prevalence and impact of physical and sexual assaults on women and girls, this type of violence has low visibility in government priorities and the criminal justice system (CJS). Many victims choose not to report to the police what happens behind closed doors and in private. In fact, more than 80 percent of rapes are not reported to police.[5] Without those police reports, gender-based violence does not get the same annual attention as other forms of violence in the media or in annual reports from police departments. This low visibility makes it harder for the issue to even get the reactive budget the problem deserves, let alone the investment in effective solutions that is so overdue.

Only in the past few decades have advocacy groups, criminologists, and health academics begun to measure the prevalence and impact of physical and sexual assault on women and to have those numbers incorporated into the gold standard of surveys in this arena: the Centers for Disease Control and Prevention's (CDC's) *National Intimate Partner and Sexual Violence Survey*, discussed in the introduction of this book.[6] Likewise, the British Crime Survey now gives annual estimates for rape and the proportion of women not reporting sexual violence to police.[7] But such surveys are not undertaken often enough nor by enough countries. Canada conducted a survey on violence against women in 1995 and is planning a more sophisticated one in 2018. Mexico has undertaken various useful surveys on violence against women as well, but none of them are as detailed as that of the CDC. Even in the United States, gender-based violence surveys are not yet annual, which would regularly remind decision makers of the urgency to do something to help abused women and girls and prevent future victimization of their mothers, sisters, daughters, and friends.

While this chapter focuses on ending violence against women and girls, I would be remiss not to note that intimate partner and sexual violence also affects men and, particularly severely, the LGBTQ community. The total number of victims who are female without necessarily being LGBTQ, however, far exceeds any other group. Also, much less is known about LGBTQ interpersonal violence and its solutions because even less research has been focused here. In fact, even countries such as Canada, England and Wales, and the United States are weak in addressing this issue. International research on this topic, therefore, must be a priority. Without information being available at this stage, though, I am not able to include suggestions for improvements on this theme in this book at this time.

I also must include a disclaimer about sex trafficking. Starting in the late twentieth century, media, politicians, and human rights organizations began to bring to light the horrific and widespread crime of human trafficking of women and children for the sex trade. Unfortunately, there has not yet been enough research on the topic for me to share solid violence prevention knowledge on effective solutions, although the reduction of sex trafficking is included in Sustainable Development Goal 5, which we will discuss shortly.

INTERNATIONAL MOVEMENT TO ACHIEVE REDUCTIONS IN GENDER-BASED VIOLENCE BY 2030

At meetings of the UN, governments resolve and resolve again to eliminate violence against women and girls (VAWG). One seminal resolution was the Beijing Declaration and Platform for Action of 1995, which provided detailed actions and objectives intended to increase gender equality and reduce VAWG.[8] To accomplish the goals, the Commission on Status of Women (CSW) was created. This body meets yearly to discuss the progress and problems of meeting the Beijing Declaration's objectives and plan strategies for moving forward, including a focus on facilitating gender equality in schools and workplaces.[9] Specifically, the Commission calls for several concrete actions, such as investment in education of girls and more balanced incomes between women and men. The group, however, has not yet focused adequately on ways of monitoring and evaluating trends to improve the outcomes of their efforts.

Similar goals are also emphasized within the World Health Assembly, which adopted a significant resolution in 2014.[10] In this resolution, the Assembly charged the WHO with the task of creating a global action plan on how to prevent VAWG and other forms of interpersonal violence.[11] In response, Caren Grown, senior director of the World Bank Group, noted:

"We have the global reach, we have the tools in terms of financing, [and] partnerships to make greater change that could be transformational."[12] Yet governments have not put their money where the evidence is, let alone taken action proportionate to the problem.

In chapter 7, we will delve into the essentials necessary to succeed in reducing violent crime, including violence against women and girls. As a sneak preview, know that one of those essentials is making goals measurable and then measuring them. With that in mind, governments of the world at the UN General Assembly in 2015 established a timeline with targets and measurable indicators to succeed in eliminating VAWG by 2030 as part of the Sustainable Development Goals (SDGs). Specifically, the target for violence against women is stated as follows in SDG 5.2: "Eliminate all forms of violence against all women and girls in the public and private spheres, including trafficking and sexual and other types of exploitation." To meet these targets by 2030, governments of the UN determined that the indicators for measuring the success of SDG 5.2 would be as follows:

> 5.2.1 Proportion of ever-partnered women and girls aged 15 years and older subjected to physical, sexual, or psychological violence by a current or former intimate partner in the previous 12 months, by form of violence and by age
>
> 5.2.2 Proportion of women and girls aged 15 years and older subjected to sexual violence by persons other than an intimate partner in the previous 12 months, by age and place of occurrence[13]

The United States is a leader in ways of measuring these two UN indicators. For example, in the introduction and chapter 1, we saw that the CDC survey provided some very clear measurement indicators of violence against women, such as "in the lifetime of an American woman," "1 in 3 experienced physical injury in intimate partner violence, of whom 1 in 5 had been victims of rape often before twenty-five years of age." We will now turn to the science of what investments would reduce the number of victims.

VIOLENCE PREVENTION SCIENCE ON VAWG

In chapters 3 and 4, I discussed the extensive science available on effective solutions to the prevention of violent crime in general. I also showcased in chapter 2 the many portals and organizations that have brought together fifty years of scientific research and culled, vetted, and disseminated it. Unfortunately, when it comes to the causes and risk factors for violence against women and girls, the science is quite limited. Without the benefit of years of surveys and research and randomized controlled trials (RCTs), we have little to go on to unequivocally advocate for specific solutions. What we do know is thanks to pioneers in just the past few decades. Whereas some proven strategies for stopping VAWG have surfaced, much more research is needed. Nonetheless, we can look to various organizations, reports, and portals, such as the following, for reviews of what VAWG prevention information is currently available:

- UN Women report (2015): *A Framework to Underpin Action to Prevent Violence Against Women*, http://www.unwomen.org/en/digital-library/publications/2015/11/prevention-framework.
- World Bank Group brief (2018): *Gender-Based Violence (Violence Against Women and Girls)*, www.worldbank.org/en/topic/socialdevelopment/brief/violence-against-women-and-girls.
- World Bank Group and partners resource guide (December 2014): *Violence Against Women and Girls Resource Guide*, http://www.vawgresourceguide.org/. A joint effort of the Global Women's Institute at George Washington University, the Inter-American Development Bank, the International Center for Research on Women, and the World Bank Group. This resource guide builds on a milestone article in the famous medical journal *The Lancet*.[14]
- World Health Assembly resolution building on existing relevant WHO work (2014): http://www.who.int/reproductivehealth/topics/violence/action-plan-endorsement/en/. WHO includes intimate partner violence (IPV) and sexual violence among its five axes for its "Violence Info" portal on prevalence, impact, and solutions to violence at http://apps.who.int/violence-info/. One particular resource featured on the site asks, "(How) Can We Reduce Violence Against Women by 50 Percent Over the Next Thirty Years?"[15]
- Funding for What Works to Prevent Violence Against Women and Girls global program: https://www.gov.uk/guidance/funding-for-what-works-to-prevent-violence-against-women-and-girls. This is a consortium led by the Medical Research Council of South Africa in partnership with the London School of Hygiene and Tropical Medicine and Social Development Direct, on behalf of the British Department of International Development. The focus of the consortium's work is funding innovation grants as well as operations research and impact evaluations of existing interventions to assess their effectiveness in preventing VAWG and meeting the needs of victims/survivors. The

program relies on an important review done for the British government, *What Works to Prevent Violence Against Women and Girls?*[16]

What we know so far shows an important consensus about some of the
drivers and underlying risk factors that affect VAWG. Social norms top
the list.[17] That is, more VAWG occurs particularly in cultures where males
have more power in intimate relationships and see wife battering as accept-
able. In addition, those men raised in families with IPV are more likely to
abuse women. We also have learned that women with the least amount of
power—perhaps due to poverty and/or social exclusion—are the most likely
victims of physical or sexual violence. Furthermore, we know that alcohol
abuse, such as binge drinking, increases the risk of IPV and that situational
opportunities, such as access to guns and the lack of safe environments or
transportation, make violence more severe or frequent.

Intimate partner and sexual violence surveys, such as that of the CDC, are
also teaching us about the high-risk years for sexual violence. Roughly from
fifteen to twenty-five are the years when date rape and sexual violence in
and around schools and university and college campuses run rampant. Some
universities that recognize the problem are undertaking surveys, looking at
rates and attitudes as well as starting to implement some components of what
we will see later are proven effective solutions. One recent survey at a US
university noted, "Among female undergraduates, 12 percent experienced
non-consensual penetration involving force or incapacitation since entering
the University of . . . and 6 percent experienced this type of assault during the
current school year."[18] In addition, the Canadian Sexual Assault Resistance
Education Centre recently reported, "As many as 1 in 4 young women will
experience attempted or completed rape before graduating from university."
The Centre is just one source that goes on to highlight the long-term devastating effects of date rape and sexual violence: "Some survivors of sexual assault drop out or change schools, many suffer loss of confidence, depression,
and/or posttraumatic stress disorder (PTSD) and other negative impacts."[19]

All this confirms the prevalence and impact of gender-based violence but
does not necessarily lead to a plan that is linked to a target reduction. As we
will see in chapter 7, linking a plan to a very specific targeted reduction goal
is an important component to getting results.

WHAT HAS NOT WORKED

One of the first things people assume is that the answer to intimate partner
and sexual violence is getting the police involved, that this will lead to heavy

sentences and the violence stopping. Actually, overrelying on policing does not work. Granted, it may be necessary to make one person accountable, but policing is not an effective solution to VAWG overall. Adopting laws to criminalize violence is also not enough. A major study of whether programs designed to stop homicide in Latin America, including Brazil and Colombia, showed that laws did not affect the number of women murdered each year.[20]

There are many reasons for the CJS not being effective in the prevention of VAWG. First, as noted earlier, many women do not report sexual violence. Government surveys in affluent countries with professional police, such as England and Wales and the United States, show that more than 80 percent of women who are raped do not report the crime to the police.[21] The reasons they remain silent run the gamut: they may associate police and the CJS with hostile treatment and a lack of respect; feel embarrassed or ashamed; or fear the blame of family and friends. Women do not report IPV for similar reasons. In addition for IPV, they are often dependent on the perpetrator for their income and feel they have nowhere to go (with their children) to escape the violence.

Even if the victimization is reported, it is often difficult for the state to get a conviction because too often there are no witnesses other than the alleged perpetrator and the victim and one or both of their testimonies may be affected by alcohol. Another interesting twist is that, in Anglo-American jurisdictions, a *criminal* court conviction requires *proof beyond a reasonable doubt*. Although few victims use it, the *civil* court process may be an easier path for getting a court decision recognizing the harm done to the victim by the perpetrator and getting reparation. This is because, in a civil court, decisions are based on the *balance of probabilities* instead of proof beyond a reasonable doubt. This is good to know because, if the perpetrator has means, the reparation may be significant.

WHAT CAN STOP VAWG: ADDRESSING THE RISK FACTORS

Effective solutions to VAWG address the established drivers and risk factors. Topping the list of effective solutions are the following:

- Altering negative attitudes and norms toward women and girls and reframing masculinity, potentially through school-based curricula
- Preventing childhood exposure to violence
- Empowering women in various ways

- Protecting women through self-defense classes; access to safe environments and transportation; and providing safe havens, such as women's
shelters
- Eliminating situational risk factors, such as access to guns and alcohol

Even when effective solutions are recognized, there are additional challenges to getting their implementation operationalized. The consensus
emphasizes that implementing effective solutions requires multisectoral
efforts, monitoring and evaluating progress, and investments proportionate
to the problem. These essential elements to successful implementation will
be discussed in detail in chapter 7 as well as in later chapters.

CHANGING NORMS AND EDUCATING MALES AT SCHOOL

Some of the most important violence prevention techniques aim at stopping boys and men from committing VAWG before it occurs through norm
changing and education. Unfortunately, school curricula often reinforce
problematic norms that lead to VAWG. As such, developing and implementing curricula that use a gender lens is valuable.[22] The WHO has identified various curricula and programs that are scientifically shown to be effective at reducing problematic gender norms.[23] While most of these programs
were tested in affluent democracies, the principles can be adapted to other
contexts. A sampling of the programs follows (see figure 5.1).

Green Dot Program

Developed originally at the University of Kentucky, Green Dot (https://
alteristic.org/services/green-dot/) has become one of the best-known effective solutions to sexual violence in high schools and on university and
college campuses. The program teaches students how to identify situations
that could lead to an act of violence (represented on incident maps by red
dots) and shows them how to intervene safely and effectively. To implement the program, advocates, such as rape crisis staff, first deliver motivational Green Dot speeches to all the students at a school. Then, educators
conduct intensive bystander training on effective intervention methods in
small groups comprising students perceived as leaders. In addition, everyone at the school receives hotline numbers, resource website information,
and access to rape crisis staff. Once implemented, when someone steps up

NAME OF STRATEGY	HOW STRATEGY WORKS	ESTIMATED REDUCTION IN OFFENDING
Changing Norms and Educating Males		
Bystander Intervention	Teaches students in schools and universities how to intervene to stop sexual violence	50%
Fourth R	Teaches students in schools about healthy sexual relationships and to respect consent	62%
SASA!	Changes individuals' attitudes and community norms and structures by supporting entire communities through a phased process of change	54%
Empowering Women		
Increase access to income	Increasing access to income for women and children through divorce and empowerment training	30%
Micro-finance with training	Provides loans to enable women to start businesses, combined with training on ending violence	50%
Gendering policing and CJS	Providing female police officers increases reporting to police and empowers women to end violence against them	N/A
Providing Protection		
Enhanced Assess, Acknowledge, Act (EAAA) Sexual Assault Resistance Program	Teaches women verbal and other self-defense skills with risk assessment to prevent violence	46%
Transportation and built environment	Provides protections for women outside of the home	N/A
Shelters/remove abuser	Provides temporary shelter for women and their children	N/A

See appendix for sources.

Figure 5.1. Effective Solutions to Ending Violence Against Women

in the school with a behavior, choice, word, or attitude that promotes safety and communicates intolerance for violence, facilitators replace the red dot on the map with a "green dot."

Outcome Those students who engaged in Green Dot bystander intervention training self-reported significantly higher intervention behaviors compared to those individuals who did not receive the training.[24] In addition, in an RCT across six schools, the program showed a greater than 50 percent reduction in the self-reported frequency of sexual violence perpetration by students at schools that received the Green Dot training, compared to a slight increase at schools that did not.[25]

Fourth R Program

The Fourth R is a program developed by a team of researchers and professionals dedicated to promoting healthy adolescent relationships and reducing risky behaviors. They develop and evaluate programs, resources, and training materials for educators and other professionals working with youth. In particular, they work with schools to promote the neglected R (for relationships) and help build this Fourth R in school climates (adding to Reading, wRiting, and aRithmetic).

Fourth R initiatives use best-practice approaches to target multiple forms of violence, including bullying, dating violence, peer violence, and group violence. In essence, the program's harm-reduction approach empowers adolescents to make healthier decisions about relationships, substance use, and sexual behavior. Fourth R members train classroom teachers to implement the curriculum, making Fourth R highly cost effective at approximately $16 per student.[26]

Outcome This program was subjected to an RCT across twenty-two schools. It reduced dating violence from 7.1 percent to 2.7 percent for the intervention group.[27] It also reduced violent delinquency among youth with high risk because of maltreatment.[28]

Safe Dates

This school-based prevention program for middle and high school students is specifically designed to stop or prevent victimization and perpetration among youth involved in a dating relationship. Available as a book with CD-ROM, *Safe Dates: An Adolescent Dating Abuse Prevention Curriculum* (http://www.violencepreventionworks.org/public/safe_dates.page), the program features school and community activities. Each of its 10 sessions is approximately 50 minutes in length and can be flexibly scheduled. Reproducible student handouts are included at the end of each session.

Outcome An RCT found that, compared to the control group, Safe Dates participants reported between 56 percent and 92 percent less physical, serious physical, and sexual dating violence perpetration and victimization. In addition, Safe Dates participants also perpetrated significantly less psychological, moderate physical, and sexual dating violence.[29]

SASA!

SASA! (http://raisingvoices.org/; http://www.cedovip.org/index.php/what-we-do/sasa-success), which means "now" in Kiswahili, is an acronym for Start, Awareness, Support, and Action—the four phases of this innovative program, which was implemented and evaluated in Uganda.[30] The main aim of this initiative is to change community norms in relation to IPV. Designed by Raising Voices and implemented in Kampala by the Center for Domestic Violence Prevention, the SASA! approach seeks to change individuals' attitudes and community norms and structures by supporting entire communities through a phased process of change. The model is likely adaptable to other countries, including developed countries.

According to the website of the Center for Domestic Violence Prevention,

> In the Start phase, community activists, regular men and women interested in issues relating to violence, are selected and trained. Police officers, healthcare providers, institutional leaders, and local governmental and cultural leaders also receive training. These activists then work through the subsequent phases of SASA!, with a central focus on discussions of power. After being introduced to new ways of thinking about power and encouraged to think about gender-related power imbalances in their own lives, the community activists are supported to engage their communities in the same critical reflection—not only about the ways in which men and women may misuse power, with consequences for their relationships and communities, but also how people can use their power positively to foster change at an individual and community level.[31]

To foster that change, SASA! recommends four strategies: local activism, media and advocacy, communication materials, and training with the specifics of intervention activities evolving in response to community priorities and characteristics.[32]

Outcome According to one evaluation, this program averted more than 1,200 cases of interpersonal violence at an estimated cost of $460 each, but the evaluation did not calculate the reductions in costs to victims or polic-ing.[33] All types of IPV (including severe forms) were lower in intervention communities compared with control communities. Past-year physical IPV was reduced from 22 percent to 9 percent in SASA! communities, and, similarly, sexual IPV was reduced from 20 percent to 14 percent. SASA! also was associated with lower onset of abuse and lower continuation of prior abuse. Plus, it was shown to be highly cost effective.[34]

Other Male-Focused Programs

There are other promising programs for which scientific evaluations have yet to confirm success. Among these projects are those aimed to train men, particularly sports leaders, to become VAWG prevention allies and to work to change the attitudes and behaviors of fellow men. One such program is Champions for Change, a Plan International project.[35] Other such pro-grams include Promundo's Program P[36] and MenCare.[37]

PREVENTING CHILDHOOD EXPOSURE TO VIOLENCE

Good role models, especially in childhood, are also essential to altering norms. For children to grow up without ACEs and thrive, they need healthy role models who protect them from any exposure to IPV. They also have a basic human right not to be abused by anyone. These types of protective measures can play a significant role in stopping the cycle of violence in families and communities. In fact, laws that ban the use of corporal pun-ishment have been proven to be effective in reducing support and use of corporal punishment, providing children with nonviolent role models, and preventing the use of violence as a form of communication.[38]

It is also important to educate parents and provide support in order to foster healthy familial relationships. In chapter 4, I discussed a number of programs, including Triple P (Positive Parenting Program), that are proven to reduce inconsistent and uncaring parenting and to mitigate the ACEs that lead to offending, drug abuse, and mental health problems.

EMPOWERING WOMEN

Some interesting and innovative steps have been taken worldwide to keep more women safe and to encourage more women to report IPV and sexual violence.

Increase Access to Income

For women to feel they have options other than living with a violent man, women must have economic independence. The classic way to improve economic independence is to push for pay equity. One such effort is to implement divorce laws that provide greater protection for women and their children. It is difficult to find studies that give a precise reduction. One study in Spain showed a 30 percent reduction in VAWG by eliminating a mandatory separation period.[39]

Microfinance with Training

In low- and middle-income countries, group savings and loans associations or microfinance education combined with gender equity training also has been proven effective in reducing and preventing VAWG. Such programs provide women with economic stability while providing men and women with lessons on healthy relationships.[40] In an RCT, microfinance and gender equity training were shown to dramatically reduce IPV in South Africa by 50 percent.[41]

Gendering Policing

Another strategy to get more women to seek help through the CJS is to increase the presence of women in police departments. Brazil and India are leading the way in this. In Brazil, all-female police units have been shown to counteract low reporting of IPV and sexual violence because women feel more comfortable reporting the abuse to another woman. Importantly, Brazil also has ensured the implementation of other social services in the police unit, encouraging consultations with psychologists and doctors.[42]

India also has several states with all-female police units. In addition, the majority of Indian police stations maintain at least two to four female police officers during the questioning of female victims to increase comfort and disclosure. Furthermore, India also employs female medical officers to whom the victims are referred for their forensic examinations (rape kit) to preserve any possible DNA involved in the rape or abuse. The country also hires female judges and prosecutors for cases involving IPV and sexual violence, which makes the legal process less traumatizing for the women and increases the chances female victims will seek enforcement from police and the justice system.[43]

Using Specially Trained Nurse Examiners

Yet other efforts to prevent VAWG involve the medical sector. Because India's police force utilizes female medical officers to administer sexual assault forensic exams, other countries are following suit. For decades, advocates of the 1994 Violence Against Women Act in the United States fought hard to institute the Sexual Assault Nurse Examiners (SANE) program (https://www.forensicnurses.org/page/aboutsane) in every state.[44] SANE nurses are registered nurses who have completed specialized and clinical preparation in the medical forensic care of patients who have experienced sexual assault or abuse. These highly trained nurses provide immediate psychological assistance and evidence collection after IPV or sexual violence. Evidence suggests the SANE program is effective in minimizing the trauma the victims face, with "75 percent of sexual assault victims describ[ing] their contact with SANE nurses as 'healing' in and of itself."[45]

PROTECTING WOMEN

Teaching women self-defense, ensuring their environment is safe, and providing safe havens also are critical in reducing risk of VAWG and mitigating repeat victimization of those who have been abused.

Sexual Assault Resistance Programs

Self-defense classes and other sexual assault resistance programs are, in fact, great violence prevention resources. One such example is the Enhanced Assess, Acknowledge, Act (EAAA) Sexual Assault Resistance program (http://sarecentre.org/), also known as "Flip the Switch." Facilitated by the Canadian Sexual Assault Resistance Education (SARE) Center, the program teaches first-year university women verbal and physical self-defense tactics, risk assessment of acquaintances, and enhanced danger appraisal. In a RCT, women who underwent EAAA training had significantly lower risk of rape and attempted rape. That is, the one-year risk of completed rape was significantly lower in the resistance group than in the control group (5.2 percent versus .8 percent), and the relative risk reduction was 46.3 percent.[46]

Transportation and Built Environment

Changing a dangerous-feeling physical environment and providing safe transportation can improve the sense of safety and confidence for women and girls. One program focusing on this effort is Women in Cities (Femmes et Villes) International (https://femmesetvilles.org/). This nonprofit organization uses awareness campaigns and education to teach individuals how to feel safe in their environment and offers ideas of individual changes that can be made to improve safety (e.g., Right to Campus). They also implement programs that increase overall community safety for women and girls.[47]

Shelters to Mitigate Repeat Victimization

Shelters for women are a crucial service aimed at reducing the harm of already victimized women. They provide a safe haven for women and girls escaping violence by offering proper care, safety planning, as well as legal assistance. Despite the fact that shelters have contributed to lowering rates of VAWG in communities, they are too few in number, and, because of overcrowding, they often must deny help to victims.

LIMITING SITUATIONAL FACTORS

As noted earlier, access to alcohol and weapons can increase the risk of VAWG. As such, implementing laws to control alcohol and weapons can prevent VAWG.[48] For instance, drinking laws should focus on minimizing heavy alcohol consumption by limiting access. Think reducing the hours and days of liquor store operation, preventing groupings of liquor stores within close proximity, as well as increasing the price of liquor. Further, laws should be enacted that set minimum drinking ages in those countries without them, to keep youth from legal consumption. These will be discussed further in chapter 9.

KEY TAKEAWAYS

- Sexual violence and IPV can be reduced by changing male norms that encourage or tolerate violence against women; programs such as Green Dot and Fourth R achieve reductions of more than 50 percent in schools and universities.
- Communities can be empowered to develop norms that do not tolerate violence against women, also with reductions of more than 50 percent.
- Women with adequate income to survive with their children on their own are less likely to be victims of violence. This can be achieved through modified divorce laws, loans, and equitable pay, accompanied with training on stopping IPV.
- Women trained in how to judge when sexual violence may occur and in ways to stop a risky situation are less often victims of sexual violence.
- Women are known to control violence against them when they know they can reach a female police officer and get protection from violence by going to a shelter.
- Physical protections designed into transportation and the built environment can save women and girls from becoming victims.
- The extent of the violence prevention science on what stops violence against women is much more limited than for gun or street violence, so governments must invest in more research and development.
- New government surveys provide more sophisticated ways to measure the prevalence and impact of VAWG as well as the effectiveness of possible solutions.

6

PUTTING VICTIMS AT ZENITH

Reimagining Justice and Support for Survivors

> So we came up with a list of seven basic rights for victims: the right to protection, the right to information and notification, the right to counsel, the right to reparations, the right to property (loss recovery) and employment, the right to due process, and the right to dignity and compassion. . . . [The] right to protection means violence prevention.
>
> —Marlene Young, Pioneer of the US and
> world movement for victim rights, 2005

In chapter 1, we saw the number of persons who are victims of violent crime and the impact of the violent crime on their lives. We saw how assessments of the harm to victims coming from civil courts give a numerical dollar value to the pain and suffering of survivors and their families. When governments adopted the Victim Magna Carta at the UN General Assembly in 1985, they recognized those multitudes of victims and the loss, injury, pain, and trauma experienced. Importantly, the UN General Assembly also recognized those losses and the trauma victims experience when collaborating with the criminal justice system (CJS). Thus, the fundamental principles in the Victim Magna Carta outline the support and justice victims of crime deserve in the way of reparation: by restitution from an offender or, if necessary, from the state. This milestone document also set out several other services and rights, all of which should receive urgent attention and investment by governments around the world.

The sad news is that, even if we reduce violent crime rates by 50 percent, as previous chapters show can be done, too many people will still be victimized and experience the pain and suffering from the perpetrator and the costs and trauma from collaborating with the CJS. We must stand with these neighbors and families, women and children, and disadvantaged young men and demand justice for them all.

Since 1985, we have learned much about effective ways to meet the needs of crime victims. We know how best to provide them with information and support them in recovering from the victimization and in coping with the CJS. We know how important it is they be given fundamental rights overlooked for too long. But we also know too little is being done, even in the most advanced jurisdictions, such as England and Wales, because a wide gap exists between the potential of best practices and the real needs and rights of victims.

There are three critical reasons to effectively meet the needs of victims of violence. The first is basic: the governments of the world have agreed on fundamental principles of justice and resolved to implement them, so we need to get governments to fulfill their agreement. The second is that, if victims' needs are not met, particularly through the CJS, then they will not report to the CJS. This means that, when needed, arrest and deter and proactive policing will have no meaning and no value to them. The third is that services and justice for victims reduce much of the anger that drives the tough-on-crime system of vengeance and retaliation. The time to act is now!

(LACK OF) PROGRESS IN OPERATIONALIZING THE FUNDAMENTAL PRINCIPLES OF JUSTICE FOR VICTIMS OF CRIME

Thankfully, since the signing of the 1985 Victim Magna Carta, myriads of new laws and international resolutions have shown good intentions.[1] The European Union's Victims' Rights Directive of 2012 sets standards for victim information, services, restitution, restorative justice, and a limited right to "participation" across more than 25 countries, reaching potentially 500 million people or more than 70 million victims.[2] Victim "participation" in the EU Directive refers to victims' procedural rights in criminal proceedings, which include getting a more active role—having the right to be heard and to be informed about the different steps of the proceedings.[3] But there is a long way to go.

To determine the extent to which the standards of the directive were being implemented across the member countries, the European Union undertook a major assessment in 2015.[4] According to the report, with regard to legal procedural rights, most of the key provisions of the directive appear to have been transposed adequately into national legislation, and some progress has been made in starting the improvement of victim services and rights in those countries that were behind in the effort. But the practice is still lacking. Police too often are not providing information and referrals. When services are provided, too often the efforts are weak, with inadequate funding. Plus, it is unclear whether restitution, compensation, and the "right to participation" are being provided. Perhaps the clearest gap in the success of the directive is the lack of funding for implementation procedures.

Looking beyond the European Union, Mexico legislated rights for victims of crime with an implementation mechanism in 2013.[5] In 2015, the federal government in Canada adopted the Bill of Rights for Victims of Crime, which focuses on the rights to information, protection, participation, and restitution, but the bill only talks about "complaint," without any real teeth.[6] The United States has the 1984 Victims of Crime Act, the 1994 Violence Against Women Act, and the 2004 Justice for All Act. While each makes progress, it is the 1984 Victims of Crime Act that provides a model for the world because it gets its funding independently of taxes through massive fines on corporations violating the federal criminal code. At the US state level, many other laws related to victims' rights have been passed. One example is Marsy's Law for All, which, as of 2017, is in six states. Marsy's Law works to get victims of crime rights equal to those already afforded to the accused and convicted.[7] But ever so much more is needed, especially given that too many of these laws often go unimplemented.

In general, there is much in common between the proposals agreed at the UN, the legislation in the United States, and the European Union's Victims' Rights Directive. Yet holes exist. The proposal, legislation, and directives identify who is a direct victim of crime, but they do not always provide provisions for family members or Good Samaritans, people who help the victims. They agree on the importance of services and assistance as well as providing information on those services and the operations of law enforcement and criminal justice. But the information and referrals are not made consistently, and services to which the referrals would be made are not adequately or sustainably funded. They agree on the importance of a gendered (such as violence against women and children) or child-sensitive approach to victims, but the countries do not always provide this,

particularly at the policing level. They agree on restitution from the offender and compensation from the state, but officials equivocate on how to
deliver on the principle and do little to assist victims in recovering costs. In
fact, every major review of victim issues has proposed a much more active
role for victims but gotten nowhere.

Another indicator of how much change is needed is a report by the
Provincial Ombudsman in Ontario, Canada's most populous and richest
province. This report rightly calls out Canada's program to provide financial
assistance to victims of violence, "adding insult to injury." In reaction, the
embarrassed government called in an elder statesman, who recently retired
as chief justice, to make recommendations. His recommendations were
pragmatic and would have led to putting Ontario at the forefront of rights
for victims.[8] But ten years later, little has changed. Police officers are not
even required to provide information and referrals, which is not costly nor
rocket science. What a disappointing indication that Canada's political and
CJS leaders are not taking the needs of victims seriously! It's no surprise
that rates for victims reporting to police in Canada are lower than in other
developed countries, such as the United States and England and Wales.
Truly, we have a long way to go to ensure that *all* victims of crime have *all*
the benefits they deserve. We cannot be satisfied with *some* crime victims
in *some* countries *some* of the time having what they need. In other words,
the challenge is getting good principles implemented and brought up to the
high standards of leading progressive countries, and we must look for ways
to accelerate the necessary changes.[9]

THE KEY TO REBALANCING JUSTICE: A MODEL COMPREHENSIVE LAW

As a move in the right direction, building on tenets similar to the European
Union's Victims' Rights Directive, experts have agreed upon the contents
of a model law on victims' rights.[10] The law starts with a relatively short pre-
amble that draws attention to the harm caused to victims by a violent crime
and through dealing with the standard CJS. The model law also outlines
the good and bad news on current actions, similar to what I have shared
in this chapter. In addition, it highlights how particular actions directly affect victims of crime; their covictims, such as family members; and Good
Samaritans. Finally, the model law clarifies the scope of action as "covering
all the relevant adult and juvenile criminal codes," including commitments
to reduce crime and prevent victimization.

For a quick outline of the main operational content of the model law to get effective solutions to support and provide justice for victims, refer to figure 6.1. In the remainder of this chapter, I will examine the six main rights delineated in this model law. The seventh, the right to prevention, is covered in the rest of the book.

Right to Recognition

It is a myth that criminal justice is justice for victims because victims historically have not been active parties in the CJS. They may report the crime and act as witnesses, but their interests in getting the truth, restitution, state action on prevention, or even punishment often have not been respected because they have not been considered CJS "participants." It is important, therefore, to be clear on who are victims of crime. In simple terms, "victims" are those harmed by an offender who committed a criminal act. Victims likely suffer loss, injury, and trauma and may suffer additional losses and trauma if they cooperate with the state in the prosecution of the offender. The model law differentiates victims who need special considerations and services because of issues such as gender, disability, or age. It also clarifies that a person still has rights, regardless of whether the state arrests or convicts an offender.

Unfortunately, too many people do not report their victimization to the police. In the United States, for example, despite the $136 billion spent on policing each year, 49 percent of serious incidents of violent crime go unreported.[11] As we saw in chapter 5, it is much worse for rape victims; more than 80 percent of them do not report to the police. What makes this situation even more disheartening is that more than 50 percent of victims of common offenses who *do* report are not satisfied with the service they receive from the police! They note as negative a lack of interest in their personal situation and a lack of information. Perhaps most notably, more than 50 percent of victims of violent crime who report their victimization are looking for the police to *prevent further offending*; only 18 percent are looking for *punishment* of the offender.[12]

Yet the common indicator of police effectiveness is not pleasing, appeasing, or supporting victims or getting more victims to report the crimes. Instead, most of today's police precincts measure success as the attainment of a high rate of "clearing offenses"—identifying the perpetrator and potentially making an arrest. Interestingly, the proportion of crimes known to police for which there is a known perpetrator has been decreasing over the years. For violent crime nationally in the United States, those numbers

RIGHTS	HOW VICTIMS NEEDS AND RIGHTS ARE MET
Support	
Right to Recognition	Defines who is a victim, family members' status, and lack of arrest does not deny victim
Right to Information	Police provide information and referral for victim to receive support, reparation, and practical services in community
Right to Assistance	
General	Services for victims to receive support, advice, and assistance with practical issues
Specialized	Services for victims of sexual and intimate partner violence and child abuse
PTSD	Expert counseling provided through free health care
Justice	
Right to Reparation	
Restitution from offender	Court organized to assess ability of offender to pay and make order
Compensation from state	Compensation board that pays victims for injuries, when offender does not
Right to Protection	
Protection	Services to advise victims on safety and provide reasonable precautions in court room
Right to Participation and Representation	
Represented by lawyer in CJS	Provide lawyer for victims with standing in CJS to address victims' interests in truth, restitution, safety, and justice, with legal aid
Outside criminal justice	Services available to support victim wanting to engage in restorative meetings with offender

Figure 6.1. Rebalancing Justice for Victims of Crime

are 30 percent for robbery, 41 percent for rape, 54 percent for aggravated assault, and 59 percent for homicide.[13] Astonishingly, in Chicago, one measure of the percentage of homicides for which there is a known perpetrator has dropped to 18 percent—a rate of impunity that should be disturbing in any country in the world and get decision makers to take action.[14]

RIGHTS	HOW VICTIMS NEEDS AND RIGHTS ARE MET
Governance	
Right to Effective Violence Prevention	(see chapters 3–5 and 7–9)
Right to Full Implementation	
Office for victims of crime	Office provides leadership for change, funding for services and evaluation, as in US Office for Victims of Crime
Standards and training	Directives on rights, support, and protection of victims that set standards and require training, as in EU directive
Monitoring and surveys	Victimization surveys assessing unmet needs and rights of victims, general and specialized for women and children
Victim advocate	Office to advocate for change from a victim's perspective, as in victim commissioner in South Australia
Research and development	Research and development on ways to meet needs and rights of victims, as in International Victimology Institute, Tilburg

See appendix for sources.

Right to Information

As noted earlier, many victims who report their victimization complain they did not receive adequate information from the police. Whereas many US states and the EU Directive require police to offer victims leaflets about social services and refer them to agencies for assistance, officers do not always follow these laws. Law enforcement, thus, must institute ways to measure respect for victim support laws during performance assessments.

Providing information to victims is one of the simplest, most cost-effective actions to improve the situation for victims of crime, plus it can be a great image builder for the police. It surprises me that commissions discuss how to improve police relations with the public in Canada, England and Wales, Mexico, and the United States, yet none of these countries has focused on this obvious, easy, and fundamental action. The commissions do study after study, oblivious to the reality that victims are shunning police with their feet by not reporting and not being available as witnesses.

On that positive note, I am impressed by the training package "Enhancing Law Enforcement Response to Victims: A Twenty-First Century Strategy," developed by victim specialists and the International Association of Chiefs of Police (IACP).[15] This wonderful guide outlines IACP's goal of putting victims at the "zenith of policing" by bringing safety, information, support, and justice to them. The thought is that such action will result in better reporting rates and, ultimately, higher clearance rates. More importantly, however, this shift from a focus on arrest and prosecution toward putting victims at the zenith will have an end result of fulfilling the basic needs and rights of crime victims. That would be a big win for policing *and* for victims. But, alas, I have yet to meet a politician or senior police officer who is aware of this great resource before I mention it.

Specifically, some key ways to put victims at the zenith of policing include the following:

- Offering compassionate options during intake. Although police must accept the decision of self-determination from the victim, they might encourage testimony in novel ways, from videotaping to providing trained victim support workers with whom the victim could discuss the tragedy.
- Empowering victims to decide how far they want to go with law enforcement and criminal justice. For example, best practices include allowing victims of sexual assault to assure evidence from a sexual assault evidence kit without being obliged to go to the police. Reports to police and crime prevention planners of the location and circumstances of sexual assault without identifying the victim can provide important data for prevention.
- Hiring more female police officers. As noted in chapter 4, there would be much more reporting by women if they knew that, if they wanted, they could work with a female officer.

Right to Assistance

Another important element of providing support and rights to crime victims is prioritizing access to support services. Too often, governments have prized projects but not the programs that provide emotional and psychological support, access to medical care, practical and community services, and safety to victims of crime. Such services must be available everywhere and must provide both basic physical and emotional support and more sophisticated assistance with psychological recovery. And these services, along with the service provider, must be free of charge to victims.

Victim experiences differ significantly because of the different nature of each crime. Consider domestic violence, sexual assault, stalking, and human trafficking. These differentially affect women more severely and generally have worse consequences for female as opposed to male victims. Further, the attitudes of predominantly male agencies, such as law enforcement, mean that women may not be treated sympathetically. Beyond this, gender is a factor that has a significant effect on how services should respond to the victimization.

The US Violence Against Women Act, passed in 1994, has the dual purpose of reducing violence against women and better serving the needs of survivors. An important component of this act is the requirement for the Office for Violence Against Women to demonstrate to Congress how the funds are reaching their targets, in other words, how effective are the funded programs in reducing violence and serving victims' needs.[16]

Because of a special one-day census, we know more about the implementation of services for victims of domestic violence than we do services for other victims. This specific census tracks how many women and children are in shelters and how many were turned away. On an average day, there are approximately 10,000 women and 10,000 children at shelters across the United States seeking protection and a range of counseling, safety planning, and legal assistance services. According to the census, those who do receive the services are overwhelmingly satisfied.[17] Unfortunately, 9,000 victims are refused services each day because the programs do not have the resources.[18] This is a serious and large gap—a travesty.

One of the strongest examples of positive action to meet the needs of victims of crime is the work done by countless dedicated individuals in sexual assault crisis centers. In the 1960s, women's groups began to provide support to victims of rape through sexual assault crisis centers across North America. In the 1970s, the center in Seattle was recognized for being the best practice among them. By the 1980s, more and more centers had opened, but all too often they lacked sustained funding.

Without a doubt, pioneers in the sexual assault crisis field struggled uphill, but their self-determinism and focus on the physical, emotional, and psychological needs of rape victims has paved the way for a variety of other victim support services around the world. By the time of the passage of the Violence Against Women Act, there were over 1,315 rape crisis centers in the United States. Whereas that number may seem impressive at first, consider that there are a million rape victims every year in the United States.[19] Obviously, the United States has nowhere near the capacity to support all the victims.

The service work related to sexual assault is not easy. Support means accompanying the victim to the hospital and, if the victim decides to report to law enforcement, dedicating a lot of time to meeting with police and going to court. Importantly, Sexual Assault Nurse Examiners (SANE) programs, listed as a key resource in chapter 4, provide healing services in a nonjudgmental atmosphere. SANEs also improve the potential for a successful prosecution because they collect evidence in the correct manner. In addition, they contribute greatly to enhanced interagency collaboration to improve overall community responses to rape.[20]

Serving child victims is also a mammoth undertaking. We know there are 700,000 children identified by child protection agencies as being abused or neglected every year in the United States.[21] In addition, there are unknown numbers of children aged twelve and under who are victims of crimes committed against them by nonfamily members. The law enforcement and criminal justice process is confusing and frightening enough to adults. Consider how much more so it is for children, especially when they don't necessarily have family members, such as parents, they can turn to for assistance.

The combination of the emotional shock of being a victim and the frightening judicial process justify many special measures, not least of which is the provision of a central care unit that can handle the many agencies involved in the child protection process. For example, unless care is taken, a child victim might be interviewed many times in many different places about the same set of facts, so a child victim advocacy unit is necessary to minimize the stress and impact on the child.

Across the United States today, more than 350 child victim advocacy clinics work to ease the experience of child victims.[22] In these clinics, police, child protection workers, prosecutors, and victim advocates are able to interview child victims in one consistent child-friendly environment. Sometimes, a video recording will be made so that repetition can be avoided; other times, professionals can watch an interview through one-way glass so the child is not disturbed. These child-focused clinics retain an intense concentration on the short- and long-term emotional and psychological health and well-being of young victims. They facilitate treatments by various child welfare agencies and other specialized healthcare workers, and some even have facilities for medical examinations. Child victim advocacy clinics are lauded for this one-stop approach to working with children who have been victims of violence because they are able to ensure that already traumatized children are exposed during the judicial process to as few new and unfamiliar circumstances as possible.

One of the areas of greatest need for victim support is therapy for those suffering from crime-inflicted trauma. One approach that has been shown to reduce the long-term harm associated with victimization is trauma-focused cognitive behavioral therapy (TF-CBT).[23] This technique focuses on addressing problematic thought patterns and emotions and providing coping mechanisms to support crime victims. One proven use of TF-CBT is in treating victims of child abuse.[24] Currently, seven other projects rated effective for reducing symptoms of posttraumatic stress disorder by Crime-Solutions.gov are also in progress.[25] These projects include successes with victims of sexual assault, children in schools who have witnessed violence, and adolescents suffering from posttraumatic stress disorder.

Right to Reparation

In addition to receiving physical and emotional support, getting financial reparation for their losses also should be a fundamental right of crime victims. Restitution from the offender is one important way to repay victim losses. Yet governmental policy around the globe does little to ensure this. Procedures must be changed to order restitution and mandate payment, wherever possible. Best practices in this effort include systems such as those in the US state of Wisconsin, where victims of crime submit a formal request for restitution together with the required documentation to back up the request. Another example of prioritizing restitution occurs in the US state of California. There, the court assesses the income and wealth of the offender at the beginning of a case; if he or she does not pay for the victim's losses, the court knows what is available and can follow up on the matter. In fact, both California and Florida have sophisticated systems to get restitution from the offender paid into a government agency which, in turn, pays the victim. More research is needed to learn how often restitution is ordered and paid to understand what works and what does not in this arena.

Another important source of compensation for victim losses is the government itself. Canada and England and Wales have robust government-supported victim compensation programs, in addition to universal health care. The health insurance is important to note because victims often end up with a mountain of medical bills. In the United States, where many victims do not have health insurance, much of victim compensation goes to pay those expenses. Also in the United States, eligible victims are supposed to be handed leaflets about state-available compensation when they report a crime. They also can find the information and appropriate forms for the state compensation on certain websites, and service providers can help them overcome the bureaucratic forms. Nonetheless, US compensation amounts should be increased to levels at least consistent with Canada and England and Wales. Furthermore, research is needed to determine the costs of compensation programs that adequately reimburse victims for pain, suffering, and mental as well as physical health care.

Right to Protection

There are many ways to provide protection. In general, victims are looking for advice on how to physically protect themselves as well as some reasonable protection in the courtroom. Yet no perfect protections exist, unless the accused is off the street, and then the protection lasts only for the duration of the detention. Granted, refuges for battered women provide some *temporary* protection, although I would remove the batterer instead of the victim from the home, as Austria and the Netherlands try to do. In the courtroom, the separation of victims and defendants is essential.

Right to Participation and Representation

France has been ahead of the field in victim-centered justice, having had relevant procedures in place since the 1960s to support victims' interests, with legal aid for those unable to pay their lawyer. (Many victim experts miss how important the legal aid provision is to operationalize what is too often a dead letter law in other jurisdictions.) But it wasn't until 1985, with the Victim Magna Carta, that all the world governments agreed to allow "the views and concerns of victims to be presented and considered at appropriate stages of the proceedings where their personal interests are affected."[26] Despite resistance from Anglo-American government lawyers, the International Criminal Court adopted pertinent procedures. Countries such as the Netherlands and Germany are believed to be catching up with France.

In the United States, the Crime Victims' Rights Act of 2004 provides some "participation," stating that victims of crime should be present and heard at all critical stages of judicial proceedings. This goes slowly toward the goal to protect victims' interests in their personal safety, reparation, privacy, justice, and truth. The US state of Oregon, specifically, now provides a mandamus procedure to ensure that constitutionally and statutorily recognized rights for victims of crime are put into practice, a procedure actually being used if in front of the right judge.

Despite all the efforts and good intentions—even the European Union's innovative Victims' Rights Directive—progress in victim-centered justice has been slow. To get more "good news," procedures must be changed to ensure that the ability of offenders to pay is ascertained early on in the judicial process so that reasonable restitution can be ordered in criminal courts. In France, 50 percent of criminal cases are settled by the payment of restitution. Victims, taxpayers, and offenders win by avoiding unnecessary incarceration.

Another strategy for ensuring victim-centered justice is to have jurisdictions experiment with joint criminal and civil court proceedings to empower victims to protect their concerns for their safety, convenience, need for services, restitution, desire for the truth, and right to justice. The best practice is the legislation, rules of procedure, and organization of the International Criminal Court, a spin-off of the UN.

As an alternative to expensive litigation, programs should be set up to provide for mediation and restorative justice, with evaluations to test for the satisfaction of victims and changes in recidivism rates. Restorative justice takes different forms, but the basic approach involves providing a context in which victim and offender can understand each other's perspectives; process the emotion; and, hopefully, arrive at a genuine apology and possibly restitution.[27] This will require national programs to train mediators in restorative justice and to spread the word to the CJS and local communities of its benefits. The evaluations show how much more satisfied victims are who go through restorative justice than those who go through the CJS.

In England and Wales, an organization called Restorative Solutions (https://www.restorativesolutions.org.uk/) promoted and developed the use of restorative justice. Their tactics were to promote the merits of restorative justice as widely as possible and to develop projects in different conflict situations both within and without the CJS. Their work provides an important trampoline toward a national policy. Among their initial achievements are the following:

- Raising $8 million to provide training and support to fund the work
- Working with a national social housing provider to use restorative justice processes to resolve neighborhood and other disputes
- Developing a neighborhood restorative justice model intended to help the police neighborhood teams and communities resolve local disputes without recourse to criminal proceeding

- Developing a program to use restorative justice to resolve disputes in schools between teachers and students, between teachers and parents, and between students, with the intent of reducing school exclusions
- Creating public relations materials, including videos, pamphlets, case studies, and a website
- Holding high-profile events aimed at engaging the interest and support of opinion formers and policy makers[28]

Right to Effective Violence Prevention

Although not listed in figure 6.1 as an effective solution for victims specifically, this right actually is an overarching right of *all humanity*. In chapters 2 to 5, I have presented the highlights of the solid violence prevention science that show that the most effective and cost-effective way to deal with crime is upstream targeted proactive policing and social development. The same goes for upstream targeted proactive policing and social development being the most effective and cost-effective way to deal with victimization. Without violence, we would have no victimization at all.

In the next part of this book, we will look at what is essential to getting proactive policing and targeted social programs implemented. The bottom line is that we know how to reduce violent crime by 50 percent or more. We should be doing that.

MECHANISMS THAT WORK

For any of the sections of the model law to become reality, funding must be radically improved and sustained. Proportionate to what is spent on the standard CJS, however, funding for victims' rights and preventive crime control remains small today. My 2011 book, *Rights for Victims of Crime: Rebalancing Justice*, proposed the investment annually should be the equivalent of 7 percent of what is currently spent on a country's CJS. About two-thirds of this would go to support services and one-third to justice, including compensation.

Adequate Funding

In the United States, the Victims of Crime Act of 1984, the Violence Against Women Act of 1994, and the Victim Rights Act of 2004 have done much to advance funding, services, and rights for victims of crime. In fact, the Victims of Crime Act provides more than $4 billion annually to states and local governments for services, compensation, and actions for vulnerable victims, such as in domestic violence cases.[29] That $4 billion is less than 2 percent of the $284 billion spent on the CJS in figure 1.1. The unique characteristic of this $4 billion is that it does not come from taxes; it comes from federal fines, significant amounts of which come from rich corporations, some of whom pay fines of over $1 billion.[30] The states also invest some of their own funds. In comparison to the needs, though, so much more money is required.

Training and Standards

Much more must be done to get real outcomes for victims of violent crime. In fact, every jurisdiction throughout the world should develop and approve a code of practice for victims of crime, such as England and Wales have done,[31] but with social science research to measure results. Importantly, any code of practice for victims of crime should have both generic standards for victim justice and specific standards that convey respect for the significant issues of gender, the needs of children, and the requirements of the elderly. Training to address such capacity is one of the keys to success. Even back in 1985, the UN General Assembly saw the need for adequate training when it stated that "[p]olice, justice, health, social service, and other personnel concerned should receive training to sensitize them to the needs of victims and guidelines to ensure proper and prompt aid."[32]

Another invaluable resource for enhancing the responsiveness of criminal justice systems to victims is Professor Benjamin Perrin's book, *Victim Law: The Law of Victims of Crime in Canada*. This peer-reviewed seminal textbook builds on the upward momentum in legislation and case law protecting the rights of victims. It may be a game changer if law schools establish courses on victim law.

Monitoring and Evaluating

Without measures and measuring, nothing will be achieved. Governments need to recognize this reality and fund surveys to identify the extent to which victims do, indeed, receive the rights proclaimed through constitutional amendments as well as to identify remedies in places where they are not receiving their due rights. Best practice is the program accompanying the US Justice for All Act.[33] The US General Accounting Office even undertook an audit of the act's implementation, including the perspective of victims. The audit determined that "increasing awareness, modifying the complaint process, and enhancing compliance monitoring" would improve implementation of the act.[34]

Mobilizing Victim Advocates

Countries also would do well to establish the position of commissioner or ombudsman for victims' rights. This person and his or her office would be responsible for assessing whether codes or laws related to victims' rights are being implemented. Australia and the United Kingdom have victims' commissioners.[35] Canada has a federal ombudsman for victims of crime.[36] Japan has implemented a comprehensive program for victims of crime.

Permanent Organizations on Victims' Rights

One of the keys to improving victims' rights and supporting them is to establish a government office for victims of crime, similar to the Office for Victims of Crime in Washington, DC. The purpose of the office would be to establish standards for what should be provided to victims, ombudsmen, or commissioners to root for change and funding equivalent to a small but real percentage of what is being spent on the CJS.

We also need to create a permanently funded institute on victims' rights. Such an institute, while requiring contributions from legal professionals, social researchers, and victims' rights agencies, must be independent of them all. This institute would likely be based out of a university and would function as a central hub for education, research, and policy observation. It would work in close cooperation with service agencies in the community, the commissioner or ombudsman for victims' rights, and legal practitioners.

One such institute has already been created in Europe and could serve as a best practices model for other countries. INTERVICT is the International Victimology Institute Tilburg. It was launched by Tilburg University in the Netherlands in 2005 and has continually expanded research on victimization and victim assistance within Europe. It also has conducted extensive evaluations of the implementation of victim legislation in the European Union and has been leading the world on issues of victimization (identity theft, human trafficking, and online victimization).

The partnership between INTERVICT and the European Forum for Victim Support changed the course of history, by demonstrating that the landmark European Framework had not made enough difference in terms of services meeting the needs of victims. As a result, the European Union modified its approach and established the 2012 Victims' Rights Directive. In the United States, the insistence that the rights in the Victims of Crime Act be evaluated by the US Congress' Government Accountability Office has ensured that improvements are being made in the act's application.

KEY TAKEAWAYS

- Even with successful implementation of effective ways of preventing violence, there will still be an unacceptable number of victims.
- In the thirty years since the governments of the world agreed to provide fundamental principles of justice for victims with the Victim Magna Carta, legislators have been busy adopting laws, including amendments to constitutions, and making modest investments in their implementation.
- Knowledge on the topic of victims' rights has accumulated, and many best practices on the topic have been developed and operationalized in different countries.
- To help victims cope with the loss, injury, and trauma from violence and get their basic rights respected, much greater effort must be devoted to adapting what is known about victims' issues and implementing effective practices to resolve them both in the CJS and outside the system in general.
- Policing needs to be improved so that victims have a better experience when they report their victimization, particularly in terms of getting information and referral to services. This may lead to more reporting to police and better access to witnesses, thereby improving policing's dismal clearance rates. The IACP has offered a training tool since 2008.
- Victims need a range of support services that already exist in England and Wales and several US states. These services must address the trauma induced by violent crime.
- Victims deserve assistance with their financial needs through restitution when possible or through compensation from the state.
- Restorative justice is an effective means of meeting the needs and rights for victims while avoiding the secondary victimization of getting involved with the CJS.
- The key to improving victims' rights and supporting them is to adopt the proposed model law, including establishing an office for victims of crime, ensuring police put victims at the zenith, and creating an institute for research and development on victim issues and policies.

III

ESSENTIALS FOR SUCCESSFUL IMPLEMENTATION

Effective models for action are available from governments which have national crime prevention structures, from cities which have established municipal crime prevention structures, and from individual projects, which have reduced various types of criminal activity.

—Paris Declaration, 1991

7

GOVERNMENTS AGREE ON ESSENTIALS

Resolving to End Violent Crime by 2030

And we're looking at things that have been done around the world, things that have been done in other jurisdictions, looking at the best evidence, the best data, to make the right decisions to make sure that we are ensuring our citizens, our communities, are safe into the future.

—Justin Trudeau, Prime Minister of Canada, 2018

In previous sections of this book, we learned about programs, projects, and policies that solid violence prevention science has shown stops violent crime. Now, we will explore how governments can put that knowledge into action, starting with what governments worldwide have agreed are the essential components of a violence prevention strategy. As noted earlier, one particularly important instrument of motivation is the 2015 UN resolution to achieve seventeen delineated Sustainable Development Goals (SDGs) by 2030. Recall that the SDGs include four goals whose targets include indicators on reducing violent crime. One particular SDG supports the all-important results-oriented approach to reaching the goals. The big question is, how do we get from where we are now to significant reductions in violent crime by 2030?

To get perspective, let's reconsider the UN General Assembly's 1985 Victim Magna Carta that drew attention to the hundreds of millions of victims suffering loss, injury, and trauma as a result of crime. To alleviate those losses and trauma, governments around the globe, through the Victim

Magna Carta, agreed to prevent victimization by attacking social causes and holding offenders accountable. Since the time of the adoption of that milestone document, there have been various attempts to meet its goals at intergovernmental organizations, including the UN Economic and Social Council (ECOSOC), the World Health Organization (WHO), UN-Habitat, and the UN Office on Drugs and Crime (UNODC). With the UN SDGs, we finally have a results-oriented framework with the potential to reduce violent crime across the world.

UN GUIDELINES ON CRIME PREVENTION

As a follow-up to the 1985 Victim Magna Carta, two seminal UN resolutions were later adopted that outlined specific guidelines on how to meet the goals of that historic resolution. These were the "Guidelines for the Cooperation and Technical Assistance in the Field of Urban Crime Prevention" (ECO-SOC Resolution 1995/9) and the "Guidelines for the Prevention of Crime" (ECOSOC Resolution 2002/13).[1] The latter includes a brief mention of violence against women. In 2010, the UNODC also published a handbook for governments on how to facilitate the implementation of the guidelines.[2]

Although several new "essentials" of crime prevention were added, the 2002 "Guidelines for the Prevention of Crime" reemphasize many of the same messages found in the 1995 guidelines. For example, both stress taking a multisectoral approach to crime prevention that involves addressing diverse issues, such as employment, education, health, housing and urban planning, poverty, and social marginalization and exclusion—with particular emphasis being placed on communities, families, children, and at-risk youth.

When they were instituted, both sets of UN guidelines were novel. Rather than waiting until crime happened and reacting to it, as the standard CJS has done prior, the new strategies intended to stop violent crime by preventing it before it happened. They also focused on strategies to reduce the risk of crime by heading off its multiple causes.[3] Such efforts included prevention through social development, locally based crime prevention, and international cooperation.

In general, the UN ECOSOC guidelines delineate basic principles and organization, methods, and approaches that science has shown are effective solutions to ending violent crime. The efforts they recommend cluster around seven essential elements, listed in the first column of figure 7.1. The second column calls out the names of the headings (with the specific paragraph numbers in parentheses) used in the 2002 ECOSOC resolution that

7 ESSENTIALS FOR IMPLEMENTING EFFECTIVE SOLUTIONS	HEADINGS IN ECOSOC-UNODC 2002 (WITH PARAGRAPH #S)	REFERENCE IN SDG 17 TO SIMILAR TARGETS	STEPS FOR ADAPTING AND IMPLEMENTING *INSPIRE***
Permanent Violence Prevention Board	Government Leadership (1, 7, 17)		
Informed by Violence Prevention Science and Data	Knowledge Base (11, 21)	17.6 ... access to science, technology and innovation ...	Select interventions, adapt interventions to local needs
Diagnosis, Planning, Implementation, and Evaluation	Planning Interventions (22, 23)	17.9**... to support national plans to implement ...	Assess needs, national and local plans of action; implement, evaluate
Mobilizing Sectors Able to Tackle Causes	Partnerships (8, 9, 19)	17.18 Data Monitoring and Accountability	Build national commitment
Adequate and Sustained Funding	Sustainability/ Accountability (10, 20)	17.17 ... public, public-private, and civil society partnerships ...	(Estimate costs, identify sources of financial support)
Standards and Training for Human Talent	Training and Capacity Building (18)	17.1 Strengthen domestic resource mobilization ...	(Develop and manage human resources)
Public Support and Engagement	Community Involvement (16)	17.9*... targeted capacity building ...	

*Brackets indicate partial match. **Refers only to developing countries. See appendix for sources.

Figure 7.1. Seven Essentials for Implementing Effective Solutions

are pertinent to the particular essential element. In the rest of this section of chapter 7, I will discuss each of the seven "essentials" in depth.

Essential Element 1: Permanent Violence Prevention Boards

The UN guidelines call for establishing a permanent national authority or responsibility center that would be the "energy" behind developing and implementing integrated crime prevention plans. To be effective, this national crime prevention board would support and collaborate with local authorities at the city and district levels because it is at the local level where crime problems are most evident and the needed services are most immediately accessible. Permanent crime prevention boards would be established at other levels, including significant cities, which would support the work of the national board as well as mobilize local talent, facilitate the exchange of information between the various sectors, and disseminate and exchange pertinent information to key stakeholders and the public.

Essential Element 2: Informed by Violence Prevention Science and Data (Knowledge-Based Approaches)

The UN guidelines specifically refer to the importance of basing crime prevention on a multidisciplinary foundation of knowledge about crime problems, their multiple causes, and promising and proven practices. The UNODC handbook, mentioned earlier, clarifies the types of knowledge as well as the importance of data. When the UN guidelines were adopted in 2002 and the handbook written in 2010, there was already considerable knowledge about dealing with crime. The handbook, thus, includes many examples of good practice.

Since 2010, however, the availability of solid violence prevention science has exploded onto portals and into national science reports, as we saw in chapter 2. Chapters 3 to 6 of this book have been written, in part, to fill a gap at the UNODC, which has not produced a guide to that new wealth of knowledge in nearly a decade. The WHO, with collaboration from the UNODC and other UN agencies, did bring some of this knowledge together in the *INSPIRE* document, which will be discussed shortly. Whereas WHO's 2016 document covers some similar ground and examples as this book, my unique contribution is to emphasize proactive policing and ways to save misspent funds from reactive policing and jails. I also focus, in chapter 10, on how effective solutions not only reap impressive reductions in violent crime but also in costs to taxpayers.

Essential Element 3: Integrated Plan Using Diagnosis, Planning, Implementation, and Evaluation (National and Local)

The 1995 "Guidelines for the Cooperation and Technical Assistance in the Field of Urban Crime Prevention" stresses the need for a local plan that mobilizes various community and economic sectors to prevent crime. According to the guidelines, that plan must be supported by the central government but be based on diagnoses of crime problems occurring locally. The plan also outlines the necessity of performance standards, targeted solutions, training protocol, and outcome evaluations.

As figure 7.2 illustrates, a successful implementation of violence prevention interventions follows an important four-step process of diagnosis, planning, implementation, and evaluation. At the core of success is centralized organization and support by a permanent violence prevention board. I like to explain this model in terms of visiting a doctor about a headache. The first step is to localize the headache and identify its cause. Next, you plan options to cure it, such as with medication. The third step is to get the medication and take it as prescribed. Finally, you assess the results and try something else if the first plan does not work. The process is basically how engineers, entrepreneurs, lawyers, and the whole world that has advanced civilization works, except for the CJS! The CJS process involves arrest, trial and sentence, and punishment without any diagnosis, plan, or evaluation of outcomes; regard of effectiveness; or cost–benefit analysis.

Essential Element 4: Mobilizing Sectors Able to Tackle Causes

Because of the nature of the risk factors that lead to crime, the permanent violence prevention board must mobilize talent able to help solve the problems. These individuals might include social workers, educators, health professionals, employment specialists, and sports figures as well as CJS workers. The police role is important because officers can actively support a municipality investing in the social, civic, and medical sectors related to crime prevention, just as heart surgeons argue for healthy lifestyles as a means to preventing disease. The International Association of Chiefs of Police guidelines for putting victims at the zenith discussed in chapter 6 are a great place for police to start with their efforts. In addition, as we saw in chapter 3 and will see again in chapter 9, police can be part of a broader strategy to use law enforcement to tackle crime risk factors, such as access to guns or knives and alcohol; to threaten persistent offenders with arrest to encourage the offenders to seek medical, emotional, mental, or social services; and to divert people in conflict with the law to community services appropriate to their particular need.

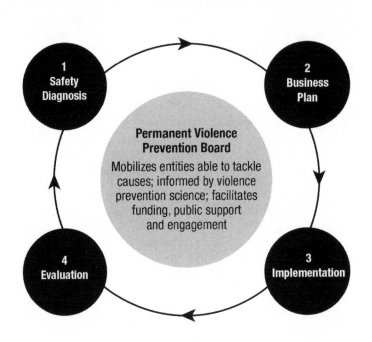

Safety Diagnosis	Systematically analyze crime problems, their causes, locations, risk factors, and consequences, in particular at the local level
Business Plan	Create a plan that draws on the most effective approach to the particular problems and adapts interventions to the specific location and context
Implementation	Organize, train, and monitor human talent to deliver interventions that are efficient, effective, and sustained
Evaluation	Monitor and evaluate the outcome of efforts with qualitative information and measured results (including comparison to targets)

See appendix for sources.

Figure 7.2.   Essential Role of a Violence Prevention Board

Essential Element 5: Adequate and Sustained Funding

Importantly, the UN guidelines also call for sustainable funding of crime prevention, noting that "Crime prevention requires adequate resources, including funding for structures and activities, in order to be sustained. There should be clear accountability for funding, implementation, and evaluation, and for the achievement of planned results."[4]

Many of the projects shown to have been effective in reducing violent crime in chapters 2 to 5 were time-limited experiments. When the experiment concluded and was shown to have been successful, too often the project ceased. For example, the HighScope Perry Preschool Project had impressive outcomes, but there has been no follow-through. Also, in the well-known Boston gun violence reduction strategy, to be discussed in more detail in chapter 9, the special budget for completing school, job training, and employment assistance disappeared (despite the police budget not being affected). Ten years later, the City of Boston had to start over.

To achieve real and sustained reductions in violent crime, an adequate and sustained budget is needed. In my book *Smarter Crime Control*, I recommended that crime prevention through social development innovations should receive the equivalent of 10 percent of what is being spent on the CJS in a country or a city. We cannot expect small and temporary projects in one or two districts to achieve the violence reduction needed across an entire city, let alone an entire country.

Essential Element 6: Standards and Training for Human Talent

For innovations to be successful, they will require the human talent capable of planning and implementing effective solutions. The ECOSOC guidelines refer to "capacity and training." I prefer to focus on "establishing standards," because many of the tasks to get effective solutions implemented require new skills. Just as we would not expect a police officer to make an arrest without training, a lawyer to prosecute without attending law school, or a prison guard to work in a jail without correction training, we should not expect the planning, community engagement, or monitoring and evaluation functions of a violence prevention strategy to happen without training human talent to standards. Nor should we expect staff members and advocates to raise awareness and get action from decision makers without some training.

Essential Element 7: Public Support and Engagement

The public can play many roles in applying violence prevention science. They can become mentors, take precautions, and help map crime. They also can be advocates to get the permanent board and funding needed to implement crime prevention strategies.

OTHER INTERNATIONAL ATTEMPTS TO DO WHAT'S NECESSARY TO STOP VIOLENT CRIME

Sadly, these important UN crime prevention guidelines have not been implemented with any serious plan, training, deadlines, or funding. It is not possible to estimate the exact number of homicides or rapes that would have been avoided if countries had acted on that seminal 2002 ECOSOC resolution. Undoubtedly, hundreds of thousands of lives would have been saved, and many millions of women would have avoided the trauma of rape. Perhaps the lack of action has to do with the fact that the requests accompanying the resolutions were vague. For example, the 2002 ECOSOC resolution requested that the Secretary-General report on the implementation of the resolution to the Commission on Crime Prevention and Criminal Justice at the next UN General Assembly, which did not lead to much action.

In 2015, UNODC held its quinquennial Congress on Crime Prevention and Criminal Justice in Doha, Qatar. The final declaration of that congress highlighted "integrating crime prevention and criminal justice into the wider United Nations agenda to address social and economic challenges and to promote the rule of law at the national and international levels, and public participation."[5] It was replete with phrases endorsing crime prevention and crime victims' rights, but, unfortunately, the declaration lacked few concrete measures. An important exception is the initiative to fund sports and life-skills training, but $50 million on this one item worldwide will do little overall. Most recently, in 2017, at the UNODC conference of the Commission on Crime Prevention and Criminal Justice, one event focused on the UNODC contribution to making cities safer.

Recent Efforts of the WHO

One organization that has been attempting to fill the void in action related to violent crime prevention worldwide is the WHO. In 2002, this prestigious international agency published an encyclopedic report on how health relates to violence issues.[6] Since then, the organization has undertaken a number of limited initiatives to get action on the recommendations outlined in this *World Report on Violence and Health*. One of its initiatives has been an annual conference of governmental and nongovernmental organizations and academic experts to share knowledge and news of innovations. This group also contributes to decisions by the World Health Assembly (WHA), the WHO's decision-making body.

Another important WHO initiative was the 2014 survey of 133 countries on the extent to which they were implementing the recommendations from the *World Report on Violence and Health*. The questionnaire explored governance plans, data collection practices, action plans, prevention laws, and trends in violence. It also included a list of "best buys," examples of solutions identified as effective in the WHO's 2009 report, solutions similar to what I presented in chapters 4 and 5. In addition, the survey outlined potential solutions for preventing violence. The gist of the WHO's list of solutions follows:

- Developing safe, stable, and nurturing relationships between children and their parents and caregivers
- Developing life skills in children and adolescents
- Reducing the availability and harmful use of alcohol
- Reducing access to guns and knives
- Promoting gender equality to prevent violence against women
- Changing cultural and social norms that support violence
- Victim identification, care, and support programs

Once all the surveys were assessed, WHO published its *Global Status Report on Violence Prevention*. This publication noted that many countries lacked basic data, particularly on youth violence and child maltreatment. Some data was available on violence against women. Some countries had national plans but not based on data. Most of the best buys had not been started in more than 50 percent of the countries. Rather, countries more often were investing in prevention programs not on a level commensurate with the scale and severity of their problems.[7] Few reported efforts to combat street violence through education. Many reported efforts to control alcohol, but those efforts were not always met with success. Many also had some type of firearms regulation, but enforcement of laws was described as woefully inadequate. In addition, the *Global Status Report* pointed out that help for victims is still very limited worldwide.

Granted, the survey is an important first step to assess implementation. It shows some small investments in starting effective solutions in some countries. But the survey was not able to report on any impact from the investments or successes in cities. Hopefully, the survey will be updated and become a regular way of assessing violence prevention progress around the globe. It truly has the potential of becoming as influential as the WHO Survey on Traffic Safety, which undoubtedly is saving many, many lives and avoiding horrible injuries.

Another important international resolution came from the WHO's governing board, the WHA. Also in 2014, the WHA committed to "Strengthening the Role of the Health System in Addressing Violence, in Particular Against Women and Girls, and Against Children" (WHA67.15).[8] This resolution urges member states to engage health systems in the prevention of violence in collaboration with other sectors, such as justice and social services. It echoes the need for scientific evidence, multiagency responses, greater use of data, and more training.

Building on Resolution WHA67.15, in 2016, the WHO adopted its *Global Plan of Action*.[9] Most of the proposals in the plan relate to the specific role of the health sector. The plan also recalls the importance of information and evidence, which includes actions related to epidemiological, social science, and intervention research; improved surveillance, including through health-information systems; and program monitoring and evaluation. All these items of the plan are important—but as part of a *comprehensive* community safety strategy, such as agreed at ECOSOC.

UN-Habitat's Responsibility for Safer Cities in the UN Urban Agenda

The UN agency responsible for human settlements and sustainable urban development is the UN Human Settlements Program (UN-Habitat). Every ten years, UN-Habitat organizes a major summit on the future of cities. As the world's population clusters increasingly in cities—and central governments neglect to support their cities—UN-Habitat draws attention to the challenges. Among these challenges are issues of street and intimate partner violence. At the most recent summit of UN-Habitat, in Quito, Ecuador, in 2016, the agency adopted what is called the "UN Urban Agenda." This document has begun to recognize street and intimate partner violence through the UN-Habitat Safer Cities program and during a special session at Habitat III. Unfortunately, the mention is minor, and there is no serious plan to implement efforts to mitigate the violence. Importantly, no measurable targets have been identified. This must change.

The UN-Habitat Safer Cities program builds on the 1995 UN ECOSOC resolution and particularly the processes illustrated in figure 7.2. That is, administrators of the Safer Cities program recommend that governments follow the four-step model of diagnosing, planning, implementing, and evaluating when addressing crime.[10] Despite its small scale, the Safer Cities program has led to various types of comprehensive community safety strategies that engage diverse sectors (for example, social service, family, schools, and health) discussed in both the ECOSOC–UNODC resolutions and in planned actions to prevent crime across municipalities. Nonetheless, while the Safer Cities program has great potential and good intentions, the road to hell is paved by good intentions. This wonderful program must become a pivot point for municipal action, with long-overdue adequate and sustained resources. In addition, collaboration with the UNODC and WHO will be instrumental in getting the SDG results for which cities strive.

UNODC Input on UN System-Wide Guidelines on Safer Cities

Most recently, in 2018, UNODC issued a report to the UN Commission on Crime Prevention and Criminal Justice, titled *UNODC Input on UN System-Wide Guidelines on Safer Cities*. This report rightly repeats many of the important principles agreed to in the ECOSOC resolutions discussed earlier. For example, the report stresses the importance of a permanent central government authority, setting of priorities, being informed by knowledge, mobilizing key sectors, and ensuring adequate and sustained funding. In addition, the report is clear about the importance of local government and recalls ways for crime prevention to succeed through a spectrum of social development through situational crime prevention and beyond. Furthermore, the report underlines the importance of managing corruption and linking local strategies with international organized crime, which is encouraging for those who want to see rates of violence reduced.

Unfortunately, this version of the UNODC report does not focus on training and capacity nor on citizen engagement, two elements critical to successful implementation of a violence prevention program. Also, whereas the WHO, in its resolutions and reports, offers examples of effective solutions—the best buys—as I also did in chapters 3 through 6 with results and savings, the UNODC report does not provide examples. Plus, it refers to

community-oriented policing and justice rather than problem-solving policing and justice.[11] There is a big difference in terms of results for citizens.

UN SDGS CALL FOR RESULTS-ORIENTED STRATEGY TO END VIOLENCE

To recap, we are close to two decades since the adoption of the 2002 ECO-
SOC "Crime Prevention Guidelines." As we have just seen, there has been
a consensus between governments in different UN fora—ECOSOC for
UNODC and UN-Habitat and WHA for the WHO—about a knowledge
base that I call solid violence prevention science. That is great. However,
the WHO is up front about the best buys, whereas the UNODC and UN-
Habitat do not share directly through a portal or document about successes.
The UNODC and UN-Habitat agree on the importance of a permanent prevention planning authority, and the WHO did for its 2014 survey. Governments through these various international entities effectively agree on the
importance of the planning process illustrated in figure 7.2. The UNODC
is clear on adequate and sustained funding. They all agree about mobilizing
the sectors that can tackle the causes. And there is some agreement on training, although public engagement does not get a lot of attention.

Why, then, is there little evidence of national reductions in violent crime
as a direct result of all these resolutions, reports, and efforts? This lack of
implementation of effective solutions is important to everyone. Had effective solutions been implemented over a five-year period, there could have
been an estimated 50 percent reduction in violent crime, as I pointed out in
Smarter Crime Control. This reduction translates into 8,500 fewer lives lost
and more than 600,000 fewer women being raped, in the United States alone.

I contend the missing link has been numbers! Enter the SDGs. As discussed earlier, in 2015, world leaders, from rich as well as poor countries,
committed to achieve by 2030 17 SDGs outlined in UN Resolution 70/1,
"Transforming Our World: The 2030 Agenda for Sustainable Development."[12] These goals offer hope to getting effective solutions implemented
to end violent crime by agreeing to focus on results. Whereas governments
talk about accountability, evaluation, and monitoring, none of what has
been discussed in this chapter thus far focuses on results, such as measuring fewer lethal tragedies and fewer women raped. But the SDGs do. They
itemize and call out specific targets and indicators.

Recall that among the 17 SDGs are two that deal specifically with victimization and crime prevention: SDG 5 calls for a significant reduction in vio-

lence against women and girls, and SDG 16 addresses a significant reduction in homicide rates. In addition, there are two other SDGs that relate to violent crime: SDG 3 includes reductions in drug abuse and traffic crashes, and SDG 11 focuses on making cities safer. Finally, SDG 17 highlights the importance of fostering partnerships for investing in capacity building, data collection, monitoring, and evaluating efforts—for all the SDGs.

The SDG process outlines many other goals in addition to tackling violence prevention. In fact, only 10 percent of "Transforming Our World's" 169 total targets are concerned specifically with reducing victimization and homicide, violence against women, traffic fatalities, and violence in cities. Nonetheless, achieving positive results for other SDGs will ultimately contribute to achieving the targets often cited as risk factors or causes for violent crime. That means less violence in our world!

Figure 7.3 highlights five SDGs. It includes the general objective for each and examples of how the results will be measured. What gets measured, gets done! Yes, governments nationally and locally need to measure these indicators and then set targets on the reductions to be achieved. If you were the king of your country or the mayor of your city, you should look at the indicators for SDG 5 and SDG 16, specifically, and decide if you would like to achieve them in the next few years—and see fewer homicides and rapes in your domain. The indicators are not how many more police you have imposed on taxpayers or how many guns were seized during a stop and frisk. They are about outcomes your citizens and voters and, hopefully, you want and deserve. But they require you to act.

Given the lives lost and ruined to violence discussed in chapter 1, the world needs to implement results-oriented strategies like the SDGs, strategies that will actually deliver an end to violent crime, not just talk about good principles to be followed. The commitment to outcomes and results iterated in "Transforming Our World" finally provides the framework for governments worldwide to identify specific indicators to achieve, such as rates of violent crime or rates of intimate partner and sexual violence. With measurable indicators, governments can set reduction targets for the indicators, and engage planning and resources to achieve those reductions by 2030.

The Results-Oriented Culture of the SDGs

This shift to a results-oriented culture is significant and spelled out in the 2018 "Discussion Guide for the Fourteenth United Nations Congress on Crime Prevention and Criminal Justice."[13] Whereas the crime prevention guidelines of the ECOSOC and WHO resolutions are about *process*,

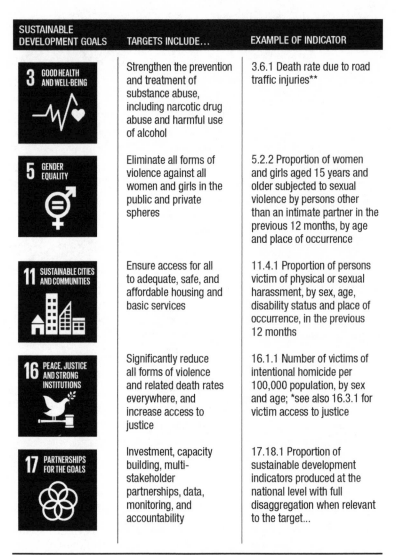

SUSTAINABLE DEVELOPMENT GOALS	TARGETS INCLUDE...	EXAMPLE OF INDICATOR
3 GOOD HEALTH AND WELL-BEING	Strengthen the prevention and treatment of substance abuse, including narcotic drug abuse and harmful use of alcohol	3.6.1 Death rate due to road traffic injuries**
5 GENDER EQUALITY	Eliminate all forms of violence against all women and girls in the public and private spheres	5.2.2 Proportion of women and girls aged 15 years and older subjected to sexual violence by persons other than an intimate partner in the previous 12 months, by age and place of occurrence
11 SUSTAINABLE CITIES AND COMMUNITIES	Ensure access for all to adequate, safe, and affordable housing and basic services	11.4.1 Proportion of persons victim of physical or sexual harassment, by sex, age, disability status and place of occurrence, in the previous 12 months
16 PEACE, JUSTICE AND STRONG INSTITUTIONS	Significantly reduce all forms of violence and related death rates everywhere, and increase access to justice	16.1.1 Number of victims of intentional homicide per 100,000 population, by sex and age; *see also 16.3.1 for victim access to justice
17 PARTNERSHIPS FOR THE GOALS	Investment, capacity building, multi-stakeholder partnerships, data, monitoring, and accountability	17.18.1 Proportion of sustainable development indicators produced at the national level with full disaggregation when relevant to the target...

*16.3.1 Proportion of victims of violence in the previous 12 months who reported their victimization to competent authorities or other officially recognized conflict resolution mechanisms. ** This indicator refers to goal to reduce traffic injuries. In 2018, deaths due to drug overdoses and organized drug trafficking did not have an indicator.
See appendix for sources.

Figure 7.3.   Sustainable Development Goals Including Violence Prevention

this discussion guide points out that the SDGs are about *outcomes*. Rather than hoping processes will lead to outcomes, a results-oriented approach to crime prevention focuses on specific results being accomplished through particular processes. More precisely, the spirit of the SDGs is to identify priorities, set targets, collect data, and measure outcomes. These goals all require a shift away from doing more of the same—spending on the same costly and largely ineffective CJS reactive responses to violence—to, instead, focusing on achieving important outcomes, such as having fewer people's lives ruined by violence. The approach means no longer spending $100 billion because someone else spent $100 billion, as mentioned in chapter 3. The results are about whether a mayor stopped 100 homicides in his or her city or Mexico stopped 10,000 homicides. The results can even be measured in a cost–benefit analysis that shows the positive impact of fewer incidents of violence on economic development.

Such benefits of a results-oriented approach to crime prevention complement evidence-based policy making, in which strategic planning and decisions are driven by the interpretation of available information and through the production and analysis of data, the review of scientific evidence, the monitoring and evaluation of policies, and the implementation of programs and projects. Integrating a review mechanism in the cycle that guarantees transparent evaluation of what works and what does not is also crucial in fostering a results-oriented culture.

In truth, the framework of the SDGs derives much of its power from the measurability of the progress made for each target, and goal indicator frameworks can help at all levels (global, regional, national, and local) to measure and evaluate the impact of crime prevention, primarily on the basis of national data and country-led evaluations. That is, indicators might derive from victimization surveys and surveys on intimate partner and sexual violence as well as homicide rates. General measures of feeling safe might also be tracked in those victimization surveys. Importantly, goal-indicator frameworks also can encourage sustainable funding because investors can know precise costs and planned benefits.

SDG 17: Partnerships for the Goals

SDG 16+ and *INSPIRE*, which I will discuss shortly, highlight actions that can lead to transformation and facilitate the achievement of violence reduction targets. The underlying challenge is developing and implementing an approach that achieves success. That's where SDG 17 comes in. SDG 17 itself calls for governments, "To strengthen the means of implementation and revitalization of the global partnership for sustainable development."[14] Ultimately, SDG 17 accentuates the importance of developing human capacity and training, partnerships, investment, use of evidence, and monitoring and evaluation to ensure rigorous implementation of specific strategies. In essence, this specific SDG is a road map, in and of itself, to success in "transforming our world."

SDGs Targeting Violence Against Women and Girls (VAWG)

As an example of how the SDGs place an emphasis on specific outcomes, consider how the UN has committed in SDG 5.2 and SDG 5.3 to the specific elimination of violence against women and girls by 2030. For instance, recall that SDG 5.2 spells out eliminating "all forms of violence against all women and girls in the public and private spheres, including trafficking and sexual and other types of exploitation."[15] This specific verbiage establishes a very clear bottom line that is operationalized into a few measurable indicators. The indicator sets out a way of measuring the results. Specifically, 5.2.2 reads, "Proportion of women and girls aged 15 years and older subjected to sexual violence by persons other than an intimate partner in the previous 12 months, by age and place of occurrence."[16]

The way the SDGs have been agreed to by governments to work is much more than agreeing to a general goal. Rather, each government has agreed to (1) set up a way to measure the indicator and then to (2) establish the targeted reduction in that indicator to be achieved by 2030. The next step is how to implement effective solutions that will achieve that targeted reduction. The implementation can apply earlier resolutions regarding sexual violence, interpersonal violence, and trafficking of women and girls.[17] It also can include other actions that will further reduce VAWG, including SDGs 4.5, 5.5, and 11.1.[18] Furthermore, the UN General Assembly has promoted the resolution of legislation and policy making, advocating that enforceable legislation should be strengthened and created to ensure gender equality and a reduction in VAWG.[19] These UN actions and resolutions stress the importance of a national commitment and contribution to end VAWG using evidence-based prevention programs, the proper allocation of resources to these evidence-based programs, national action plans, and ongoing monitoring and evaluation of techniques.

The Role of Cities in Relation to the SDGs

We cannot leave the discussion of the SDGs without addressing local crime prevention efforts. As noted earlier, community engagement is paramount to delivering effective violence reduction and achieving well-being at the local level. Getting investments *upstream* before violence ruins lives, not just paying more *downstream* to react to crime after it has happened, takes a comprehensive community safety strategy. This approach calls for mobilizing all the services needed to successfully tackle the risk factors that lead to crime and violence, including law enforcement, education, health, social services, and environmental design. As UN-Habitat stresses in its Safer Cities program, safety will be achieved only through a coordinated, multidisciplinary community effort to address the multiple root causes of delinquency, violence, and insecurity.[20]

Two Missing Pieces of the SDGs

There are two issues not addressed by UN Resolution 70/1, "Transforming Our World." The first is how to achieve the targets outlined in the SDGs. However, this is a solvable problem. The ECOSOC guidelines and reports by the UNODC, WHO, and UN-Habitat all clearly delineate the essential elements of a crime prevention program, as evidenced in figure 7.1. Combining these "seven essentials" with effective solutions is the key to success. The second missing piece of the puzzle is how to generate the political support and action necessary to stop people killing each other and men raping women. This will be the focus of chapters 10 through 12.

GETTING GOVERNMENTS TO ACT

Slowly but surely, the SDGs are gathering momentum. Governments, organizations, and agencies around the world, including some "pathfinder" governments, are committing to action. Pathfinder governments are those who are early adopters and leading the charge. Some of them are preparing road maps on how to achieve the SDG targets by 2030, starting from 2015—a short time to "transform the world." Herein, I will discuss two major examples of these road maps: *INSPIRE* and SDG 16+. In addition, two other initiatives deserve special mention: the Inter-American Development Bank (IDB) is influencing better investment to end violent crime in Latin America, and stellar international organizations are advocating for victims' rights and support around the world.

INSPIRE: Major UN Agencies Agree on Seven Key Strategies to End Violence Against Children

One particularly influential road map is *INSPIRE*, a 2016 WHO publication endorsed by the UN Children's Fund (UNICEF), UNODC, World Bank Group, and a variety of other governmental and nongovernmental agencies.[21] It uses compelling data on the number of victims and the tragedies caused to those victims to remind decision makers of the urgency of action and implementation of crime prevention strategies. It shows in a similar way as chapter 1 the outrageous and tremendous human and financial loss the world currently faces due to violence. It presents seven broad strategies for different government ministries to implement along with examples of effective solutions taken from the science of violence prevention. It also highlights an important list of essential elements for implementation. In 2018, UNICEF also published a handbook to provide guidance on indicators for measuring progress on the implementation of *INSPIRE*'s outlined strategies.[22] This should be a great addition to violence prevention efforts.

INSPIRE is an acronym for the way the WHO grouped the effective solutions around the actions of different sectors to reduce violence affecting children and youth:

Implementation and enforcement of laws includes legislation from the justice sector to control alcohol, guns, and corporal punishment of children.

Norms and values includes actions in the education, health, and social welfare sectors to change gender norms, such as those discussed in chapter 5.

Safe environment includes actions in the policing sector, such as those discussed in chapter 3.

Parent and caregiver support includes actions in the family sector, similar to those in chapter 4.

Income and economic strengthening includes actions in the labor sector.

Response and support services includes actions for victims in the welfare, health, and justice sectors, similar to those discussed in chapter 6.

Education and life skills includes actions for victims in the school sector, including life-skills training, as discussed in chapter 4.

For operationalizing the seven recommended strategies, *INSPIRE* proposes a process with nine components. I have grouped these components in the fourth column of figure 7.1, to show how they line up with the UNODC seven essentials for implementing effective solutions. Note that *INSPIRE*'s overall approach, unfortunately, does not include a permanent violence prevention board, though it does include building national commitment, which it discusses in terms of mobilizing different sectors. It stresses being informed by violence prevention science in the selection of interventions and their adaptation to local needs. Plus, it includes all four components of the planning process, as illustrated in figure 7.2. *INSPIRE* also proposes actions to estimate costs and identify sources of support and assumes that funding will come from building national commitment. It calls for the development and management of human resources but does not focus on standards. Finally, as we discussed earlier, monitoring and evaluating the actions to achieve the SDGs is crucial—perhaps the silver bullet for success. Thus, in accordance with SDG 17, the *INSPIRE* framework emphasizes the importance of determining the elements of a national action plan. This plan involves selecting goals, objectives, and targets as well as defining appropriate indicators to monitor program implementation. The *INSPIRE* framework also affirms the importance of including mechanisms to facilitate monitoring through ongoing data collection and analysis. As noted in *INSPIRE*,

> Monitoring should be an ongoing process of collecting and analyzing information about implementation of the INSPIRE package. It should involve regular assessment of whether and how activities are being carried out as planned so that problems can be discussed and addressed. Monitoring should follow the progress of planned activities, identify problems, provide feedback to managers and staff, and solve problems before they cause delays. Data should be processed and analyzed promptly. Results of analysis should be passed to those in a position to take action.[23]

Despite the significance of its contribution to reaching the SDGs, *INSPIRE* does have some drawbacks: Whereas the report's main focus is on reducing violence against children (inclusive of SDG 16) and logically incorporates SDG 11 (making cities safer), it does not mention violence against women (SDG 5) nor drugs and traffic safety (SDG 3). A critical challenge for *INSPIRE* is how to get funding, which I will discuss in chapters 10 to 12. Specifically, *INSPIRE* refers to developing national commitment and identifying sources of funding, but it does not discuss how governments will acquire the funding for the necessary actions. Furthermore, although the recommended process surely will require a "backbone" organization to organize and implement its steps as well as public support and engagement for its sustainability, *INSPIRE* does not emphasize these. In chapters 10 to 12, I will discuss both, specifically highlighting the importance of public support as part of sustaining political will. Only once these issues are addressed will this model succeed.

Center on International Cooperation's SDG 16+

Another important road map to achieve the SDGs is called "SDG 16+."[24] This road map is outlined in the document titled *The Roadmap for Peaceful, Just and Inclusive Societies*, published in 2017 by the Center on International Cooperation. The pathfinder governments that launched the process are Brazil, Sierra Leone, and Switzerland. The group of governments supporting the initiative is expanding, with Canada, England and Wales, and Mexico on that list.

Those governments, international organizations, global partnerships, and other partners who have agreed to this road map focus on action to be taken in 2017 through 2022 that will cover all targets within the SDG goals that will achieve SDG 16 as well as the targets and measurable outcomes that aim for peaceful, just, and inclusive societies. See figure 7.3. Specifically, the SDG 16+ road map calls for the implementation of strategies that will lead not only to change but also to the radical transformation needed to turn 16-plus SDG violence reduction targets into reality. These targets include eliminating gender-based violence, street violence, and violence against children. Actions to achieve the envisioned transformation include the following:

- Scaling up violence prevention for women, children, and vulnerable groups
- Building safe, inclusive, resilient cities
- Targeted prevention for countries and communities
- Increasing justice and legal empowerment
- Empowering people as agents of change
- Respecting all human rights and promoting gender equality[25]

According to SDG 16+, implementation of these actions requires the mobilization of and the financial support from national, international, public, and private sources. SDG 16+ also highlights the importance of increased investment in the knowledge, data, and evidence that are needed to inform decision making. In addition, the road map recommends working with political champions; recommitting to *INSPIRE* (including investing in the implementation of globally agreed strategies); and engaging other sectors, such as justice, education, and health. The cost of inaction related to SDG 16+ can be counted in terms of lives lost and damaged, economic costs, and diminished investment across all SDGs.

How the Inter-American Development Bank (IDB) Is Helping

IDB's 2014 "Citizen Security and Justice Sector Framework Document"[26] also offers some hope for transformation of governments to end violent crime. Over the years, the IDB has had a sustained interest in ending violent crime. In 2018, they published an important report on better spending for better lives. This included a chapter providing a comprehensive analysis of crime trends, public opinion, and government spending for Latin American and Caribbean countries.[27] This chapter focuses on citizen security—violence prevention—and argues for being smart on crime. It shows smart on crime between the two extremes of soft on crime or tough on crime, which have been presented politically to deal with crime. Soft on crime refers to policies of socioeconomic restructuring that reduce poverty, provide education, and create jobs. In fact, it is being soft on potential criminals because it provides positive opportunities, such as jobs for them. Tough on crime refers to increases in policing and longer prison sentences. Actually, it is being tough on criminals in the hope of deterring them from offending.

"Smart on Crime" focuses on the outcomes of reducing violent crime. It is using the solid prevention science to invest in solutions that are effective and cost effective in stopping crime. The IBD chapter is echoing generally not only the smart on crime movement discussed earlier and my book on smarter crime control but also decisions by the Organization of American States. It concludes that prevention is the most cost effective way to end violent crime but that political traction is needed to implement it. This report is particularly important because it uses extensive data to stress five major conclusions:

- These countries have high levels of violence, 9 percent of the world's population but 33 percent of the world's homicides.
- Violence has been increasing while income has been increasing.
- Public opinion often favors more security spending.
- Of the countries that increased security spending the most, only a minority saw their security indicators improve.

- Smarter spending is
  - more preventive and less reactive,
  - more focused and less broad based, and
  - more based on scientific evidence and less on intuition.[28]

The challenge is how to get political traction. The scientific evidence is available, as we have seen in the second part of this book, but political traction is much more than knowledge being available. It is also a question of identifying the essentials for successful implementation; examples of that implementation are discussed in this chapter and chapters 8 and 9. It is about how to get buy-in as well, as will be discussed in chapters 10, 11, and 12.

Victimologists Call for Urgent Action

In 2006, victimologists drafted a cogent text for a "UN Convention on Justice and Support for Victims of Crime and Abuse of Power," which includes special references to the actions discussed in chapter 6.[29] This was prepared by two international organizations that focus specifically on evidence and good practice for the rights of victims. The International Victimology Institute (INTERVICT) at Tilburg University in the Netherlands (https://www.tilburguniversity.edu/research/institutes-and-research-groups/intervict/about/) promotes and executes interdisciplinary research that can contribute to a comprehensive, evidence-based body of knowledge on the abuse of power and the empowerment and support of victims of crime. The World Society of Victimologists (http://www.worldsocietyofvic timology.org/) advances victimological research and practices around the world; encourages interdisciplinary and comparative work and research in this field; and advances cooperation between international, national, regional and local agencies, and other groups concerned with the problems of victims. These experts know their field and have agreed on a model law that provides minimal rights for victims in criminal courts.[30] Yet, despite the expertise that has gone into this particular road map, there have been few examples of jurisdictions adopting the ideas.

Unfortunately, victims remain the orphans of social policy. Victimologists and other experts on victim care and rights, thus, are calling on governments—international, regional, statewide, and local—to act, and to act now. In those jurisdictions that have made some advances, more can be done. In the rest of the world where achieving progress in victims' rights and services has been slow, trumpets should be sounding the alarm that violence must be stopped and victims must be supported.

KEY TAKEAWAYS

- Governments have agreed at ECOSOC on the importance of crime prevention and on a list of seven essentials for success.
- The seven essential elements include permanent crime prevention boards, knowledge-based crime prevention approaches, integrated national and local planning processes, sustainable and adequate funding, training to develop human talent, and engagement of the public.
- Governments have agreed at the WHA on effective solutions and the importance of preventing violence against women and children.
- Governments have agreed at UN-Habitat on the importance of making cities safer, particularly emphasizing the planning processes from the ECOSOC–UNODC guidelines.
- The WHO *Global Survey of the State of Violence Prevention* shows that some governments use violence prevention science some of the time.
- The UN SDGs stress a results-oriented approach that is measurable. In four of the SDGs, the goals include some aspect of stopping violence, such as achieving reductions in street and gender-based violence and making cities safer by 2030.
- Some governments, organizations, and agencies are preparing road maps on how to achieve the SDG targets by 2030, such as WHO's *INSPIRE* (on violence against children) and the Center on International Cooperation's SDG 16+.
- The IDB has set out cogent arguments for using smarter spending to end violence, including prevention, focus, and evidence.
- Other initiatives, such as those from victimology organizations, may also contribute to an end of violence.
- Whereas all these efforts provide essential steps, they do not solve the challenges of political will, cogent implementation, and funding, which will be discussed in the next chapters.

LEARNING FROM EARLY ADOPTERS

Keys to Success and Avoiding Failure

Facts are stubborn things; and whatever may be our wishes, our inclinations, or the dictates of our passions, they cannot alter the state of facts and evidence.

—US President John Adams

Several governments were early adopters of national strategies to end violent crime, but most of them ignored the consensus at ECOSOC about utilizing certain essential elements for success. As US President John Adams noted, "facts are stubborn things." Without paying attention to the facts of what is needed for effective implementation of a violence prevention program, failure was likely inevitable. Nonetheless, we can learn just as much from those failures—magnificent disasters—as we can from the successes of violence prevention pioneers.

Before we dig into an exploration of the actions of early adopters, I would like to recap what has been covered thus far. In chapters 3 through 6, we saw examples of projects in proactive policing and different social development sectors that have reduced crime much more than the standard CJS. These results and their cost benefits constitute a solid violence prevention science. In chapter 7, we learned that governments have formally announced their consensus on the importance of crime prevention, through their resolutions, particularly at the UN Economic and Social Council (ECOSOC) coming from the UN Office on Drugs and Crime (UNODC).

We also now know, through those resolutions, that prevention programs can be operationalized if they incorporate certain essential ingredients: a permanent crime prevention board; evidence-based knowledge; an integrated plan that features a cycle of diagnosing the problem(s), implementing a targeted plan, and evaluating the outcome; multisector talent; engaging the public; and sustainable and adequate funding. We also saw in chapter 7 that governments have committed to results-oriented transformations to achieve the Sustainable Development Goals (SDGs) by 2030. Unfortunately, however, most governments are still reacting to violent crime after it has happened by enlarging the standard criminal justice system, doing more of the same that others are doing.

Although the shift to implementing effective solutions has been timid, a few countries and communities have gotten the ball rolling. In the early 1970s, Scandinavian countries started small crime prevention councils to promote citizen responsibility to take precautions for prevention. Denmark went further by establishing a national social development partnership between schools, social services, and police. And various cities in the United States, the United Kingdom, and Latin America have stepped forward with their own efforts, as we will explore in chapter 9. Some of these efforts focus on limiting access to alcohol and guns, whereas other efforts boast a marriage of smart proactive policing and upstream social programs to reduce homicide rates. There are even a few governments that have started ambitious strategies along the lines of the UNODC resolutions, although they have not been sustained. One particularly exciting project found ten governments in Latin America collaborating to develop national plans.

My goal with this chapter is to share insights about various national violence prevention programs and projects. My discussion will explore the positive lessons from these early adopters as well as reasons several of them met an early demise. The more one knows, the better one does.

ARE EARLY ADOPTERS MEETING ECOSOC GUIDELINES?

Belgium, France, and Sweden are often thought to be at the forefront of crime prevention. Their initiatives are consistent with several elements of the ECOSOC guidelines discussed in chapter 7. These early adopters, however, have not focused on evaluating their impact on violent crime rates, so they are not yet in the results-oriented culture of the SDGs. Because of this, we do not know if these three countries are on track to meet the SDGs by 2030.

Belgium

For nearly twenty years, Belgium has required municipalities, via a contract, to develop a comprehensive community safety strategy, and a federal central crime prevention center oversees those contracts. As part of the agreement, the municipalities analyze or audit their crime problem; develop and implement a plan to tackle the problem; and then evaluate their efforts, as in the comprehensive community safety strategy illustrated in figure 7.2 in chapter 7. In the past few decades, the Belgian Council of Ministers has approved hundreds of programs targeting at-risk populations and communities. Through evaluations of the processes for these initiatives, they conclude they have met over 90 percent of their objectives, but they need to verify the extent to which the funded programs have contributed to less violent crime.[1]

In checking off the "essentials" of a successful crime prevention program, note that Belgium is doing several things right: the country has a central crime prevention agency, local multisectoral plans, and some sharing of best practices. Recently, it has talked about evaluation.[2] Because the efforts are not tracked as data, however, we do not know how much violent crime has actually been stopped.

France

In 1986, France supported six of its cities in pioneering collaborative comprehensive community safety strategies. By 2018, almost every municipality in the country had some form of a comprehensive community safety strategy. France continues to provide national support for these multisectoral strategies, including through the *Stratégie nationale de prévention de la délinquance*. This detailed action plan provides the framework for a multisectoral strategy aimed at improving public safety by reducing fear of crime and targeting at-risk youth and prevention of violence against women.[3] This important document demonstrates sustained funding, local multisectoral approaches, and talks about evaluation—meeting many of the ECOSOC "essentials" guidelines. But we do not know how much violent crime has been stopped as a result of the efforts. There needs to be more analysis of the extent to which cities are implementing proven solutions and whether these cities are achieving greater reductions than the national trends.

Sweden

Sweden established a national crime prevention council in 1974. Today, this council not only manages crime prevention research and data analysis, but it also supports local crime prevention efforts. Its official reports rightly refer to the importance of helping local initiatives use evidence-based strategies, applying violence prevention knowledge, and facilitating collaboration among various sectors.[4]

Some of Sweden's crime prevention work is consistent with the ECO-SOC guidelines in relation to fostering local, multisectoral approaches to violence prevention; creating and implementing evidence-based plans; and providing adequate training. Whether there is sustained and adequate funding for the crime prevention efforts, however, is unclear. In addition, Sweden has not yet moved toward a results-oriented framework, though individual cities, such as Malmö, are moving in that direction. Again, without a results-oriented framework, we do not know how much violent crime has been stopped in Sweden and what work still needs to be done.

LESSONS FROM SUCCESS

As we discussed earlier in the book, research has uncovered various risk factors that act as "facilitators of violence." From firearms and alcohol to poverty and lack of employment—all these can be targeted in crime prevention efforts. The logic is, if the risk factor is eliminated or reduced, violence can be reduced or even purged completely in a community. With this theory in mind, some countries and municipalities across the globe have developed a number of innovations to tackle various facilitators of violence.

Limiting Access to Alcohol in the Former USSR

Reducing the availability of alcohol is well established as a way to reduce violence. In the mid-1980s, the government of the former USSR enforced various alcohol-related measures, including restricting liquor store hours as well as the number of outlets for alcohol purchase. This strict alcohol regulation led to a dramatic fall in violence.[5] Programs in cities in chapter 9 further demonstrate how restricting access to alcohol reduces homicides.

Firearm Control in Canada and Australia

Canada introduced commonsense regulations to require gun owners to have a license and to restrict ownership of any guns other than rifles for hunting. The program was evaluated in terms of results, and evaluations showed reductions in homicides and robberies.[6] In another "win," Australia organized a massive buyback of guns and instituted much stricter rules for owning a gun. The initiative is credited by researchers with a more than 50 percent drop in murders and suicide in that country. In addition, as of the writing of this book in 2018, there have been no mass shootings in Australia since the gun buyback program and policy changes.[7]

Preventing Gun Violence in the United States

Whereas Canada and Australia seem to have moderated gun violence at this time, such is not the case in the United States. According to the Giffords Law Center to Prevent Gun Violence:

> Gun violence is one of the most urgent public health crises of our time, with nearly 115,000 Americans killed or injured by bullets each year. Nowhere is this more evident than in historically underserved urban communities, many of which suffer from gun death rates that dwarf the national average. The inequalities faced by these communities are real—Black men make up a mere 6 percent of the population in the United States, but account for more than half of all gun homicide victims each year. That staggering toll is unconscionable.[8]

In an effort to mitigate the tragedies occurring in the United States at the hands of gunmen, the Giffords Law Center has examined concrete ways state leaders could support and scale community-driven solutions that have a real and lasting impact on gun violence in urban neighborhoods. They were searching for a strategy that saves lives from gun violence while also generating cost savings for taxpayers and lifting up communities. Their research has taken them to three of the five states that fund and support evidence-based urban violence prevention and intervention programs: Massachusetts, Connecticut, and New York. All three have had remarkable success cutting gun violence rates, as you will learn by reading on.

In Massachusetts, one of the nation's leaders when it comes to investing in urban gun violence reduction, a statewide initiative is dramatically cutting violence and incarceration rates by offering critical services to the young men most likely to pick up a gun, providing nonviolent alternatives, and saving taxpayers $7 for each dollar invested. Specifically, between 2010 and 2015, gun homicide rates in the state fell by 35 percent, while gun homicide rates nationally increased 14 percent during that same period.[9]

In Connecticut, the statewide gun homicide rate fell by 16 percent in the same time period. In addition, violence rates have dropped by more than 50 percent in three of Connecticut's major cities since 2011, with help from a state-funded violence intervention program that brings together a powerful partnership of law enforcement officers, community members, and social service providers. At a total cost of less than $1 million per year, this program has prevented shootings while generating an annual savings of $7 million.[10]

Meanwhile, in the state of New York, gun homicide rates fell 23 percent in those years. With the number of evidence-based violence reduction programs increasing in the state—programs funded and coordinated in part by the state—New York gun violence rates continue to plunge, especially in New York City. Interestingly, the state's $20 million investment in its gun violence reduction effort pales in comparison to the overall cost of gun violence in New York State—an estimated $5.6 billion per year.[11] Increasing the $20 million investment likely would increase the reductions in gun violence even further.

Based on the successes noted above, additional research, and their knowledge of the essentials of a quality prevention program, the Giffords Law Center advocates that six key elements be present in any state plan to arrest urban gun violence:

- Provide robust state-level coordination (permanent violence prevention board)
- Implement evidence-based strategies (informed by violence prevention science and data)
- Focus on high-risk people and places (diagnosis, planning, implementation)
- Conduct regular program evaluations (evaluation)
- Commit to long-term, stable funding (adequate and sustained funding)
- Facilitate community input and engagement (public support and engagement)

These six key elements coincide with the ECOSOC essential elements, as shown by the essential elements noted in parentheses. That Giffords Law Center would advocate for these key elements, therefore, is not a coincidence. In addition, it is important to note that the cost to taxpayers to support and scale proven programs is minuscule compared to what gun violence currently costs—an estimated $229 billion annually nationwide in the United States.[12] Plus, these programs have nothing to do with the regulation of firearms, making them more likely to receive bipartisan support. Decision makers who want to end gun violence deaths and injuries should pay attention to this information. There truly is no excuse for inaction.

LESSONS FROM META-ANALYSES

As discussed in chapter 2, with more and more peer-reviewed articles on violence prevention programs readily available, experts can now review the lessons learned from the most scientifically sound articles. Such meta-analyses provide a compelling basis for the conclusion that preventive strategies are the most effective and cost-effective ways to reduce the number of and the harm to crime victims. Three particularly invaluable meta-analyses in the field of crime prevention science follow:

- *What Works in Reducing Community Violence: A Meta-Review and Field Study for the Northern Triangle* (https://www.usaid.gov/sites/default/files/USAID-2016-What-Works-in-Reducing-Community-Violence-Final-Report.pdf), prepared for the US Agency for International Development in February 2016 by Thomas Abt and Christopher Winship
- *Mapping of Homicide Prevention Programs in Latin America and the Caribbean* (http://www.lav.uerj.br/docs/rel/2016/Relato%CC%81rio%20Final%20Ingle%CC%82s.pdf), prepared for the Laboratório de Análse da Violência, Universidade do Estado de Rio de Janeiro in 2016 by Ignacio Cano, Emiliano Rojido, and João Trajano Sento-Sé
- *Regional Model for a Comprehensive Violence and Crime Prevention Policy* (http://sia.eurosocial-ii.eu/files/docs/1461686840-DT_33-_Modelo%20regional%20Prevencion%20Violencia%20(ENG).pdf), a remarkable meta-analysis done in collaboration with officials representing Mexico and nine other Latin American governments

The Search for Solutions to Community Violence in the Northern Triangle

For *What Works in Reducing Community Violence*, researchers Thomas Abt and Christopher Winship examined more than forty reviews and visited twenty sites in Central America and the United States to identify lessons for the prevention of community violence. Their methodology grouped situations for programs rather than individual programs. They were positive about citywide strategies, discussed in chapter 9, that combined focused deterrence by police with services for high-risk individuals known to police. They also highlighted Chicago's Becoming a Man strategy, referenced in chapter 4, and the well-known reintegration strategy of cognitive behavioral therapy, which reduces some of the harm from "too little too late" in corrections. In addition, Abt and Winship's analysis identified six "elements of effectiveness," shared by the most impactful interventions. Those six elements of effectiveness follow herein, with the coinciding ECOSOC essential elements in parentheses:

- A well-defined and understood theory of change (partial—informed by violence prevention science and data)
- Maintaining a specific focus on those most at risk for violence (partial—diagnosis and evaluation)
- Proactive efforts to prevent violence before it occurs, whenever possible (partial—planning, implementation)
- Active engagement and partnership with critical stakeholders (mobilizing sectors able to tackle causes)
- Careful attention to program implementation and fidelity (partial—standards and training for human talent)
- Increasing the perceived and actual legitimacy of strategies and institutions (partial—public support and engagement)[13]

Note that the effort to identify essential elements is important but only touches on some of the seven essential elements agreed upon by the governments of the world. Two vital elements are missing: a permanent prevention planning board and adequate and sustained funding. Focusing on the ECOSOC and SDG guidelines would significantly increase the potential to reduce violence in both Latin America and the United States.

The Search for Effective Homicide Prevention in Latin America and the Caribbean Islands

The meta-analysis by Ignacio Cano, Emiliano Rojido, and João Trajano Sento-Sé identified ninety programs whose direct or indirect ambition was to reduce homicides in Latin America and the Caribbean Islands. They also identified strategies that were probably successful. Among those strategies were controlling risk factors, such as firearms and alcohol, and reducing impunity in criminal justice. Because the successful strategies in this awesome report were at the city level, they will be discussed more in chapter 9.

Regional Model for a Comprehensive Violence and Crime Prevention Policy in Latin America[14]

This nonbinding declaration is a comprehensive regional violence and crime prevention policy framework of a group of Latin American countries, including Chile, Colombia, Costa Rica, Ecuador, El Salvador, Honduras, Mexico, Nicaragua, Panama, and Uruguay. It is the result of a joint project of the European Forum for Urban Safety and the International Juvenile Justice Observatory and was organized by Veronica Martinez-Solares.

The *Regional Model for a Comprehensive Violence and Crime Prevention Policy* opens with an agreement that the origin of violence and crime is multidimensional in nature and, therefore, countries must go beyond the standard CJS and tackle the myriads of causes and risk factors for violence by implementing programs affecting families, early childhood, adolescence, and social cohesion.[15] As you are reading this after the earlier chapters, this statement may seem self-evident, but sustained success in ending violent crime requires a radical transformation by governments in thinking and in action—the ultimate goal of this book and my life's work.

Wisely, the model outlines seven elements important to the success of those programs. These elements are as follows, with the corresponding essential elements from ECOSOC in parentheses:

- Good governance and institutionalization (permanent violent prevention board)
- Appropriation of knowledge (informed by violence prevention science)
- Focus and results (diagnosis, planning, implementation, and evaluation)
- Coordination and integration (mobilizing sectors able to tackle causes)
- Sustained funding (adequate and sustained funding)
- Conditions for it to function (standards and training of human talent)
- Inclusion and equity and gender perspective (partial—public engagement and support)

The last element is particularly important. The ECOSOC guidelines did refer to a gender perspective but only briefly. This particular element stresses the need to look at how to involve people who are excluded for reasons such as race or gender. It also focuses on the need to have a gender perspective, for the analysis and the strategies (such as those discussed in chapter 5) as well as for engaging the public.

What is especially exciting is that the *Regional Model* adds three essential elements that go beyond the ECOSOC resolutions and *INSPIRE* to achieve the SDGs. Violence and crime prevention programs, not only in Latin America but around the world, would be wise to incorporate these in future efforts. These three stellar additions include the following:

- Strong political will and leadership
- Management and ethics
- Regional collaboration

Let's break down these three key elements. In the next part of this book, we will discuss how to develop strong "political will"—in part by showing the affordability, achievability, and benefits of investments in violence prevention, but also by showing how to get political buy-in. "Management and ethics" comprises issues of corruption, particularly when funds for upstream investment are often flexible and vulnerable to exploitation. Sometimes, corruption takes the form of illegal skimming off of funds, but it also can be less visible, such as when managers allocate more funds to the constituencies supporting the current government. "Regional collaboration" is important because successes in one country can often inspire another country.

LESSONS FROM FAILURE

Just as valuable as learning about what works and about the international consensus on the essential elements is learning about what does not work. To that end, let's explore some lessons from national crime reduction and prevention programs and efforts that failed to be sustained. Those efforts that I will discuss are listed in figure 8.1. The chart also shows the seven essential elements and the extent to which the program adhered to those elements. I worked in various capacities with each of these pioneering strategies, celebrated their successes, and watched their demise, often imploring them to pay more attention to all the essential elements. It was and is particularly striking that these wonderful evidence-based programs were cut short in their prime, when they could have saved so many lives, so many tragedies, and so much money. In hindsight, the lack of two essential elements contributed to the magnificent disasters. That is, those programs that failed most often neglected (1) establishing standards and training for

ALBERTA, CANADA (2007 TO 2013)	MEXICO PRONAPRED (2013 TO 2015)	SOUTH AFRICA, (1998, RESTARTED 2016)	UK (1998–)	UK (1999–2001)

7 ESSENTIALS FOR IMPLEMENTING EFFECTIVE SOLUTIONS

Permanent Violence Prevention Board				
No	No*	No	Yes	No

Informed by Violence Prevention Science and Data				
Yes	No	Yes	Yes	Yes

Diagnosis, Planning, Implementation, and Evaluation				
Yes	Innovative statistical survey of needs	Yes	Yes	No

Mobilizing Sectors Able to Tackle Causes				
Yes	Yes	Yes	Yes	No

Adequate and Sustained Funding				
Yes	Yes	No	Yes	No

Standards and Training for Human Talent				
Yes	No	No	Yes	No

Public Support and Engagement				
No	No	No	No	No

Duration				
6 years	3 years	1 year**	20 + years (ongoing)	2 years

Reason for Demise				
Loss of political understanding of role of interministerial collaboration	Insufficient political will and concern about misspent funds	Insufficient political will and return to CJS	N/A	Bureaucratic inertia, including capacity and cultural resistance

*Mexico had legislated a permanent crime prevention center (Ley General para la prevención social de la violencia y de la delincuencia) but funded its strategy outside the center. **Restarted in 2016.
See appendix for resources.

Figure 8.1. Reasons for Demise of Governmental Violence Prevention Efforts

human talent and (2) nurturing public support and engagement. In the next chapter, we will see these highlighted in the city successes, and, in the last part of the book, I will emphasize their importance in mobilizing implementation to achieve strategy effectiveness.

Alberta, Canada

One of the best-thought-out and longest-lasting government initiatives to stop violent crime was developed by the government of Alberta, a Canadian province with a population close to four million. In 2006, Alberta established a provincial task force to investigate crime reduction, community safety, and public attitudes about these issues.[16] The recommendations of the task force, outlined in its 2007 *Keeping Communities Safe* report, included improvements in law enforcement, treatment, and prevention. In fact, the recommendations became part of the electoral platform for the long-standing conservative party of Alberta, and additional funding of $500 million flowed over three years—significant funding for a small province, even when divided between the three priorities. A key component of this "tough-on-crime, tough-on-causes" initiative was the establishment of the Safe Community Innovation Fund, which became part of the budget base and seemed permanent.[17]

As part of Alberta's efforts, 80 new treatment beds in community mental health centers were created, 200 new police officers were hired, and $60 million was slated for prevention programs. The province was also forward thinking in establishing a community safety secretariat made up of senior-level bureaucrats from various ministries—including housing, social services, youth, and health—cooperating with law enforcement, justice, and municipal affairs.

Alberta's task force is an important "best practice" to emulate. This task force gave birth to the strategy that was based in the best violence prevention science available. In addition, the task force worked from the "diagnosis-to-evaluation" approach and recommended this approach be followed by all the funded innovations. The task force also made funding decisions based on the evidence and diagnosis. Its core group was brilliant at mobilizing sectors able to tackle causes and to provide sustained and adequate funding for implementing effective solutions. In fact, comprehensive crime reduction strategies such as Alberta's are effective because they work on short-term actions to achieve long-term success. Alberta's only weakness was the lack of attention to engaging public and constituency support. That is, the task force needed to elicit and ensure support from interest groups, such as victims, and administrators, such as mayors.

Violence prevention success absolutely depends on political and public buy-in. Tragically, however, when the funding for the brains of the program was cut to save a very modest amount of money, there was no reaction from victim groups or mayors! Those close to the amazing program were stunned to see such a magnificent program killed in its prime for no good reason.

Mexico

Between 1990 and 2006, Mexico had a homicide rate hovering around nine murders per 100,000 people, just below the US homicide rate of the early 1990s. In 2006, however, President Calderón began his six-year term vowing to fight a war against the cartels. He chose to do this by increasing resources for the army and policing. This faulty, shortsighted, nonevidence-based strategy resulted in the homicide rate climbing nearly 300 percent by 2012, to 24 murders per 100,000 people. In the last year of Calderón's presidency, however, two significant initiatives were enacted that might have changed the trajectory of Mexico's war on crime.

In January 2012, the Mexican Congress adopted a general law for the social prevention of violence and crime. This law established a national crime prevention directorate whose responsibilities comprised tackling the risk factors of violence by coordinating action across different sectors and orders of government. In essence, this was a model for a law and a framework to get effective violence prevention strategies implemented that was consistent with the ECOSOC guidelines.

In the next presidential election in 2012, the candidates did not clearly address how to implement violence prevention. As noted in the introduction to this book, poet and activist Javier Sicilia took up the mantle. Sicilia had lost his own son to drug-related violence, so he was motivated to mobilize other Mexican families affected by violent crime. Not only did he lead rallies to keep the cause in the forefront, but he also helped to develop legislative proposals that included legalization of drugs and the establishment of a truth and reconciliation commission and proposed these strategies to the presidential candidates whom he accused of ignoring the issues.[18] His words were searing: "The 60,000 dead, the more than 20,000 who've disappeared, the hundreds of thousands of people displaced, wounded and hunted, the tens of thousands of widows and orphans that this stupid war against drugs is costing us, do not exist for you and your parties."[19]

Enrique Peña Nieto won the election. After becoming president, Peña Nieto committed to "launch a new national-security strategy to reduce violence and fight drug cartels."[20] A key component of this strategy was called the National Program for the Social Prevention of Violence and Crime (PNPSVD).[21] The undersecretary of prevention and citizen participation in the powerful central Ministry of Home Affairs was charged with the key responsibility for the program, including managing the federal funding, known by the acronym as PRONAPRED. The funds were intended to develop diagnostics as well as to design, implement, and evaluate preventive interventions to address the risk and protective factors linked to violence and crime. The program also aimed to increase the coresponsibility of citizens and social actors in social prevention, reduce vulnerability in populations requiring priority attention, and strengthen capacity. It looked hopeful, particularly as, all told, the Mexican government allocated about US$100 million to finance the PRONAPRED actions in each of the years from 2013 to 2016.[22]

One of the significant achievements of that period was the completion of the country's remarkable survey on "Social Cohesion for the Prevention of Violence and Crime" in 2014. The survey is the work of Mexico's well-respected statistical agency, the National Institute of Statistics and Geography (http://www.inegi.org.mx/), which is a model for the world and is rightly being used by the UN to help countries develop the statistics needed to measure the SDG indicators. Specifically, the survey was designed to provide data on what influences young people. The idea was that, "With this comprehensive perspective, the authorities will be able to generate measures and policies to detect, correct, and prevent those elements and dynamics that affect in a negative the development of youth and heads of household in Mexico."[23]

This extraordinary survey was focused on young people aged twelve to twenty-nine, the well-known age range during which offending peaks. It was conducted in forty-seven Mexican metropolitan areas and included data on risk factors known to correlate with offending: conflict within the family and how youth reacted, youth employment and unemployment, use of alcohol and other drugs, role models, and attitudes about neighborhood crime. It looked at victimization, including child abuse, bullying, and street violence. Among many other things, the survey results showed a considerable lack of confidence in the police by young Mexicans.

Coincidentally or not, by 2016, homicide rates in Mexico had fallen—from 24 per 100,000 in 2013 to 17 per 100,000 in 2016. But, after only four years, funding for PRONAPRED died, even though it had been the government's key instrument for shifting the direction and scope of the security policy in Mexico toward an effective prevention agenda. Some say the PNPSVD was new and innovative and had room to grow. One expert commented on some weaknesses.[24] Nonetheless, since the demise of PRONAPRED and the programs that funding supported, Mexico's homicide rate has exploded again, with 29,000 homicides in 2017, or 22 murders per 100,000 people. In contrast to ending PRONAPRED funding, Mexico increased its security expenditures from 2010 to 2017 by 61 percent, to US$11 billion annually.[25] This has led to a growth in the number of police officers but not necessarily to an improvement in the quality of police officers nor their effectiveness.[26] Importantly, it has not led to a reduction in homicides.

Despite the size of the challenge and the funds available, the PNPSVD had major weaknesses, which could have been overcome. Facilitators did not pay enough attention to violence prevention science, nor did they train and guide those individuals involved in the efforts. Some would say that, like the Crime Reduction Program in the United Kingdom, everything happened too fast; not enough time nor energy was invested in the human talent nor in learning from success stories what procedures would be most effective. Even PNPSVD's own permanent violence prevention staff were ignored, even though the best thinking internationally had gone into the center's development. On a positive note, following the demise of the PRO-NAPRED funding, the regional model described earlier was developed, which provides a more robust basis for trying again.

South Africa White Paper on Safety and Security

In 1998, the South African minister for Safety and Security developed an important white paper, a document outlining violence reduction objectives and a framework for how to achieve those goals. This white paper built on the 1996 National Crime Prevention Strategy, which had established the importance of both criminal justice and social development as part of a crime reduction strategy. Thus, South Africa's White Paper on Safety and Security identified how South Africa's approach to crime prevention would be two pronged and integrate effective policing and social crime prevention. Its social development actions were to be achieved through actions informed by violence prevention science at the time and included the likes of supporting at-risk youth, families, and groups and promoting socioeconomic interventions to undercut causes of crime.[27] Local government was given substantial authority to carry out social crime prevention programs that were to be informed by diagnosis and planning. The white paper also emphasized that crime prevention should also take place at national and provincial levels and be collaborative and multidisciplinary.

Unfortunately, the document did not spell out the need for a permanent violence prevention board. Within a year, South Africa's white paper on safety and security fell victim in the transition from Mandela to Mbeke as president. Under President Mbeke's tenure, prevention was downgraded and shifted into the national policing service. In part, this demise of a good plan was the government's knee-jerk reaction to public concern that crime in the country was intolerable. Had a permanent violence prevention board been in place to educate the new administration about violence prevention science and make the case for implementing the good ideas of the White Paper on Safety and Security, the plan might have had a chance. Engaging the public to stand up and demand social programs would also have helped.

Thankfully, after a continuing moral crisis about violent crime in South Africa and a review of the pluses and minuses of the 1998 South Africa White Paper on Safety and Security, South Africa's government agreed to a new version of the plan in 2016. A Directorate for Safety, Crime, and Violence Prevention now reports to the president and has a special cause of victim support. This permanent violence prevention unit is responsible for planning and evaluating programs as well as developing the human talent to implement those programs. The directorate focuses efforts on three themes consistent with violence prevention science: (1) ensuring an effective criminal justice system, (2) intervening early to prevent crime and violence, and (3) promoting safety, particularly through environmental design. The directorate also has prioritized effective and integrated service delivery for safety, security, and violence and crime prevention and active public and community participation. It is too early to know whether this strategy will accomplish its goal of ending violent crime. The links that remain to be operationalized are adequate and sustained funding guided by violence prevention science.

Tackling Youth Violence in the United Kingdom

The UK Youth Justice Board was created in 1998. It spearheaded the implementation of a Youth Inclusion Program in seventy-two high-risk priority zones. Evaluations of this intervention, as we saw in chapter 4, highlighted significant reductions in arrests. It still exists today but would need to be strengthened to get sustained implementation of effective solutions.

In 1996, the British Audit Commission published a report with the poignant title "Misspent Youth." The report was an analysis of the returns that British taxpayers got from paying for reactive and standard law enforcement, courts, and corrections as a way to respond to young people and crime. The report concluded rightly that the resources spent catching, convicting, and "correcting" youth could be much better used, that is, that upstream crime prevention is much more effective and cost-effective than reactive cure. In sum, the report found that taxes were being misspent on youth and that youths' lives were allowed to drift into crime so their lives also were being misspent as a result. That's a powerful condemnation to be sure and repeats much of the violence prevention science now available.

The report made a number of recommendations about how the money should be reallocated. These recommendations ranged from providing parents with parenting skills, to supporting teachers, to providing positive leisure opportunities for youth. As a result, just two years later, the newly installed government of Prime Minister Tony Blair acted to create a permanent Youth Justice Board, mandated to stop crime and reorganize the youth justice system by using *evidence* for effective practice. This agency draws on leaders in law enforcement, social services, education, and more. The result is that England leapt ahead of other countries with the potential to multiply successful upstream crime prevention programs across problem places. It tested successfully setting specific goals relating to the reduction of youth offending, and it wanted to hold its funding recipients accountable for helping to meet those goals. It did develop the important model of a Youth Inclusion Program to stop youth from drifting into offending.[28]

But its potential as a permanent crime prevention board has not yet been realized. As of the summer of 2018, a committee of the Parliament for England and Wales is working on a report on solutions to youth violence. The committee is a commendable collaboration between politicians from all the parties and a university. Their interim report diagnoses the causes, risk factors, and failures of public policy that lead to youth violence. It uses the best violence prevention science available and recommends actions at the city level, during early childhood and adolescence, in schools, and for employment. It also advocates for interfacing with police.[29] So far so good. These recommendations are largely consistent with my conclusions in chapters 3 and 4 and those to be discussed in chapter 9. Strikingly missing from their early recommendations, however, is how to sustain the work of the commission and get the solutions implemented. The Youth Justice Board provides one vehicle, but it would need to be strengthened with trained staffing, adequate and sustained funding, and public support.

UK Crime Reduction Program

In 1999, the UK Home Office in London implemented a crime reduction program. This large and evidence-based program grew out of collaboration between the powerful British Treasury and the UK Home Office, the ministry responsible for policing, prisons, crime research, and more. Chris Nuttall, from the Home Office, and Richard Price, from the Treasury, worked together on persuading the Home Office and Treasury, rightly, that a big investment in what works would pay off in large crime reductions. The basis of the program was an impressive review of what had worked internationally. Titled *Reducing Offending: An Assessment of Research Evidence on Ways of Dealing with Offending Behaviour*, the report was an excellent review of the best violence prevention science at the time and summarized evidence on the following:

- Promoting a less criminal society by preventing the development of criminality among young people and investing in situational crime prevention to reduce the opportunities for crime
- Preventing crime in the community by acting on the social conditions that sustain crime in residential communities and implementing effective police strategies for reducing crime
- Criminal justice interventions through changes in sentencing policy or extending the use of effective interventions with offenders and drug users[30]

In sum, this program was based on the best violence prevention science at the time. It was the most-ambitious, best-resourced, and most-comprehensive effort for driving down crime ever attempted in an affluent democracy and still would be today. But I did not say the best implemented. And it disappeared within two years. There are two assessments of why the UK Crime Reduction Program failed. Both assessments directly and indirectly stress the lack of attention to the human talent committed to the program's goals in central government.[31] Some of this gap can be put at the feet of the retirement of its main advocate and expert. The lesson is that knowledge of violence prevention science is not common and the emotional commitment to its use is even less common.

KEY TAKEAWAYS

- Belgium, France, and Sweden have been early adopters of crime prevention strategies and demonstrate sustained commitment to crime prevention but not necessarily crime reduction because we do not know how successful they are in terms of ending violence.
- Three meta-analyses on violence prevention reinforce the ECO-SOC guidelines. They include *Mapping of Homicide Prevention Programs in Latin America and the Caribbean*, *What Works in Reducing Community Violence: A Meta-Review and Field Study for the Northern Triangle*, and the *Regional Model for a Comprehensive Violence and Crime Prevention Policy*.
- The *Regional Model for a Comprehensive Violence and Crime Prevention Policy* provides a stellar framework that builds on the seven essential elements from ECOSOC and UNODC, but the meta-analysis adds attention to gender and equity, management of funds and implementation, and regional collaboration to its list of elements needed to prevent and reduce violence and crime.
- Most crime prevention programs informed by violence prevention science that failed in only a few years were missing one or more of the seven elements essential to success.
- Serious efforts to implement effective solutions must focus on the seven essential elements, with a particular focus on having a permanent violence prevention board, ensuring sustainable funding, and using indicators to set targets and accounting mechanisms and performance standards to measure whether those targets are being achieved.
- Priority must be given to developing the human talent involved in implementing effective solutions, raising awareness and commitment to those solutions among politicians and the public, and measuring and evaluating the results of the efforts.

9

CITIES LEADING THE WAY

Using Essentials to Implement
Effective Solutions Ends Violent Crime

Less crime means less harm to citizens and less need for expensive reactive services. Municipalities can play a key role in targeting those preventive services to where they are most needed but require financial and other support from other orders of government.

—Canadian Municipal Network on Crime Prevention, 2016

Starting with Bogotá in the 1990s, cities have put the ideas in the opening quote into practice. Some have even been able to reduce street violence significantly within a few short years. Bogotá succeeded because it applied the "essentials" of an effective crime prevention program, which were outlined in chapter 7. With integrative planning and a focus on data, that Colombian city was able to achieve a reduction in homicides within ten years that was 50 percent better than the national plan, and its permanent prevention planning unit has sustained this success into several decades.[1] Boston, Massachusetts, in the United States reduced shootings and homicides within three years by applying some of the essentials, such as planning, mobilizing key sectors, and utilizing data. Without a permanent prevention planning organization, however, Boston was not able to sustain its efforts. Ten years later, the city started over.[2] Glasgow in Scotland applied essentials, such as planning, mobilizing key sectors, and using data, to cut homicides and street violence by close to 50 percent within three years of implementing that city's crime prevention plan. It has a permanent violence reduction unit that has sustained its success.[3] Most importantly, all three cities chose to go beyond the standard criminal justice system (CJS) to invest in upstream multisector strategies to tackle the causes of violence, thereby reducing the prevalence of crime within their city's limits.

CITIES DEMONSTRATE THE POWER OF UPSTREAM VIOLENCE PREVENTION ON A LARGE SCALE

Recall, from part II of this book, that randomized controlled trials (RCTs) were used to measure the impact of particular upstream programs and projects on stopping violent crime. Many of the effective programs and projects demonstrate crime reductions of 50 percent or more as well as important social returns on investment of $7 or more. Inevitably, however, these RCT projects are small scale. Even the highly lauded multisystemic therapy, which boasts results on 48,000 cases, is a small player.[4] Proactive policing success stories are also mostly small scale and short lived in terms of proof. So citywide strategies with much more impressive numbers provide even more impressive proof of the efficacy of the effectiveness of putting into practice the essential elements of a crime prevention program. As a reminder, those essential elements, as identified in the UN Economic and Social Council resolutions of 1996 and 2002, are included in figure 9.1.

Consider that Bogotá is home to 8.5 million people. Glasgow's population is 600,000, and there are approximately 700,000 people living in Boston. The success of these three cities in applying the essentials of crime prevention and actually reducing rates of violence among large numbers of people is extremely strong evidence that other cities, small and large, can also reduce violence within their borders and boundaries by administering a similar results-oriented crime prevention program. My main message here is that, to stop violent crime, cities must apply the essentials presented in chapter 7.

In this chapter, we will take a close look at the success stories of these three model cities and explore a number of other cities also showing significant reductions in crime. We will discuss the practical application of some of the essential strategies as the model cities and others followed those. It will be important to note that most of the world cities that have been successful have included the collaborative community safety strategies described in figure 7.2: they have rightly developed crime prevention programs based on a cycle of *diagnosing* the causes and specific locations of

STREET VIOLENCE			GUN VIOLENCE			ALCOHOL-RELATED VIOLENCE		
BOGOTÁ	BOSTON	GLASGOW	CHICAGO	CIUDAD JUÁREZ	STOCKTON	CARDIFF	COAHUILA	DIADEMA
7 ESSENTIALS FOR IMPLEMENTING EFFECTIVE SOLUTIONS								
Permanent Violence Prevention Board								
Yes	No	Yes	No	No	No	Yes	No	No
Informed by Violence Prevention Science and Data								
Yes	Yes	Yes	Yes	Yes	Yes	Yes	Yes	Yes
Diagnosis, Planning, Implementation, and Evaluation								
Yes	Partial	Yes	No	Yes	Yes	Yes	Yes	Yes
Mobilizing Sectors Able to Tackle Causes								
Yes	Partial	Yes	No	Yes	Yes	Yes	Yes	Yes
Adequate and Sustained Funding								
Yes	Time limited	Yes	Time limited	Time limited	Time limited	Yes	Time limited	Time limited
Standards and Training for Human Talent								
Yes	Partial	Yes	No	No	Yes	Yes	No	No
Public Support and Engagement								
Yes	Yes	Yes	No	No	No	No	Yes	No
Citywide Reductions								
50%	66%*	50%	32%**	83%	55%	44%	70%	66%
Sustained Success								
Yes	No	Yes	No	No	No	Yes	No	No

* Boston reconstituted its Operation Ceasefire in 2007, thus showing lack of sustained focus. It acquired skills from a successful project in Lowell. The evaluation showed a more modest reduction of 31%. ** Chicago has no citywide program. It has three different projects where evaluations have shown similar reductions, including a Safe Neighborhood Project, which was enriched by adding notifications for convicted felons, a Cure Violence project, and a focused deterrence project.

Figure 9.1. Reasons for Success of City Violence Prevention Efforts

crime within the city, *planning* how to tackle the particular causes, *implementing* the plan, and *evaluating* the outcomes.

Unfortunately, each city did not always apply *every* essential. Most often, the missing links to long-term and widespread replication of success have been lack of a permanent violence prevention authority, acquiring adequate sustained funding, and recruiting and training multisector talent. Yet the size of the reductions for relatively small investments in our model cities is good news and strongly supports the case for achieving a 50 percent reduction nationally with investment equivalent to 10 percent of current expenditures on the standard CJS. This specific proposal will be explored more in chapter 10 as a compelling case for the national and local investments needed to reach targets for the Sustainable Development Goals.

The bad news is that these successes have been emulated with measured results by only a small number of other cities. It is not so much that there are no other cities enacting some part of the essentials strategy; rather, more often than not, the step to evaluate outcomes is not taking place. For example, although the European Forum for Urban Security (EFUS) has some 300 members across southern Europe and advocates this essentials strategy, the EFUS member cities have not measured their outcomes. Thus, little is known about whether their crime prevention efforts are working or not. Fortunately, Glasgow is a significant European city that did measure the outcomes of its crime prevention plan. At least Glasgow can be used as a poster child of violence reduction success based on applying the essentials.

One interesting simulation study looked at the impact of Cure Violence and directed police patrol in New York City over the past thirty years.[5] It concluded there was a 13 percent reduction in violent victimization because of the Cure Violence program, which is lower than many evaluations showed. When combined with directed police patrol, however, the reduction of violence in the simulation would increase to 19 percent. Add one outreach worker on top of those two interrupter initiatives, and there would be a 24 percent reduction in homicide rate. Compare that to a 150 percent increase in police force over 20 years to achieve the same result! Granted, this was only a simulation model and does not look at the potential with the essential elements, but it is interesting, nonetheless, to pay attention to the numbers. Now, back to Bogotá, Boston, and Glasgow.

STREET VIOLENCE: MODEL PRACTICES

Combating Urban Gun Violence in Bogotá, Colombia

It may seem strange to say that cities in North America can learn from Latin America, but the city of Bogotá, Colombia, presents an inspiring example of how a city can reduce violence by tackling the risk factors that cause violence.

Bogotá has a population of 8.5 million, which is marginally bigger than that of New York City. Its homicide rate peaked in 1993 at 80 per 100,000, close to the national rate for Colombia at that time. Ten years later, the city rate was 23 and the national rate was 50. The reduction for the city is spectacular, but it keeps on getting better because the permanent violence prevention unit has fostered continuing reductions. In 2017, for example, its rate of 14 murders per 100,000 population is well below the national Colombian rate of 23. In comparison, it is still well above New York City at 3 but well below Chicago at 23.[6]

Bogotá illustrates the dramatic reductions that can be achieved through the leadership of the mayor, or in this case, three mayors, in establishing a permanent crime prevention planning office. With that centralized unit reporting to the mayor, continuity has been built into the program as the next mayor and then the next and beyond oversee the office. Granted, a particular mayor could have decided or chosen to decide in the future to dismantle the unit, but in Bogotá, mothers of men being killed are having none of that: they have lobbied loud and clear for the program to continue.

The job of Bogotá's permanent crime prevention planning office is to analyze the location of violence and the risk factors causing that violence, recommend actions to tackle those risk factors, monitor implementation, and evaluate the results. When analyses of coroners' reports identified too many handguns and too much alcohol in the bodies of victims in the high-violence areas, it was obvious that solutions needed to focus on having police remove handguns and limit access to alcohol during high-violence evenings. The office also established services to help victims of violence—and of insults. Mitigating retaliation is one preventive strategy.

Combating Urban Gun Violence in Boston, Massachusetts

As noted in the introduction to this chapter, some cities have reduced urban gun violence citywide by 50 percent or more within just a few years. The benefits for the city and taxpayers, when measured, are $7 or better for every dollar invested. The cities with these significant reductions used as the basis for their success some type of comprehensive community safety strategy coupled with government support. One great example of an effective campaign to deal with urban gun violence is Boston, Massachusetts.

Boston achieved a significant reduction in gun-related homicides through deliberate policy.[7] Its comprehensive strategy involved problem-oriented policing, provision for outreach services to youth at risk of using handguns, and the mobilization of mothers and the community to stop the violence. Importantly, there were no changes in gun laws. Prior to the comprehensive community effort, two entities were working separately to combat gun violence in the city: the police department was working in isolation and looking at its data in terms of how enforcement might crack down on the main offenders, and the School of Public Health at Harvard University was diagnosing the social and other risk factors that lead to violence. When these two efforts came together, they produced a synergy that resulted in positive policy to stop violence. In line with the conclusions from police data analysis and the public health diagnosis, Boston launched a full spectrum of policing and social initiatives in 1996, which successfully stemmed a rising wave of gang violence involving young men in problem places.

The law enforcement portion of Boston's gun violence reduction initiative was termed Operation Ceasefire. It focused police efforts on a range of enforcement procedures to seize guns and to threaten to put persons persistently carrying guns behind bars. The objective was to make at-risk youth believe they would experience heavy and predictable punitive consequences for carrying handguns and engaging in violence. To this end, the police used whatever laws they could to intervene, including aggressive enforcement of liquor, traffic, and probation violations, but, again, without any change in laws to register or control firearms directly.[8] Notably, these interventions specifically targeted men known to police; they weren't just stop and frisks based on a gut feeling about furtive behavior.

The social component, guided by the public health analysis, included prevention programs that included having social workers reaching out to youth in street gangs to help them and their families access much-needed social services.[9] In addition, Boston increased its services for runaways and established mentoring programs to reduce school dropout rates. Importantly, Boston also enhanced job training programs and mobilized local firms to create jobs for at-risk youth. For instance, the John Hancock Mutual Life Insurance Company invested in a summer program that gave

Boston's inner-city youth a greater chance of completing high school and going on to college.

The third component involved in Boston's success story was mobilizing the mothers of at-risk young men. Both privately and in street demonstrations, these proactive moms pressured political leaders to focus action on solving the problem. They also encouraged their sons to abandon violent lifestyles that put them at risk of death and injury from street violence and police enforcement.

Evidence for the effectiveness of Boston's combination of smart policing with targeted social outreach and proactive community engagement is strong: homicide in the city fell, from an average of 44 persons per year murdered in the period of 1991 to 1995, to 15 in 1998; and none of those 15 homicides involved youth gun violence. While some of this decline might have correlated with general declines in violence across the United States and the numbers are small because Boston was home to only 600,000 people at the time, the size and speed of the drop of 63 percent is remarkable.[10]

Granted, the police component was clearly an active ingredient in the quick drop. Importantly, however, Boston's success in combating gun violence cannot be reduced to the police operation on its own. The social component was also vital. Unfortunately, however, with the decrease in homicides, funding was cut for many of the community services that likely contributed to the reduction in gun violence, although the police budget did not change. It's no wonder gun violence in Boston started creeping up again.[11] Less than ten years later, the city had to reinvent the program, hiring the police chief from Lowell, a smaller city in Massachusetts. While not as successful in percentage terms, a similar project in Lowell had also reduced gun violence.[12]

There are two lessons from Boston's original success followed by its recurrence of crime. First, to prevent gun violence, you need both smarter policing *and* social outreach services. Second, you need a permanent leadership center in the city—and not one based in the isolationist police department—so that the partnership continues and funding is sustained for the targeted social development programs as much as for policing.

Lowering Murder Rates in Glasgow, Scotland

As I have already noted in other places in this book, Glasgow brought down its murder rates by 50 percent. The city did this through smart law enforcement in combination with programs targeted to youth, family, health, and other sectors in problem places.[13] Glasgow's violence prevention success also shows how a permanent violence prevention board can maintain and accelerate progress. In fact, the decline in homicide rates that started in Glasgow in 2008 has continued and been extended to the whole of Scotland.[14]

Here is a quick recap of how Glasgow succeeded in lowering its murder rates: To deal with its entrenched levels of violent crime, Glasgow established a violence reduction unit (VRU) in 2005. The VRU implemented a diagnosis of the city's crime problems and their location and causes.[15] Once the diagnosis was completed, the VRU instituted the Community Initiative to Reduce Violence (CIRV) to tackle the risk factors identified in the diagnosis. Those efforts took a three-pronged approach: "A zero-tolerance police warning that, if the violence doesn't stop, life is going to get very tough for every single gang member; a pledge from assorted agencies and charities that, if youths do renounce violence, they can get help with education, training, job-finding; and a powerful, personal message" from mothers and community members.[16]

In other words, Glasgow combined a diagnosis and plan that was implemented through focused deterrence using proactive policing and targeted social development programs aimed at problem areas. The social development component included early childhood education, parenting support, youth conflict resolution in schools, street outreach, rehabilitation and treatment, and interventions in hospitals to mentor people out of violence.[17] Leaders of Glasgow's efforts also prioritized measurement of the results. And they measured outcomes in terms of fewer acts of violence, not by how many arrests or convictions occurred or did not occur each year.

According to a 2014 evaluation of the program in the peer-reviewed journal *Aggression and Violent Behavior*, not only is the program effective in saving lives, but the cost benefit of the CIRV program is also outstanding: "The CIRV programme cost some £4.8m over its first two years, with funding provided by the Scottish government and from partners and services in kind. . . . [W]ith the most straightforward murder inquiry costing £1.3m, and a year in prison working out at £49,000, we don't have to prevent many killings for it to become worthwhile."[18]

Interestingly, whereas Glasgow's successful VRU program is tied directly to the city's police department, most experts see this organizational placement as unusual. UN guidelines would place the crime prevention board in city hall in any other city, as would I. But the two personalities that got Glasgow's successful program going made such a placement work.

EXAMPLES OF IMPORTANT PLAYERS IN COMBATING VIOLENCE

The bottom line is that cities reduce crime when they develop comprehensive community safety strategies based on diagnosing problems, planning solutions, investing in what is cost effective, and evaluating outcomes in terms of less victimization. Besides building on a diagnosis, the strategies involve both proven upstream prevention and focused proactive policing. The police role is to tackle access to alcohol and weapons and to use focused deterrence to get high-risk individuals to consider accessing upstream prevention services. The upstream prevention includes the likes of early childhood intervention, youth outreach, school completion, job creation, and life-skills training. The actions are coordinated through some type of permanent violence prevention board, which in Glasgow is the VRU (http://actiononviolence.org/), working alongside the police.

In Europe, the go-to organization on crime prevention is the European Forum for Urban Security (EFUS) (https://efus.eu/en/). This respected organization is a network of cities across Europe that have endorsed the processes in figure 7.2 in chapter 7. Launched in 1987, EFUS now consists of some 300 cities that meet to discuss ways to improve community safety. Out of that collaboration over the years and the work of a team of experts has come an important and user-friendly guide on good governance of community safety and city crime prevention.[19] Specifically, EFUS's 2016 *Methods and Tools for a Strategic Approach to Urban Security* outlines how to implement the four-step process of diagnosis, planning, implementation, and evaluation for strategic approaches to community safety. It also sets out both the key steps and arguments to implement particular strategies and is consistent with the Safer Cities strategy proposed by UN-Habitat. With little known about the extent to which EFUS or its guide has actually helped to end any violent crime, we still do not have the numbers to determine the organization's effectiveness in Europe.

In the United States, there are a few coalitions that have been formed to build community safety in cities through comprehensive multisectoral strategies that other countries and cities can emulate. Examples of these important players in combating violence and supporting community resilience follow:

- National Forum on Youth Violence Prevention (National Forum), a US government-sponsored network of communities and federal

agencies dedicated to resolving the crisis of youth and gang violence (https://youth.gov/youth-topics/about-national-forum)
- National Network for Safe Communities, a project of the John Jay College of Criminal Justice (https://nnscommunities.org/who-we-are/mission)
- Urban Network to Increase Thriving Youth (UNITY), a Prevention Institute initiative (https://www.preventioninstitute.org/unity/general/unity-about-us)

Specifically, the National Forum on Youth Violence Prevention, established in 2010 at the direction of President Obama, brings together people from diverse professions and perspectives to develop comprehensive solutions to violence on the local as well as national levels. The National Forum website is a great resource for information on violence prevention research and the home to the "Logic Model" of violence prevention. Like the UN Economic and Social Council resolutions, the National Forum Logic Model stresses similar essential elements of a crime prevention program: understanding the problem, identifying solutions, setting goals, evaluating progress, involving multisectors, and ensuring sustainability. The National Forum website even has a link to a valuable "Strategic Planning Toolkit" that focuses on four areas of youth violence: prevention, intervention, enforcement, and reentry.[20]

Among the US cities using the National Forum model is St. Louis. In 2013, that city announced the development of a youth violence task force based on the National Forum framework.[21] But it was not until 2017 that St. Louis actually acquired the necessary funding for the task force efforts, and then it is *project* funding rather than permanent funding.[22] The jury is still out as to whether St. Louis' efforts will be successful and sustainable.

Similar to the National Forum, the National Network for Safe Communities focuses on supporting cities implementing proven strategic interventions to reduce violence and improve public safety.[23] The National Network for Safe Communities was launched in 2009 and is directed by David Kennedy, a major player in the focused deterrence component of the Boston strategy. Among the key principles of the National Network for Safe Communities are getting deterrence right, reducing the overreliance on arrest and incarceration in the United States, and focusing crime prevention efforts on the high-risk 0.5 percent of the population who are responsible for 50 percent to 75 percent of homicides.

Steeped in research, the National Network for Safe Communities boasts a comprehensive website on violence prevention that features a list of evaluations of projects across the United States that have shown reductions in gun violence. The organization also offers a free brochure titled, "Proven Strategies for Reducing Violence and Strengthening Communities."[24] Whereas the National Network for Safe Communities does impressive work, it does not stress the essentials of a sustained crime prevention program, which were discussed in the previous chapters.

Finally, the Prevention Institute's UNITY promotes community planning and implementation of comprehensive community safety plans that include prevention and intervention. The initiative offers training and consultation, organizes violence prevention events, develops and disseminates tools and materials, and conducts network-building activities. Yet UNITY's website notes, "Too many communities lack the resources to do what is needed."[25] Several US cities have adopted UNITY's plans, for example, consider Milwaukee's Blueprint for Peace program,[26] but it is too early to know the outcomes.

In Canada, the Canadian Municipal Network on Crime Prevention (http://safercities.ca/) was launched through the University of Ottawa in 2006. By 2009, it had gained enough momentum to continue on its own. In 2014, financial support from Public Safety Canada has been used to strengthen and grow the network around the theme of harnessing evidence for crime prevention. CMNCP currently has approximately thirty members, many of whom have some type of comprehensive community safety strategy. The members have been helped to get to know solid violence prevention science through short action briefs designed for decision makers, workshops and webinars for members, and a series of regional and national meetings providing opportunities to strengthen the network around the evidence.[27]

OTHER EXAMPLES OF CITIES WITH VIOLENCE PREVENTION SUCCESSES

There are not myriads of examples of cities tackling violent crime. The examples we do have, however, showcase that success is possible through comprehensive partnerships and the implementation of the essentials of crime prevention. Some of the examples also highlight how, despite spectacular success, a project can disappear, and violence can return if all the essentials are not addressed.

GUN VIOLENCE

Chicago, A Pioneer of Success Without the Essentials to Sustain That Success

Chicago experiences more than 600 murders each year, most of them gun related,[28] and approximately 10,000 rapes, based on Centers for Disease Control and Prevention's survey rates. Its homicide rate per capita is 24 per 100,000, higher per capita than Mexico and seven times that of New York City.[29] Yet it spends $1.5 billion on its city police alone[30] and has one of the largest local jails in the United States, the Cook County jail.[31]

In a concerted effort to get violence under control, Chicago leaders implemented and evaluated two focused deterrence projects at different times in limited areas, one called Project Safe Neighborhood. Chicago also is where a few of the most effective social development solutions to violent crime were invented and proven. These include Cure Violence, Becoming a Man, and summer jobs with mentoring. Each of these projects has been shown to reduce homicides by 30 percent or better. At one time, Chicago had 14 Cure Violence projects going, but they eventually were reduced to one. When I visited the city in 2018, none of the social programs were implemented across multiple areas where social problems and violent crime are high.

My reason to include Chicago here, alas, is not because it is a magnificent success. Instead, Chicago is a good example of what happens if you do not have all the essentials in place. Clearly, with so many proven successes, someone in the city is informed by violence prevention science and data, but "someone" is not enough. Chicago has no permanent violence prevention board or citywide plan, does not invest in violence prevention in a sustained and adequate manner, does not develop human talent other than for specific projects, and has done little to mobilize the public.

But Chicago *could* be a magnificent success. Using the benefit–cost logic to be explained in chapter 10, a $3 million investment in a permanent violence prevention board to develop the capacity and plans for an investment of $300 million in effective solutions would save the city 325 lives, 5,000 rapes, and $800 million in taxes within five years.

Reducing Homicides in Ciudad Juárez, Mexico

One of the most dramatic examples of violence prevention success is the reduction in homicides in Ciudad Juárez, Mexico—from over 3,000 homicides in 2010[32] (200 per 100,000 people) to approximately 600 in 2016 (40 per 100,000).[33] Most of the deaths are young disadvantaged men shooting each other with handguns. Some of the fights are over drug territory; a few are over girls and pride. A city of approximately 1.4 million people, Ciudad Juárez is across the border from El Paso, Texas. Ironically, El Paso has one of the lowest homicide rates in the United States.

This violence prevention success story started in 2008 with a clear challenge. Ciudad Juárez had experienced a rapid increase in deaths by violence; in 2008, some 300 persons had been killed, whereas by 2010, the number of homicides had grown to over 3,000.[34] This increase was associated partly with the economic crisis in the United States, which resulted in employment cutbacks in the maquilas in Juárez, and partly with President Calderón's policy of using the army to fight the organized Mexican drug cartels.

Desperate to stop the violence in Ciudad Juárez, Mexican officials designated $200 million in 2011 and again in 2012 for various crime prevention efforts grouped under the program title Todos Somos Juárez: Reconstruyamos la Ciudad ("We Are All Juárez: Let's Rebuild Our City"). Not only was the federal government behind the program, but so also were the Chihuahua state government, the Ciudad Juárez municipal government, and civil society, despite the fact that expenditures for Todos Somos Juárez were equivalent to the total spending on prevention elsewhere in all of Mexico.[35]

Components of the comprehensive Todos Somos Juárez program included (1) increased investment focused on reducing crime and violent behavior, (2) social programs, (3) situational crime prevention, and (4) improving the operation of the CJS. To implement program strategies, a quarter of the budget was devoted to public safety and three-quarters of the budget was divided among various other sectors, including employment, health, education and sports, and social development. The public safety initiatives improved the response to emergency calls, added prosecutors and detectives to reduce impunity, and clamped down on car theft. Employment initiatives included entrepreneur and job training as well as efforts to increase the numbers of full- and part-time jobs. Health-related crime prevention activities encompassed emergency care and mental health and addiction treatment. Education initiatives improved schools and expanded extracurricular offerings in sports and music. Social development made improvements in housing and day care. Each sector had significant involvement from civil society, although a top federal government official coordinated the Todos Somos Juárez program.

The results of this program were impressive. By 2013, there were only 600 murders—about 40 per 100,000—compared to the 2010 high of more than 3,000 homicides. Plus, the city's homicide rate has continued to hover near this level, with 700 homicides recorded in 2017.[36] Logically, the program interventions must have contributed significantly to the declines in violent crime, although other social trends may have helped. If this citywide strategy had been an RCT, we would know more precisely what factors affect the results. But such a comprehensive effort cannot be broken down and evaluated the same as RCTs can. Nonetheless, we do know the interventions were positive for people in Ciudad Juárez, regardless of ending violent crime, and almost certainly were major contributors to many fewer lethal tragedies.

Stopping Gun Violence in New Haven, Connecticut

Connecticut is one of a few US states to invest in Group Violence Intervention (GVI), an evidence-based violence intervention strategy recommended by the National Network for Safe Communities and modeled on Boston's Operation Ceasefire. This strategy is based on the insight that, in most American cities, a small and readily identifiable segment of the population is responsible for the vast majority of gun violence. These individuals are often affiliated with loose social networks that exist in a fluid state of competition and violent rivalry. In cities across the country, these groups constitute less than 0.5 percent of a city's population but are linked to up to 70 percent of shootings and homicides.[37]

In response to their growing level of gun violence, leaders in New Haven, Connecticut, announced the launch in 2012 of what they call Project Longevity, an effort to implement the GVI strategy in their city of approximately 130,000 people. They formed a partnership of community members, law enforcement officials, and social service providers to lead the program. The way GVI and Project Longevity work is that program coordinators first identify the small population of those most at risk for involvement with gun violence. Then, they bring those individuals together in an in-person meeting, a "call-in," a meeting similar to what we discussed in chapter 3 in relation to the proactive policing strategy called focused deterrence. During the call-in, the at-risk individuals are given a powerful message that their criminal behavior must end. This message comes from the moral voice of the community, often represented by clergy members, victims of gun violence, and reformed former perpetrators. Law enforcement representatives also deliver a message, in the most respectful terms possible, that if the community's plea is ignored, swift legal action will be taken against any group or individual responsible for a new act of lethal violence. In addition, during a call-in, social service providers make a direct offer of meaningful and immediate help to attendees, including educational opportunities and job training. The call-in process is repeated until the intervention population understands that, at the request of the community, all promises made during the call-ins will be kept.

Since its founding in 2012, Project Longevity has had impressive results. A Yale University study conducted in 2015 showed a 37 percent decrease in total shootings per month in New Haven and a 73 percent decrease in group-related shootings per month. These same researchers stated that "Three years into its implementation, our results suggest that the decrease in group-related shootings and homicides are because of Project Longevity."[38] In addition to just being good news of a program that really works, these findings also bolster research confirming the efficacy of focused deterrence and social outreach approaches to reducing gun violence. Potentially, Project Longevity could receive sustained funding from the state. That would ensure its long-term success.

Working to Stop Homicides in New Orleans, Louisiana

Another US city following the National Network's advice and implementing the GVI strategy is New Orleans. Recognizing that law enforcement alone could not solve the city's historically high murder rate, the city's mayor launched the "NOLA for Life" program in 2012. With the targeted aim of reducing group-related gun violence, NOLA for Life takes a holistic approach to get to the root of the problem and implements initiatives under five pillars: (1) Stop the Shooting, (2) Invest in Prevention, (3) Promote Jobs and Opportunity, (4) Strengthen the NOPD, and (5) Get Involved and Rebuild Neighborhoods.[39]

Fueled by the Mayor's Innovation Delivery Team in partnership with public safety and public health experts and local service providers, NOLA for Life showed promising results, reducing gang-related homicides by 55 percent between 2011 and 2013. The reductions were maintained for the next three years. Unfortunately, the rates of homicide increased in the first half of 2017.[40] We will have to wait to see whether those numbers improve with sustained intervention through the NOLA for Life program.

Reducing Gun Violence, Again and Forever, in Stockton, California

Stockton is included herein because it achieved a large reduction in gun-related homicides in 1997, then had to repeat the program in 2012. Now, however, this city of approximately 250,000 people has a permanent violence prevention office and a mayor who is prioritizing adequate funding for crime prevention efforts. In essence, Stockton was magnificent briefly and is now magnificent again.

Here is Stockton's story. In 1997, Stockton had 37 murders per year. Leaders analyzed the problem and determined that gun violence needed to be tackled. Inspired by Boston's Operation Ceasefire, Stockton implemented a focused deterrence strategy with some community services. Within one year, the number of homicides had dropped to 19, a close to 50 percent reduction.[41] Over a decade later, though, the number of people murdered was skyrocketing again. In 2012, 71 people had been murdered. With renewed commitment, Stockton once again implemented elements of Operation Ceasefire. By 2013, the efforts resulted in a 55 percent reduction in homicides while the police force had been reduced by 25 percent.[42]

A few years later, the numbers were creeping up yet again. In 2016, Stockton had 49 homicides. But then, a dynamic new mayor was elected. Mayor Michael Tubbs has supported Stockton's Office of Violence Prevention by adopting a comprehensive and evidence-based strategy focusing on youth outreach and financial incentives for youth who stay crime free. He has secured over $20 million in philanthropic capital to launch the Stockton Scholars, a place-based scholarship that aims to triple the number of Stockton students entering and graduating from college. He brought Advance Peace to Stockton, a data-driven program that works to reduce gun violence in communities, similar to Cure Violence. He also has launched a municipal level basic income pilot project.

The ability of Stockton's charismatic young mayor to tackle economic issues and foster the permanent violence prevention office as well as to take part in Mayors for Smart on Crime makes Stockton's prospects of being "magnificent" well into the future look promising. But we will have to see. The chances would be increased with greater sustained investment, a commitment to developing human talent, and proactive outreach to encourage public participation in violence prevention efforts.

ALCOHOL-RELATED VIOLENCE

Dealing with Alcohol-Related Tragedies in Cardiff, England

The Cardiff Violence Prevention strategy is a well-known best practice among violence prevention specialists. The strategy involves collecting data about the circumstances in which injuries take place that lead to people being admitted to hospital emergency rooms. From the data, policy makers can identify hot spots for violence, that is, locations where injuries related to alcohol use or abuse occur most frequently. The data enable smart policing and law enforcement to focus on managing the source of the risk factor (excessive alcohol), thereby reducing the violence.

The results of the Cardiff strategy are impressive: it has been shown to bring about reductions in violence of more than 40 percent in problem places within a year. Analyses suggest that every $1 spent on this strategy results in a savings of $19 in criminal justice costs. Overall, a US Centers for Disease Control and Prevention cost–benefit analysis shows a return of more than $80 per $1 related to the Cardiff strategy.[43]

A popular program, the Cardiff Violence Prevention strategy has been used successfully in various cities, such as Milwaukee in Wisconsin. Amsterdam in the Netherlands also has recently decided to tackle the alcohol-related roots of its violence using this strategy. It is an obvious quick win for cities, with huge savings in costs to hospitals and to police in calls for service, not to mention reductions in the number of victims of violent and sexual assaults. Jonathan Shepherd, founder of Cardiff University's Violence Prevention Group, offers an excellent TEDx presentation on the model.[44]

Special Law to Control Sale and Consumption of Alcohol in Coahuila, Mexico

Another strategy to prevent alcohol-related tragedies was instituted in the state of Coahuila in northern Mexico. In 2012, this state adopted a special law to control the sale and consumption of alcohol, which was enforced by the police. The law resulted in the confiscation of 37,000 liters of alcohol, the closure of 1,600 establishments, and 30,000 arrests for public consumption of alcohol. Not only did the law have a small effect on the reduction of traffic crashes, but it resulted in more than 70 percent fewer homicides related to alcohol and to 70 percent fewer street gang-related homicides.[45]

Another Homicide Prevention Effort in Diadema, Brazil, with a Twist of Alcohol

This Brazilian city reduced rates of homicide from 100 per 100,000 in 2000 to 34 per 100,000 by 2004.[46] Their strategy was quite targeted. At the turn of the century, the mayor of Diadema established a public safety and social justice group to look at how to address the loss of life to violence in Diadema. They recruited an academic institute to analyze the situation. The results of the study showed that one of the main causes of the high number of homicides in Diadema was alcohol abuse. Following the lead of Bogotá, Colombia, which successfully reduced homicides in the 1990s by restricting alcohol access (Ley Zanahoria [Carrot Law]), Diadema passed a law to restrict the availability of alcohol after 11:00 pm (Ley Seca [Dry Law]), and police strictly enforced the law. As in Bogotá, there was also significant public support for the law, with members of the public reporting violations.

Due to the new law, not only did Diadema see its homicide rates decline, but neighboring municipalities also experienced some decline. Diadema's significant drop in homicide rates in four years provides reasonable evidence of a contribution to a significant reduction in homicides associated with the law and its enforcement to limit access to alcohol.

MULTISECTORAL VIOLENCE PREVENTION

Gang Reduction in Los Angeles

The Los Angeles Gang Reduction and Youth Development (GRYD) Program has been described as one of the best examples of a comprehensive approach to violence reduction in the United States.[47] With an annual budget exceeding $20 million, GRYD manages or coordinates a wide range of violence prevention services, gang intervention services, violence interruption activities, and proactive peacemaking activities. The program is undertaken in partnership with several local universities that research what works, how to improve the program, and whether it actually affects rates of violence.

In general, GRYD's efforts are people and place focused. Using a specially designed tool, the program identifies youth at elevated risk for gang involvement. Then GRYD offers programs and services to these youth to help them deal with family issues, trauma, or retaliatory violence. A recent evaluation of the GRYD interventions to stop retaliatory violence showed a reduction of 185 gang-related violent crimes, including 10 fewer homicides, for 2014 and 2015. Put differently, every 100 gang-related incidents affected by GRYD allowed only 13.6 retaliations compared to 24 for those not treated by GRYD.[48] This alone saves $55 million a year in harm to victims and their families.

Dealing with Youth Violence in Minneapolis, Minnesota

Another striking example of the successes that can happen when you mobilize community resources comes from Minneapolis in the US state of Minnesota. Concerned with the high rates of serious injuries and deaths and the related costs to taxpayers, Minneapolis City Council declared youth violence a public health issue. Called Blueprint in Action, their comprehensive plan to deal with youth violence had four objectives: mentor at-risk youth, intervene at the first signs of risk, focus on reintegrating youth, and commit to changing the culture of violence.[49] This led to a 62 percent reduction in youth gunshot victims, a 34 percent reduction in youth victims of crime, and a 76 percent reduction in youth arrests with a gun from 2007 through 2015.[50]

A key component of the sustained success of Blueprint in Action program is the implementation of a permanent office led by the city's mayor. In fact, Minneapolis' success has led to the passage of the Youth Violence Prevention Act, which has defined youth violence as a public health issue.[51]

Tackling Auto Theft in Winnipeg, Canada

While not usually thought of as a violent crime, auto theft in the City of Winnipeg in Canada had resulted in serious injuries and deaths when joyriders lost control of the stolen car. After establishing a task force in 2004 to diagnose the problem areas and the risk factors, the task force received $40 million to implement a three-pronged plan tailored specifically to the city's auto theft problem. The plan included (1) intensive community supervision of high-risk youth, (2) a program requiring compulsory vehicle immobilizers for the most at-risk vehicles, and (3) youth programming to address the root cause of the vehicle thefts.

Evaluations show that this comprehensive strategy was a significant success, reducing auto theft an impressive 76 percent within six years. Furthermore, the investment of $40 million has contributed to annual reductions in insurance premiums of $30 million or more over several years—perhaps a return alone of $5 for every dollar, with other savings in health and policing costs.[52]

SOCIOECONOMIC DEVELOPMENT REDUCING VIOLENCE

Cleaning Up Violent Crime in New York City

New York City (NYC) has seen homicide rates drop from a peak at 2,200 murders in 1990 to less than 300 in 2017.[53] The disturbing trends in the 1990s were discussed in chapter 4. In the 2000s, it is likely that much of the decline in homicide rates was the continuation of economic recovery that contributed in the 1990s, but the city has innovated several other actions since then. For example, NYC has instituted 18 Cure Violence projects in high-crime problem places. Two of these were the subject of an evaluation by researchers from John Jay College. The evaluation showed promising results, including a reduction from 44 to 22 shootings in one area and 54 to 13 in the other. In addition, the NYC Cure Violence projects triggered a significant change in attitudes about resolving disputes with guns.[54]

Unfortunately, NYC does not have a transparent plan for the prevention of violent crime, although the city has established a special office for the reduction of gun violence with an annual budget of $22 million.[55] This supports a range of wraparound services, such as school conflict mediation, employment programs, and mental health services. In addition, the New York Police Department appointed a deputy commissioner for partnerships, who has encouraged various crime prevention projects, including Cure Violence. This is good news and should reap benefits.

KEY TAKEAWAYS

- Bogotá, Boston, and Glasgow provide important examples of how cities that use the essential elements, including collaborative and comprehensive community safety strategies, can reduce violent crime across the city by 50 percent or more. If they have a permanent violence prevention unit, they can sustain and increase the reductions.
- The organizations in Canada, Europe, and the United States that provide advice and training for cities looking for effective violence prevention strategies include the Canadian Municipal Network on Crime Prevention, European Forum for Urban Safety, National Forum on Youth Violence Prevention (National Forum), National Network for Safe Communities, and the Prevention Institute's Urban Network to Increase Thriving Youth (UNITY).
- Successful sustained comprehensive community safety strategies have a permanent office, are informed by violence prevention science, mobilize key sectors around a problem-solving and results-oriented plan, develop human talent, and mobilize the public for support.
- Cities that combined focused deterrence and outreach services have reduced their rates of gun violence by 50 percent or more, but they do not sustain the success without a permanent violence prevention office.
- Cities, such as Cardiff in the United Kingdom and others in Latin America, that focus on controlling alcohol have reduced their rates of violence by 50 percent or more.
- Although estimating the social return on the investments in a precise way is difficult for cities, a few US cities can show returns of seven dollars for every one dollar invested in crime prevention.

IV

SECRETS TO GET BUY-IN

When people are determined, they can overcome anything.

—Nelson Mandela

❿

BIG BENEFITS FROM SMART INVESTMENT

Effective Solutions Reduce Deaths, Sexual Violence, and Wasted Taxes

An ounce of prevention is worth a pound of cure.

—Benjamin Franklin

In part I, we looked at the urgency to end preventable human tragedies and the long-term costs and consequences of violent crime. In part II, we explored the range of upstream interventions shown by violence prevention science to actually end violence. In part III, we examined the consensus among governments about how to implement violence prevention, the problems with national strategies that do not follow enough of the guidelines, and the magic that can happen when communities succeed by adhering to the "essentials" for operationalizing the effective solutions. In sum, we learned about the potential opportunity for radical transformation in ending homicide and rapes in our world—if only we could get governments to shift from looking at the standard criminal justice system as the only solution. Now, we turn to how to be persuasive in that effort.

In this final part of the book, I start by discussing the compelling financial case for making the investment in violence prevention. That logic model is obvious: adequate and sustained investments now in violence prevention planning boards and national and citywide effective solutions will deliver significant reductions in violent crime and less need for the standard, reactive criminal justice system (CJS) and so generate funds for jobs and more. Ultimately, this lucrative cost–benefit scenario requires a transformation from a reactive, standard CJS to a smart, results-oriented governance of violent crime issues.

In chapter 7, we saw that the Inter-American Development Bank called for governments across Latin America and the Caribbean to make this transformation to "smart on crime."[1] This chapter shows just how lucrative smart on crime is in terms of numbers of lives saved and rapes avoided; taxes reduced because they are not needed to pay for oversue of policing and incarceration; and increases in GDP, that flow from greater community safely.

COST–BENEFIT LOGIC FOR INVESTING IN EFFECTIVE SOLUTIONS

My logic model is influenced by the work over several decades of the Washington State Institute for Public Policy (WSIPP). With highly sophisticated methodology, WSIPP has taken cost–benefit analysis a long way.[2] Pertinent to this book, this well-respected organization has undertaken an impressive number of project reviews related to juvenile and adult (as well as some prekindergarten to age twelve) criminal justice, albeit *after* a crime and arrest have taken place. Though WSIPP has not yet presented an analysis of investment in a package of upstream prevention and proactive policing in relation to street violence or violence against women, the organization has assessed individual projects in terms of project cost versus benefits to the victim (less harm and so on) and potentially less costs for the standard CJS.[3]

Using the logic and work of WSIPP as a springboard, the model I present in this chapter provides a compelling case for transforming our ways of coping with violent crime. Investing in operationalizing "effective solutions" with the "essentials" for success, including adequate and sustained funds, will end much violent crime. This, consequently, will reduce the pain and costs to victims and the losses to their families and communities. In turn, that reduction will diminish the need and, therefore, the costs of the reactive CJS and its negative consequences, thereby freeing up taxes to create other jobs and so improving our quality of life and prosperity.

To understand this model more clearly, let's consider how investment in effective violence prevention solutions would affect the United States, referring to figure 10.1 for visual reinforcement. If the United States were to make an annual investment equivalent to 10 percent of its current CJS costs, for which there are good reasons to suppose is sufficient, the benefits would include a reduction of $262 billion in tangible and intangible costs

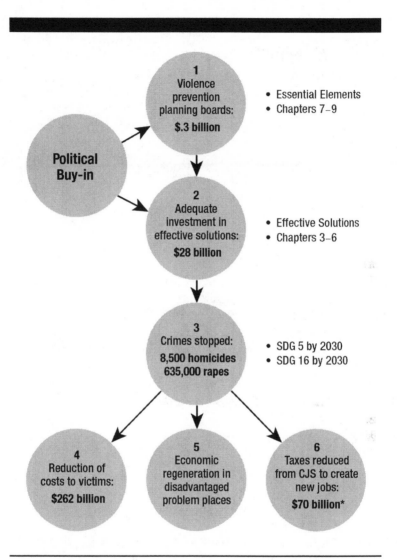

*20% reduction in policing and courts and 70% reductions in incarceration
to 1965 level after investing in effective solutions.

For source of numbers on saving lives, incarceration, and CJS costs,
see figure 10.2 and text of chapter.

**Figure 10.1. Benefits of 10% Investment in Violence Prevention
in the US**

to victims of homicide and rape (noted as number 4 in figure 10.1). This would result from stopping 50 percent of violent crime—8,500 homicides and 635,000 rapes (noted at number 3 in figure 10.1). In addition, there would be many fewer other violent crimes, including 250,000 fewer robberies and half a million or more fewer aggravated assaults. The 50 percent reduction in violent crime also would potentially free up close to $70 billion in spending on standard CJS (noted as number 6 in figure 10.1), including gradually reducing policing levels by 20 percent and reducing incarceration to rates from the 1960s, when police-recorded crime rates were similar to today's. In broader terms, with investments starting now, the United States would be able to achieve significant crime reduction results by 2030, the deadline of the Sustainable Development Goals, and have money left over for reinvesting in its citizens.

At first glance, a 50 percent reduction in violent crime may seem ambitious. Yet recall that a 50 percent reduction in homicides has been achieved in cities such as Boston, Glasgow in Scotland, and Bogotá in Colombia with comprehensive prevention programs and without radical shifts in unemployment, social welfare, or gun control. In addition, New York City has seen a 50 percent reduction happen twice, first from 1990 to 2000 and then from 2000 to 2015, largely from improvements in the job market.

OPERATIONALIZING COSTS AND BENEFITS

Ultimately, the challenge to decision makers is how to reduce the human and financial costs of violent crime so as to achieve well-being. Those costs include the following:

- Costs to victims caused by violent crime, including costs to society and neighborhoods
- Costs to taxpayers for the standard CJS
- Costs to offenders, their families, and communities for engagement with the CJS

To reduce those costs, decision makers need to make upstream investments in effective solutions. From part II of this book, we know what solid violence prevention science identifies as effective solutions. From part III, we know that governments agree that implementation of effective solutions requires permanent prevention planning boards; adequate, sustained investment; multisectoral human talent; data; and so on. So, the bottom line is that, to reduce the human and financial costs of violent crime (the three previous bullet items), governments must make core investments to fund permanent prevention planning boards and the other essential elements. (See numbers 1 and 2 in figure 10.1.) Every essential element costs money! With a permanent violence prevention planning board in place that can guide adequate and sustained investment in effective solutions to tackle risk factors, communities can experience up to a 50 percent reduction in violent crime within five years (noted as number 3 in figure 10.1). This reduction in crime will result in the following:

- Reduced costs to victims (noted at number 4 in figure 10.1)
- Economic regeneration of disadvantaged problem places because the consequences of incarceration will be reduced (noted as number 5 in figure 10.1)
- Reduced costs for the CJS (noted as number 6 in figure 10.1)

To delve deeper into the logic and numbers, let's explore each of the costs in depth in relation to the United States.

Costs to Victims Caused by Violent Crime

In chapter 1, we learned that the United States had 17,000 homicides and 1,270,000 or more rapes in 2016 and 2017. There were also half a million robberies and a million or more serious assaults.[4] Clearly, tangible and intangible losses are associated with these tragedies. Although different ways of assigning a dollar value to these losses exist,[5] for this chapter I am using the WSIPP method of assigning a dollar value, which gives lower estimates than some other systems.[6] For just the violent crimes of homicide and rape, my estimate of the dollar value for losses to victims in the United States in figure 1.2 in chapter 1 was a staggering $524 billion per year.

But it is not just costs to victims. For the World Economic Forum, the director of the Institute of Economics and Peace, Camilla Schippa, wrote an article in which she beautifully captures the additional costs of violence:

[V]iolence and the fear of violence can fundamentally alter the incentives faced by business. Consequently, with greater levels of violence it is likely that we might expect lower levels of employment and economic productivity over the long term, as the incentives discourage new employment creation and longer-term investment. Beyond that, violence also affects economic development, including reduced productivity on the job, decreased investment and saving, distortion of government resource allocation, and the flight of human and financial capital.[7]

These are not just losses in high-violence areas of Mexico or Latin America; they also are losses in high-violence neighborhoods of London, Toronto, and Chicago. Enough said.

Costs to Taxpayers for the Standard CJS

We also learned in chapter 1 that the latest estimates of expenditures on the standard CJS in the United States total $284 billion, of which, $135 billion went to policing, $61 billion to courts, and $87 billion to corrections.[8] These estimates date from 2015 but likely increase every year as decision makers continue more of the same.

Costs to Offenders, Families, and Their Communities for Engagement with the Standard CJS

Unfortunately, that staggering $284 billion budget with its policing, courts, and corrections line items is not the end of the costs relative to an individual getting caught up in the CJS industry. In its 2014 report, *The Growth of Incarceration in the United States*, the National Academy of Sciences outlined additional consequences of arrest and incarceration. Overall, the overwhelming list of consequences offered by the National Academy of Sciences is collectively difficult to quantify in dollars, but that cost is extremely high.

Among those consequences is limited access to occupations and vocational licenses for offenders, particularly men released from incarceration. This real cost affects the economic prosperity of not only the individuals but also the criminals' families and the problem places where they are concentrated. Plus, this reality perpetuates the revolving door of arrest and rearrest.[9]

Another costly consequence noted in the National Academy of Sciences report relates to having a parent in prison. Recall that having an incarcerated parent is one of the adverse childhood experiences (ACEs) which increase the probability of offending, mental health issues, and drug abuse. And consider that more than two million children have an incarcerated father. Now, imagine the ramifications of that!

In addition, policing and incarceration fall disproportionately on disadvantaged and minority populations, such as Blacks in the United States and indigenous people in Canada. Thus, overpolicing and overincarceration do not reduce the much higher risk of these populations being affected by violent crime. Plus, these costs are exacerbated by the impact of violent crime on economic activity, as described above.

HOW TO ACHIEVE REDUCTIONS IN THESE COSTS TO VICTIMS, CONSEQUENCES TO NEIGHBORHOODS, AND EXPENDITURES ON THE CJS

After understanding the three categories of costs, the next step is to understand the solutions to reducing those costs. Figure 10.1 provides a good illustration of the cost reductions and the downstream impacts of those reductions.

Core Investments to Fund Permanent Prevention Planning Boards and the Essentials

The functions of permanent violence prevention planning boards start with the vision and framework for investments in upstream prevention. They include informing local policy based on violence prevention science, organizing the diagnosis, planning, implementing the plan, and evaluating the strategy outcomes as well as mobilizing actions in the youth, family, police, school, health, and related sectors. Prevention boards also must mobilize and engage the public and keep decision makers interested and up to date. In addition, they must develop effective education and training programs, facilitate data gathering and analysis for monitoring and evaluation of results, and solicit and guide investment in effective solutions.

There is no clear standard for resourcing these functions, but some experience from Canada suggests that two dollars per person per year would be a minimum.[10] This is 0.3 percent of current expenditures, of which half would be provided to local government and half to other orders of government.

Once again, to succeed, prevention investments must be based on the following:

- **Diagnosis:** Data for diagnosis must include geographic concentration, measurement of risk factors, analysis of social context of victims and perpetrators, and situational issues, such as alcohol and guns. The diagnosis also must be inspired by knowledge of social factors, such as

ACEs, parenting, poverty, difficulties in primary school, and alcohol, using developmental criminology and practical experiences of successful cities as resources. It is much more than CompStat or predictive policing that focuses on efficient arrest and rearrest. Rather, the diagnosis phase is about focusing on where and how to target social development and proactive policing—and in that order.

- **Plan of how to address the risk factors:** The plan must identify what innovations in different sectors would address the risk factors identified in the diagnosis. This must be inspired by violence prevention science on what has worked in randomized controlled trials; in other research; and, particularly, in successful citywide role models.

- **Implementation in a range of sectors:** The sectors might include youth outreach and mentoring, job training and job creation, family, school, hospital emergency, sports and life skills, and proactive policing. It will require developing the human talent and staffing in each of those sectors to undertake the innovations needed. Just as police officers must be trained to arrest, lawyers defend, and prison guards to guard, so street workers must be trained to outreach, sports coaches must be trained in developing life skills for their players, and so on.

- **Monitoring and evaluation:** Of critical importance is (1) covering performance standards of what is needed to tackle the risk factors and (2) transparent measuring of the outcomes (for example, fewer crimes, money saved, and so forth). Remember, what gets measured gets done!

The diagnosis, planning, implementation, and evaluation process must be done competently. Success requires training planners to standards. It includes the development of the business case for those plans. As mentioned in chapter 9, the European Forum for Urban Safety (EFUS) has developed an excellent guide on how to do this, and their report for EUROsociAL identifies how to avoid many of the booby traps.[11] The hopeful starts and then disappointing failures of national efforts to end violent crime in chapter 8 are a warning to make sure this four-step process is done right. The magnificent disaster of Mexico's failure to utilize international expertise and experience despite significant funding is the hardest lesson to be learned in terms of lives lost.[12]

Proportionate Investment for Effective Solutions to Tackle Risk Factors

Refer to the box titled "Recap of Effective Solutions" for proven upstream strategies to prevent violence. It is important to remember that programs that reduce ACEs, including child abuse, take longer to deliver results in terms of street violence and violence against women because their impact on crime is in the period when adult males are passing through the high-crime years of fifteen to twenty-five. However, the benefits from these investments are significant, so they must be a part of the prevention portfolio.

RECAP OF EFFECTIVE SOLUTIONS

- Comprehensive community safety strategies achieving citywide reductions:
  - Bogotá focused on sustained reductions, including tackling access to alcohol and guns as well as retaliatory killings[13]
  - Glasgow focused on sustained reductions, using a combination of
    - smart policing (for example, focused deterrence and call-ins) with a focus on knives,
    - youth outreach,
    - parenting–family empowerment,
    - limiting access to alcohol, and
    - hospital emergency room intervention.
  - Boston achieved time-limited reductions, as have some other US cities, such as New Haven, Connecticut, as highlighted by Giffords Law Center to Prevent Gun Violence. New Haven achieved its success through
    - focused deterrence by police and
    - enhanced social services.[14]
- Various programs, projects, and efforts proven to be effective and cost effective via randomized controlled trials on limited populations:[15]
  - Youth mentoring and outreach, such as through Cure Violence[16]
  - Parenting support and family therapy[17]
  - School curriculum enhancement for life-skills training[18]

- ○ Job training and mentoring[19]
- ○ Hospital emergency social interventions[20]
- ○ Proactive policing[21]
- Various programs, projects, and efforts using effective strategies:
  - ○ National programs, such as Job Corps[22] and the Youth Inclusion Program[23]
  - ○ Sports and life-skills training[24]
- Programs that reduce poverty, provide a social safety net, and support positive parenting[25]
- Reducing impunity by increasing the professionalism of policing (public confidence, training, pay, and accountability)[26]
- Legalizing drugs:
  - ○ Legalizing marijuana has momentum in Canada and in a growing number of states in the United States.
  - ○ The homicide rates in both Mexico and the inner cities of the United States will be reduced significantly by removing the financial incentive for street gangs of selling drugs.[27]

Reduction in Homicides and Rapes

Investments in smart prevention are expected to achieve reductions of 50 percent or more in homicides, rapes, armed robberies, and aggravated assaults. My book *Smarter Crime Control* makes the case for a new investment equivalent to 10 percent of the expenditures on policing, courts, and corrections being enough to achieve a 50 percent reduction in national rates of homicides, rapes, and armed robberies. Note that, in chapter 9, cities have achieved such reductions within three years and many of the project evaluations in different sectors in both chapter 3 on proactive policing and chapter 4 on targeted social development reduced violence by 50 percent or more.

The social return on investment shows many of the programs and at least one city's strategies returning $7 for each one invested. Of this, maybe a third are savings on the standard CJS.[28] A stitch in time saves seven. An ounce of prevention is worth seven pounds. Maybe not as wonderful as the original proverbial phrases but applicable just the same! Who can get a seven-dollar return on a pension nest egg within five years? And this is not just money we are talking about. It involves well-being and life itself.

As highlighted earlier and in figure 10.1, a 50 percent reduction in homicides and rapes means 8,500 fewer homicide victims and 635,000 fewer rapes in the United States. It also means 250,000 fewer robberies, 500,000 fewer aggravated assaults, and 240,000 fewer victimizations involving a firearm, but I have not included these statistics in figure 10.1 in the interest of simplicity. These are significant reductions and achieve results for the Sustainable Development Goals in 2030 that are great for the United States and would be a model for other countries.

Reduction in Costs to Victims

All this means much less tangible loss and lost productivity for the victims and their families and much less intangible trauma and pain from violent crime. These numbers signify an impressive avoidance of tragedies that ruin so many lives, families, and communities. Research puts the reduction in monetarized loss for just homicide and rape in the United States at $262 billion a year.[29] Approximately $26 billion of that is related to lost productivity based on 10 percent of the tangible and intangible losses for homicide, which I have not included in figure 10.1 for the sake of simplicity.[30]

Economic Regeneration in Disadvantaged Problem Places

A 50 percent reduction in crime also would reduce the negative consequences of arrest, conviction, and jail time, particularly on young disadvantaged and racial minorities while stimulating economic development in problem places. Unfortunately, the National Academies report did not quantify this, but the combination of more men without the burden of conviction and incarceration and lower violent crime rates will help economic regeneration significantly. It will have a multiplier effect.

Taxes Reduced from the CJS to Create New Jobs

To be cautious, I have used in figure 10.1 a scenario in which $98 billion is saved (using current dollars) by reducing police and court expenditures by 20 percent and incarceration to the rate in 1965, when police statistics were similar to 2017 and before the exponential growth in incarceration commenced. But the investment in violence prevention planning boards and effective solutions would cost about $28 billion, so this must be deducted from the $98 billion. The net benefit then would be $70 billion, as noted in figure 10.1. The savings could be used to create 1.5 million jobs at an annual average wage of $44,000 a year. The jobs could achieve national priorities in health care, education, or even exploration of space, or the savings could be used to reduce taxes by that amount.

Here are the details of the assumptions of this conservative scenario: In relation to policing, some of the effective solutions to achieve the reductions require police resources to be transferred into proactive policing. That means that large cuts to policing would be counterproductive. England and Wales, for instance, achieved a 20 percent reduction in policing expenditures, most of which was achieved within three years of the start of the government's general austerity program. That significant reduction was achieved *without* immediate political consequences, labor unrest, or medium-term explosions in crime rates. Thus, if I use the more conservative estimate of 20 percent reduction in policing expenditures, which is $27 billion, this would allow a 20 percent cost reduction in courts ($12 billion), while still providing more court time per arrest and possibly reducing impunity.

In relation to incarceration, the reductions in violent crime would have a big impact on the number of people incarcerated because more than half of those in state prison are convicted of a violent crime.[31] It is harder to know the proportion of inmates in jails for violent crime, but many prisoners spend months or years on pretrial detention for offenses that eventually lead them to state prisons. Reducing violent crime, therefore, would help reduce levels of incarceration in both local jails and state prisons. The impact on the federal prison population would not be so great because many federal prisoners are incarcerated for other reasons than violence.

As noted, I have chosen to target the reduction to a conservative rate, which is the 1965 level, when US police-recorded crime rates were similar to those of today.[32] This is also the year when the incarceration explosion started. As we shall see in chapter 11, figure 11.3, the 1965 rate is much higher than other G7 countries and Mexico; therefore, much bigger savings could come from achieving a rate such as that in Canada or England and Wales or, indeed, Germany. Even this conservative 1965 rate, however, provides for savings of $58 billion. In contrast, the long-term trend for large reductions in homicides in New York City, combined with greater use of less punitive charges, has reduced local rates of incarceration by approximately the same proportion. There are also direct savings in tangible costs to victims ($26 billion), so total savings would be even greater, at $96 billion.

REDUCTIONS IN COSTS AND INCREASES IN GDP

With investments in effective crime prevention strategies, lives will be saved, rapes prevented, and money saved, as figure 10.2 so clearly shows for Canada, England and Wales, Mexico, and the United States, which have readily available statistics. These four countries offer good examples of how the model of balancing reactive CJS expenditures with a percentage of investment in violence prevention can reap great rewards. (Note that I have created draft charts similar to figure 10.1 for Canada, England and Wales, and Mexico as well as for some cities, including Chicago, but for this book I am presenting only the numbers for these countries in figure 10.2.)

Canada

A 50 percent cut in homicides would prevent 320 families from losing a member. If the number of rapes is at a per capita rate similar to the rate in the United States, there would be 70,000 Canadian women who avoid being victims of rape, which is the number I use because "rape" is more serious than the technical definition for "sexual assault" used in Canadian surveys. These numbers can be compared to the Canadian victimization survey in 2014, which estimated 200,000 sexual assaults and 2.2 million violent victimizations. That said, a 50 percent reduction would amount to 100,000 fewer sexual assaults and a million fewer violent victimizations in Canada.[33] Crime is estimated to cost Can$55 billion, or 2.5 percent of GDP.[34] A 50 percent reduction, thus, would bring down the cost to Can$28 billion, or 1.25 percent of GDP.

With that 50 percent reduction in victimization, the annual savings from the CJS in Canada would be close to Can$6 billion—out of total annual expenditures on policing, courts, and corrections in Canada, which was Can$22 billion in 2017.[35] If we use assumptions similar to those we used for the US scenario for police and courts, we would save Can$2.8 billion on policing (20 percent of Can$14.2 billion) and Can$0.8 billion on courts (20 percent of Can$4 billion). For corrections, a 50 percent cut in the prison population would reduce the rate below that of Germany but above that of Japan, which seems feasible. This would save Can$2.3 billion (50 percent of Can$4.6 billion) in operating costs and avoid significant capital costs because many provinces, such as Ontario, are building bigger and better jails.[36]

The investment in planning and effective solutions would cost approximately Can$2 billion, so this must be deducted from the Can$6 billion. The net benefit, thus, would be Can$4 billion. The savings could be used

	CANADA	ENGLAND & WALES	MEXICO	USA
Number of Lives Saved by homicides prevented to nearest 100 for a recent year	300	350	14,500	8,500
Rate of Homicides per 100,000 total population	0.8	0.6	11.7	2.6
Approximate number of women where **Prevention Stopped Rapes** occurring	70,000	114,000	243,000	635,000
Number of People for whom incarceration averted on an average day to nearest 1,000	20,000	42,000	109,000	1,472,000
Rate of Persons Incarcerated per 100,000 total population	57	70	88	200
Population in millions	36	58	124	324
Total Expenditures on police, courts, and prisons in billions	Can$16	£17	Mex$288	$186
Expenditure on Effective Solutions in billions	Can$2	£2	Mex$28	$28
Total Savings in billions	Can$4	£2	Mex$0	$70
Potential Jobs Created outside of CJS at average wage	80,000	74,000	80,000	1,522,000

See appendix for sources.

Figure 10.2. Prevention Saves Lives, Stops Rapes, and Reduces the CJS

to create 80,000 jobs at an annual average wage of Can$51,000 per year. The jobs could achieve national priorities in health care, education, or even saving the environment, or the savings could be used to reduce taxes by that amount.

England and Wales

There were 702 persons murdered in 2017 in England and Wales and, according to the proportion noted in the Centers for Disease Control and Prevention (CDC) survey, 228,000 rapes.[37] Thus, a 50 percent cut in homicides will prevent 350 families from losing a member, and a 50 percent reduction in rapes will save 114,000 women from that violent crime.

I get similar numbers for rape using British data instead of the CDC rate. The British Crime Survey in 2017 estimated 144,000 rapes.[38] But this is not a specialized survey on intimate partner and sexual violence, and so it is likely to significantly underestimate the number of rapes.[39] Another way is to use the fact that only 20 percent of rape victims report to police.[40] So we must add another 80 percent to the police-recorded numbers of 54,000. Then, the total number of rapes in England and Wales annually is 260,000, close to the estimate using the CDC data.

This book focuses on homicide and rape, but the smart solutions will reduce other common violent crimes. The British Crime Survey estimated 1,259,000 "incidents of violence" in 2017, including 74,000 robberies and 39,000 knife-related crimes.[41]

With recommended investment and the consequent reduction in crimes, the annual savings from the CJS in England and Wales would be close to £4 billion out of total annual expenditures on policing, courts, and corrections, which was £21 billion in 2017.[42] Because England and Wales has already cut police by 20 percent, I do not see any significant cuts or savings in policing from £11 billion. However, the reductions in cases going to courts and in the numbers of criminals going to prisons should provide savings. For instance, a 20 percent cut to courts from £5 billion would save £1 billion. A 50 percent cut from prisons at £5 billion would save £2.5 billion because most of the costs are salaries. This would reduce the rate to about that of Germany, save operating costs, and avoid significant capital costs because there have been proposals to build bigger and better prisons there as well as in Canada. (Note that a 50 percent cut in the prison population has been proposed by key leaders no longer in power in England and Wales.[43])

The investment in planning and effective solutions in England and Wales would cost approximately £2 billion, so this must be deducted from the £4 billion. The net benefit, thus, would be £2 billion. The savings could be used to create 74,000 jobs at an annual average wage of £27,000. The jobs could achieve national priorities in health care, education, or even undersea exploration, or, again, the savings could be used to reduce taxes by that amount.

There are no clear estimates for the cost of violent crime in England and Wales.[44] It is likely the costs are in the ballpark of £30 billion a year, so a 50 percent cut would be £15 billion, or 1 percent of GDP.

Mexico

A 50 percent decrease in homicides from current levels of 29,000 would save nearly 15,000 lives in Mexico.[45] A 50 percent decrease in rapes would save 243,000 women from being raped. My calculation estimates that the number of women raped in Mexico is proportionate to that in the United States. I use these numbers because it is difficult to use Mexico's National Institute of Statistics and Geography data to arrive at a clear estimate at this stage.[46]

Total expenditures on policing, courts, and corrections in Mexico is estimated at 288 billion pesos.[47] Mexico needs to invest significantly in increasing the capacity of its police and courts to reduce impunity.[48] The country, thus, would be wise to freeze the numbers of police and, instead, focus on raising the integrity and effectiveness of its police force. Under this scenario, there would no savings from policing. Mexico might even need to shrink the numbers of police but pay the individual officers more as the country improves the professional capabilities of its police force. Quality not quantity is essential to success.

As background to this logic, let us delve deeper into policing in Mexico. Mexico has close to double the number of police compared to the other thirty-four members of the Organization for Economic Co-operation and Development, but the country also suffers from very high rates of impunity.[49] The bottom line is that proactive policing cannot succeed without catching, convicting, and incarcerating persistent violent offenders. Nonetheless, in past years, Mexico has increased expenditures on policing and related repression by 61 percent, despite the fact, as we learned in chapter 3, that policing numbers do not affect violence rates. Instead, I recommend that Mexico focus on improving the professionalism of its current police officers; raise admission and promotion standards; link pay for supervisors to increases in reporting, clearance, and lack of corruption; and increase the number of judges.

Ultimately, a 50 percent decrease in violent crime should allow Mexico's incarcerated population to stay steady, despite more offenders getting convicted. Their focus to get the violence-reduction dividend must be (1) improving the professionalism of policing and courts to achieve less impunity and more proactive policing, and (2) investing adequately and sustainably in effective solutions to social causes of violence. This book's chapters 4 and 5 and, for the city level, chapter 9, would be great resources to jump-start the effort.

Under my proposed scenario of investing in upstream solutions, Mexico would not see savings from the CJS, but it would from economic growth in GDP. Seven percent is quite a significant loss in GDP, and the number may be larger given the full Global Peace Index (GPI) estimate. I am using a 7 percent loss to GDP from violence, based on the most recent data.[50] A 50 percent cut in violent crime would generate 3.5 percent of the GDP—600 billion pesos or 60,000 jobs at 65,000 pesos per year.[51] This estimate of loss to GDP in Mexico from violent crime at 7 percent is also midway between the Inter-American Development Bank estimate of 1.9 percent and the 13 percent estimate of the GPI, World Economic Forum, and World Bank. Note that the loss from violent crime can be estimated in various ways.[52] The GPI and World Economic Forum broaden what is included in the costs to victims and the CJS to reach 13 percent of GDP, equivalent to two months of wages for an average Mexican worker.[53] The World Bank has calculated the loss to GDP from violent crime for Latin American countries in a similar range.[54]

KEY TAKEAWAYS

- Most governments pay more and more for standard police, courts, and corrections despite evidence that the increases in expenditures do not usually stop violence.
- An investment equivalent to 10 percent of what is currently spent on the standard CJS would achieve significant benefits.
- The smart investment must go into the permanent violence prevention boards at all levels of government—in the United States $1 per capita—and adequate and sustained investment in smart effective solutions—in the United States equivalent to 10 percent of current expenditures on the CJS.
- Using the UN Economic and Social Council essentials to guide investments in effective solutions, governments can cut violence in half, avoid harm to victims, regenerate economic development, and save taxes and so generate employment outside the CJS.
- As crime is reduced, savings in taxes can be generated by modest decreases in expenditures on policing over time, except in Mexico, where the quality of policing must be improved, and by significant reductions in numbers of people incarcerated.
- Police budgets must be shifted to proactive policing and reducing impunity.
- Investments in targeted social development and its impact on reducing consequences of incarceration and neighborhood decline will increase economic development in problem places.
- In high-violence neighborhoods and countries, reductions in violence will cut the loss to GDP, thus generating employment.

AFFORDABLE AND ACHIEVABLE

Adequate Investment in Effective Solutions

The public wants education and prevention more than police, lawyers, and prisons.

—Gallup

With the exception of the government in England and Wales, governments around the world have found more and more money to spend on their reactive criminal justice systems (CJSs). We have seen that much of this funding has had little or no effect on ending violent crime. In other words, funding has been available but just not used in the most effective or cost-effective ways to stop violence.

Enough is enough! With so many lives lost and destroyed by violence, even now cannot be soon enough to heed the advice of violence prevention experts and academics who have conducted studies, surveys, and randomized controlled trials to prove what really works to end violent crime. It is time to follow the guidelines that governments have agreed are needed to operationalize success. We *must* get decision makers across the world on board. I call on marketing experts in the next chapter to create compelling videos and cartoons and conduct engaging high-level workshops to persuade those decision makers to become aware and take action. We must pull out all the stops and do whatever it takes to reduce violence in our world.

This chapter will examine the art of what is politically possible and how to support decision makers in making the transition from a reactive CJS to a transformative violence prevention program.

WE CAN AFFORD PREVENTION

As discussed numerous times, many governments have increased expenditures on reactive CJS significantly. If they could afford to pay for more of the strategies now known to be of limited effectiveness, then they can afford to invest in effective and cost-effective strategies that will reduce violent crime and save their taxpayers money. This is not just an issue for national and regional governments; it applies to municipal governments as well.

United States of America

Most of the expansion in policing and incarceration in the United States occurred in the 1980s and 1990s, but it also has continued in the 2000s. Some of these increases have been due to inflation, but most of them have been due to growth in CJS employment and salaries.[1] Whatever the reason, two things are for certain: the United States was able to increase spending rapidly in the name of fighting crime, and the spending was not based on what was cost effective in reducing crime. Specifically, in 1980, the United States was spending close to $20 billion on policing and just under $10 billion each on corrections and courts. By 2000, these numbers had reached $75 billion for policing, $55 billion for corrections, and $38 billion for courts. This growth was followed by yet another spurt; by 2010, the United States was spending $124 billion for policing, $80 billion for corrections, and $55 billion for courts, numbers that increased by about 10 percent by 2015.

While spending more on the CJS, the United States has not been spending more on sectors likely to have an impact on ending violent crime. One important comparison for CJS expenditure increases must be with investment in education, especially given that two-thirds of inmates in US state prisons have not completed high school. According to a 2016 news release from the US Department of Education, "Over the past three decades, state and local government expenditures on prisons and jails have increased about three times as fast as spending on elementary and secondary education. At the postsecondary level, the contrast is even starker: From 1989-90 to 2012–13, state and local spending on corrections rose by 89 percent, while state and local appropriations for higher education remained flat."[2] What does that say about priorities?

Mexico

Mexico has a similar story of massive increases to reactive security and CJSs without equivalent expenditures on proven prevention. As discussed in chapter 8, Mexico's spending on police and its army rose by 61 percent between 2008 and 2015.[3] Despite this increased funding of the CJS, Mexico's homicide rates spiked and have gone on rising significantly since then. Looking for reasons for this trend, one think tank has pointed to the lack of increased investment in upstream prevention and stresses the importance of reducing impunity.[4] Also of interest is that, during this time, Mexico transformed its court system to operate similarly to that of the United States, but these courts are underfunded, which likely has contributed to impunity.

Canada

Canada increased expenditures on policing by 100 percent, a 43 percent increase over inflation, also without spending on proven effective solutions. The total costs of policing have grown from $6 billion in 2000 to $14.7 billion in 2017, mostly by increasing salaries.[5] It is also interesting to note that two-thirds of policing costs in Canada are paid out of municipal budgets. Thus, as a result of the increase in CJS expenditures, municipalities have had to cut other services. In fact, the Federation of Canadian Municipalities says that the unsustainable increases in the costs of public safety are crowding out early intervention and prevention.[6] The Council of Canadian Academies also has drawn attention to these trends and has argued for greater recognition of the spectrum of agencies, other than policing, that can affect crime rates. The Council also points out the need to recruit police executives who work in the "partnership" environment.[7] Think Glasgow, youth services, schools, housing, and so on. It is time to spend where it matters, which would also reduce police workload.

If Canadian municipalities do shift from spending more on policing to spending more on effective solutions, they need to be sure to spend smartly—and locally. Municipalities represent the level of government best suited to identify local issues and problems and the conditions contributing to the problems. Yet municipal government accesses only 8 percent of the total revenue from taxes in Canada, and these taxes come largely from property taxes. It is clear, therefore, that federal and provincial funding is needed to provide stable and timely funding for municipal crime prevention, as in other advanced countries.

England and Wales

England and Wales is a different story. Starting in 2011, in the name of austerity, the government cut all expenditures except education and health—without politicians being thrown out of power for the reductions. Policing costs, over time, were cut by close to 20 percent.[8] Simultaneously, similar cuts were made to those services likely to reduce the need for policing, such as children's services. The result? Police-recorded crime data showed no major changes due to the police staffing reductions, which occurred between 2011 and 2013.[9]

Interestingly, though, the reduction in funding to social sectors that influence crime levels increased the portfolio of what police are doing with their time, even without significant increases in crime. As we discussed in the past, because police officers are available 24/7 through a national emergency telephone number—in England and Wales, that number is 999—they are the obvious fallback for any and every public crime, dispute, or problem. In a 2015 report, the UK chief inspector of police confirmed that, with increasing pressures on public services, such as housing, mental health, drug addiction, and education, the police are increasingly being left filling the gaps in social services. He stated, "Society should no longer tolerate conditions in which these illnesses and disorders are neglected until they land at the feet of the police, in circumstances of violence, disorder, and desperation."[10]

That said, despite the rates of crime remaining flat during the years of police cutbacks from 2011 to 2013, there has been an increase in police-recorded crime, including homicide, in 2016 and 2017.[11] (The rates per capita still remain much lower than homicide rates in the United States and, indeed, Canada.) At first glance, the recent trends in England and Wales cannot eliminate the possibility of a delayed impact from lower police numbers, but the trends also cannot confirm that having fewer police officers on the street is the only reason for these rising crime numbers. There are several other plausible explanations, including a domino effect from cuts to social sectors, such as children's services.[12]

Conclusions from solid violence prevention science, underscored in chapter 3, prove that ending violent crime does not depend on the number of police officers but on how the police officers are used. Think proactive policing. We also learned, in chapter 4, that crime rates can be reduced much more cost effectively by investing in upstream social programs than, once again, by expanding the traditional CJS. If England and Wales want to reduce violent crime, the violence prevention science in this book underlines the importance of using police resources better and increasing smart investment in targeted social development.

GETTING AN OUNCE OF PREVENTION: TITHING

Benjamin Franklin told us that "an ounce of prevention is worth a pound of cure." Yet we have just shown that governments are spending a pound on cure—and a whole lot more—but not investing in the ounce of prevention. One way to get the ounce of prevention is to fix the amount that will go to prevention in proportion to spending on reaction. In other words, tie the prevention investment to the reaction expenditures. Typically, the amount needed for targeted upstream prevention is just a fraction of what is needed for reaction. Granted, it is easier to get funds to "pick up the pieces" because the tragedies of violent crime are evident and emotionally wrenching. For strategies that prevent those tragedies, the urgent need for investment is not so obvious.

In my book *Smarter Crime Control*, I propose that governments spend on prevention the equivalent of 10 percent of what they are spending on the CJS. This amount could be found gradually over five years and is approximately the same as inflation. Because many of the upstream programs discussed in chapter 4 are relatively inexpensive, 10 percent is estimated to provide enough to get a 50 percent reduction in crime. Once crime comes down further with the investment, it is easier for governments to stop hiring more CJS personnel, so they could afford equal investment in preventive, positive actions by reallocating the saved CJS funds. Leading the way, the International Organization for Victim Assistance proposed at the 2015 UN Congress on the Prevention of Crime and Criminal Justice that one-tenth of 1 percent of GDP be invested in harnessing this knowledge through good governance strategies to achieve the violence reduction targets of the Sustainable Development Goals (SDGs). As yet, however, governments have not shifted to making the investments needed to get the reductions in homicides and rapes foreseen in the vision of the SDGs. Hopefully, this book will empower them to act.

In Canada, specifically, a number of proposals relative to this approach have been made. One option in funding crime prevention in Canada comes from the 1993 parliamentary committee known as the Horner Commission. This commission recommended that 5 percent of what is spent on policing, criminal justice, and corrections be invested in prevention. If this recommendation had been followed, crime rates would be much lower, and the demand for policing considerably diminished. Another resolution, adopted in 2008 at the Annual Congress of the Federation of Canadian Municipalities, called for one dollar for crime prevention for every additional dollar spent on policing. If this had been followed, municipal crime prevention in Canada would be in a much stronger position today. Cities would have fewer homicides and fewer rapes.

PREVENTION IS WHAT THE MAJORITY OF PEOPLE WANT

In democracies, government officials are supposed to be representing their constituents. If legislators actually did this, crime prevention would be the law of the land and adequately supported and funded because research shows that the majority of people prefer prevention over punishment. Figure 11.1 shows an analysis from the US National Crime Victim Survey of what victims of violence want when they report to police. As noted earlier in the book, they want prevention more than punishment. Furthermore, figure 11.2 shows that 64 percent of Americans prefer to lower crime through putting money and effort into education and jobs; only 32 percent of Americans prefer police and prisons as the answer to crime.[13]

The proportion of local spending on policing varies widely between cities. From one study of ten major US cities and two US counties, we learned that police spending today vastly outpaces expenditures in vital community resources and services. In those cities, per capita police spending ranged from as low as $133 in St. Louis County to as high as $772 in Baltimore. The city with the highest percentage of its general fund expenditures going to police, sheriff, and corrections, at 41.2 percent, was Oakland, California.[14]

This study—conducted by the Center for Popular Democracy along with Law for Black Lives and the Black Youth Project 100—reported that all twelve jurisdictions involved in the study had consistent community safety priorities. Most notable among their demands were the following:

- Educational opportunities
- Health care

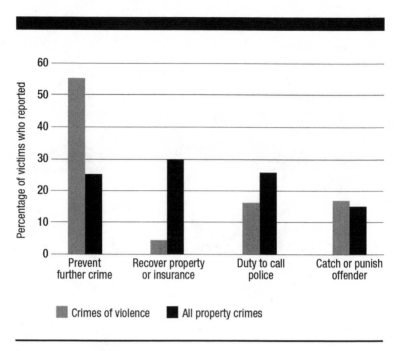

Crimes of violence   All property crimes

See appendix for sources.

Figure 11.1. Reasons for Victims to Report to Police

- Mental health services and treatment
- Affordable housing
- Transit access
- Investments in youth

In the words of the leaders of those US cities and counties, "When we have a mental health crisis, we want a mental health professional, not a police officer to show up. If someone we love is struggling with drug addiction, we want them to receive treatment and rehabilitation, not a jail sentence."[15] The cities and counties also call for community budgeting, so those most affected by the problems can recommend where funding should be invested. From a bird's-eye view, note that these are the same categories of programs and services for which solid violence prevention science advocates.

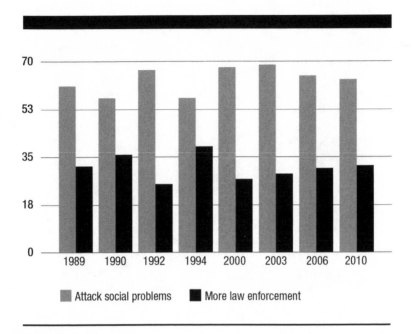

See appendix for sources.

Figure 11.2. Citizens Prefer Spending on Social Programs Rather Than on Police and Prisons

Politicians Who Expand the Punishment Empire Misspend Taxes

Not only is expansion of police and punishment not what the majority of voters want, but that expansion also does not achieve what politicians say. It leads to more, not less, street and gender violence and increases and misspends taxes. In the United States, for example, forty years of criminal justice bills and efforts to expand policing and prisons have pushed criminal justice taxes per capita to exceed those of any other major affluent democracy, without reducing homicide rates to anything close to those of other democracies. Consider, as the first two columns of figure 11.3 show, that the United States is the G7 country with a national rate of incarceration of 655 per 100,000, more than four times that of England and Wales and eight times that of Germany. Even with so many perpetrators behind bars, the murder rate in the United States is 5 per 100,000, more than four times higher than that of England and Wales and six times higher than that of Germany.

As explored in chapter 10, if the United States were to invest $28 billion a year in prevention—10 percent of what it spends on the standard CJS—

COUNTRY	HOMICIDES	INCARCERATION	COST TO US PROPORTIONATE TO RATE OF INCARCERA-TION OF G7 COUNTRY	ANNUAL NET SAVINGS TO US TAXPAYERS
	Rate per 100,000 population		Rate per billions of US dollars	
USA	5.2	655	$87	$0
Canada	1.8	114	$15	$72
England and Wales	1.2	141	$19	$68
France	1	102	$14	$73
Italy	0.9	90	$12	$75
Germany	0.8	76	$10	$77
Japan	0.3	45	$6	$81
USA (1965)	5.1	215	$29	$58
Mexico	23.4	176	$23	$64

Figure 11.3. Savings if US Reduced Incarceration to Rates of Other G7 Countries

the country could bring down its astronomical incarceration rates. I used the 1965 rate for the calculations in figures 10.1 and 10.2, which saves $58 billion. But it could save from $68 billion to $81 billion, depending on the rate for other G7 countries.[16] Even after deducting the $28 billion investment, the savings are massive—from $30 billion at 1965 rates to $53 billion at Japan's rate—while also halving the homicide rate.

Unfortunately, in major part because of the misspending on the CJS and the misguided thinking about the potential outcome of CJS practices and policies, the United States has not been investing in those preventive programs that science says unequivocally will put an end to violence. On a whole, the country, thus, is stuck in a no-win situation when it comes to crime. Thankfully, some cities and states are implementing prevention strategies. Without federal government dollars and support, however, those efforts are fragile.

Not Just a Red Problem

I must point out that not just right-wing politicians prioritize the CJS over public services. In the United States, in addition to Republican presidents, Democratic president Bill Clinton also played a role in getting the United States to where it is today when it comes to the bloated CJS. In England, Jeremy Corbyn, the left-leaning leader of the Labour Party, wanted to spend more money on policing in 2017. In response, a major British newspaper, *Independent*, ran an article titled "Criminal Justice after Austerity: Are There Radical Possibilities?" The article rightly called for a shift from spending on the police to spending on public services that reduce harm and meet the needs of individuals and communities. The article's subheading captured the point adeptly: "Promising greater police numbers may suit the current political mood, but Jeremy Corbyn's Labour should be looking at more creative alternatives when it comes to protecting the public."[17] Bingo. In fact, the opportunity lost by misspending on police would actually have the opposite effect of what Corbyn assumed policing would provide. And Corbyn is not alone. Too many politicians treat policing at budget time as if it equated stopping crime. It does not. There is absolutely no evidence to support the myth politicians propagate that more police will bring less crime. Better, proactive policing, yes! Also, the evidence earlier in this chapter does not support that pandering to the public with more police is what the public wants. They do not.

Politicians who run on a tough-on-crime, tough-on-causes platform get elected and by large margins. Just look at Tony Blair in England and Wales, Nelson Mandela in South Africa, and the conservative government in Alberta discussed in chapter 8. But such leaders must invest in effective solutions as well as smarter CJS to bring their agendas to fruition.

PREVENTION PROVIDES MORE THAN VIOLENCE REDUCTION

When determining budgets and setting policies regarding the CJS and violence prevention, government leaders must take into account not only quantitative but also qualitative information. The evidenced-based truth is that violence prevention actions improve the lives of young people and disadvantaged groups—whether or not they stop crime. Consider all the positive outcomes of many of the preventive programs highlighted in chapters 4 and 5: more youth completing school, more young men getting jobs, more women living lives free of fear, more children growing up without abuse, fewer young men behind bars.

Violence prevention is also a catalyst for economic development, particularly in poor cities and developing countries. Think about this proven cycle: targeted social development leads to less violence, which leads to less overpolicing, which leads to less crime and fear, which leads to more investment in the economy, which leads to the ability to invest in more targeted social development. Intergovernmental groups, such as the World Bank and the Inter-American Development Bank (IDB), understand this and support violence prevention. Recall my calling attention to the 2017 report published by the IDB titled *The Costs of Crime and Violence: New Evidence and Insights in Latin America and the Caribbean.*

So important is violence prevention to the IDB that its leaders are investing in research on the topic. Truly, the IDB as well as the World Bank, both of which are heavily supported by the United States, have major untapped ways of implementing effective prevention solutions in high-violence countries. It is time that world leaders, such as the United States, China, and the European Union, see the light and join these two intergovernmental agencies in investing in effective violence prevention strategies as a means to implementing the SDGs around the globe, for the well-being of all people, especially those in poor and developing nations.

Issues That Need Kid-Glove Care

While major social and economic benefits will result from investing in effective crime prevention solutions, some potential side effects may need special attention. For example, with decreased rates in victimization and less money being spent on the standard CJS, the number of CJS jobs will diminish. This may create some resistance from those earning a living in the CJS, unless this human resource issue is well managed with empathy.

Let's first examine how reductions in CJS funding might affect police. We have already seen that England and Wales was able to reverse the increasing expansion of police staffing as part of an austerity program started in 2011. Over time, through attrition and encouragement to retire, a reduction in spending close to 20 percent and decreases in numbers of police of 15 percent were achieved. Note the reductions occurred through attrition and retirement—over time. I want to point out that by "reducing CJS funding," I do not mean reducing incomes. Decent wages are important to the quality of the personnel because low incomes can result in loss of efficacy of police, courts, and corrections and can lead to corruption, human rights violations, and organized crime. The bottom line is, we need high-quality staff to organize and engage in effective proactive policing and to partner in comprehensive community safety strategies.

As police become more professional, it is important to compare their vision to that of other professions, such as doctors. In the modern version of the medical Hippocratic Oath, for example, one line reads, "I will prevent disease whenever I can, for prevention is preferable to cure." Police might follow suit and promise to prevent *crime* whenever they can, for prevention is preferable to *jail*. This is so because "arrest and deter" does harm offenders as well as their families and communities.[18] Nonetheless, it is the Peel Principles police leadership often quote. Unlike the focus on "doing no harm" in the Hippocratic Oath, the Peel Principles stress that lack of crime and disorder is the sign of effective policing. Yes, the heavy hand this "lack of crime and disorder" implies is justified in some instances. Violence prevention science, however, has uncovered the truth that heavy-handed policing is justified much less than it is used. Police would be better to shift to a philosophy of it is better to do no harm, unless the harm outweighs the benefits to the public as well as to the offender.

For prison guards, CJS reductions may be more complicated. As with policing, attrition and retirements are the way to begin shrinking the corrections industry; the explosion in incarceration took place approximately thirty years ago, so many guards may be anticipating retirement. If layoffs and job eliminations are necessary, city or community jails may be easier to deal with than state prisons. This is because, in cities and more urban communities, the guards most likely would be able to find other employment; such is likely the case with those guards losing their jobs as New York City's Rikers Island prison complex closes over the next decade. On the other hand, those working in state prisons, which are often in isolated rural communities where unemployment was high before the prison was built, might have to move to find work. Layoffs are never easy, but they often follow the realization that more cost-effective solutions exist. Consider that progress in many sectors, from car manufacturing to universities to hospitals, leads to layoffs. In the case of incarceration, part of the "prevention dividend" may be the availability of job retraining or job placement in more lucrative positions for those losing their CJS job. The bottom line is that the staff must be treated fairly and with empathy.

Finally, guns! Talk about a hot-button topic, especially in the United States. As we discussed in previous chapters, limiting the availability of firearms is an important strategy in violence prevention. If the objective is to save the most lives, the challenge is to limit the illegal, harmful use of handguns, especially in disadvantaged areas in US cities. Doing so does not necessarily mean fighting the powerful gun-rights lobbying group, the National Rifle Association, or rewriting the US Second Amendment. Rather, in chapter 9, I showcased a variety of alternative actions, such as focused deterrence, that can be effective in reducing gun-related homicides. For more ideas, check out the website of Giffords Law Center to Prevent Gun Violence (http://lawcenter.giffords.org/). This leading-edge organization offers comprehensive resources on US policies related to firearms as well as fact sheets, reports, toolkits, and other publications that feature up-to-date and critical information about US firearms laws and the most effective solutions to gun violence.

MAKING THE TRANSITION

The conclusions from part II of this book are that effective solutions require more proactive policing and more investments in targeted social development across several sectors. The conclusions from part III are that operationalizing the implementation of effective solutions requires seven necessary and essential actions. These smart innovations will save many lives and prevent many rapes, but they require adaptation and concretization at different orders of government. The tried and tested way to make these governmental transformations is through commissions, task forces, and conferences/congresses that engage the different stakeholders in finding common ground, leveraging research and resources, and making pragmatic recommendations to decision makers on how to proceed.

Role of National Commissions

Often, significant transformation comes from a major commission. In the 1960s, three major US presidential commissions looked at different aspects of crime and violence. For instance, the Katzenbach Commission on the Challenge of Crime in a Free Society examined the causes and solutions to violent crime.[19] Its recommendations led to the Law Enforcement Assistance Act and Administration that invested significant federal funds in launching the movement toward professional police, functioning courts, and adequate incarceration. Its recommendations included the need to tackle the causes of violent crime. (Although a private commission was established in 1996 to update and replicate the Katzenbach Commission, it did not result in government action.[20])

In 1983, at the instigation of Mothers Against Drunk Drivers (MADD), another US presidential commission examined the problem of drunk driving. This commission made a number of recommendations that were transformed into law and action, thus radically changing attitudes toward drinking and driving. A year later, in 1984, the Presidential Task Force on Victims of Crime looked at the state of victim services and rights across the United States. Its recommendations led to the Victims of Crime Act, which established the influential Office for Victims of Crime—a model for the world.

In England and Wales, across "the pond" from the United States, a Commission on Youth Violence is scheduled to release its report in 2018. This joint project, between a parliamentary committee and a university, is expected to present the latest research and make recommendations on youth violence solutions for England and Wales. Its interim report recommends actions from chapters 3 and 9.[21] For instance, it proposes greater use of the Glasgow model, a focus on early years, transformation of youth services, boosting support in schools, increasing employment, fostering better reporting to police, and studying the decriminalization of drugs.

City Task Forces

As we saw in chapter 9, the mayors of some cities have established task forces to examine how violent crime might be prevented in their local communities. These task forces have led to permanent crime prevention boards, which steer the development and implementation of crime prevention plans for the cities.

THE POWER OF "SMART ON VIOLENCE" PREVENTION

In the introduction, I mentioned the growing movement in the United States and elsewhere to get those holding the purse strings to make spending decisions that are (1) most cost effective and (2) in line with current knowledge and science. These two factors support a logic that appeals to some decision makers and many ordinary citizens. In other words, I am advocating for being "smart on violence prevention" while being "smart on crime." Thankfully, we are seeing some early adopters and leaders.

United States of America

If the federal government is not taking the lead on crime prevention in the United States, states and cities are stepping up to fill the void. In fact, some US states are investing small amounts to encourage cities to end violent crime by using violence prevention knowledge and evidence. For instance, Connecticut, Maryland, Massachusetts, and New York all have statewide strategies.[22] In addition, two groups recently were formed to tackle violence in America: a consortium called States for Gun Safety is attempting to tackle gun violence, and Mayors for Smart Crime strives to reduce crime rates through sharing evidence-based research and strategies and supporting each other's efforts.

Specifically, States for Gun Safety was launched in 2017 by governors from Puerto Rico and six northeastern states (Connecticut, Delaware, Massachusetts, New Jersey, New York, and Rhode Island). This consortium includes some of the states that have already established state-wide strategies and reduced gun violence. Nonetheless, this new alliance proposes to undertake significant research on all aspects of gun violence by engaging experts from various sectors, including public health, social welfare, public policy, and criminal justice. The group also intends to inform the public about research findings, provide evidence- and data-informed policy recommendations to reduce shootings, and share between the states information about background checks and illegally used guns.[23]

The second group, Mayors for Smart on Crime, also founded in 2017, was launched by the Center for American Progress. I mentioned this network in the introduction. As of early 2018, its membership consists of fourteen US mayors. They are committed to four "pillars" related to being smart on crime:

- Data- and evidence-driven solutions
- Just and proportional responses
- Fair laws and enforcement of the laws
- Comprehensive investments[24]

In their outreach efforts, Mayors for Smart on Crime plan to focus every six months on one of their four pillars. Their ultimate goal is to help all US cities advance toward fairer and more effective crime prevention. Their inclusion of two of the "essential" elements—being evidence driven and ensuring investment—is particularly important.

Canada

In Canada, municipalities have come together to form the Canadian Municipal Network on Crime Prevention (CMNCP). This alliance of officials with responsibility for comprehensive community safety strategies has spearheaded greater use of violence prevention science in Canada. The group stresses the importance of going beyond reactive policing and investing in effective and cost-effective prevention that involves innovations in youth and family services, schools, and other community sectors as well as shifting policing to a partnership and problem-solving role. To their credit, the CMNCP focuses on some of the essential elements, including being evidence based, planning, mobilizing multisector talent, and providing training for that talent. The group also has developed some important tools for fostering adequate and sustained funding, which will be discussed in chapter 12.

Europe

In 1987, a group of mayors from across Europe launched the European Forum for Urban Safety (EFUS). Since then, EFUS has been the champion for local collaborative and comprehensive strategies to prevent crime and promote community safety through evidence- and data-informed approaches. Every ten years, EFUS holds a major conference, the most recent one having been in Barcelona in 2017, the thirtieth anniversary of the organization's founding. Impactful, EFUS has helped to form national forums for urban safety with similar objectives in Belgium, France, Italy, Portugal, and Spain.

In Germany, an annual conference was started in the 1990s to discuss recommendations from their own violence prevention commission. Now an influential movement, the German Crime Prevention Congress brings together thousands of German participants to focus on spreading knowledge and eliciting action on effective solutions and essential elements for violence prevention. So influential, this conference has spun off a smaller international conference on violence prevention aimed at getting effective solutions implemented across the world.[25]

In England and Wales, the government established police and crime commissions. These commissions, in turn, have formed an Association of Police and Crime Commissioners. These commissioners oversee policing in their communities, but they also bring together community safety and criminal justice partners to make sure local priorities are consistent. The organization has not yet taken on the "smart on crime" mantra, but some signs suggest that its partnership with the College for Policing may go in that direction.

Latin America

In a short, provocative article for the Open Society Foundations, Michelle Marinho and Dandara Tinoco write:

> [T]here is a murder in Latin America every 15 minutes. Every day, 400 people suffer violent deaths. Every year, 144,000 join them. It should come as no surprise, then, that Latin America is the most violent region in the world. Despite being home to only 8 percent of the global population, Latin America accounts for 38 percent of all homicides in the world. In the years between 2000 and 2016, more than 2.6 million human beings were killed. The violence is on a scale that only the war zones of the Middle East and Central Asia can match. And if nothing is done, the problem will only get worse. Absent concerted and determined action, by 2030, the homicide rate could increase from 21 to 35 per 100,000. But Latin America is not doomed. This open wound can be healed; the blood flow can be stanched. If appropriate measures are taken, consistently and sustainably, there can be hope.[26]

According to the Open Society Foundations, that is the belief of nearly thirty separate organizations—from Brazil, Colombia, El Salvador, Guatemala, Honduras, Mexico, and Venezuela—behind Instinto de Vida, a new region-wide network of nongovernmental organizations created in 2017 that is devoted to homicide reduction in Latin America. With policy makers and scientists working together and using solid data science to support their decisions, Instinto de Vida hopes to reduce homicide rates in the region by 50 percent within ten years.[27] Some of the group's objectives include setting targets, focusing on the most affected areas, and sharing successes. Specific strategies involve pressuring decision makers to change policies and stimulating empathy for preventive actions. Instinto de Vida also is collaborating with the IDB and the Organization of American States, so its efforts are comprehensive.

KEY TAKEAWAYS

Prevention is affordable:

- In past decades, most governments demonstrated their ability to pay for fighting violent crime by increasing spending significantly on standard CJS.
- Given violence prevention science, expenditures on prevention must be an adequate and sustained component of spending. (Think 10 percent rule for investment.)
- Tithing expenditures on CJS for prevention and matching increases in CJS with prevention would foster investment in prevention. (Think "an ounce of prevention is worth a pound of cure"!)
- Under its austerity program, England and Wales reduced government expenditures, including close to a 20 percent cut in costs of policing, without strikes or increases in crime.

Prevention is achievable:

- The public is in favor of prevention. Victims of violence in the United States report to police to get violence *prevented*, not so much to get the offender *punished*.
- The public wants social and mental health services, not the CJS.
- Issues such as reducing policing and prisons need to be achieved carefully, associated with reduction in workload, and have a clear human resource strategy.
- A key component in reducing gun violence is reducing the demand for handguns through strategies referenced in chapter 9.

Being smart on crime:

- In Mexico, impunity is a major challenge. It must be met by professionalizing the CJS and achieving large reductions in workload through prevention strategies.
- Politicians who run on "tough on crime, tough on causes" win elections.

- Making the transition from overrelying on the standard CJS to the appropriate balance can be eased through task forces, commissions, and conferences that engage the different stakeholders in finding common ground and leveraging research and resources.
- The smart on crime movement is providing some momentum for others to join.

12

MARKETING POLITICAL BUY-IN

Getting the Decisions That Matter

For the harm done by the offender, he is responsible. For the harm done because we do not use the best knowledge when that is available to us, we are responsible.

—Lord Butler

Getting effective solutions implemented to end violent crime has been my life's work. I cannot imagine a more urgent calling. To fulfill my mission, I can bemoan the tragic stories of violent crime's many victims; spout statistics and benefit–cost ratios; share the contact information for effective, evidence-based prevention programs; and expound upon exactly how to implement a successful crime prevention program. But none of these efforts will get results—unless politicians buy in! So this chapter may be the most important one of the book.

Ultimately, the arguments I make in this book must be sold to decision makers at all levels of government. As with any other new idea or way of thinking, adoption can take time. But lives are at stake! In addition, 2030, the year governments agreed upon to achieve the UN Sustainable Development Goals (SDGs), is just around the corner. Perhaps these SDGs, and the possibility of governments being liable for uninformed decision making, will encourage some shift; in our modern, connected world, it is becoming harder to ignore the pressures for change. We have our work cut out for us! We must forge ahead in building awareness about and interest in the power of violence prevention over the reactive CJS. Then, that awareness and interest must shift into action and long-term commitment.

How can this be done? In our digital age—with social media, videos, action briefs, cartoons, and more. With collaborative human engagement—through training to standards, conferences, workshops, in-depth journalism and research, school curricula, and university and college courses. By teaming up with like-minded individuals—in organizations, rallies, public talks, and legislative lobbying. The rest of this chapter will explore these tactics in depth.

E-Marketing Media
- Videos
- Social media
- Action briefs
- Cartoons

Human Engagement
- Training, workshops, webinars
- School curricula
- University and college courses
- In-depth media and research

Transformation
- Act on SDG results orientation
- Use commissions for transition
- Respect ethical and legal responsibility
- Have intergovernmental banks put their money where their mouth is

Knowing Who Wants Violence Prevention
- Mothers and families
- Movements (e.g., #MeToo)

Figure 12.1. Key Strategies Likely to Foster Buy-in by Decision Makers

E-MARKETING TO RAISE AWARENESS AND INTEREST TO SAVE LIVES AND MONEY

As noted in chapter 11, the majority of the public support prevention over punishment, but politicians are not generally aware of this. Nor do they know about solid violence prevention science, the myriads of effective national programs, and the examples of progressive cities that have reduced violent crime. So we need to look at affordable and effective ways to make them aware, get them interested, and get them to act.

In today's world, we all use computers, cell phones, and social media to communicate quickly and easily, even with large audiences. The trick is to reduce messages to short headlines, with longer, more in-depth material to support the message. Any of these tech tools can be used to engage politicians, most of whom are now using Facebook and Twitter. One member of a police services board said that it is not just teenagers who watch screens more than listening to a parent's wisdom! When experts reported to his board on evidence, the board members were too often obsessed with their screens. So we need to get the information onto their screens.

Building Awareness through the Video World

Mayors and politicians can learn about violence prevention science painlessly in two minutes or less. One video (https://www.theatlantic.com/video/index/526584/a-new-understanding-of-the-childhood-brain/?utm_source=eb) shows how preventable adverse childhood experiences affect adult life and where to invest to prevent the violence against young children. Another animation (https://www.youtube.com/watch?v=DC8qD9D7tQI), prepared for mayors, explains why it is better to be smart on crime than tough on crime. Yet one more video (https://youtu.be/55rW5a-6mlY) includes testimony from three major US mayors on why they believe in smart on crime and are making it happen.

There are several other videos that are a must:

- Edna Chavez, quoted in chapter 1 (https://www.youtube.com/watch?v=BinNvKznltA) can inspire anyone to change the world to stop violence.
- Mark Bellis (http://www.youtube.com/watch?v=kHjMArLTi4I) provides erudite numbers on violence prevention science.

A growing number of TED and TEDx talks on the subject are also inspiring. Here are three examples:

- Jackson Katz (https://www.ted.com/speakers/jackson_katz) on violence against women as a men's issue
- Gary Slutkin (https://www.ted.com/speakers/gary_slutkin) on Cure Violence
- My own TEDx (http://www.youtube.com/watch?v=FgVorJJa2cM) on smarter crime control

Exerting Pressure through the Hashtag World

Powerful movements such as #MeToo (https://metoomvmt.org/) and #BlackLivesMatter (https://blacklivesmatter.com/) demonstrate how quickly public awareness of issues can gather momentum by using high-profile cases to illustrate what happens all too frequently. Part of the reason these movements are so successful is that they draw attention to the victims rather than to the offenders, and they are a rally cry for solutions to stop victimization.

Sharing What Is Possible through Op-Eds, Blogs, Action Briefs, and More

Twitter and Facebook provide easy platforms to introduce decision makers to short extracts of information and what they should do with the information. Op-eds, blogs, and action briefs are equally impactful and can reach millions of potential advocates who can amplify the messages policy makers need to hear.

EXAMPLES OF HARNESSING E-MARKETING MEDIA IN CANADA

Let's now take a look at how these e-marketing tools have been put to use in Canada. As mentioned before, several municipalities in Canada, including the country's most populous cities and several other cities, created the Canadian Municipal Network on Crime Prevention (CMNCP). The network comprises individuals assigned as a representative by the mayor of each member city. These individuals are not selected from the police ranks. Rather, they are people whose specific job is to oversee community safety and crime prevention. The members meet and otherwise collaborate with the aim of harnessing the latest information about evidence-based crime prevention for the good of their cities.[1]

One of the first things the CMNCP members learned was that they were facing an uphill battle when it came to convincing their mayors to shift from the old, reactive ways to the new, preventive ways of ending violent crime. This is because most mayors and city councilors in the country still believe solutions to crime lie in hiring more police officers. Not many municipal leaders seem to be interested in learning about violence prevention science or investing in the essentials that reduced violence in Glasgow, Boston, and Bogotá. Realizing this, the CMNCP decided to produce a variety of tools to convince the municipal leaders to shift their thinking. Enter clever, twenty-first-century marketing measures!

The CMNCP's strategy started with getting me to help them produce four short action briefs of fewer than 2,000 words each. These briefs provide an overview of violence prevention science on issues such as why to invest in crime prevention; what programs have been effective; and which city strategies, like those in Glasgow, had succeeded. Each brief starts with a short overview of a problem and then outlines four or five actions a municipal politician might take to mitigate the problem.

These action briefs are available on the CMNCP website for easy download in Canada but can be accessed easily across the world in both English and French. They also have been distributed in printed form at events organized by the network or by others wanting to prevent crime. Cities can use the briefs with municipal politicians and senior officials in the municipality and their network of citizens taking an interest in crime prevention. The ultimate aim is to get municipal leaders to make decisions informed by violence prevention science and to rebalance spending on reaction with investments in upstream effective solutions.

The CMNCP realized also that municipalities needed to change the mindsets of other orders of government that control most of the taxes in Canada, including the funds needed to invest in effective solutions, as noted in chapter 11. Ultimately, to have adequate and sustained funding for effective solutions in Canada, the lion's share would need to come from provincial and federal governments. The action briefs, thus, were also targeted to provincial, regional, and national events, particularly those attended by municipal stakeholders. The CMNCP also prepared policy proposals for other orders of government.

In addition to the action briefs, one of the CMNCP's member cities, Winnipeg, created an innovative short video to tackle its gang problem.

Cleverly, the production was instrumental as part of the antigang strategy. The way the project worked was that a team of seasoned producers taught at-risk street youth how to use computer equipment to make music and videos. Their final project for the CMNCP was the creation of a video focused on the main points for investing in violence prevention. That video, called "Investing in Youth for Safer Cities," while not hyper-sophisticated "Hollywood," is reality, with authentic human stories and the challenging facts. And the kids had fun in the process! Check out the video at https://www.youtube.com/watch?v=ZfzyfkIae3M.

The CMNCP also did other short videos in TEDx style and started a Twitter campaign to highlight the main arguments for different aspects of prevention; it also has facilitated webinars on many issues related to violence prevention. All these innovative tools are available at http://safercities.ca/. Although the CMNCP's promotional materials, efforts, and collaboration are exciting, only time will tell whether they use them to their advantage with the various orders of government and do more than raise awareness. Perhaps the greatest challenge is to close the gap between people working for cities who know solid violence prevention science and those who make the political decisions and control the purse strings in government.

COLLABORATIVE HUMAN ENGAGEMENT

Politicians are busy people with a lot on their plates. They might watch a video, read an action brief, or crack a smile with a funny cartoon, but that might not be enough to tip them into being violence prevention advocates who make decisions based on that science. Another key strategy likely to foster their buy-in is to offer more opportunities for face-to-face engagement about the power of violence prevention science through conferences. In addition, human talent makes things work, so we must educate and train people in violence prevention science and in the essentials for successful implementation, especially people capable of influencing political buy-in. Think "smart on violence prevention" training and workshops on being smart on crime. All these will go a long way toward developing the human talent necessary to carry out the mission of ending violent crime. Looking long term, building information about violence prevention science into grade school, high school, college, and university curricula will give the next generations of leaders a head start on being smarter on crime than many of our leaders today.

Training, Workshops, and Webinars

By attending workshops or training courses specifically focused on getting violence prevention implemented, decision makers and practitioners can expand their horizons and gain expertise on the subject. Such opportunities must become a priority at conferences for political parties and mayors. For example, EFUS offers workshops for mayors and practitioners. In addition, the CMNCP has developed training modules for strategy planning and promotion of investment in effective solutions.

Curriculum on Violence Prevention in Schools

An important long-term strategy is to supplement school curriculum with materials on violence prevention science, the limits and consequences of the standard CJS, and the essentials for achieving the Sustainable Development Goals. The future of youth actually depends on the successful achievement of these goals!

As demonstrated in part II of this book, a broad range of sources—from WHO to the National Institute of Justice of the US Department of Justice and many other agencies—agree on the risk factors of crime and their solutions. But adolescents and their teachers are not aware of this knowledge or the possibilities of ending victimization. So much more can be done to help youth learn how they can be actors in reducing violence and promoting peace, how they can be "upstanders" and intervene as bystanders.

Curriculum at Universities and Colleges

Public feelings and knowledge on violent crime are driven by media headlines that highlight the sensational and exceptional without context or solutions. It is time to establish mandatory courses for every first-year college or university student that provide tools to cope with personal and relational problems. At a minimum, the courses must require a passing grade on prevention of intimate partner and sexual violence, managing alcohol, helping with mental illness, and positive parenting. These courses must include insights into the science, essentials, and secrets of violence prevention.

As I mentioned in chapter 6, the world would be a better place if law schools established courses on victim law, including restorative justice. A valuable resource for such a course would be Benjamin Perrin's book, *Victim Law: The Law of Victims of Crime in Canada.* Other curriculum at universities and colleges could focus on crime prevention in criminology courses and the like.

Collaboration and Sharing of Information

Just as with everything in life, we have much to learn from each other relative to violence prevention science. For example, with such innovative strategies, the CMNCP has attracted the attention of the European Forum for Urban Safety (EFUS), German Crime Prevention Congress, and UN-Habitat as well as some Mexican and US cities. Many of these organizations and municipalities have invited representatives of the CMNCP to come to their countries to share their secrets to getting effective solutions to violence prevention implemented.

In addition to getting international attention, the CMNCP also has developed partnerships with progressive police leadership in Canada, who share much of the same vision. In both Ontario and Saskatchewan, exceptional police leadership has joined the bureaucracy with the CMNCP mantras such as "We cannot arrest our way out of violence" and "What gets measured gets done!" Recently, even the Canadian prime minister used a phrase close to the CMNCP vision in searching for solutions for a surge of gun violence in Toronto. He said: "And we're looking at things that have been done around the world, things that have been done in other jurisdictions, looking at the best evidence, the best data, to make the right decisions to make sure that we are ensuring our citizens, our communities, are safe into the future."[2] There is hope!

TRANSFORMATION

Joining e-marketing and human engagement, a third key strategy likely to foster buy-in by decision makers is focusing attention on transformation to a results-oriented culture grounded in violence prevention science. Unfortunately, too many politicians still are spending their constituents' money the way they did last year, the way their predecessors and colleagues have done for decades.[3] Should they be held accountable for the outrageous levels of street violence and violence against women that is still occurring because they are not using the solid violence prevention science available today, that has been available for more than a decade? And the leadership of intergovernmental banks that can be instrumental in encouraging governments to be proactive about crime prevention have been sitting on the sidelines. We need action!

Politicians Need to Act on SDG Results Orientation

Recall that the UN set the stage for the world to end violent crime and violence specifically against women with results-oriented targets and measurement built into the SDGs. With the agreement among governments to reach the SDGs by 2030, some nations are starting to, at least, think about being results oriented regarding crime prevention. Some have committed to beginning to measure indicators that will establish a baseline for their efforts. These indicators would include homicide rates, victimization surveys, and surveys that focus on intimate partner and sexual violence.

As an example, in Canada, the CMNCP prepared a special action brief on the implications of the SDGs for crime prevention and community safety in Canadian municipalities. That action brief asserts that Canadian cities must find effective solutions to violent crime and invest in them so that rates of violent crime are reduced consistent with the SDG vision. This sets out a logic totally opposite of how many city councilors operate, so an immediate challenge is to get governments at all levels to organize to measure these indicators and then set targets for 2030.

Recall that many of the cities in chapter 9 identified homicides as the target crime to reduce. Setting the target is an essential part of achieving the target. Yet, even in Canada, with its proactive CMNCP, it is not easy getting governments to avoid spending billions on the "same old, same old" and to invest in getting results instead. For example, whereas the Ontario government passed legislation requiring every municipality to have a community safety and well-being plan, it is not known whether this will be implemented with investments in the human talent and other essentials, such as planning, being informed by violence prevention science, and public engagement.

Use Commissions for Transition

As we saw in chapter 11, much of the expansion of the CJS came from Presidential Commissions in the United States in the 1960s. Mothers Against Drunk Driving got sweeping changes to laws to prevent drunk driving through a President's Task Force in the 1980s. The revolution to recognize the needs and rights for victims of crime also came from the renowned President's Task Force on Victims of Crime. In 2014, the President's Task

Force reported on twenty-first-century policing. All good stuff! But now, given the availability of violence prevention science and the essentials for its implementation, we need a task force on ending violent crime.

In England and Wales, the Youth Violence Commission (http://yvcom mission.com/) has done its homework on violence prevention science but not yet on the essentials. Nonetheless, it provides a model for the United States and other countries.

The Youth Violence Commission was set up following a debate in the British Parliament on rising youth crime and violence. It is chaired by an opposition MP with members from all the other parties. It was supported by a team from the University of Warwick and the Active Communities Network. It brought together extensive research on the causes and solutions to youth violence from across the English-speaking world as well as a unique survey of the needs of youth.

Its interim report in 2018 concluded that "The root causes of youth violence include: childhood trauma, undiagnosed and untreated mental health issues, inadequate state provision and deficient parental support, poverty and social inequality."[4] The solutions to tackling these causes will "involve collaboration across central and local government as well as between practitioners, service providers, charities and community leaders at the local level. . . . It will need to have the voice of young people themselves at its core."[5] It cautioned that implementation will take time and need support from the cross section of political parties. It proposes six axes for action that parallel the conclusions on effective solutions in part II:

- **Developing a national public health model:** This axis is inspired by the sustained success of the holistic model implemented in Glasgow, Scotland, which diagnosed the problems as the basis for implementing proven solutions encompassing proactive policing, youth outreach, parenting programs, and so on.
- **A focus on early years and early intervention:** This axis is designed to tackle adverse childhood experiences and so reduce the need for expensive services as the youth grow up, including reducing the number of young men without employment, education, or training. Efforts call for a greater focus on dealing with trauma and expanding early childhood centers.
- **Fundamental reform of youth services:** This axis will give priority to youth services, including more support for grassroots organizations that are good at working with youth and reducing unnecessary competition for funding.

- **Boosting support in schools:** This axis calls for schools to do better providing career advice, high quality healthy relationship counselling, support services, and reforming the use of excluding youth from schools.
- **Increasing employment opportunities:** This axis involves more teaching of basic skills, encouragement to aspire to jobs, and providing role models and apprenticeship for minorities.
- **Investment in community policing and a systematic review of the CJS's approach to drug use:** This axis specifically wants more police youth can trust and not stop and search. It calls for action to reduce illicit trafficking of drugs, including considering decriminalization similar to the Canadian and Portugal models.[6]

Their final report is expected in late 2018. It is too early to see the impact of their work, but this commission is an example of an important intermediary step between the solid violence prevention science and application because it engages politicians and indirectly political parties in buy-in.

Already, the Mayor of London has acted on some of their recommendations, including establishing the all-important permanent violence reduction planning unit.[7] Because of the importance of London in the world, this is likely to foster more cities in the English-speaking world, including Canada, the United Kingdom, and the United States, to consider a similar innovation.

At the city level, many of the innovations for effective violence prevention have come out of a mayor's task force that brings together leaders of social services, education, policing, and others. Good examples of such city-level task forces include those found in Minneapolis in the United States and Edmonton in Canada.

Politicians Should Take Ethical and Legal Responsibility: It's Public Money!

John Carnochan tweeted, "The science of prevention in relation to violence is solid. If government agencies are not applying that science, they should be challenged to explain why. It's public money! It's public safety!"[8] Likewise, the quote at the beginning of this chapter stresses accountability for harm: "For the harm done by the offender, he is accountable. For the harm done because we do not use the best knowledge when that is available to us, we are responsible."[9]

These statements are not just empty rhetoric. They emphasize the responsibility of government to act on solid violence prevention science using the essential actions to which they have agreed through the UN Economic and Social Council (ECOSOC). We know what actions to take to end violent crime. It is up to politicians to finally pay attention to the science and the examples and act for the safety and well-being of their constituents. As Carnochan says, if they do not use the best knowledge available when making decisions with public money, politicians should be challenged to explain why. This is an issue of ethics!

In addition to being held accountable by their constituents for their ethical violation of public trust, government officials may also find themselves facing legal liability. The costs allowable by civil courts for homicide are significant, as we saw earlier.[10] For example, the losses for an average murder are $10 million. That means that not paying attention to prevention that would save 100 lives allows $1 billion in harm to victims' families!

Typically the families of murder victims do not sue the offender because he or she has insufficient means to repay and besides, has been sent to prison. But there are exceptions. The families of the victims of O.J. Simpson sued him successfully for wrongful death and got an award of $33 million.[11] Unfortunately collection has not been easy.[12] Further, efforts by families of victims in the Sandy Hook mass shooting have been suing the manufacturer of the gun used, but it is not clear how far they will get.[13]

Whereas liability of different orders of government is not clear and governments in most countries are protected from civil suit by sovereign immunity, various countries, states, or cities may have a court-ordered mandamus procedure requiring the government to act on "best knowledge." (The details of this go beyond this book.[14]) In Canada, for instance, when a constitutional guarantee, such as the right to life, is ignored, courts are allowed "to obtain such remedy as the court considers appropriate and just in the circumstances." Regardless of the niceties of laws and their interpretation, there is certainly an ethical duty for government to use the best knowledge available when making decisions. In the case of violence prevention, the best knowledge is unequivocally available!

Development Banks Must Walk the Talk

As discussed in chapters 7 and 10, the World Bank and the Inter-American Development Bank have a significant interest in persuading governments to invest in violence prevention: they know violence prevention directly correlates with economic development. Up to now, however, they talk the talk but do not walk it.

The way to walk the talk is to encourage governments to develop strategies to end violent crime based on parts II and III of this book. "Encouragement" can take a variety of forms. Some ideas include the following:

- Incorporate a condition for crime prevention in loans or grant programs
- Raise awareness at the political level through meetings and briefings
- Offer technical assistance in training officials to necessary standards on the science and essentials for their application
- Develop survey and data technology for diagnosis of a community's problem(s)
- Help to establish measured indicators and targets for crime prevention in countries
- Provide access to examples of successful programs implemented in similarly situated countries

GROUPS FIGHTING TO END VIOLENCE

And we must add our time, energy, and money to the movements that share our goals. Thankfully, we are living in an age when vision, philanthropic support, and social media have generated some well-organized, effective groups already leading the charge. Many of these organizations are powered by women and parents motivated to see a better world for their children. In fact, several of the most successful transformations from the standard CJS to an effective violence prevention solution have come from those who have experienced the tragic loss of a child.

Drawing on a panel of 264 cities spanning more than twenty years in the United States, a researcher demonstrated that every ten organizations focusing on crime and community life in a city with 100,000 residents leads to a 9 percent reduction in the murder rate, a 6 percent reduction in the violent crime rate, and a 4 percent reduction in the property crime rate.[15] Without a doubt, mobilization of the public sustains violence prevention. Public pressure also plays an essential role in keeping policies to end violent crime crossing over from one political era to another. In fact, some of the best national violence prevention programs that offered hope disappeared because there was no active and articulate cry from the public to have them continue. To sustain effective strategies to end violent crime, we must vigilantly develop a constituency who feels strongly about getting the prevention investments and keeping victimization policies that work.

One particularly influential group when it comes to facilitating change in politics and in the world, particularly relating to violence, is mothers. Often, the most vocal and visible of mothers are those whose children have been murdered, injured, or incarcerated. Channeling their deep grief into action, they can move mountains and may be one of the strongest partners we have in getting our message of crime prevention heard by policy makers.

But it is not just women who are mothers who stand up and fight. We saw in chapter 1 the extent to which women are victims at rates similar to men for street violence. We also saw the unacceptably high rates of intimate partner violence that harms women more than men and sexual violence that is predominantly against women. In sum, there are good reasons for women, whether mothers or not, to be working hard to end violent crime. Their lives depend on it.

A few examples of influential advocacy groups follow.

Mothers Against Drunk Driving (MADD)

Though focusing on traffic safety, MADD presents an important example of how mothers can change the world. MADD (https://www.madd.org/) grew out of the tragic losses of children killed by drunk drivers; thus, the group advocates holding accountable drivers who drive drunk. Initiated by Candy Lightner in California, MADD has spread across the United States and other affluent English-speaking countries. Not only is MADD a great resource on research about what is most effective in stopping this violent crime, but MADD's members also sit in courtrooms and shame judges into harsher or more effective sentences for drunk drivers. Most notably, in the 1980s, MADD was successful in getting President Reagan to establish a national task force to look at the problem of driving drunk and its solutions. This task force recommended a series of measures, including changing laws to foster the use of breathalyzers and increasing penalties when a person is killed.

Moms Demand Action for Gun Sense

Moms Demand Action for Gun Sense (https://momsdemandaction.org/) in America was founded by stay-at-home mom Shannon Watts in 2012, in response to the devastating shooting at Sandy Hook Elementary School. The organization quickly flourished into a leading force for gun violence prevention, with chapters in all fifty states and a powerful grassroots network of moms that has successfully effected change at the local, state, and national levels. In December 2013, Moms Demand Action partnered with Mayors Against Illegal Guns to unite a nationwide movement of millions of Americans working together to change the game and end the epidemic of gun violence that affects every community.[16] In the United States, women, in particular, are stepping up and voting for commonsense gun legislation as well as running for election in 2018 and getting elected. Stay tuned.

Everytown for Gun Safety

In 2006, former New York City Mayor Michael Bloomberg and former Boston Mayor Thomas Menino founded Mayors Against Illegal Guns as a coalition of fifteen mayors. Since then, they have built a bipartisan group of more than a thousand current and former mayors from nearly every US state to fight for commonsense gun laws.[17] The movement is now called Everytown for Gun Safety (https://everytown.org/). It describes itself as a movement of Americans working together to end gun violence and build safer communities.

March for Our Lives

Tragically, gun violence can touch every town in America. For too long, change has been thwarted by the Washington gun lobby and by leaders who refuse to take commonsense steps that will save lives. But something is changing. Following the February 14, 2018, massacre at Marjory Stoneman Douglas High School in Parkland, Florida, a massive movement grew to hold politicians accountable for their lack of action to end mass shootings in schools and gun violence, more generally. That movement, called March for Our Lives (https://marchforourlives.com/), made news headlines when, on March 24, 2018, more than four million mayors, moms, cops, teachers, survivors, gun owners, and everyday Americans marched together in Washington, DC, to make their own communities safer. Together, they are fighting for changes they know will save lives.

EXAMPLES OF CITIES MOBILIZING TO SUSTAIN VIOLENCE PREVENTION

Public mobilization is not just hopeful at the national level. It is public engagement that has kept the feet of politicians to the fire in model cities leading the world in violence reduction. Let's end this chapter with a quick look at how public engagement has sustained a few successful citywide crime prevention initiatives.

Bogotá

In 1992, Antanas Mockus was elected mayor of Bogotá in Colombia. In that year, there were 4,452 murders. By 2001 and two different mayors later, the number of murders had been reduced to 1,993. Mockus took the actions that ECOSOC recommends for governments. He set up a crime prevention office to analyze why and where Bogotá had so many murders and to propose solutions.[18] The analysis led the city to programs controlling access to alcohol and guns as well as to persuading victims of violence not to retaliate. How could this program last through the three administrations with different political philosophies? The answer is that Mockus encouraged a constituency of mothers who wanted their sons to live and this group lobbied to keep the violence prevention programs in place in successive elections.

Boston

Different versions exist of how Boston reduced its homicide rate. One version claims the "Boston Miracle" was due to a policing strategy that targeted the young men most involved in carrying guns and drugs.[19] Another version emphasizes the outreach to those same young men offering them ways of finishing school, getting job training, and getting jobs.[20] Another version talks about the 10-point coalition of ministers who defused some of the racism.

According to Howard Spivak and Deborah Prothrow-Stith in an article in *Applied Developmental Science*, the answer is clear:

> The public health movement intentionally enlisted the participation of community residents, youth themselves, and, maybe most important, survivors of violence—all of whom were clearly the key stakeholders in the needed responses and who also brought a passion and commitment to the effort no one else could bring. In particular, parent and sibling survivors have become the backbone of the larger national violence prevention programs around the country.[21]

KEY TAKEAWAYS

- Violent crime will only end if politicians buy in to violence prevention science and use the essential elements to put into practice what the science says.
- Presidential and mayoral commissions and task forces facilitate buy-in by providing consensus recommendations for a country or city.
- E-marketing is one important way to interest politicians and inspire them to act. We need to engage various tools, such as action briefs, videos, and cartoons, to convince policy makers of the importance of balancing their reactive CJS expenditures with an adequate and sustained investment in upstream violence prevention.
- Educating and training human talent to manage implementation is another powerful tool to get violence prevention science successfully implemented.
- Learning for a world free of violent crime must be mandatory so that school children and university students get to know violence prevention science and how they can use it.
- The results-oriented nature of the SDGs, agreed to by governments around the world, is a framework for all governments—local, regional, and national—to become results oriented and be successful in ending violent crime.
- Governments are ethically, and potentially legally, responsible to their constituents for using evidence-based crime prevention solutions.
- Development banks must play a greater role in getting governments to invest in effective solutions to violent crime by fostering political interest in buy-in and developing human talent.
- Public-based advocacy groups can make a huge impact on shifting politicians from doing more of the same (that does not work) to being results oriented and prevention focused. Mothers and parents of children who have been killed, injured, or incarcerated are a particularly powerful group.

EPILOGUE

The Time Has Come: Ending Violent Crime—For All

Greater than the tread of armies is an idea whose time has come.

—Victor Hugo

Given the horrendous toll of the tragedies caused by violent crime in every corner of the world, from across Latin America and the Caribbean to South Africa to the United States, the time for action is long overdue. The implementation of smart on crime, which leverages the solid violence prevention science, will stop lives being cut short and ruined for countless women and girls, young men and children, and particularly the disadvantaged. They do not need to suffer the pain, loss, and trauma of shootings, rape, robberies, assault, and other violent crimes. We cannot let another day go by without taking a step toward ending violence—for all.

The good news in today's bleak domain of unacceptable homicide and rape statistics, of off-the-chart numbers of young men spending the prime of their lives behind bars, of millions of dollars washed down the drain of courts and corrections is that we now know how to plug the dike—for good. Thanks to the work of the titans of solid violence prevention as well as academics, advocacy groups, nongovernmental agencies, criminologists, victimologists, and enlightened government and law enforcement officials across the globe, we know for certain what programs and practices can stop crime in its tracks.

But solid violence prevention is not enough; we also have agreement from all the governments of the world—through the leadership of the UN—on the essential elements needed to operationalize those efforts. Plus, we have compelling logical, ethical, and financial arguments for investing in crime prevention. We even have some success stories of early adopters and the commitment of all governments to achieve less violence by 2030.

Yet politicians worldwide seem to have missed the memo. Too many stick with the old way of doing crime—arrest and deter and more police and jails. If it does not work, then spend more on the same—a way that obviously is not working. Too many seem to think their only tools are reactive policing and incarceration. While these have a role in reacting to, and even stopping, crime, clearly we cannot arrest ourselves out of all the ugly faces of violence! Violence at these levels is not inevitable; it is preventable.

What needs to happen next for a sea change to take place and violence prevention to work its magic is for our world's policy makers to act. If you are a policy maker reading this book, that means you need to take the information you have learned from my words and put it into practice. Call on your advisers to explain the solid violence prevention science and its conclusions on practical actions that are effective and cost effective in ending violent crime, as I have done in part II of this book. It is at their fingertips on multiple websites and various portals, including those of no lesser organizations than the US Department of Justice and the World Health Organization. It has been reviewed and is being dispensed by the national academies and leading think tanks.

Prevention is better than cure, but most countries today have not legislated a permanent violence prevention board. They have acted on cure through parole boards but not prevention through prevention boards. So, create a permanent crime prevention board to ensure sustained leadership in implementing smart solutions! It must have the human talent and tools to diagnose your local crime problems, draw up your plan to solve the problem, get capable people in the key sectors to implement it, and build in monitoring and evaluation. It must have sustained and adequate funding, equivalent to 10 percent of what is spent now on reacting and "picking up the pieces" when violence occurs.

The recipe for success is actually very simple. What is stopping you? Truly, you have an ethical and financial—perhaps even moral—obligation to do right by your constituents! They voted you into office to protect them. Do your job, and do it smartly. By ending the epidemic of tragedies, investing in futures for young people, and creating the context for positive economic growth. The benefits will be monumental.

If you are not a policy maker reading this book, know that you also have a significant role to play in changing the course of crime in your community.

You need to take up the banner and join the "idea" army on smart on crime, about which Victor Hugo spoke when he so poetically wrote, "Stronger than the tread of armies is an idea whose time has come." Let your voice be heard. Join Moms Demand Action for Gun Sense, rally with the #MeToo or #BlackLivesMatter movements, and support March for Our Lives, and lobby your legislators. Perhaps you can create your own organization focused on a particular type of crime. And vote. In democratic societies, politicians are in office only because you put them there. And they know it.

Before I literally close the book, I would like to leave everyone with one more tool to add to your crime prevention toolbelt: a list of seven proven steps to reach success in ending violence in your community (figure E.1). Follow these steps to motivate and empower politicians to enact effective

1) Develop Tools to Raise Awareness
- Videos, social media, leaflets, and more

2) Mobilize Multisector Talent
- Educate and share the science and the essentials

3) Support Violence-Prevention Advocacy Groups
- Apply awareness tools and agree on joint effective and essential proposals

4) Engage Decision Makers
- Use awareness tools to get buy-in for effective and essential actions, particularly at election time

5) Rally Funders
- Help banks, foundations, and other funders to prioritize effective prevention solutions

6) Help Governments Be Smart on Crime
- Help governments to use the essentials

7) Stay the Course
- Make results measurable and measure them

Figure E.1.   Seven Next Steps to Get Effective Solutions Implemented

crime prevention solutions. Follow them to take back your streets and save the lives of your young and vulnerable.

STEP 1: RAISE AWARENESS WITH EFFECTIVE TOOLS

Unfortunately, at this stage, only a small group of aficionados in the UN, various governments, and academics are aware of the grand potential of evidence-based violence prevention solutions. We must find ways to share the good news of solid violence prevention science; the essentials for success; the city successes; the compelling arguments; and, particularly, what will be achieved if a groundswell of support gets smart solutions and prevention programs implemented. To this end, pull out all the stops. As I pointed out in chapter 12, a strong marketing campaign, which is what violence prevention needs, takes advantage of all the media available today: social networking, in-depth journalism, TED Talks and other videos, action briefs, and even cartoons. Use them all! For examples of effective marketing of crime prevention strategies, check out the work of the Canadian Municipal Network on Crime Prevention (http://safercities.ca/) discussed in chapter 12. The CMNCP is a great role model.

STEP 2: MOBILIZE MULTISECTOR TALENT

Getting the message of crime prevention's secret sauce out to the masses— and more importantly to politicians—may require the skills of seasoned marketing professionals. Likewise, implementing successful crime prevention programs will take a whole cadre of people of different ages from various disciplines with specialized skills. Seek them out. Implementing effective solutions to end violent crime will take integrating knowledge of violence prevention science with the implementation essentials. Key players in the game will be needed to harness the latest digital technology. Others will advance the cause through education and training to achieve standards on comprehensive community safety strategies. And still more will be the engine behind the "essential" of monitoring and evaluation.

As I have stressed more than once in this book, of equal or more importance to gathering a good team is having a centralized agency or board at the helm. In Latin America, a commission modeled after the Global Commission on Drugs (https://www.globalcommissionondrugs.org/the-five-pathways-to-drug-policies-that-work/) may advance the cause. Within countries, national commissions such as the Youth Violence Commission (http://yvcommission.com/) in the UK may be helpful. At the UN, the quinquennial Congresses on Crime Prevention and Criminal Justice in the context of the SDGs and the High Level Political Forum on SDG 16 present special opportunities for quarterbacking crime prevention efforts globally. Just remember to integrate into your permanent violence prevention board a particular emphasis on raising awareness and urgency. Nothing will get accomplished without those twin pillars of success.

STEP 3: SUPPORT ADVOCACY GROUPS

Some of the most important allies for getting effective solutions implemented are those advocating for a particular cause. I shared several such groups in chapter 12. Think Moms Demand Action for Gun Sense and the students from Marjory Stoneman Douglas High School in Parkland, Florida, who precipitated the 2018 March for Our Lives. The choir of voices of these passionate advocates may be loud enough and sustained long enough to reach the souls of those government officials who have the power to change policies and save lives. It is important to engage with these mothers and fathers, women and students, not only to support their advocacy but also to share with them the violence prevention science and essentials for implementation. Add to their toolboxes!

STEP 4: ENGAGE DECISION MAKERS

It is not enough to just raise awareness. The need for action is urgent. To that end, politicians and policy makers in all orders of government must be brought to the crime prevention table and outfitted with new tools to stop violence. Once you find an open ear, foster the relationship and cultivate a political champion who can lead his or her colleagues in the chambers of government to make wiser choices to end crime.

STEP 5: RALLY FUNDERS

As we saw in chapter 8, even some of the best-laid plans for tackling violent crime failed. One of the too-frequent culprits for demise of a promising crime prevention program is lack of adequate, sustainable funding. In chapters 10 and 11, I crunched the numbers and shared with you the mathematical proof that implementing an effective crime prevention program is achievable as well as affordable—in any country or community. Not only can program funding be gleaned from savings on CJS cutbacks, but the outcomes of a successful program reap dividends that can be reinvested in the economy, or in more upstream crime prevention.

In addition, there are some benevolent, forward-thinking organizations in the world that can be helpful resources to tap for support. For example, development banks such as the Inter-American Development Bank (IDB) and the World Bank can use their influence to encourage governments to invest in effective solutions to violent crime as a development goal that will increase GDP in low- and middle-income countries. Another great resource are foundations. For example, Bloomberg Philanthropies (https://www.bloomberg.org/about/) invests in using data-driven approaches to global change. Mike Bloomberg, the founder of Bloomberg Philanthropies, does this in many different ways—such as by funding Moms Demand Action for Gun Sense, a number of WHO projects, and many other important activities. Likewise, philanthropist George Soros has committed to building vibrant and tolerant democracies whose governments are accountable and open to the participation of all people. His foundation, Open Society Foundations (https://www.opensocietyfounda tions.org/), has funded some of the work in Latin America discussed in this book.

STEP 6: HELP GOVERNMENTS BE SMART ON CRIME

Again, as I have reiterated over and over, governments will not succeed in eliminating crime without establishing permanent national violence prevention boards, using violence prevention science, mobilizing multisector talent, creating results-driven plans and implementing them, monitoring and evaluating program outcomes, and providing adequate and sustained funding. We know this as fact and have consensus on this by governments and experts throughout the world. Yet knowledge about using these "essentials" to implement a successful crime prevention program is more rudimentary. Thus, this book. That is also why, as governments and cities invest in effective solutions, they need to learn from their sister cities and countries what works and what does not. This is particularly true of gender-based violence, for which the pool of knowledge is newer and shallower. That is where steps 1 through 5 come in. Taking those successive steps can lead governments to be smart on crime—and get prevention right.

STEP 7: STAY THE COURSE—WITH MONITORING AND EVALUATION

The most important way to transform our world and end violent crime is to make our efforts measurable and to measure them. Remember the adage, "What gets measured gets done." This cannot be overstated. We have the means: police and health data on homicides, surveys of victimization from assaults and robberies, and surveys on intimate partner and sexual violence. These measurements must become a routine part of monitoring implementation and evaluating outcomes and results. Ending violent crime by 2030 as foreseen in SDGs 3, 5, 11, and 16 cannot be achieved without an emphasis on data. Data highlights the truth and points the way to success.

CONCLUSION

In closing, allow me to say that I am humbled by the interest you have demonstrated by reading my book. The more people around the world who are inspired by my message, the more action will happen for the good of our brothers and sisters, friends and family, all around the world.

Truly, I hope by reading this book and reviewing its many charts that you feel empowered to lend your voice, your hands, your votes, and even your money to our worthy mission of peace in the world. Only with your help will our children and future generations live lives free from the tragedies of violent crime. Only with your help will we be able to invest in the futures of disadvantaged youth, creating economic development for all, and safeguarding democracy and rule of law with justice. This world's future is one worth using science, common sense, and common decency to achieve. Let it be so.

APPENDIX

Figures and Their Sources

Figure 1.1—Number of Victims of Homicide and Estimated of Rape (with number of persons incarcerated and standard CJS expenditures for Canada, England and Wales, Mexico, and the United States for 2017 or closest year)

Sources: Homicide—Canada, 2016: https://www150.statcan.gc.ca/n1/daily-quotidien/171122/dq171122b-eng.htm; England and Wales, 2017: https://www.ons.gov.uk/peoplepopulationandcommunity/crimeandjustice/articles/homicideinenglandandwales/yearendingmarch2017; Mexico, 2017: https://www.cbc.ca/news/world/mexico-record-homicide-rate-1.4497466; and United States, 2016: https://www.fbi.gov/news/stories/2016-crime-statistics-released. US rape/sexual assault, 2016: https://www.cdc.gov/violenceprevention/pdf/NISVS_Report2010-a.pdf. Incarceration and population, 2016: http://www.prisonstudies.org/world-prison-brief-data. Spending—Canada, 2015: https://www.publicsafety.gc.ca/cnt/rsrcs/pblctns/2015-s022/2015-s022-en.pdf; England and Wales, 2016: Matt Ford, Trends in Criminal Justice Spending, Staffing and Populations (London: Centre for Crime and Justice Studies, 2017); Mexico, 2015: https://ethos.org.mx/wp-content/uploads/2017/07/SeguridadFnlDigital.compressed.pdf; and United States, 2015: https://www.bjs.gov/index.cfm?ty=pbdetail&iid=6310.

Figure 1.2—Tangible and Intangible Costs for Homicide and Rape in the United States

Sources: K. E. McCollister, M. T. French, and H. Fang, "The Cost of Crime to Society: New Crime-Specific Estimates for Policy and Program

Evaluation," *Drug and Alcohol Dependency* 108, no. 1 (2010): 98–109; and World Health Organization, UNODC, UNDP, *Global Status Report on Violence Prevention* (Geneva: World Health Organization, 2014).

Figure 2.1—Sectors Showing Numbers of Programs and Practices Identified as Effective (on CrimeSolutions.gov of the US National Institute of Justice)
Source: Web portal of the National Institute of Justice, accessed May 22, 2018, https://www.crimesolutions.gov/.

Figure 3.1—Rates of Homicide and Incarceration for Each US State (in 2016)
Sources: "2016 Crime in the United States," *FBI: UCI*, accessed July 20, 2018, https://ucr.fbi.gov/crime-in-the-u.s/2016/crime-in-the-u.s.-2016/tables/table-3; and Danielle Kaeble and Mary Cowhig, "Correctional Populations in the United States, 2016," *Bureau of Justice Statistics*, April 2018, https://www.bjs.gov/content/pub/pdf/cpus16.pdf.

Figure 3.2—Examples of Effective Solutions Using Proactive or Reduced Policing (with range of improvement over CJS and comment on evidence)
Source: See discussion in chapter 3.

Figure 4.1—Effective Solutions Using Targeted Social Development (showing % reduction in offending and savings to victims and CJS per $1)
Source: See discussion in chapter 4.

Figure 4.2—Illustration of Reduction to Cost of Standard CJS with the Intervention of a Combination of Three Upstream Effective Programs
Source: From *Tyler's Troubled Life* (2016). Used with permission from Community Safety and Countering Crime Branch, Research Division, Public Safety Canada, Ottawa, ON.

Figure 5.1—Effective Solutions for Ending Violence against Women (showing % reduction)
Source: See discussion in chapter 5.

Figure 6.1—Effective Solutions for Providing Support and Rights for Victims of Crime
Sources: See discussion in chapter 6 and Irvin Waller, *Rights for Victims of Crime: Rebalancing Justice* (Lanham, MD: Rowman & Littlefield, 2011), 173–83.

Figure 7.1—Seven Essentials for Implementing Effective Solutions (based on government resolutions at the ECOSOC from the UNODC, compared to SDG 17 and *INSPIRE*)

Sources: UN Economic and Social Council, Resolution 2002/13, "Guidelines for the Prevention of Crime," July 24, 2002, https://www.unodc.org/documents/justice-and-prison-reform/crimeprevention/resolution_2002-13.pdf; UN Office on Drugs and Crime, *Handbook on the Crime Prevention Guidelines: Making Them Work* (Vienna: United Nations, 2010), https://www.unodc.org/pdf/criminal_justice/Handbook_on_Crime_Prevention_Guidelines_-_Making_them_work.pdf; "Goal 17: Revitalize the Global Partnership for Sustainable Development," United Nations, accessed July 28, 2018, https://www.un.org/sustainabledevelopment/globalpartnerships/; and World Health Organization, *INSPIRE: Seven Strategies for Ending Violence Against Children* (Geneva: World Health Organization, 2016), http://apps.who.int/iris/bitstream/10665/207717/1/9789241565356-eng.pdf.

Figure 7.2—Essential Planning of Interventions by National and Local Permanent Violence Prevention Planning Boards (Comprehensive Community Safety Strategy)

Sources: Adapted from UN Economic and Social Council, Resolution 2002/13, "Guidelines for the Prevention of Crime," July 24, 2002, para. 22–23, https://www.unodc.org/documents/justice-and-prison-reform/crimeprevention/resolution_2002-13.pdf; and the UN-Habitat Safer Cities program. See, for example, figure 1 in *Safer Cities: A Safer and Just City for All*, accessed August 30, 2018, https://unhabitat.org/safer-cities-a-safer-and-just-city-for-all/.

Figure 7.3—Sustainable Development Goals Whose Targets Include Indicators on Ending Violent Crime

Source: Sustainable Development Knowledge Platform website, United Nations, accessed May 22, 2018, https://sustainabledevelopment.un.org/.

Figure 8.1—Governments That Pioneered Implementation (showing my subjective assessment of the extent to which the essential elements were respected as well as the timing and general reason for the demise)

Source: See discussion in chapter 8.

Figure 9.1—Cities That Achieved Significant Reductions in Homicides (showing essential elements and whether success was sustained)

Sources: See discussion in chapter 9; Anthony A. Braga, Andrew V. Papachristos, and David M. Hureau, "The Effects of Hot Spots Policing on Crime: An Updated Systematic Review and Meta-Analysis," *Justice Quarterly* 31, no. 4 (2014): 633–63, doi.org/10.1080/07418825.2012.673632; and
Andrew V. Papachristos and David S. Kirk, "Changing the Street Dynamic: Evaluating Chicago's Group Violence Reduction Strategy," *Criminology and Public Policy* 14, no. 3 (August 2015): 525–58, doi.org/10.1111/1745-9133.12139.

Figure 10.1—For the United States, Impact of Investment in Effective Violence Prevention Solutions (assuming investment is equivalent to 10 percent of CJS expenditures and a 50 percent reduction in violent crime)
Source: See discussion in chapter 10.

Figure 10.2—Number of Lives Saved and Rapes Prevented Each Year as a Result of Effective Violence Prevention (with number of incarcerations averted and reductions possible for CJS expenditures for Canada, England and Wales, Mexico, and the United States before 2030, assuming no population growth and no change in value of currency to current values)
Sources: See sources for figure 1.1 and explanation in chapter 10. For average annual income in national currency—Canada: Can$51,000, https://careers.workopolis.com/advice/how-much-money-are-we-earning-the-average-canadian-wages-right-now/; England and Wales: £26,832, https://www.ons.gov.uk/employmentandlabourmarket/peopleinwork/earnings and workinghours; United States: $46,000, https://www.thebalance.com/what-is-average-income-in-usa-family-household-history-3306189; Mexico: Mex$65,000, based on an average hourly wage of Mex$31 for 40 hours a week, https://www.reuters.com/article/us-mexico-economy-analysis-idUSKBN0ED20H20140602. For Mexico GDP in billions in pesos: Mex$15,461 in 2017, converted at 13 pesos to $1 for GDP $1,150 trillion, https://countryeconomy.com/gdp/mexico?year=2017.

Figure 11.1—Reasons for Victims to Report Their Victimization to Police
Sources: Irvin Waller, *Rights for Victims of Crime: Rebalancing Justice* (Lanham, MD: Rowman & Littlefield, 2011), 60–62; based on original analysis of the National Crime Victimization Survey, in particular, using US Department of Justice, Bureau of Justice Statistics, "Criminal Victimization, 2008," NCJ 227777, September 2009, https://www.bjs.gov/content/pub/pdf/cv08.pdf.

Figure 11.2—Preference of US Citizens to Solve Crime Problems by Spending on Social Programs Rather than on Police and Prisons

Sources: Sourcebook of Criminal Justice Statistics Online, Table 2.28.2010, University at Albany, State University of New York, accessed August 28, 2018, https://www.albany.edu/sourcebook/pdf/t2282010.pdf, which is based on Gallup, "Crime," December 21, 2010, http://www.gallup.com/poll/1603/Crime.aspx.

Figure 11.3—Rates per 100,000 for Homicide and Incarceration for G7 Countries (showing savings to US citizens if US incarceration rate were reduced to each G7 country rate, with savings at US 1965 and Mexico rates)

Sources: Canada, 2016, https://www150.statcan.gc.ca/n1/daily-quotidien/171122/dq171122b-eng.htm; England and Wales, 2017, https://www.ons.gov.uk/peoplepopulationandcommunity/crimeandjustice/articles/homicideinenglandandwales/yearendingmarch2017; United States, 2016, https://www.fbi.gov/news/stories/2016-crime-statistics-released; other G7 countries, 2013, UN Office on Drugs and Crime, *Global Study on Homicide 2013* (Vienna: UNODC, 2014); incarceration, 2016, http://www.prisonstudies.org/world-prison-brief-data; and expenditures in United States, 2012, https://www.bjs.gov/index.cfm?ty=pbdetail&iid=5239.

NOTES

INTRODUCTION

1. Edna Chavez, "March for Our Lives (Full Speech)," video, 7:48, posted by Community Coalition, March 28, 2018, https://www.youtube.com/watch?v=BinNvKznltA.

2. Temi Mwale, "Ending Youth Violence through Community Healing," video, 18:42, filmed June 2017 at TEDxHamburg, Hamburg, DE, http://www.tedxhamburg.de/ending-youth-violence-through-community-healing-temi-mwale.

3. "Audette Shephard Marks 10th Anniversary of Son Justin's Murder," *City News*, published June 27, 2011, http://toronto.citynews.ca/2011/06/27/audette-shephard-marks-10th-anniversary-of-son-justins-murder/.

4. "Audette Shephard," Ontario Office for Victims of Crime, accessed May 25, 2018, http://www.ovc.gov.on.ca/board-members/audette-shephard/; and Cate Buchanan, ed., *Gun Violence, Disability, and Recovery* (Sydney: Surviving Gun Violence Project, 2014).

5. Javier Sicilia, "Carta abierta a politicos y criminales: 'Estamos hasta la madre,'" personal copy of the letter and poem, trans. Arturo Cervantes Trejo; also see "Javier Sicilia: Estamos hasta la madre . . . (Carta abierta a politicos y criminales)," Circulo de Poesía (in Spanish), published April 3, 2011, https://circulodepoesia.com/2011/04/javier-sicilia-estamos-hasta-la-madre-carta-abierta-a-los-politicos-y-a-los-criminales/; and Randal C. Archibold, "Violence Suffocated a Father's Poetry, But Not His Voice," *New York Times*, May 13, 2011, https://www.nytimes.com/2011/05/14/world/americas/14sicilia.html.

6. Catherine E. Shoichet, "Mexican Poet Becomes Crusader for Peace after Son's Slaying," *CNN*, modified May 5, 2011, http://www.cnn.com/2011/WORLD/americas/05/05/mexico.poet.activist/index.html?hpt=Sbin.

7. Archibold, "Violence Suffocated a Father's Poetry."

8. "Youth Violence: Facts at a Glance 2016," CDC, National Center for Injury Prevention and Control, accessed July 27, 2018, https://www.cdc.gov/violencepre vention/pdf/yv-datasheet.pdf.

9. Molly Pahn, Anita Knopov, and Michael Siegel, "Gun Violence in the US Kills More Black People and Urban Dwellers," *The Conversation*, November 8, 2017, https://theconversation.com/gun-violence-in-the-us-kills-more-black-people-and-urban-dwellers-86825.

10. "Black Americans Are Only 13% of the US Population Yet Represent 51% of Homicide Victims," Violence Policy Center, accessed July 28, 2018, http://www.vpc.org/wp-content/uploads/2018/04/blackhom2018400.jpg.

11. Pahn, Knopov, and Siegel, "Gun Violence in the US."

12. Ibid.

13. Jamie Ducharme, "President Trump Targeted London's Knife Crime at NRA—But London's Murder Rate Is Lower than Every Big US City's," *Time*, May 5, 2018, http://time.com/5266759/donald-trump-london-knife-crime-murder-rate/.

14. Ibid. See this book's chapter 1 for rates for other cities.

15. UN Office on Drugs and Crime, *Global Study on Homicide, 2013* (Vienna: UNODC, 2014), https://www.unodc.org/documents/gsh/pdfs/2014_GLOBAL_HOMICIDE_BOOK_web.pdf.

16. Mary Allen, "Police-Reported Crime Statistics, 2017," *Juristat*, Canadian Center for Justice Statistics, published July 23, 2018, https://www150.statcan.gc.ca/n1/en/pub/85-002-x/2018001/article/54974-eng.pdf?st=vKFnqVWY; and Jean-Denis David, "Homicide in Canada, 2016," *Juristate*, Canadian Center for Justice Statistics, published November 22, 2017, https://www150.statcan.gc.ca/n1/en/pub/85-002-x/2017001/article/54879-eng.pdf?st=-YBmPyLv.

17. Tristin Hopper, "As Toronto's Tragedies Mount, Is Crime in Canada Spiraling Out of Control?" *National Post*, July 25, 2018, https://nationalpost.com/news/as-torontos-tragedies-mount-is-canadian-gun-crime-spiralling-out-of-control.

18. James Fredrick, "Mexico Registers Its Highest Number of Homicides on Record," Parallels, *NPR*, January 25, 2018, https://www.npr.org/sections/paral lels/2018/01/25/580239712/mexico-registers-its-highest-homicides-on-record.

19. Laura Jaitman, ed., *The Costs of Crime and Violence: New Evidence and Insights in Latin America and the Caribbean* (Washington, DC: Inter-American Development Bank, 2017), https://publications.iadb.org/bitstream/handle/11319/8133/The-Costs-of-Crime-and-Violence-New-Evidence-and-Insights-in-Latin-America-and-the-Caribbean.pdf?sequence=7&isAllowed=y.

20. Centers for Disease Control and Prevention, *National Intimate Partner and Sexual Violence Survey (NISVS): 2010 Summary Report* (Atlanta, GA: CDC,

2011), 62–63, tables 6.1 and 6.2, https://www.cdc.gov/violenceprevention/pdf/NISVS_Report2010-a.pdf.

21. Ibid., 38, tables 4.1 and 4.2.

22. Ibid., 18, table 2.1. This includes forced completed penetration at 620,000; attempted forced penetration at 519,000; and completed alcohol-/drug-facilitated penetration at 781,000.

23. "2016 Crime Stats Released: Violent Crime Increases, Property Crime Decreases," FBI, published September 25, 2017, https://www.fbi.gov/news/stories/2016-crime-statistics-released.

24. Irvin Waller, *Rights for Victims of Crime: Rebalancing Justice* (Lanham, MD: Rowman & Littlefield, 2011), 60.

25. Jennifer Bronson, "Justice Expenditure and Employment Extracts, 2015—Preliminary," Bureau of Justice Statistics, Office of Justice Programs, US Department of Justice, NCJ 251780, June 29, 2018, https://www.bjs.gov/index.cfm?ty=pbdetail&iid=6310.

26. Ibid., and Irvin Waller, *Smarter Crime Control: A Guide to a Safer Future for Citizens, Communities, and Politicians* (Lanham, MD: Rowman & Littlefield, 2014), 14.

27. Irvin Waller, *Less Law, More Order: The Truth about Reducing Crime* (Westport, CT: Praeger, 2006), 9–10.

28. "Gross Domestic Product (GDP)," Organization for Economic Co-operation and Development (OECD), accessed July 27, 2018, https://data.oecd.org/gdp/gross-domestic-product-gdp.htm.

29. Jose A. Del Real, "The U.S. Has Fewer Crimes. Does That Mean It Needs Fewer Police?" *New York Times*, January 7, 2018, https://www.nytimes.com/2018/01/07/us/crime-police.html?smid=tw-share.

30. Dan Hinkel and Jennifer Smith Richards, "Despite Hiring Push, Chicago Police Still Falling Short in Attracting Black Officers," *Chicago Tribune*, May 4, 2018, http://www.chicagotribune.com/news/local/breaking/ct-met-chicago-police-hiring-20180503-story.html.

31. Ryan Marx, "Chicago Homicide Data Since 1957," *Chicago Tribune*, March 2, 2016, http://www.chicagotribune.com/news/local/breaking/ct-chicago-homicides-data-since-1957-20160302-htmlstory.html; and "Final 2017 Totals," HeyJackass!, accessed July 27, 2018, https://heyjackass.com/category/2017-stats/.

32. David Topping, "Metrocide: A History of Violence," *Torontoist*, July 22, 2008, https://torontoist.com/2008/07/metrocide_historical_homicides/.

33. "Table 3: Municipal Police Services Serving a Population of 100,000 or More, Canada, 2017," Canadian Center for Justice Statistics, Government of Canada, accessed July 27, 2018, https://www150.statcan.gc.ca/n1/pub/85-002-x/2018001/article/54912/tbl/tbl03-eng.htm.

34. "World Prison Brief Data," Institute for Criminal Policy Research and Birkbeck University of London, accessed July 27, 2018, http://www.prisonstudies.org/world-prison-brief-data.

35. See figures 1.1 in chapter 1 and 11.3 in chapter 11 in this book for more details.

36. Irvin Waller and J. Chan, "Prison Use: A Canadian and International Comparison," in *Correctional Institutions*, 2nd ed., ed. L. T. Wilkins and D. Glazer (Philadelphia: J. B. Lippincott, 1976), 41–60.

37. Greg Berman and Julian Adler, "How New York City Reduced Crime and Incarceration," *City and State New York*, March 7, 2018, https://www.cityandstateny.com/articles/opinion/commentary/how-new-york-city-reduced-crime-and-incarceration.html.

38. "Netherlands: World Prison Brief Data," Institute for Criminal Policy Research and Birkbeck University of London, accessed July 27, 2018, http://www.prisonstudies.org/country/netherlands.

39. "Further Drop in Registered Crime and Suspect Rates," CBS Netherlands, September 10, 2017, https://www.cbs.nl/en-gb/news/2017/41/further-drop-in-registered-crime-and-suspect-rates; and Tom Coggins, "Why Crime Rate in the Netherlands Is So Low?" *Culture Trip*, modified October 18, 2017, https://theculturetrip.com/europe/the-netherlands/articles/why-crime-rate-in-the-netherlands-is-so-low/.

40. "The Big Graph," Eastern State Penitentiary, accessed July 27, 2018, https://www.easternstate.org/explore/exhibits/big-graph.

41. Waller and Chan, "Prison Use."

42. See figure 11.3 in chapter 11 of this book.

43. Waller and Chan, "Prison Use." The United States incarcerates 655 people per 100,000, compared to Canada, at 114 per 100,000; Mexico, 176 per 100,000; and England and Wales, 141 per 100,000.

44. Waller, *Smarter Crime Control*, 245–54.

45. "2016 Crime Stats Released."

46. US Department of Education, "Report: Increases in Spending on Corrections Far Outpace Education," news release, published July 7, 2016, https://www.ed.gov/news/press-releases/report-increases-spending-corrections-far-outpace-education.

47. Christopher Woody, "These Were the 50 Most Violent Cities in the World in 2017," *Business Insider*, March 6, 2018, https://www.businessinsider.com/most-violent-cities-in-the-world-2018-3.

48. Elliott C. McLaughlin, "With Chicago, It's All Murder, Murder, Murder . . . But Why?" *CNN*, modified March 6, 2017, https://www.cnn.com/2017/03/06/us/chicago-murder-rate-not-highest/; "Final 2017 Totals"; and Mitchell Armentrout, "Chicago Homicides Down Sharply in 2017, Still Over 670 Slain," *Chicago Sun-Times*, December 31, 2017, https://chicago.suntimes.com/news/chicago-murders-homicides-2017-steep-decline/.

49. "Home," Smart on Crime, accessed July 18, 2018, https://www.smarton crime.us. Also see Smart on Crime, "America's Mayors Are Getting Smart on Crime," video, 1:51, posted by "seeprogress," January 31, 2018, https://youtu. be/55rW5a-6mlY; #ENDViolence, https://www.unicef.org/end-violence; and Center for American Progress, https://www.americanprogress.org.

CHAPTER I

1. World Health Organization, *Global Plan of Action to Strengthen the Role of the Health System Within a National Multisectoral Response to Address Interpersonal Violence, In Particular Against Women and Girls, and Against Children* (Geneva: World Health Organization, 2016), http://apps.who.int/iris/bitstream/han dle/10665/252276/9789241511537-eng.pdf;jsessionid=AB507F304BFB10B3D1C1 4B43D081AC05?sequence=1.

2. UN General Assembly, 40th Session, Resolution 34, "Declaration of Basic Principles of Justice for Victims of Crime and Abuse of Power," A/RES/40/34, November 29, 1985, in *Resolutions and Decisions of the UN General Assembly 1985*. New York: United Nations, 1985. http://www.un.org/documents/ga/res/40/a40r034. htm.

3. Ibid.

4. Irvin Waller, *Rights for Victims of Crime: Rebalancing Justice* (Lanham, MD: Rowman & Littlefield, 2011), 173–83.

5. UN General Assembly, 40th Session, Resolution 34.

6. Waller, *Rights for Victims of Crime*, 1–9.

7. World Health Organization, *INSPIRE: Seven Strategies for Ending Violence Against Children* (Geneva, Switzerland: WHO, 2016), apps.who.int/iris/bitstr eam/10665/207717/1/9789241565356-eng.pdf.

8. Total violent victimizations are at a rate of 1 in 50 (21.1 victimizations per 1,000 persons) age 12 or older. The rate of stranger violence (8.2 per 1,000 persons) was higher than the rate of intimate partner violence (2.2 per 1,000). In 2016, US households experienced 15.9 million property crimes—a rate of 119.4 per 1,000 households. See Rachel Morgan and Grace Kena, "Criminal Victimization, 2016," Bureau of Justice Statistics, Office of Justice Programs, US Department of Justice, NCJ 251150, December 2017, https://www.bjs.gov/content/pub/pdf/cv16.pdf.

9. Ibid., 9, table 8.

10. Jan van Dijk, J. van Kesteren, and P. Smit, *Criminal Victimization in International Perspective: Key Findings from the 2004-2005 ICVS and EU ICS* (The Hague: Boom Legal Publishers, 2008).

11. "LAPOP, 2014," cited in Serrano, Rodrigo, and Mejorando, "La seguridad de los Latinoamericanos a través de un gasto público más preventivo, focalizado e inteligente," chapter in preparation by IBD for the Report on Development in the Americas. LAPOP is the Latin American Public Opinion Survey, which includes

victimization data. See also Elizabeth J. Zechmeister, *Cultura política de la democracia en las Américas, 2014: Gobernabilidad democrática a través de 10 años del Barómetro de las Américas*, USAID, May 2016, https://www.vanderbilt.edu/lapop/ab2014/AB2014_Comparative_Report_Spanish_V1_042017_W.pdf.

12. World Health Organization, *Global Status Report on Road Safety 2015* (Geneva: WHO, 2016), http://www.who.int/violence_injury_prevention/road_safety_status/2015/en/.

13. "Number of Murders Committed per 100,000 Inhabitants in Mexico from 2000 to 2017," Statista, accessed July 21, 2018, https://www.statista.com/statistics/714113/mexico-homicide-rate/.

14. James Alan Fox and Marianne W. Zawitz, "Homicide Trends in the United States," Bureau of Justice Statistics, accessed August 19, 2018, https://www.bjs.gov/content/pub/pdf/htius.pdf.

15. Claire McEvoy and Gergely Hideg, *Global Violent Deaths 2017: Time to Decide* (Geneva: Small Arms Survey, Graduate Institute of International and Development Studies, 2017), http://www.smallarmssurvey.org/fileadmin/docs/U-Reports/SAS-Report-GVD2017.pdf.

16. Morgan and Kena, "Criminal Victimization, 2016."

17. Waller, *Rights for Victims of Crime*, 60.

18. Centers for Disease Control and Prevention, *National Intimate Partner and Sexual Violence Survey (NISVS): 2010 Summary Report* (Atlanta, GA: National Center for Injury Prevention and Control, 2011), https://www.cdc.gov/violenceprevention/pdf/NISVS_Report2010-a.pdf; and Waller, *Smarter Crime Control*, 164–66.

19. Centers for Disease Control and Prevention, *National Intimate Partner and Sexual Violence Survey*.

20. Patricia Tjaden and Nancy Thoennes, *Full Report of the Prevalence, Incidence, and Consequences of Violence Against Women* (Washington, DC: National Institute of Justice and the Centers for Disease Control and Prevention, 2000), https://www.ncjrs.gov/pdffiles1/nij/183781.pdf.

21. Dean Kilpatrick et al., *Drug-Facilitated, Incapacitated, and Forcible Rape: A National Study*, unpublished report prepared for the National Institute of Justice, US Department of Justice, February 1, 2007, Doc. 219181, https://www.ncjrs.gov/pdffiles1/nij/grants/219181.pdf, 2.

22. "Child Abuse, Neglect Data Released," Administration for Children and Families, US Department of Health and Human Services, published January 19, 2017, https://www.acf.hhs.gov/media/press/2017/child-abuse-neglect-data-released.

23. Ibid.

24. David Farrington, "Family Influences on Delinquency," in *Juvenile Justice and Delinquency*, ed. D. W. Springer and A. R. Roberts (Sudbury, MA: Jones and Bartlett, 2010), 203–22.

25. L. Musu-Gillette et al., *Indicators of School Crime and Safety: 2017*, National Center for Education Statistics, Institute of Education Sciences, NCES

2018-036/NCJ 251413 (Washington, DC: US Department of Education and US Department of Justice, Office of Justice Programs, 2018), https://nces.ed.gov/pubs2018/2018036.pdf.

26. Justin W. Patchin, "Millions of Students Skip School Each Year Because of Bullying," *Cyberbullying Research Center*, published January 3, 2017, https://cyberbullying.org/millions-students-skip-school-year-bullying.

27. "High School Students Carrying Weapons," Child Trends, published August 23, 2016, https://www.childtrends.org/indicators/high-school-students-carrying-weapons.

28. "Indicator 1: Violent Deaths at School and Away from School," National Center for Education Statistics, modified March 2018, accessed July 21, 2018, https://nces.ed.gov/programs/crimeindicators/ind_01.asp.

29. Graham Farrell and Ken Pease, eds., *Repeat Victimization* (New York: Criminal Justice Press, 2001).

30. "Table 3: Crime in the United States by State, 2016," FBI, accessed August 28, 2018, https://ucr.fbi.gov/crime-in-the-u.s/2016/crime-in-the-u.s.-2016/tables/table-3.

31. "Guerrero, Estado de Mêxico y Chihuahua, los Estados con Más Asesinators" ("Guerrero and Chihuahua, the Mexican States with the Most Murders"), *Emequis*, July 25, 2016, http://www.m-x.com.mx/2016-07-25/guerrero-estado-de-mexico-y-chihuahua-los-estados-con-mas-asesinatos-en-2015-inegi/.

32. "Homicide Victims, Number and Rates," table 35-10-0068-01, Statistics Canada, accessed August 28, 2018, https://www.statcan.gc.ca/tables-tableaux/sumsom/l01/cst01/legal12b-eng.htm.

33. "Las 50 Ciudades Más Violentas del Mundo 2017" ("The 50 Cities of the World with the Most Violence"), Seguidad Justica y Paz (Security, Justice, and Peace), accessed July 28, 2018, https://www.seguridadjusticiaypaz.org.mx/biblioteca/prensa/download/6-prensa/242-las-50-ciudades-mas-violentas-del-mundo-2017-metodologia; and Christopher Woody, "These Were the 50 Most Violent Cities in the World in 2017," *Business Insider*, March 6, 2018, http://www.businessinsider.com/most-violent-cities-in-the-world-2018-3.

34. Dominic Casciani, "Reality Check: Has London's Murder Rate Overtaken New York's?" *BBC News*, April 4, 2018, https://www.bbc.com/news/uk-43628494; Joe Tidy, "In Context: Just How Bad Is London's Murder Rate?" *Sky News*, April 4, 2018, https://news.sky.com/story/in-context-just-how-bad-is-londons-murder-rate-11315585; "TPS Crime Statistics—Homicide," Toronto Police Service Public Safety Data Portal, accessed July 23, 2018, http://data.torontopolice.on.ca/pages/homicide.

35. See, generally, National Academies of Sciences, Engineering, and Medicine, *Proactive Policing: Effects on Crime and Communities* (Washington, DC: National Academies Press, 2018), https://doi.org/10.17226/24928.

36. "2016 Crime Stats Released: Violent Crime Increases, Property Crime Decreases," FBI, September 25, 2017, https://www.fbi.gov/news/stories/2016-crime-statistics-released.

37. "Nonfatal Physical Assaults—Related Injuries Treated in Hospital Emergency Departments—United States, 2000," Centers for Disease Control and Prevention, May 31, 2002, https://www.cdc.gov/mmwr/preview/mmwrhtml/mm5121a3.htm.

38. Centers for Disease Control and Prevention, *National Intimate Partner and Sexual Violence Survey*.

39. World Health Organization, *INSPIRE: Seven Strategies for Ending Violence Against Children* (Geneva: WHO, 2016), apps.who.int/iris/bitstream/10665/207717/1/9789241565356-eng.pdf; and World Health Organization, UNODC, and UN Development Program, *Global Status Report on Violence Prevention 2014* (Geneva: World Health Organization, 2014), http://www.who.int/violence_injury_prevention/violence/status_report/2014/en/.

40. Ted Miller, Mark Cohen, and Brian Wiersema, *Victim Costs and Consequences: A New Look* (Washington, DC: National Institute of Justice, US Department of Justice, 1996), https://www.ncjrs.gov/pdffiles/victcost.pdf.

41. World Health Organization, *The Economic Dimensions of Interpersonal Violence* (Geneva: World Health Organization, 2004), http://apps.who.int/iris/bitstream/10665/42944/1/9241591609.pdf.

42. Waller, *Rights for Victims of Crime*, chap. 1.

43. Miller, Cohen, and Wiersema, *Victim Costs and Consequences*.

44. Kathryn E. McCollister, Michael T. French, and Hai Fang, "The Cost of Crime to Society: New Crime-Specific Estimates for Policy and Program Evaluation," *Drug and Alcohol Dependency* 108, no. 1-2 (April 2010): 98–109, https://doi.org/10.1016/j.drugalcdep.2009.12.002. See also Washington State Institute for Public Policy (http://www.wsipp.wa.gov/) for how these estimates are used to assess the cost–benefit of effective solutions.

45. "Why Invest in Crime Prevention in Municipalities: Strategic Overview," Canadian Municipal Network on Crime Prevention, action brief 2016.1, September 12, 2016, http://safercities.ca/wp-content/uploads/2016/12/CMNCP_AB1_FINAL_digital_sept12.pdf. See also Thomas Gabor, *Costs of Crime and Criminal Justice Responses*, Research Report 2015—R022 (Ottawa, ON: Public Safety Canada, 2015), https://www.publicsafety.gc.ca/cnt/rsrcs/pblctns/2015-r022/2015-r022-en.pdf; and World Health Organization, *The Economic Dimensions of Interpersonal Violence*.

46. Richard Dubourg, Joe Hamed, and Jamie Thorns, The Economic and Social Costs of Crime Against Individuals and Households 2003/04, *The National Archives*, June 2005, http://webarchive.nationalarchives.gov.uk/20100408123402/http://www.crimereduction.homeoffice.gov.uk/statistics/statistics39.htm.

47. Laura Jaitman, ed., *The Costs of Crime and Violence: New Evidence and Insights in Latin America and the Caribbean* (Washington, DC: Inter-American Development Bank, 2017), https://publications.iadb.org/bitstream/handle/11319/8133/The-Costs-of-Crime-and-Violence-New-Evidence-and-Insights-in-Latin-America-and-the-Caribbean.pdf.

48. World Bank, *World Development Report 2011: Conflict, Security, and Development* (Washington, DC: International Bank for Reconstruction and Development/The World Bank, 2011), https://siteresources.worldbank.org/INTWDRS/Resources/WDR2011_Full_Text.pdf.

49. Ibid.

50. Ibid.

51. Ibid.

CHAPTER 2

1. Irvin Waller, *Smarter Crime Control: A Guide to Safer Futures for Citizens, Communities, and Politicians* (Lanham, MD: Rowman & Littlefield, 2014); Ignacio Cano, "Breaking Down the Silos between Latin America's Homicide Reduction Programs," *Open Society Foundations*, published September 22, 2016, https://www.opensocietyfoundations.org/voices/breaking-down-silos-between-latin-america-s-homicide-reduction-programs.

2. David P. Farrington, "The Developmental Evidence Base: Psychosocial Research," in *Forensic Psychology*, ed. Graham J. Towl and David A. Crighton (Chichester, UK: Wiley, 2015), 161–81; and David P. Farrington, ed., *Integrated Developmental and Life-Course Theories of Offending*, vol. 14, *Advances in Criminological Theory* (London: Routledge, 2017).

3. David P. Farrington and Brandon C. Welsh, "Saving Children from a Life of Crime: The Benefits Greatly Outweigh the Costs!" *International Annals of Criminology* 52, no. 1–2 (2014): 67–92, https://doi.org/10.1017/S0003445200000362.

4. National Research Council et al., *Juvenile Crime, Juvenile Justice* (Washington, DC: The National Academies Press, 2001), 3–4, https://www.nap.edu/catalog/9747/juvenile-crime-juvenile-justice.

5. "Definition: What Is an ACE?," Minnesota Department of Health, accessed July 18, 2018, http://www.health.state.mn.us/divs/cfh/program/ace/definition.cfm.

6. "About the CDC-Kaiser ACE Study," Centers for Disease Control and Prevention, modified June 14, 2016, https://www.cdc.gov/violenceprevention/acestudy/about.html.

7. "Definition: What Is an ACE?"

8. "Adverse Childhood Experiences (ACEs)," Centers for Disease Control and Prevention, modified April 1, 2016, https://www.cdc.gov/violenceprevention/acestudy/index.html.

9. Cathy S. Widom and Michael G. Maxfield, "An Update on the 'Cycle of Violence,'" *Research in Brief* (Washington, DC: US Department of Justice, National Institute of Justice, 2001), http://www.ncjrs.gov/pdffiles1/nij/184894.pdf.

10. James A. Reavis et al., "Adverse Life Experiences and Adult Criminality: How Long Must We Live before We Possess Our Own Lives?" *The Permanente*

Journal 17, no. 2 (Spring 2013), 44–48, https://www.ncbi.nlm.nih.gov/pmc/articles/PMC3662280/.

11. "Adverse Childhood Experiences," Center for the Application of Prevention Technology, Substance Abuse and Mental Health Services Administration, US Department of Health and Human Services, modified July 9, 2018, https://www.samhsa.gov/capt/practicing-effective-prevention/prevention-behavioral-health/adverse-childhood-experiences.

12. World Health Organization, *INSPIRE: Seven Strategies for Ending Violence Against Children* (Geneva: World Health Organization, 2016), 16–17, http://apps.who.int/iris/bitstream/handle/10665/207717/9789241565356-eng.pdf;jsessionid=597E369ED7B4D6618C940507139FE704?sequence=1.

13. Keith McQuirter, dir., *Milwaukee 53206* (New York: Transform Films, Inc., 2016), https://www.milwaukee53206.com/.

14. World Health Organization, *Violence Prevention: The Evidence* (Geneva: World Health Organization, 2009), http://apps.who.int/iris/bitstream/handle/10665/77936/9789241500845_eng.pdf?sequence=1.

15. Lawrence W. Sherman et al., "Preventing Crime: What Works, What Doesn't, What's Promising," *Research in Brief*, National Institute of Justice, July 1998, https://www.ncjrs.gov/pdffiles/171676.pdf; and Lawrence W. Sherman et al., *Evidence-Based Crime Prevention* (New York: Routledge, 2002).

16. "Home," CrimeSolutions.gov, US National Institute of Justice, accessed July 13, 2018, https://www.crimesolutions.gov/.

17. "Benefit–Cost Results," Washington State Institute for Public Policy, modified December 2017, http://www.wsipp.wa.gov/BenefitCost.

18. National Research Council, *Fairness and Effectiveness in Policing: The Evidence* (Washington, DC: The National Academies Press, 2004), https://www.nap.edu/catalog/10419/fairness-and-effectiveness-in-policing-the-evidence.

19. National Research Council, *The Growth of Incarceration in the United States: Exploring Causes and Consequences* (Washington, DC: The National Academies Press, 2014), https://www.nap.edu/catalog/18613/the-growth-of-incarceration-in-the-united-states-exploring-causes.

20. Council of Canadian Academies, *Policing Canada in the 21st Century: New Policing for New Challenges* (Ottawa, ON: Expert Panel on the Future of Canadian Policing Models, Council of Canadian Academies, 2014), http://www.scienceadvice.ca/uploads/eng/assessments%20and%20publications%20and%20news%20releases/policing/policing_fullreporten.pdf.

21. The National Academies of Sciences, Engineering, and Medicine, *Proactive Policing: Effects on Crime and Communities* (Washington, DC: The National Academies Press, 2018), https://doi.org/10.17226/24928.

22. Youth Violence Commission, "Interim Report," July 2018, http:yvcommission.com/interim-report.

23. "Smart Spending on Citizen Security: Beyond Crime and Punishment," Inter-American Development Bank, accessed November 11, 2018, https://flagships.

iadb.org/sites/default/files/dia/chapters/Chapter-7-Smart-Spending-on-Citizen-Se
curity-Beyond-Crime-and-Punishment.pdf.

24. Laura Jaitman, ed., *The Costs of Crime and Violence: New Evidence and Insights in Latin America and the Caribbean* (Washington, DC: Inter-American Development Bank, 2017), https://publications.iadb.org/bitstream/handle/11319/8133/The-Costs-of-Crime-and-Violence-New-Evidence-and-Insights-in-Latin-America-and-the-Caribbean.pdf?sequence=7&isAllowed=y.

25. Ignacio Cano, Emiliano Rojido, and João Trajano Sento-Sé, *Mapping of Homicide Prevention Programs in Latin America and the Caribbean* (Rio de Janeiro: Laboratório de Análse da Violência, Universidade do Estado de Rio de Janeiro, 2016), http://www.lav.uerj.br/docs/rel/2016/Relato%CC%81rio%20Final%20Ingle%CC%82s.pdf.

26. Thomas Abt and Christopher Winship, *What Works in Reducing Community Violence: A Meta-Review and Field Study for the Northern Triangle* (Bethesda, MD: Democracy International, 2016), https://www.usaid.gov/sites/default/files/USAID-2016-What-Works-in-Reducing-Community-Violence-Final-Report.pdf.

CHAPTER 3

1. Barry Friedman, "We Spend $100 Billion on Policing. We Have No Idea What Works." *Washington Post*, March 10, 2017, https://www.washingtonpost.com/posteverything/wp/2017/03/10/we-spend-100-billion-on-policing-we-have-no-idea-what-works/?nid&utm_term=.fbeafcaaa50c.

2. Jose A. Del Real, "The U.S. Has Fewer Crimes. Does That Mean It Needs Fewer Police?" *New York Times*, January 7, 2018, https://www.nytimes.com/2018/01/07/us/crime-police.html.

3. Tiffany Ford and Wesley Epplin, "Letter: Does Chicago Really Need More Police Officers?" *Chicago Tribune*, October 6, 2017, http://www.chicagotribune.com/news/opinion/letters/ct-letters-chicago-police-budget-violence-20171005-story.html; and "CPD Defends Budget Increases for 2018, to Hire More Officers and Implement Reforms," CBS Chicago, published November 2, 2017, http://chicago.cbslocal.com/2017/11/02/police-department-budget-hearings/.

4. Toronto Police Service, *Action Plan: The Way Forward*, January 2017, http://www.tpsb.ca/items-of-interest/send/29-items-of-interest/546-action-plan-the-way-forward-modernizing-community-safety-in-toronto.

5. "Final 2017 Totals," HeyJackass!, accessed July 31, 2018, https://heyjackass.com/category/2017-stats/; and Mike Tobin, "Chicago Records 762 Homicides in 2016, Up 57 Percent from Previous Year," *Fox News*, modified July 5, 2017, http://www.foxnews.com/us/2017/01/01/1-chicagos-bloodiest-years-ends-with-762-homicides.html.

6. "TPS Crime Statistics—Homicide," Toronto Police Service Public Safety Data Portal, accessed July 31, 2018, http://data.torontopolice.on.ca/pages/homicide;

and "Homicide 2004-2017," *Business Intelligence & Analytics*, accessed July 31, 2018, https://app.powerbi.com/view?r=eyJrIjoiNmFiNjgyYzYtMjlhZi00ODA4LThkNjgtNDZmZWFjYjhhY2IyIiwidCI6Ijg1MjljMjI1LWFjNDMtNDc0Yy04ZmI0LTBmNDA5NWFFlOGQ1ZCIsImMiOjN9.

7. Jennifer Bronson, "Justice Expenditure and Employment Extracts, 2015—Preliminary," US Department of Justice, Bureau of Justice Statistics, NCJ 251780, June 29, 2018, https://www.bjs.gov/index.cfm?ty=pbdetail&iid=6310.

8. Ibid.

9. Irvin Waller, *Smarter Crime Control: A Guide to a Safer Future for Citizens, Communities, and Politicians* (Lanham, MD: Rowman & Littlefield, 2014), 30; and, "Total Police Personnel per 100,000 Residents in Canada and the U.S. from 2003 to 2015," Statista, accessed July 31, 2018, https://www.statista.com/statistics/529925/police-personnel-rate-in-canada-and-us/.

10. Council of Canadian Academies, *Policing Canada in the 21st Century: New Policing for New Challenges* (Ottawa, ON: Council of Canadian Academies, 2014), http://www.scienceadvice.ca/uploads/eng/assessments%20and%20publications%20and%20news%20releases/policing/policing_fullreporten.pdf.

11. Daniel R. Deakin, "Freeze! The World's 10 Biggest Police Forces," *The Richest*, published February 27, 2014, https://www.therichest.com/rich-list/the-biggest/freeze-the-10-biggest-police-forces-in-the-world/.

12. Caroline Kuritzkes, "Increased Mexico Security Spending Not Delivering Security Gains: Report," *InSight Crime*, published August 14, 2017, http://www.insightcrime.org/news/brief/increased-mexico-security-spending-not-delivering-security-gains-report.

13. Ibid.

14. See figure 1.1 in chapter 1 of this book and, more generally, World Prison Brief Data at http://www.prisonstudies.org/world-prison-brief-data.

15. Alex Vitale, *The End of Policing* (New York: Verso, 2017).

16. For US opinion polls, see chapter 11.

17. Niall McCarthy, "Private Security Outnumbers the Police in Most Countries Worldwide," *Forbes*, published August 31, 2017, https://www.forbes.com/sites/niallmccarthy/2017/08/31/private-security-outnumbers-the-police-in-most-countries-worldwide-infographic/#4c4233e6210f.

18. Ibid.

19. Claire Provost, "The Industry of Inequality: Why the World Is Obsessed with Private Security," *The Guardian*, May 12, 2017, https://www.theguardian.com/inequality/2017/may/12/industry-of-inequality-why-world-is-obsessed-with-private-security.

20. Lawrence W. Sherman, "The Rise of Evidence-Based Policing: Targeting, Testing, and Tracking," *Crime and Justice* 42, no. 1 (2013): 377–451, https://doi.org/10.1086/670819; and Lawrence W. Sherman, "Attacking Crime: Police and Crime Control," *Crime and Justice* 15 (January 1992): 159–230. https://doi.org/10.1086/449195.

21. "Over 200 Dead after Anarchy Breaks Out during Brazil Police Strike," Global News Canada, modified February 9, 2017, https://globalnews.ca/news/3238535/over-100-dead-anarchy-brazil-police-strike/; and "'State of Emergency Declared in Brazil as Police Strike,'" Telesur TV, published January 6, 2018, https://www.telesurtv.net/english/news/State-of-Emergency-Declared-in-Brazil-as-Police-Strike-20180106-0027.html.

22. National Research Council, *Fairness and Effectiveness in Policing: The Evidence* (Washington, DC: The National Academies Press, 2004), https://www.nap.edu/catalog/10419/fairness-and-effectiveness-in-policing-the-evidence.

23. Waller, *Smarter Crime Control*, 40–41.

24. Ibid., 33–34; and National Research Council, *Fairness and Effectiveness in Policing*.

25. Waller, *Smarter Crime Control*, 32–33.

26. Niall McCarthy, "How Much Do U.S. Cities Spend on Policing?" *Statista*, published August 7, 2017, https://www.statista.com/chart/10593/how-much-do-us-cities-spend-on-policing/.

27. The reductions translate to a reduction of 18 percent in police staffing and a 15 percent reduction in police officers while the population grew by 5 percent. This is based on, as of March 31, 2010, a total staff of 244,500 and 143,700 police officers and, as of March 31, 2018, a total staff of 199,700 and 122,400 police officers. The population of England and Wales grew from 55.9 million in 2010 to 58.7 million in 2017. See Ravi Mulchandani and Jenny Sigurdsson, "Police Service Strength: England and Wales," *Home Office Statistical Bulletin*, July 23, 2009, http://webarchive.nationalarchives.gov.uk/20110220110009/http://rds.homeoffice.gov.uk/rds/pdfs09/hosb1309.pdf; and "Statistical News Release: Police Workforce, England and Wales," Home Office, July 19, 2018, https://assets.publishing.service.gov.uk/government/uploads/system/uploads/attachment_data/file/726404/hosb1118snr.pdf.

28. See generally, "Police Funding in England and Wales," Full Fact, September 28, 2018, https://fullfact.org/crime/police-funding-england-and-wales/; and Matt Ford, *Trends in Criminal Justice Spending, Staffing and Populations* (London: Centre for Crime and Justice Studies, 2017), https://www.crimeandjustice.org.uk/sites/crimeandjustice.org.uk/files/Trends%20in%20criminal%20justice%20spending%2C%20staffing%20and%20populations%2C%20Dec%202017.pdf.

29. "London's Surge of Violence: 2018's Victims," Sky News, accessed July 31, 2018, https://news.sky.com/story/londons-year-of-horror-so-far-the-victims-in-the-first-weeks-of-2018-11315362.

30. Kuritzkes, "Increased Mexico Security Spending."

31. Irvin Waller and J. Chan, "Prison Use: A Canadian and International Comparison," *Criminal Law Quarterly* 17, no. 1 (1974): 47–71; and "World Prison Brief," accessed July 31, 2018, http://www.prisonstudies.org/.

32. Waller, *Smarter Crime Control*; and Jeremy Travis and Bruce Western, eds., *The Growth of Incarceration in the United States: Exploring Causes and Consequences* (Washington, DC: The National Academies Press, 2014).

33. Jan Van Dijk, Andromachi Tseloni, and Graham Farrell, eds., *The International Crime Drop: New Directions in Research* (London: Palgrave Macmillan, 2012).

34. Travis and Western, *The Growth of Incarceration in the United States*.

35. William Spelman, "The Limited Importance of Prison Expansion," in *The Crime Drop in America*, ed. Alfred Blumstein and Joel Wallman (Cambridge: Cambridge University Press, 2000), 97–129.

36. Travis and Western, *The Growth of Incarceration in the United States*; and Daniel S. Nagin, "Deterrence in the Twenty-First Century," *Crime and Justice* 42, no. 1 (2013): 199–263, https://doi.org/10.1086/670398.

37. Ford, *Trends in Criminal Justice Spending*.

38. Ibid.

39. Michael Savage and Mark Townsend, "Exclusive: Shock Figures Reveal Crisis State of Prisons in England and Wales," *The Guardian*, February 17, 2018, https://www.theguardian.com/society/2018/feb/17/uk-brutal-prisons-failing-violence-drugs-gangs.

40. Ryan J. Reilly, "Rikers Population Drops While New York City Crime Rate Remains at Record Low," *Huffington Post Canada*, published March 23, 2017, https://www.huffingtonpost.ca/entry/rikers-island-population-drop_us_58d3c995e4b02d33b7490825.

41. Irvin Waller, *Less Law, More Order: The Truth about Reducing Crime* (Westport, CT: Praeger, 2006), 74–80.

42. James Austin and Michael P. Jacobson, *How New York City Reduced Mass Incarceration: A Model for Change?* (New York: New York University School of Law, 2013), https://www.brennancenter.org/sites/default/files/publications/How_NYC_Reduced_Mass_Incarceration.pdf.

43. Waller, *Smarter Crime Control*, chap. 4.

44. Adam Gelb and Tracy Veláquez, "The Changing State of Recidivism: Fewer People Going Back to Prison," *Pew Charitable Trusts*, published August 1, 2018, http://www.pewtrusts.org/en/research-and-analysis/articles/2018/08/01/the-changing-state-of-recidivism-fewer-people-going-back-to-prison.

45. Mariel Alper, Matthew R. Durose, and Joshua Markman, "2018 Updates on Prisoner Recidivism: A 9-Year Follow-up Period (2005-2014)," US Department of Justice, Bureau of Justice Statistics, NCJ 250975, May 2018, https://www.bjs.gov/content/pub/pdf/18upr9yfup0514.pdf.

46. Nancy Fishman, "Justice Reinvestment Initiative," *Vera Institute of Justice*, accessed August 8, 2018, https://www.vera.org/projects/justice-reinvestment-initiative.

47. "35 States Reform Criminal Justice Policies Through Justice Reinvestment," Pew Charitable Trusts, July 2018, http://www.pewtrusts.org/-/media/assets/2018/07/pspp_reform_matrix.pdf.

48. The National Academies of Sciences, Engineering, and Medicine, *Proactive Policing: Effects on Crime and Communities* (Washington, DC: The National Academies Press, 2018), https://doi.org/10.17226/24928.

49. Ibid.

50. John Rappaport, "Jeff Sessions Is Scapegoating the ACLU for Chicago's Murder Rate Spike," *Slate*, May 11, 2018, https://slate.com/news-and-politics/2018/05/jeff-sessions-is-scapegoating-the-aclu-for-chicagos-murder-rate-spike.html.

51. "Impact: Results," National Network for Safe Communities at John Jay College, accessed August 8, 2018, https://nnscommunities.org/impact/results.

52. Anthony A. Braga, David Weisburd, and Brandon Turchan, "Focused Deterrence Strategies and Crime Control: An Updated Systematic Review and Meta-Analysis of the Empirical Evidence," *Criminology and Public Policy* 17, no. 1 (2018): 205–50.

53. Sam Kuhn and Stephen Lurie, *Reconciliation Between Police and Communities: Case Studies and Lessons Learned* (New York: John Jay College, 2018), https://nnscommunities.org/uploads/Reconciliation_Full_Report.pdf.

54. "Impact: Results."

55. "Project Profile: Project Safe Neighborhoods," CrimeSolutions.org, National Institute of Justice, profile posed February 9, 2016, https://www.crimesolutions.gov/ProgramDetails.aspx?ID=448; and Waller, *Smarter Crime Control*, 47–48, 142–44.

56. Andrew V. Papachristos, Tracey L. Meares, and Jeffrey Fagan, "Attention Felons: Evaluating Project Safe Neighborhoods in Chicago," *Journal of Empirical Legal Studies* 4, no. 2 (July 2007), 223–72.

57. Nadia Ahmed, "The Deteriorating Impact of the Project Safe Neighborhoods Program in Chicago," *Chicago Policy Review*, published March 8, 2018, http://chicagopolicyreview.org/2018/03/08/the-deteriorating-impact-of-the-project-safe-neighborhoods-program-in-chicago/.

58. Anthony A. Braga, David M. Hureau, and Andrew V. Papachristos, "Deterring Gang- Involved Gun Violence: Measuring the Impact of Boston's Operation Ceasefire on Street Gang Behavior," *Journal of Quantitative Criminology* 30 (2014): 113–39.

59. "Practice Profile: Problem-Oriented Policing," CrimeSolutions.org, National Institute of Justice, accessed August 28, 2018, https://www.crimesolutions.gov/PracticeDetails.aspx?ID=32.

60. L. W. Sherman, "Attacking Crime: Police and Crime Control," *Crime and Justice* 15 (January 1992): 159–230, https://doi.org/10.1086/449195; and, more generally, see Anthony A. Braga and David L. Weisburd, *Policing Problem Places: Crime Hot Spots and Effective Prevention* (New York: Oxford University Press, 2012).

61. Braga and Weisburd, *Policing Problem Places*, 164–66; and "Program Profile: Problem-Oriented Policing in Violent Crime Places (Jersey City, NJ), Crime Solutions.org, National Institute of Justice, profile posted March 26, 2012, https://www.crimesolutions.gov/ProgramDetails.aspx?ID=227.

62. "Advanced Search: Keyword 'problem-place policing,'" CrimeSolutions.org, National Institute of Justice, https://www.crimesolutions.gov/advsearch.aspx.

63. "Program Profile: Hot Spots Policing (Lowell, Mass.)," CrimeSolutions.org, National Institute of Justice, profile posted December 20, 2011, https://www.crime solutions.gov/ProgramDetails.aspx?ID=208.

64. The National Academies of Sciences, Engineering, and Medicine, "Proactive Policing," 128.

65. Ibid., 132–35.

66. Chris Weller, "There's a Secret Technology in 90 US Cities That Listens for Gunfire 24/7," *Business Insider*, published June 27, 2017, https://www.businessin sider.com/how-shotspotter-works-microphones-detecting-gunshots-2017-6.

67. Matt Finn, "ShotSpotter Technology Makes Dent in Chicago's Crime—But Raises Privacy Concerns," *Fox News*, published January 23, 2018, accessed August 8, 2018, http://www.foxnews.com/us/2018/01/23/shotspotter-technology-makes-dent-in-chicagos-crime-but-raises-privacy-concerns.html.

68. "Advanced Search: Keyword 'problem-place policing.'"

69. "Program Profile: Philadelphia Policy Tactics Experiment: Offender-Focused Policing," CrimeSolutions.org, National Institute of Justice, profile posted February 29, 2016, https://www.crimesolutions.gov/ProgramDetails.aspx?ID=449.

70. "Program Profile: Kansas City (MO) Gun Experiment," CrimeSolutions.org, National Institute of Justice, profile posted May 4, 2012, https://www.crimesolu tions.gov/ProgramDetails.aspx?ID=238.

71. Joseph A. Ferrandino, "The Effectiveness and Equity of NYPD Stop and Frisk Policy, 2003–2014," *Journal of Crime and Justice* 41, no. 2 (October 2018), https://www.tandfonline.com/doi/abs/10.1080/0735648X.2016.1249385.

72. Paul Quinton, Matteo Tiratelli, and Ben Bradford, *Does More Stop and Search Mean Less Crime? Analyses of Metropolitan Police Services Panel Data 2004–14* (London: College of Policing, 2017), http://whatworks.college.police.uk/Research/Documents/SS_and_crime_report.pdf.

73. Christopher Ingraham, "A Brief History of DARE, the Anti-Drug Program Jeff Sessions Wants to Revive," *Washington Post*, July 12, 2017, https://www.washingtonpost.com/news/wonk/wp/2017/07/12/a-brief-history-of-d-a-r-e-the-anti-drug-program-jeff-sessions-wants-to-revive/?utm_term=.f9abf628c504.

74. Waller, *Smarter Crime Control*, 219–21; and David Forrester et al., *The Kirkholt Burglary Prevention Project: Phase II* (London: Home Office, 1990), http://library.college.police.uk/docs/hopolicers/fcpu23.pdf.

75. Charles C. Branas et al., "Citywide Cluster Randomized Trial to Restore Blighted Vacant Land and Its Effects on Violence, Crime, and Fear," *Proceedings of the National Academy of Sciences* 115, no. 12 (March 20, 2018): 2946–51, https://doi.org/10.1073/pnas.1718503115.

76. Ailsa Chang, "'Insane': America's Three Largest Psychiatric Facilities Are Jails," podcast, 8:16, *All Things Considered*, Health News from NPR, April 25, 2018, https://www.npr.org/sections/health-shots/2018/04/25/605666107/insane-americas-3-largest-psychiatric-facilities-are-jails?utm_campaign=storyshare&utm_source=twitter.com&utm_medium=social.

77. Malcolm Gladwell, "Million-Dollar Murray: Why Problems Like Homelessness May Be Easier to Solve than to Manage," *The New Yorker*, February 13, 2006, https://www.newyorker.com/magazine/2006/02/13/million-dollar-murray.

78. Vitale, *The End of Policing*.

79. "Fatal Force," a program of the *Washington Post* tracking the fatal shootings by police officers in the line of duty, accessed August 8, 2018, https://www.washingtonpost.com/graphics/national/police-shootings-2017/.

80. Michelle Alexander, *The New Jim Crow: Mass Incarceration in the Age of Color Blindness* (New York: New Press, 2012).

81. The National Academies of Sciences, Engineering, and Medicine, "The Growth of Incarceration in the United States," pp. 56–64.

82. Katie Reilly, "Sesame Street Reaches Out to 2.7 Million American Children with an Incarcerated Parent," *FactTank*, Pew Research Center, published June 21, 2013, http://www.pewresearch.org/fact-tank/2013/06/21/sesame-street-reaches-out-to-2-7-million-american-children-with-an-incarcerated-parent/.

83. Austin and Jacobson, "How New York City Reduced Mass Incarceration."

84. Dale R. McFee and Norman E. Taylor, *The Prince Albert Hub and the Emergence of Collaborative and Risk-Driven Community Safety* (Ottawa, ON: Canadian Police College, 2014).

85. Global Commission on Drug Policy, *Advancing Drug Policy Reform: A New Approach to Decriminalization* (Geneva: Global Commission on Drug Policy, 2016), http://www.globalcommissionondrugs.org/wp-content/uploads/2016/11/GCDP-Report-2016-ENGLISH.pdf.

86. Jamie Doward, "Legal Marijuana Cuts Violence Says US Study, As Medical-Use Laws See Crime Fall," *The Guardian*, January 13, 2018, https://www.theguardian.com/world/2018/jan/14/legal-marijuana-medical-use-crime-rate-plummets-us-study.

87. Jack K. Reed, *Marijuana Legalization in Colorado: Early Findings* (Denver: Colorado Department of Public Safety, 2016), https://cdpsdocs.state.co.us/ors/docs/reports/2016-SB13-283-Rpt.pdf; Drug Policy Alliance, *From Prohibition to Progress: A Status Report on Marijuana Legalization* (New York: Drug Policy Alliance, 2018), http://www.drugpolicy.org/sites/default/files/dpa_marijuana_legalization_report_v6_0.pdf, chart 2; and Drug Policy Alliance, *Marijuana Facts* (New York: Drug Policy Alliance, 2017), http://www.drugpolicy.org/sites/default/files/dpa_marijuana_booklet_january2018_0.pdf.

CHAPTER 4

1. "Gun Violence Must Stop. Here's What We Can Do to Prevent More Deaths," Prevention Institute, accessed July 22, 2018, https://www.preventioninstitute.org/focus-areas/preventing-violence-and-reducing-injury/preventing-violence-advocacy.

2. Deborah Prothrow-Stith, "Preventing Youth Violence," video, 2:03, posted by "APB Speakers," August 1, 2018, https://www.youtube.com/watch?v=NeVSkgLmFBQ.

3. Tom MacInnes et al., *Monitoring Poverty and Social Exclusion 2014*, Joseph Rowntree Foundation (York, UK: New Policy Institute, 2014), https://www.jrf.org.uk/sites/default/files/jrf/migrated/files/MPSE-2014-FULL.pdf.

4. Mimi Kirk, "The Crisis of Unemployment Among Chicago Youth," *City Lab*, published June 19, 2017, https://www.citylab.com/life/2017/06/the-chicago-youth-experiencing-severe-joblessness/530643/.

5. Megan L. Rogers and William Alex Pridemore, "How Does Social Protection Influence Cross-National Homicide Rates in OECD Nations?" *Sociological Quarterly* 58, no. 4 (2017): 576–94, https://uncw.edu/soccrm/programs/Rogers%20Pridemore%202017%20TSQ.pdf; and William Alex Pridemore, *Poverty Reduction and Social Protection as Sustainable Development Goals for Violence Prevention* (Albany, NY: University of Albany School of Criminal Justice, 2015), http://www.who.int/violence_injury_prevention/violence/7th_milestones_meeting/Pridemore_Targets_1.3_and_10.2_poverty_and_social_protection.pdf.

6. "Home," Triple P—Positive Parenting Program, accessed August 8, 2018, https://www.triplep.net/glo-en/home/.

7. "New York Crime Rates," Disaster Center, accessed June 13, 2018, http://www.disastercenter.com/crime/nycrime.htm.

8. Adam Lusher, "Is London's Murder Rate Really Worse Than New York's?" *Independent*, April 3, 2018, https://www.independent.co.uk/news/uk/crime/london-murder-rate-new-york-compare-worse-stabbings-knife-crime-teenagers-statistics-figures-a8286866.html.

9. "Broken Windows Policing," Center for Evidence-Based Crime Policy, Department of Criminology, Law, and Society, George Mason University, accessed August 8, 2018, http://cebcp.org/evidence-based-policing/what-works-in-policing/research-evidence-review/broken-windows-policing/.

10. Irvin Waller, *Less Law, More Order: The Truth about Reducing Crime* (Westport, CT: Praeger, 2006), 74–80.

11. Ibid.

12. Irvin Waller, *Smarter Crime Control: A Guide to a Safer Future for Citizens, Communities, and Politicians* (Lanham, MD: Rowman & Littlefield, 2014), chap. 9.

13. Wesley G. Skogan et al., *Evaluation of CeaseFire-Chicago*, unpublished report, June 2009, NCJ 227181, https://www.ncjrs.gov/pdffiles1/nij/grants/227181.pdf.

14. Charlie Ransford, "The Relationship between Cuts to the Cure Violence Model and Increase in Killings in Chicago," *Cure Violence* (Blog), September 22, 2016, http://cureviolence.org/post/why-is-chicago-violence-skyrocketing/.

15. "Results/Scientific Evaluations," Cure Violence, accessed August 2, 2018, http://cureviolence.org/results/scientific-evaluations/.

16. "New York City Evaluation (John Jay)," Scientific Evaluations, Cure Violence, accessed July 22, 2018, http://cureviolence.org/results/scientific-evaluations/nyc-evaluation-johnjay/; and "Category: Cure Violence," John Jay College of Criminal Justice Research and Evaluation Center, City University of New York (CUNY), accessed July 22, 2018, https://johnjayrec.nyc/category/work-products-by-project/cure-violence-project-materials/.

17. "Results/Scientific Evaluations."

18. "About Us," Youth Justice Board, accessed August 2, 2018, https://www.gov.uk/government/organisations/youth-justice-board-for-england-and-wales/about.

19. Richard Ives and Barbara Wyvill, *Evaluation of the Junior Youth Inclusion Program* (Camden, UK: Camden Children's Fund, 2007), http://www.castlehaven.org.uk/static/uploads/documents/Educari-Report.pdf.

20. "What Is the Youth Justice Board Resource Hub?" Youth Justice Board, accessed August 2, 2018, https://yjresourcehub.uk/training-development/what-is-the-yj-resource-hub.html.

21. Morgan Harris Burrows, *Evaluation of the Youth Inclusion Program: End of Phase 1 Report* (London: Youth Justice Board, 2003); and Waller, *Smarter Crime Control*, 127.

22. "Research on Big Brothers Big Sisters," Big Brothers Big Sisters of America, accessed July 27, 2018, http://bbbs.org/research.

23. Michael Shiner et al., "Mentoring Disaffected Young People: An Evaluation of 'Mentoring Plus,'" *Joseph Rowntree Foundation*, published June 16, 2004, https://www.jrf.org.uk/report/mentoring-disaffected-young-people-evaluation-mentoring-plus.

24. "Program Profile: Perry Preschool Project," CrimeSolutions.gov, National Institute of Justice, profile posted June 14, 2011, https://www.crimesolutions.gov/ProgramDetails.aspx?ID=143.

25. "Perry Preschool Project," HighScope Educational Research Foundation, accessed July 22, 2018, https://highscope.org/perrypreschoolstudy.

26. Ibid.

27. James J. Heckman, "Invest in Early Childhood Development: Reduce Deficits, Strengthen the Economy," *Heckman Equation*, published December 7, 2012, https://heckmanequation.org/resource/invest-in-early-childhood-development-reduce-deficits-strengthen-the-economy/.

28. See, for instance, James A. Reavis et al., "Adverse Childhood Experiences and Adult Criminality: How Long Must We Live before We Possess Our Own Lives?" *The Permanente Journal* 17, no. 2 (2013): 44–48, https://www.ncbi.nlm.nih.gov/pmc/articles/PMC3662280/; and Jessica M. Craig, "The Potential Mediating Impact of Future Orientation on the ACE–Crime Relationship," *Youth Violence and Juvenile Justice* (February 8, 2018), https://doi.org/10.1177/1541204018756470. Also, generally, see "Adverse Childhood Experiences," Substance Abuse and Mental Health Services Administration, accessed August 7, 2018, https://www.

samhsa.gov/capt/practicing-effective-prevention/prevention-behavioral-health/ad verse-childhood-experiences; and, in particular, Rebecca Rebble et al., "Adverse Childhood Experiences among Youth Aging Out of Foster Care: A Latent Class Analysis," *Child Youth Services Review* 74 (March 2017): 108–116, https://www. ncbi.nlm.nih.gov/pmc/articles/PMC5404688/.

29. "Courses for Parents of Teens," Triple P—Positive Parenting Program, accessed August 7, 2018, https://www.triplep-parenting.ca/can-en/get-started/triple-p-courses-for-parents-of-teens/.

30. "The Numbers," Triple P—Positive Parenting Program, accessed August 7, 2018, https://www.triplep.net/glo-en/the-triple-p-system-at-work/cost-effective/ the-numbers/; and "Program Profile: Triple P—Positive Parenting Program," CrimeSolutions.gov, National Institute of Justice, accessed August 7, 2018, https:// www.crimesolutions.gov/ProgramDetails.aspx?ID=80.

31. For population level return, see "Benefit–Cost Results," Washington State Institute for Public Policy, modified December 2017, http://www.wsipp.wa.gov/ BenefitCost. This updates S. Lee et al., *Return on Investments: Evidence-Based Options to Improve Statewide Outcomes*, Document No. 12-04-1201 (Olympia, WA: Washington State Institute for Public Policy, 2012).

32. "The Numbers," Triple P—Positive Parenting Program.

33. "Program Profile: Multisystemic Therapy (MST)," CrimeSolutions.gov, National Institute of Justice, profile posted June 27, 2011, https://www.crimesolutions. gov/ProgramDetails.aspx?ID=192.

34. "MST Is a Scientifically Proven Intervention for At-Risk Youth," MST Services, accessed July 22, 2018, http://www.mstservices.com/.

35. "Program Profile: Multisystemic Therapy (MST)." Also see D. Gorman-Smith, A. Kampfner, and K. Bromann, "What Should Be Done in the Family to Prevent Gang Membership?" in *Changing Course: Preventing Gang Membership*, ed. Nancy M. Ritter, Thomas R. Simon, and Reshma R. Mahendra (Washington, DC: US Department of Justice and US Department of Health and Human Resources, 2013), 75–89; Jon Shute, "Family Support as a Gang Reduction Measure," *Children and Society* 27, no. 1 (January 2013): 48–59; and "Cost-Effectiveness," MST-UK, accessed August 6, 2018, http://www.mstuk.org/mst-outcomes/cost-effectiveness.

36. "Clinical Model," Functional Family Therapy, accessed August 8, 2018, https://www.fftllc.com/about-fft-training/clinical-model.html.

37. For population level return, see "Benefit–Cost Results."

38. "Program Profile: Multidimensional Treatment Foster Care—Adolescents," CrimeSolutions.gov, National Institute of Justice, profile posted June 10, 2011, https://www.crimesolutions.gov/ProgramDetails.aspx?ID=141.

39. "Treatment Foster Care Oregon (TFCO)," Child Trends, modified December 12, 2016, https://www.childtrends.org/programs/multidimensional-treatment-foster-care-mtfc.

40. "Benefit–Cost Results."

41. "Program Profile: Nurse-Family Partnership," CrimeSolutions.gov, US National Institute of Justice, profile posted June 15, 2011, https://www.crimesolutions.gov/ProgramDetails.aspx?ID=187.

42. J. Eckenrode et al., "Long-Term Effects of Prenatal and Infancy Nurse Home Visitation on the Life Course of Youths: Nineteen-Year Follow-Up of a Randomized Trial," *Archives of Pediatrics and Adolescent Medicine* 164 (2010): 9–15.

43. Waller, *Smarter Crime Control*, 128–31.

44. "Program Profile: Drug Abuse Reduction Education (DARE) (1983-2009)," CrimeSolutions.gov, National Institute of Justice, profile posted June 3, 2011, https://www.crimesolutions.gov/ProgramDetails.aspx?ID=99.

45. "Resource Fact Sheet," LifeSkills Training, accessed August 7, 2018, https://www.lifeskillstraining.com/fact-sheet/.

46. Ibid.

47. "Cost–Benefit Studies," LifeSkills Training, accessed August 1, 2018, https://www.lifeskillstraining.com/cost-benefit-studies/; and "Benefit–Cost Results."

48. "Home," Youth Guidance, accessed August 2, 2018, https://www.youth-guidance.org/.

49. "Crime Lab: Becoming a Man," Urban Labs, accessed August 1, 2018, https://urbanlabs.uchicago.edu/projects/becoming-a-man.

50. Sara Heller et al., "Thinking Fast and Slow? Some Field Experiments to Reduce Crime and Dropout in Chicago," *The Quarterly Journal of Economics* 132, no. 1 (2017): 1–54.

51. "Benefit–Cost Results."

52. "Program Profile: SNAP® Under 12 Outreach Program," CrimeSolutions.gov, National Institute of Justice, profile posted April 9, 2012, https://www.crimesolutions.gov/ProgramDetails.aspx?ID=231.

53. Ibid.

54. David Farrington and Christopher Koegl, "Monetary Benefits and Costs of the Stop Now And Plan Program," *Journal of Quantitative Criminology* 31, no. 2 (2015): 263–87.

55. Ibid.

56. "Keys to Collaboration between Hospital-Based Violence Intervention and Cure Violence Programs," National Network of Hospital-Based Violence Intervention Programs, accessed August 7, 2018, http://nnhvip.org/2018/07/11/nnhvip-releases-a-brief-on-collaboration-with-street-outreach/.

57. "Shock Trauma Violence Intervention Program Aims to Cut Down on Repeat Victimization," video, 2:30, posted by CBS News Baltimore, October 26, 2017, https://baltimore.cbslocal.com/video/3752458-shock-trauma-violence-intervention-program-aims-to-cut-down-on-repeat-victims/.

58. Carolyn Snider et al., "Wraparound Care for Youth Injured by Violence: Study Protocol for a Pilot Randomized Control Trial," *BMJ Open* 5, no. 5 (May 2015): 1–6, https://doi.org/10.1136/bmjopen-2015-008088.

59. Vincent E. Chong et al., "Hospital-Centered Violence Intervention Programs: A Cost-Effectiveness Analysis," *American Journal of Surgery* 209, no. 4 (April 2015): 597–603.

60. Jonathan Purtle et al., "Hospital-Based Violence Intervention Programs Save Lives and Money," *Journal of Trauma and Acute Care Surgery* 75, no. 2 (August 2013): 331–33, doi: 10.1097/TA.0b013e318294f518.

61. New York Times Editorial Board, "Jobs for the Young in Poor Neighborhoods," *New York Times*, March 14, 2016, https://www.nytimes.com/2016/03/14/opinion/jobs-for-the-young-in-poor-neighborhoods.html.

62. David P. Farrington, Brandon C. Welsh, and Doris Layton MacKenzie, *Evidence-Based Crime Prevention*, ed. Lawrence W. Sherman (London: Routledge, 2002), 215–17, 232.

63. "Program Profile: Job Corps," CrimeSolutions.gov, National Institute of Justice, profile posted September 10, 2012, https://www.crimesolutions.gov/ProgramDetails.aspx?ID=270.

64. Martha Ross, "Let's Invest in Summer Jobs Programs to Maximize Their Impact," *The Avenue, Brookings Institution*, published February 23, 2018, https://www.brookings.edu/blog/the-avenue/2018/02/23/lets-invest-in-summer-jobs-programs-to-maximize-their-impact/.

65. New York Times Editorial Board, "Jobs for the Young in Poor Neighborhoods."

66. Sara B. Heller, "Summer Jobs Reduce Violence among Disadvantaged Youth," *Science* 346, no. 6214 (December 5, 2014): 1219–23, https://doi.org/10.1126/science.1257809.

67. Alicia Sasser Modestino, "How Can Summer Jobs Reduce Crime among Youth? An Evaluation of the Boston Summer Youth Employment Project," *Brookings Institution*, published January 5, 2018, https://www.brookings.edu/research/how-can-summer-jobs-reduce-crime-among-youth/.

68. Tim Murphy, "Did This City Bring Down Its Murder Rate by Paying People Not to Kill?" *Mother Jones*, July/August 2014, https://www.motherjones.com/politics/2014/06/richmond-california-murder-rate-gun-death/.

69. New York Times Editorial Board, "Jobs for the Young in Poor Neighborhoods."

70. "Crime Prevention—Research Highlights 2017—H03-CP—Sports-Based Crime Prevention Programs," Public Safety Canada, modified December 12, 2017, https://www.publicsafety.gc.ca/cnt/rsrcs/pblctns/2017-h03-cp/index-en.aspx.

71. "Sports, Keeping Youth Away from Crime," Doha Declaration: Promoting a Culture of Lawfulness, UNODC, published February 26, 2018, https://www.unodc.org/dohadeclaration/en/news/2018/02/sports--keeping-youth-away-from-crime.html.

72. "Tyler's Troubled Life—Research Summary," Public Safety Canada, modified May 8, 2017, https://www.publicsafety.gc.ca/cnt/rsrcs/pblctns/2016-s005/index-en.aspx.

CHAPTER 5

1. Centers for Disease Control and Prevention, *National Intimate Partner and Sexual Violence Survey (NISVS): 2010 Summary Report* (Atlanta, GA: National Center for Injury Prevention and Control, 2011).

2. "Violence against Women: Key Facts," World Health Organization, published November 29, 2017, http://www.who.int/news-room/fact-sheets/detail/violence-against-women.

3. Nata Duvvury et al., *Intimate Partner Violence: Economic Costs and Implications for Growth and Development* (Washington, DC: World Bank Group, 2013), http://documents.worldbank.org/curated/en/412091468337843649/pdf/825320WP0Intim00Box379862B00PUBLIC0.pdf.

4. "Gender-Based Violence (Violence Against Women and Girls)," World Bank, published October 5, 2018, http://www.worldbank.org/en/topic/socialdevelopment/brief/violence-against-women-and-girls.

5. Irvin Waller, *Rights for Victims of Crime: Rebalancing Justice* (Lanham, MD: Rowman & Littlefield, 2011), 60.

6. Centers for Disease Control and Prevention, *National Intimate Partner and Sexual Violence Survey*.

7. "How Prevalent Are Sexual Assaults?," UK Office for National Statistics, accessed August 15, 2018, https://www.ons.gov.uk/peoplepopulationandcommunity/crimeandjustice/articles/sexualoffencesinenglandandwales/yearendingmarch2017#how-prevalent-are-sexual-assaults.

8. "Beijing Declaration and Platform for Action," UN Fourth World Conference on Women, September 15, 1995, http://www.un.org/womenwatch/daw/beijing/pdf/BDPfA%20E.pdf.

9. "Commission on the Status of Women," UN Women, accessed July 27, 2018, www.unwomen.org/en/csw.

10. World Health Assembly, "Strengthening the Role of the Health System in Addressing Violence, in Particular against Women and Girls, and against Children," (Geneva: World Health Organization, 2014), http://apps.who.int/iris/handle/10665/162855.

11. "Sixty-Seventh World Health Assembly Adopts Resolution on Addressing Violence," World Health Organization, accessed July 28, 2018, http://www.who.int/violence_injury_prevention/media/news/2014/24_05/en/.

12. Maria Caspini, "The Hidden Cost of Violence against Women," World Economic Forum, published December 5, 2014, https://www.weforum.org/agenda/2014/12/the-hidden-cost-of-violence-against-women/.

13. "Sustainable Development Goal 5," UN Sustainable Development Knowledge Platform, accessed July 28, 2018, https://sustainabledevelopment.un.org/sdg5.

14. Mary Ellsberg et al., "Prevention of Violence against Women and Girls: What Does the Evidence Say?" *The Lancet* 385, no. 9977 (April 18, 2015): 1555–66, https://doi.org/10.1016/S0140-6736(14)61703-7.

15. Rachel Jewkes, "(How) Can We Reduce Violence Against Women by 50% over the Next 30 Years?" *PLOS Medicine* 11, no. 11 (November 25, 2014): e1001761.

16. Rachel Jewkes, *What Works to Prevent Violence against Women and Girls? Evidence Review of the Effectiveness of Response Mechanisms in Preventing Violence against Women and Girls*, June 2014, https://www.gov.uk/government/uploads/system/uploads/attachment_data/file/337622/evidence-review-response-mechanisms-H.pdf.

17. "Gender-Based Violence (Violence Against Women and Girls)."

18. David Cantor et al., *Report on the AAU Campus Climate Survey on Sexual Assault and Sexual Misconduct* (Philadelphia: University of Pennsylvania, 2015), http://www.upenn.edu/ir/surveys/AAU/Report%20and%20Tables%20on%20 AAU%20Campus%20Climate%20Survey.pdf.

19. "About the Enhanced Assess, Acknowledge, Act (EAAA) Sexual Resistance Program," Sexual Assault Resistance Education (SARE) Centre, accessed July 28, 2018, http://sarecentre.org/.

20. Ignacio Cano, Emiliano Rojido, and João Trajano Sento-Sé, *Mapping of Homicide Prevention Programs in Latin America and the Caribbean* (Rio de Janeiro: Laboratório de Análse da Violência, Universidade do Estado de Rio de Janeiro, 2016), http://www.lav.uerj.br/docs/rel/2016/Relato%CC%81rio%20 Final%20Ingle%CC%82s.pdf.

21. Waller, *Rights for Victims of Crime*, 59–60.

22. Margaret E. Greene et al., *A Girl's Right to Learn Without Fear: Working to End Gender-Based Violence at School* (Ottawa, ON: Plan Canada, 2012), https://plancanada.ca/Downloads/Reports/Plan-Right-To-Learn-Without-Fear-ENG.pdf. In other words, school personnel must be trained to eliminate harmful norms in the classroom and, instead, to use methods and techniques that educate boys to be nonviolent and empower girls to reduce their risk of victimization.

23. World Health Organization and Joint UN Program on HIV/AIDS (UN-AIDS), *Addressing Violence against Women and HIV/AIDS: What Works?* (Geneva, Switzerland: World Health Organization, 2010), http://www.who.int/repro ductivehealth/publications/violence/9789241599863/en/; and "Violence Prevention Information System (Violence Info)," World Health Organization, accessed July 28, 2018, http://apps.who.int/violence-info/.

24. Keith Hautala, "'Green Dot' Effective at Reducing Sexual Violence," news release, University of Kentucky, published September 10, 2014, https://uknow.uky. edu/research/green-dot-effective-reducing-sexual-violence.

25. Ann L. Coker et al., "RCT Testing Bystander Effectiveness to Reduce Violence," *American Journal of Preventive Medicine* 52, no. 5 (May 2017): 566–78.

26. "Home," The Fourth R, accessed August 3, 2018, https://youthrelationships. org.

27. "Fourth R Research & Evaluation," The Fourth R, accessed August 3, 2018, https://youthrelationships.org/fourth-r-findings; and D. A. Wolfe et al., "A Universal

School-Based Program to Prevent Adolescent Dating Violence: A Cluster Random-ized Trial," *Archives of Pediatric and Adolescent Medicine* 163, no. 8 (August 2009): 692–99, https://doi.org/10.1001/archpediatrics.2009.69; and "Program Profile: 4th R Curriculum," CrimeSolutions.gov, National Institute of Justice, profile posted June 8, 2011, https://www.crimesolutions.gov/ProgramDetails.aspx?ID=109.

28. Claire V. Crooks et al., "Impact of a Universal School-Based Violence Prevention Program on Violent Delinquency: Distinctive Benefits for Youth with Maltreatment Histories," *Child Abuse and Neglect* 35, no. 6 (June 2011): 393–400.

29. "Program Profile: Safe Dates," CrimeSolutions.gov, National Institute of Justice, profile posted June 11, 2011, https://www.crimesolutions.gov/ProgramDetails.aspx?ID=142.

30. Tanya Abramsky et al., "The Impact of SASA!, A Community Mobilisation Intervention, On Women's Experiences of Intimate Partner Violence: Secondary Findings from a Cluster Randomised Trial in Kampala, Uganda," *Journal of Epidemiology & Community Health* 70, no. 8 (2016): 818–25, https://jech.bmj.com/content/70/8/818.

31. See note 30, p. 819; see also "Activist Kit for Preventing Violence Against Women and Children," Center for Domestic Violence Prevention, accessed August 3, 2018, http://www.cedovip.org/index.php/activist-kit.

32. "SASA! Success," Center for Domestic Violence Prevention, accessed July 28, 2018, http://www.cedovip.org/index.php/what-we-do/sasa-success/.

33. Christine Michaels-Igbokwe et al., "Cost and Cost-Effectiveness Analysis of a Community Mobilisation Intervention to Reduce Intimate Partner Violence in Kampala, Uganda," *BMC Public Health* 16 (2016): 196, https://doi.org/10.1186/s12889-016-2883-6.

34. Ibid.

35. "Ugandan Men Are Becoming Girls' Rights Allies," Plan International, accessed July 28, 2018, https://plan-international.org/uganda/ugandan-men-confront-stigma-fight-equality.

36. "Program P," Promundo, accessed July 28, 2018, https://promundoglobal.org/programs/program-p/.

37. MenCare website, accessed July 28, 2018, https://men-care.org/.

38. "Violence Prevention Information System (Violence Info)."

39. Pablo Brassiolo, *Domestic Violence and Divorce Law: When Divorce Threats Become Credible* (Barcelona, Spain: Universitat Pompeu Fabra, 2011), http://conference.iza.org/conference_files/SUMS2012/brassiolo_p7630.pdf.

40. World Health Organization, *INSPIRE: Seven Strategies for Ending Violence Against Children* (Geneva, Switzerland: World Health Organization, 2016), http://apps.who.int/iris/bitstream/10665/207717/1/9789241565356-eng.pdf.

41. Ibid.

42. Waller, *Smarter Crime Control*, 173.

43. Vibha Hetu, *Victims of Rape: Rights, Expectations, and Restorations* (Noida, India: Thomson Reuters, 2017).

44. Waller, *Smarter Crime Control*, 174.

45. Ibid.

46. Charlene Y. Senn et al., "Efficacy of a Sexual Assault Resistance Program for University Women," *New England Journal of Medicine* 372, no. 24 (June 11, 2015): 2326–35.

47. "Our Work: Programming, Technical Assistance, Research, and Events Programming," Women in Cities International, accessed August 3, 2018, http://femmesetvilles.org/our-work/our-work/.

48. World Health Organization, *INSPIRE*.

CHAPTER 6

1. Marc Groenhuijsen and Rianne Letschert, *Compilation of International Victims' Rights Instruments* (Tilburg, Netherlands: Wolf Legal Publishers, 2012).

2. "Support and Protection of Victims," European Commission, accessed July 28, 2018, https://ec.europa.eu/info/strategy/justice-and-fundamental-rights/criminal-justice/victims-rights_en; and Amandine Scherrer et al., *The Victims' Rights Directive 2012/29/EU: European Implementation Assessment* (Brussels: European Parliament, 2017), http://www.europarl.europa.eu/RegData/etudes/STUD/2017/611022/EPRS_STU(2017)611022_EN.pdf.

3. European Commission, "The Victims' Rights Directive: What Does It Bring?" February 2017, http://ec.europa.eu/newsroom/document.cfm?doc_id=43139.

4. Scherrer et al., *The Victims' Rights Directive 2012/29/EU*.

5. "General Law of Victims," General Congress of the United States of Mexico, DOF 03-01-2017, in Spanish, http://www.diputados.gob.mx/LeyesBiblio/pdf/LGV_030117.pdf; and "Letter of the Rights of Crime Victims," infographic, United Mexico Against Crime for Project Justice, published April 7, 2016, in Spanish, http://proyectojusticia.org/carta-derechos-denunciantes-victimas/.

6. "Canadian Victims Bill of Rights," Justice Laws, accessed August 3, 2018, http://laws-lois.justice.gc.ca/eng/acts/C-23.7/; and "The Canadian Victims Bill of Rights," Office of the Federal Ombudsman for Victims of Crime," accessed August 3, 2018, http://www.victimsfirst.gc.ca/serv/vrc-dvc.html.

7. "About Marsy's Law: Justice with Compassion," accessed July 28, 2018, https://marsyslaw.us/about-marsys-law/.

8. The former chief justice recommended eight specific actions, including guiding police to provide information to victims, an office that would pursue the interests of victims, and ways to measure progress. "Financial Assistance for Victims of Violent Crime in Ontario," Ontario Ministry of the Attorney General, accessed May 28, 2018, https://www.attorneygeneral.jus.gov.on.ca/english/about/pubs/mcmurtry/.

9. National Victims' Constitutional Amendment Passage website, accessed July 28, 2018, http://www.nvcap.org/.

10. Irvin Waller, *Rights for Victims of Crime: Rebalancing Justice* (Lanham, MD: Rowman & Littlefield, 2011), 173–83.

11. Rachel Morgan and Grace Kena, "Criminal Victimization, 2016," US Department of Justice Bureau of Justice Statistics, NCJ 251150, December 2017, https://www.bjs.gov/content/pub/pdf/cv16.pdf.

12. Waller, *Rights for Victims of Crime*, 58–62.

13. "2016 Crime in the United States: Clearances," Federal Bureau of Investigation, accessed May 28, 2018, https://ucr.fbi.gov/crime-in-the-u.s/2016/crime-in-the-u.s.-2016/topic-pages/clearances.

14. Frank Main, "Murder 'Clearance' Rate in Chicago Hit New Low in 2017," *Chicago Sun-Times*, February 9, 2018, https://chicago.suntimes.com/news/murder-clearance-rate-in-chicago-hit-new-low-in-2017/.

15. International Association of Chiefs of Police (IACP), *Enhancing Law Enforcement Response to Victims: A Twenty-First Century Strategy*, 2 vol. (Alexandria, VA: IACP, 2008), https://www.theiacp.org/sites/default/files/all/i-j/IG_repaginated_09_Final.pdf.

16. US Department of Justice, Office on Violence Against Women, *2006 Biennial Report to Congress on the Effectiveness of Grant Programs Under the Violence Against Women Act* (Washington, DC: US Department of Justice, Office on Violence Against Women, 2006), http://citeseerx.ist.psu.edu/viewdoc/download?doi=10.1.1.218.5392&rep=rep1&type=pdf; and US Department of Justice, Office on Violence Against Women, *S.T.O.P. Program Services, Training, Officers, Prosecutors: Annual Report 2006* (Washington, DC: US Department of Justice, Office on Violence Against Women, 2006).

17. Eleanor Lyon, Shannon Lane, and Anne Menard, *Meeting Survivors' Needs: A Multi-State Study of Domestic Violence Shelter Experience, Final Report*, unpublished document, NCJ 225025, October 2008, prepared for National Institute of Justice, https://www.ncjrs.gov/pdffiles1/nij/grants/225025.pdf.

18. Ten thousand beds relative to 20,000 means that the daily shortfall is 50 percent. A daily rate of 20,000 is equivalent to 300,000 over a year, or a factor of 15. So the shortfall is 10,000 × 365/15, or 243,000.

19. Dean Kilpatrick et al., *Drug-Facilitated, Incapacitated, and Forcible Rape: A National Study* (Washington, DC: US Department of Justice, 2007).

20. "Sexual Assault Nurse Examiners," International Association of Forensic Nurses, accessed August 3, 2018, https://www.forensicnurses.org/page/aboutsane.

21. US Department of Health and Human Services, *Child Maltreatment 2016* (Washington, DC: US Department of Health and Human Services, 2018), https://americanspcc.org/wp-content/uploads/2018/03/2016-Child-Maltreatment.pdf.

22. National Children's Alliance website, accessed August 3, 2018, http://www.nationalchildrensalliance.org/.

23. Courtney Ackerman, "Trauma-Focused Cognitive Behavioral Therapy (TF-CBT): How Far We've Come from Freud," *Positive Psychology Program*, January

11, 2018, https://positivepsychologyprogram.com/trauma-focused-cognitive-behav ioral-therapy/.

24. Michael K. Slade and Russell T. Warne, "A Meta-Analysis of the Effectiveness of Trauma-Focused Cognitive Behavioral Therapy and Play Therapy for Child Victims of Abuse," *Journal of Young Investigators*, June 1, 2016, https:// www.jyi.org/2016-june/2017/2/26/a-meta-analysis-of-the-effectiveness-of-trauma-focused-cognitive-behavioral-therapy-and-play-therapy-for-child-victims-of-abuse; and Alessandra Pereira Lopes et al., "Systematic Review of the Efficacy of Cognitive Behavior Therapy-Related Treatments for Victims of Natural Disasters: A Worldwide Problem," *PLOS ONE* 9 (October 8, 2014): 10, http://journals.plos.org/ plosone/article?id=10.1371/journal.pone.0109013.

25. "Advanced Search: Keyword 'trauma,'" CrimeSolutions.gov, National Institute of Justice, accessed November 9, 2018, https://crimesolutions.gov/advsearch. aspx.

26. UN General Assembly, 40th Session, Resolution 34, "Declaration of Basic Principles of Justice for Victims of Crime and Abuse of Power," A/RES/40/34, November 29, 1985, in *Resolutions and Decisions of the UN General Assembly 1985* (New York: United Nations, 1985), http://www.un.org/documents/ga/res/40/ a40r034.htm, para. 6.B.

27. UN Commission on Crime Prevention and Criminal Justice, UN Economic and Social Council, "Outcome of the Expert Group Meeting on Restorative Justice in Criminal Matters: Report of the Secretary-General," February 19, 2018, E/CN.15/2018/13, http://undocs.org/E/CN.15/2018/13 http://undocs.org/E/ CN.15/2018/13.

28. Personal communication with Nigel Whiskin, one of the pioneers and fundraisers for the organization.

29. National Association of VOCA Assistance Administrators website, accessed July 28, 2018, http://www.navaa.org/.

30. One example of significant fines ordered is a fine on Credit Suisse AG for $1.1 billion: United States vs. Credit Suisse AG, 1:14-CR-188 (4th Cir. 2014), http://lib.law.virginia.edu/Garrett/corporate-prosecution-registry/agreements/ credit-suisse-2014.pdf.

31. "Statutory Guidance: The Code of Practice for Victims of Crime and Supporting Public Information Materials, UK Ministry of Justice, modified December 18, 2015, https://www.gov.uk/government/publications/the-code-of-practice-for-victims-of-crime.

32. UN General Assembly, Resolution A/RES/40/34, "Declaration of Basic Principles of Justice for Victims of Crime and Abuse of Power," November 29, 1985, para. 16, http://www.un.org/documents/ga/res/40/a40r034.htm.

33. "The Justice for All Act," Office for Victims of Crime, Office of Justice Programs, US Department of Justice, accessed August 18, 2018, https://www.ovc.gov/ publications/factshts/justforall/welcome.html.

34. "Crime Victims' Rights Act: Increasing Awareness, Modifying the Complaint Process, and Enhancing Compliance Monitoring Will Improve Implementation of the Act," US Government Accountability Office, December 15, 2008, https://www.gao.gov/products/GAO-09-54.

35. Victims' Commissioner website, Government of the UK, accessed August 18, 2018, https://victimscommissioner.org.uk/; and Commissioner for Victims' Rights website, Government of South Australia, accessed August 18, 2018, http://www.voc.sa.gov.au/.

36. Office of the Federal Ombudsman for the Victims of Crime website, Government of Canada, accessed July 28, 2018, http://www.victimsfirst.gc.ca/.

CHAPTER 7

1. UN Office on Drugs and Crime, *United Nations Standards and Norms in Crime Prevention at Your Fingertips: For a Future Without Fear*, accessed November 10, 2018, https://www.unodc.org/pdf/criminal_justice/UN_standards_and_norms_in_crime_prevention_at_your_fingertips.pdf. See particularly, UN Economic and Social Council, Resolution 2002/13, "Guidelines for the Prevention of Crime," July 24, 2002, para. 9, https://www.unodc.org/documents/justice-and-prison-reform/crimeprevention/resolution_2002-13.pdf.

2. UN Office on Drugs and Crime and International Centre for the Prevention of Crime, *Handbook on the Crime Prevention Guidelines: Making Them Work* (Vienna: UNODC, 2010), https://www.unodc.org/pdf/criminal_justice/Handbook_on_Crime_Prevention_Guidelines_-_Making_them_work.pdf.

3. UN Economic and Social Council, Resolution 2002/13, "Guidelines for the Prevention of Crime," para. 3.

4. Ibid., point 10.

5. UN Office on Drugs and Crime, *Doha Declaration on Integrating Crime Prevention and Criminal Justice into the Wider United Nations Agenda and to Promote the Rule of Law at the National and International Levels, and Public Participation* (Vienna, United Nations, 2015), https://www.unodc.org/documents/congress/Declaration/V1504151_English.pdf.

6. World Health Organization, *World Report on Violence and Health* (Geneva: World Health Organization, 2002), http://www.who.int/violence_injury_prevention/violence/world_report/en/.

7. World Health Organization, UN Office on Drugs and Crime, and UN Development Program, *Global Status Report on Violence Prevention 2014* (Geneva: World Health Organization, 2014), 5, http://apps.who.int/iris/bitstream/10665/145086/1/9789241564793_eng.pdf?ua=1&ua=1.

8. World Health Assembly, *Strengthening the Role of the Health System in Addressing Violence, in Particular Against Women and Girls, and Against Children* (Geneva: World Health Organization, 2014), http://apps.who.int/iris/handle/10665/162855.

9. World Health Organization, *Global Plan of Action to Strengthen the Role of the Health System Within a National Multisectoral Response to Address Interpersonal Violence, in Particular, Against Women and Girls, and Against Children* (Geneva: World Health Organization, 2015), http://apps.who.int/iris/bitstream/handle/10665/252276/9789241511537-eng.pdf?sequence=1.

10. UN-Habitat, *Safer Cities Program: Special Issues Paper for Habitat III.* (New York: United Nations, 2015), http://habitat3.org/wp-content/uploads/Habitat-III-Issue-Paper-3_Safer-Cities-2.0.pdf.

11. UN Office on Drugs and Crime, Commission on Crime Prevention and Criminal Justice, "UNODC Input for United Nations System-Wide Guidelines on Safer Cities," March 6, 2018, E/CN.15/2018/CRP.2, https://www.unodc.org/documents/commissions/CCPCJ/CCPCJ_Sessions/CCPCJ_27/E_CN15_2018_CRP2_e_V1801267.pdf.

12. "Transforming the World: The 2030 Agenda for Sustainable Development," UN Sustainable Development Knowledge Platform, accessed July 28, 2018, https://sustainabledevelopment.un.org/post2015/transformingourworld.

13. UN Office on Drugs and Crime, "Discussion Guide for the Fourteenth United Nations Congress on Crime Prevention and Criminal Justice," February 9, 2018, E/CN.15/2018/CRP.1, https://cms.unov.org/dcpms2/GetDocument.drsx?UniqueStamp=-1345862110&DocId=61cfa830-6177-4e0f-88b8-6235bb78e32c.

14. "Goal 17: Revitalize the Global Partnership for Sustainable Development," United Nations, accessed July 28, 2018, https://www.un.org/sustainabledevelopment/globalpartnerships/.

15. "Sustainable Development Goals," Sustainable Development Goals Knowledge Platform, accessed July 28, 2018, https://sustainabledevelopment.un.org/sdgs.

16. Ibid.

17. "Work of the General Assembly on Violence Against Women," UN Women, accessed July 28, 2018, http://www.un.org/womenwatch/daw/vaw/v-work-ga.htm.

18. UN General Assembly, "Elimination of All Forms of Violence Against Women, Including Crimes Identified in the Outcome Document of the Twenty-Third Special Session of the General Assembly, Entitled 'Women 2000: Gender Equality, Development, and Peace for the Twenty-First Century,'" February 4, 2003, https://www.iom.int/jahia/webdav/shared/shared/mainsite/policy_and_research/un/57/A_RES_57_181_en.pdf.

19. UN General Assembly, Resolution 70/1, "Transforming Our World: The 2030 Agenda for Sustainable Development," September 25, 2015, http://www.un.org/ga/search/view_doc.asp?symbol=A/RES/70/1&Lang=E; "Open Working Group Proposal for Sustainable Development Goals," UN Sustainable Development Platform, accessed July 28, 2018, https://sustainabledevelopment.un.org/focussdgs.html; and UN General Assembly, Resolution 67/144, "Intensification of Efforts to Eliminate All Forms of Violence Against Women," December 20, 2012, http://www.un.org/ga/search/view_doc.asp?symbol=A/RES/67/144&Lang=E.

20. "Safer Cities Programme," UN-Habitat, accessed July 28, 2018, https://un-habitat.org/urban-initiatives/initiatives-programmes/safer-cities/.

21. World Health Organization, *INSPIRE: Seven Strategies for Ending Violence Against Children* (Geneva: World Health Organization, 2016), http://apps.who.int/iris/bitstream/10665/207717/1/9789241565356-eng.pdf.

22. UN Children's Fund, *INSPIRE Indicator Guidance and Results Framework—Ending Violence Against Children: How to Define and Measure Change* (New York: UN Children's Fund, 2018), https://www.unicef.org/peru/spanish/INSPIRE_Indicator_Guidance_and_Results_Framework.pdf.

23. Ibid., 90.

24. Pathfinders for Peaceful, Just and Inclusive Societies, *The Roadmap for Peaceful, Just and Inclusive Societies: A Call to Action to Change Our World* (New York: Center on International Cooperation, 2017), https://cic.nyu.edu/sites/default/files/sdg16_roadmap_en_20sep17.pdf.

25. Ibid.

26. Inter-American Development Bank, "Citizen Security and Justice Sector Framework Document, July 2014, https://issat.dcaf.ch/download/102482/1814890.

27. "Smart Spending on Citizen Security: Beyond Crime and Punishment," Inter-American Development Bank, accessed November 10, 2018, https://flagships.iadb.org/sites/default/files/dia/chapters/Chapter-7-Smart-Spending-on-Citizen-Security-Beyond-Crime-and-Punishment.pdf.

28. "Smart Spending on Citizen Security."

29. World Society of Victimology, "UN Convention on Justice and Support for Victims of Crime and Abuse of Power," cogent draft, November 14, 2006, http://www.worldsocietyofvictimology.org/publications/Draft%20Convention.pdf.

30. Irvin Waller, *Rights for Victims of Crime: Rebalancing Justice* (Lanham, MD: Rowman & Littlefield, 2011), 173–83.

CHAPTER 8

1. "Permanent Secretariat of Prevention Policy, Belgium," International Center for the Prevention of Crime, accessed August 18, 2018, http://www.crime-prevention-intl.org/en/directory-organizations-prevention/annual.html?org=32&cHash=f8977ef6c1.

2. Belgische Kamer Van Vollksvertegenwoordigers (Belgian Chamber of Representatives), *Algemene Beleidsnota: Veillgheid en Cinnenlandse Zaken (General Policy Note: Security and Home Affairs)*, October 18, 2017, http://www.lachambre.be/doc/flwb/pdf/54/2708/54k2708008.pdf.

3. Secrétariat Général du Comité Interministériel de Prévention de Délinquance (Secretary General of the Interdepartmental Committee for the Prevention of Delinquency), *Stratégie nationale de prévention de la délinquance: 2013-2017*

(National Strategy on the Prevention of Delinquency), June 2013, https://www.interieur.gouv.fr/SG-CIPDR/Strategie-nationale.

4. Government Office of Sweden, Ministry of Justice, *Combating Crime Together: A National Crime Prevention Program*, accessed August 8, 2018, https://www.government.se/49d966/contentassets/f2054a68786949d9a321dbc4b50cd02b/combating-crime-together.pdf.

5. World Health Organization, *Violence Prevention: The Evidence; Preventing Violence by Reducing the Availability and Harmful Use of Alcohol* (Geneva: World Health Organization, 2009), http://www.who.int/violence_injury_prevention/violence/alcohol.pdf.

6. Elisabeth Scarff, Decision Dynamics Corporation, *Evaluation of the Canadian Gun Control Legislation: Final Report* (Ottawa, ON: Communication Division, Solicitor General, Government of Canada, 1983).

7. Will Oremus, "In 1996, Australia Enacted Strict Gun Laws. It Hasn't Had a Mass Shooting Since," *Crime: Slate* (Blog), October 2, 2017, http://www.slate.com/blogs/crime/2012/12/16/gun_control_after_connecticut_shooting_could_australia_s_laws_provide_a.html; http://fortune.com/2018/02/20/australia-gun-control-success/; and "Fact Check Q&A: Did Government Gun Buybacks Reduce the Number of Gun Deaths in Australia?," excerpts from a conversation between Q&A audience member Diana Melham and former deputy prime minister Tim Fischer on Q&A, *The Conversation*, published October 19, 2017, https://theconversation.com/factcheck-qanda-did-government-gun-buybacks-reduce-the-number-of-gun-deaths-in-australia-85836.

8. "Investing in Intervention: The Critical Role of State-Level Support in Breaking the Cycle of Urban Gun Violence," Giffords Law Center to Prevent Gun Violence, modified December 18, 2017, http://giffordslawcenter.org/intervention.

9. Giffords Law Center to Prevent Gun Violence, Pico National Network, and Community Justice Reform Coalition, *Investing in Intervention: The Critical Role of State-Level Support in Breaking the Cycle of Urban Gun Violence* (San Francisco: Giffords Law Center to Prevent Gun Violence, Pico National Network, and Community Justice Reform Coalition, 2018), https://lawcenter.giffords.org/wp-content/uploads/2018/02/Investing-in-Intervention-02.14.18.pdf.

10. Ibid.

11. Ibid.

12. Michelle Singletary, "The Enormous Economic Cost of Gun Violence," *Washington Post*, February 22, 2018, https://www.washingtonpost.com/news/get-there/wp/2018/02/22/the-enormous-economic-cost-of-gun-violence/?utm_term=.7e9814498d28.

13. Thomas Abt and Christopher Winship, *What Works in Reducing Community Violence: A Meta-Review and Field Study for the Northern Triangle* (Bethesda, MD: Democracy International, 2016), https://www.usaid.gov/sites/default/files/USAID-2016-What-Works-in-Reducing-Community-Violence-Final-Report.pdf.

14. EUROsociAL Programa, *Regional Model for a Comprehensive Policy for the Prevention of Violence and Crime*, Collection of Working Documents 33 (Madrid: EUROsociAL Program, 2015), http://sia.eurosocial-ii.eu/files/docs/1461686840-DT_33-_Modelo%20regional%20Prevencion%20Violencia%20(ENG).pdf.

15. Ibid., 27.

16. Alberta Government, Alberta's Crime Reduction and Safe Communities Task Force, *Keeping Communities Safe: Report and Recommendations* (Edmonton, AB: Government of Alberta, 2007), https://open.alberta.ca/dataset/4a051c27-945f-4cb3-bcf1-fff1f1930f14/resource/3d5f24f7-263c-4716-bdc4-de4f3819e9a1/down load/keepingcommunitiessafe-v3-sm.pdf.

17. Alberta Government, "New Safe Communities Fund Aims to Help People at Risk and Reduce Crime," news release, December 11, 2008, https://www.alberta.ca/release.cfm?xID=2493026b5ba12-d118-67b1-629c31089913a904.

18. Enrique Krauze, "Can This Poet Save Mexico?" *New York Times*, October 1, 2011, https://www.nytimes.com/2011/10/02/opinion/sunday/can-this-poet-save-mexico.html.

19. Ed Vulliamy and Jo Tuckman, "Mexico Elections: Failure of Drugs War Leaves Nation at the Crossroads," *The Guardian*, June 23, 2012, https://www.the-guardian.com/world/2012/jun/23/mexico-elections-drugs-war.

20. "Mexico's Moment: Enrique Peña Nieto, Mexico's Newly Elected President, Sets Out His Priorities," *The Economist*, November 21, 2012, https://www.economist.com/news/21566314-enrique-pe%C3%B1a-nieto-mexicos-newly-elect ed-president-sets-out-his-priorities-mexicos-moment.

21. "Qué es el program nacional para la prevención social de la violencia y el delito?" ("What is the National Program for the Social Prevention of Violence and Crime?"), Mexico Evalúa, Proyecto Prevención del Delito (Mexico Evaluate, Crime Prevention Project), accessed August 8, 2018, http://mexicoevalua.org/prevencion/conoce-el-proyecto/que-es-el-programa-nacional-para-la-prevencion-social-de-la-violencia-y-la-delincuencia-pronapred/.

22. "Lineamientos para el otorgamiento de apoyos a las entidades federativas en el marco del Ppograma Nacional de prevención del delito" ("Guidelines for the Granting of Support to the States in the Framework of the National Program for the Prevention of Crime"), United States of Mexico Ministry of the Interior, published February 15, 2016, http://www.dof.gob.mx/nota_detalle.php?codigo=54256 03&fecha=15/02/2016.

23. *Encuesta de cohesion social para la prevención de la violencia y el delito 2014: Principales resultados (Survey on Social Cohesion for the Prevention of Violence and Crime 2014: Principal Results)*, Mexico's National Institute of Statistics and Geography, August 2015, http://internet.contenidos.inegi.org.mx/contenidos/productos/prod_serv/contenidos/espanol/bvinegi/productos/nueva_estruc/promo/ecopred14_presentacion_ejecutiva.pdf.

24. "What Is the National Program for the Social Prevention of Violence and Crime?"

25. Caroline Kuritzkes, "Increased Mexico Security Spending Not Delivering Security Gains: Report," *InSight Crime*, published August 14, 2017, http://www.insightcrime.org/news-briefs/increased-mexico-security-spending-not-delivering-security-gains-report.

26. Ibid.

27. Ingrid Palmary, "Social Crime Prevention in South Africa's Major Cities," City Safety Project, Center for the Study of Violence and Reconciliation, June 2001, http://www.csvr.org.za/docs/urbansafety/socialcrimeprevention.pdf.

28. Irvin Waller, *Smarter Crime Control: A Guide to a Safer Future for Citizens, Communities, and Politicians* (Lanham, MD: Rowman & Littlefield, 2014), chap. 5.

29. "Interim Report," Youth Violence Commission, July 2018, http://yvcommis sion.com/interim-report/.

30. Christopher P. Nuttall, dir., and Peter Goldblatt and Chris Lewis, eds., *Reducing Offending: An Assessment of Research Evidence on Ways of Dealing with Offending Behaviour* (London: Home Office Research and Statistics Directorate, 1998), http://nomsintranet.org.uk/roh/official-documents/HomeOfficeResearch Study187.pdf.

31. Peter Homel et al., *Investing to Deliver: Reviewing the Implementation of the UK Crime Reduction Programme* (London: Home Office Research and Statistics Directorate, 2004); and Mike Maguire, "The Crime Reduction Programme in England and Wales: Reflections on the Vision and the Reality," *Criminology and Criminal Justice* 4, no. 3 (2004): 213–37, doi.org/10.1177/1466802504048463.

CHAPTER NINE

1. Irvin Waller, *Less Law, More Order: The Truth about Reducing Crime* (Westport, CT: Praeger, 2006), 114–15.

2. Ibid., 80–82.

3. Waller, *Smarter Crime Control: A Guide to a Safer Future for Citizens, Communities, and Politicians* (Lanham, MD: Rowman & Littlefield, 2014), 144–45; and Claire Stewart, "Homicide in Scotland 2016-17 Figures," *Violence Reduction Unit*, published October 10, 2017, http://www.actiononviolence.org.uk/news-and-blog/homicide-in-scotland-2016-17-figures.

4. "Proven Results," MST Services, accessed August 8, 2018, http://www.mstser vices.com/proven-results. This is the number for the research. They have reached more than 200,000 families.

5. Magdalena Cerdá, Melissa Tracy, and Katherine M. Keyes, "Reducing Urban Violence: A Contrast of Public Health and Criminal Justice Approaches," *Epidemiology* 29, no. 1 (January 2018): 142–50.

6. "Crime and Security in Bogota," Colombia Reports Data, published July 23, 2018, https://data.colombiareports.com/bogota-crime-security-statistics/.

7. Waller, *Smarter Crime Control*, 140–42.

8. David Kennedy, *Don't Shoot: One Man, A Street Fellowship, and the End of Violence in Inner-City America* (New York: Bloomsbury, 2011).

9. For a leading perspective on the public health approach to gang violence in the United States, see Deborah Prothrow-Stith and Howard Spivak, *Murder Is No Accident: Understanding and Preventing Youth Violence in America* (San Francisco: Jossey-Bass, 2004).

10. David Kennedy et al., *Reducing Gun Violence: The Boston Gun Project's Operation Ceasefire* (Washington, DC: National Institute of Justice, 2001), 57–66.

11. Anthony A. Braga, David Hureau, and Christopher Winship, "Losing Faith? Police, Black Churches, and the Resurgence of Youth Violence in Boston," *Ohio State Journal of Criminal Law* 6 (2008): 141–72.

12. Anthony A. Braga, David Weisburd, and Brandon Turchan, "Focused Deterrence Strategies and Crime Control: An Updated Systematic Review and Meta-Analysis of the Empirical Evidence," *Criminology and Public Policy* 17, no. 1 (2018): 205–50.

13. Gary Younge and Caelainn Barr, "How Scotland Reduced Knife Deaths Among Young People," *The Guardian*, December 3, 2017, https://www.theguard ian.com/membership/2017/dec/03/how-scotland-reduced-knife-deaths-among-young-people.

14. Philip Conaglen and Annette Gallimore, *Violence Prevention: A Public Health Priority*, Scottish Public Health Network, December 2014, www.scotphn. net/wp-content/uploads/2015/10/Report-Violence-Prevention-A-Public-Health-Priority-December-2014.pdf; and Stewart, "Homicide in Scotland 2016-17 Figures."

15. Younge and Barr, "How Scotland Reduced Knife Deaths Among Young People."

16. Jon Henley, "Karyn McCluskey: The Woman Who Took on Glasgow's Gangs," *The Guardian*, December 19, 2011, https://www.theguardian.com/soci ety/2011/dec/19/karyn-mccluskey-glasgow-gangs.

17. *Case Study: Preventative Criminal Justice in Glasgow, Scotland: Violence Reduction Unit, Scotland*, November 2014, http://www.reform.uk/wp-content/up loads/2014/11/Preventative_criminal_justice_in_Glasgow_Scotland.pdf.

18. Damien J. Williams et al., "Addressing Gang-Related Violence in Glasgow: A Preliminary Pragmatic Quasi-Experimental Evaluation of the Community Initiative to Reduce Violence (CIRV)," *Aggression and Violent Behavior* 19, no. 6 (November-December, 2014): 686–91, https://doi.org/10.1016/j.avb.2014.09.011.

19. European Forum for Urban Security, *Methods and Tools for a Strategic Approach to Urban Security* (Paris: European Forum for Urban Security, 2016).

20. "Strategic Planning Toolkit," National Forum on Youth Violence Prevention, accessed July 28, 2018, https://youth.gov/youth-topics/preventing-youth-violence/strategic-planning-toolkit.

21. "Youth Violence Task Force," St. Louis, MO, published October 15, 2013, https://www.stlouis-mo.gov/government/departments/mayor/news/Youth-Violence-Task-Force.cfm.

22. *St. Louis American* staff, "Youth Violence Is 'a Public Health Emergency,'" *St. Louis American*, November 9, 2017, http://www.stlamerican.com/your_health_matters/health_news/youth-violence-is-a-public-health-emergency/article_e7cb9380-c4e4-11e7-90bd-63b70baf07c5.html.

23. "Who We Are," National Network for Safe Communities at John Jay College of Criminal Justice, accessed July 28, 2018, https://nnscommunities.org/who-we-are/mission.

24. National Network for Safe Communities at John Jay College of Criminal Justice, *Proven Strategies for Reducing Violence and Strengthening Communities*, 2015, accessed July 28, 2018, https://nnscommunities.org/uploads/NNSC_Brochure_2015.pdf.

25. "Blueprints & Plans," Prevention Institute, accessed July 28, 2018, https://www.preventioninstitute.org/unity/strategic-plans/examples.

26. "414 Life: Milwaukee Blueprint for Peace," Milwaukee, Wisconsin, Office of Violence Prevention, accessed July 28, 2018, http://city.milwaukee.gov/414Life/Blueprint#rates.

27. Canadian Municipal Network on Crime Prevention website, accessed August 13, 2018, www.safercities.ca.

28. "Final 2017 Totals," HeyJackass!, accessed August 28, 2018, https://heyjackass.com/category/2017-stats/.

29. See figure 1.1 and its sources, listed in the appendix.

30. City of Chicago, *2018 Budget Recommendations*, accessed August 28, 2018, https://www.cityofchicago.org/content/dam/city/depts/obm/supp_info/2018Budget/2018_Budget_Recommendations.pdf.

31. Cook County Sheriff, "Sheriff's Daily Report," April 3, 2018, https://www.cookcountysheriff.org/wp-content/uploads/2018/04/CCSO_BIU_DailyCCDOC_v8_2018_04_03.pdf. For information about other large jails, check out City of New York, "Mayor de Blasio and City Council Reach Agreement to Replace Rikers Island Jails with Community-Based Facilities," news release, February 14, 2018, https://www1.nyc.gov/office-of-the-mayor/news/094-18/mayor-de-blasio-city-council-reach-agreement-replace-rikers-island-jails-with/#/0; and Esther Lim and Daisy Ramirez, *Orange County Jails: American Civil Liberties Union of Southern California Jails Project*, June 2017, https://www.aclusocal.org/sites/default/files/ocjails2017-aclu-socal-report.pdf.

32. Nick Valencia and Arturo Chacon, "Juarez Shedding Violent Image, Statistics Show," *CNN*, January 5, 2013, https://www.cnn.com/2013/01/05/world/americas/mexico-juarez-killings-drop/index.html.

33. Lorena Figueroa, "Juarez Among Most Dangerous Cities in the World," *El Paso Times*, modified April 14, 2017, https://www.elpasotimes.com/story/news/2017/04/13/jurez-among-most-dangerous-cities-world/100425962/.

34. Cano, Rojido, and Sento-Sé, *Mapping of Homicide Prevention Programs in Latin America and the Caribbean*.

35. Ibid.

36. Ibid.

37. Giffords Law Center to Prevent Gun Violence, PICO National Network, and Community Justice Reform Coalition, *Investing in Intervention: The Critical Role of State-Level Support in Breaking the Cycle of Urban Gun Violence* (San Francisco: Giffords Law Center to Prevent Gun Violence, 2018), https://lawcenter.giffords.org/wp-content/uploads/2018/02/Investing-in-Intervention-02.14.18.pdf.

38. Michael Sierra-Arevalo, Yanick Charette, and Andrew V. Papachristos, "Evaluating the Effect of Project Longevity on Group-Involved Shootings and Homicides in New Haven, Connecticut," *Crime and Delinquency* 63, no. 4 (April 10, 2016): 446–67, http://journals.sagepub.com/doi/pdf/10.1177/0011128716635197.

39. "New Orleans," National Network for Safe Communities at John Jay College, accessed August 8, 2018, https://nnscommunities.org/impact/city/new-orleans.

40. City of New Orleans, *NOLA for Life: 2016 Progress Report*, accessed August 8, 2018, http://nolaforlife.org/files/nolaforlife_progressreport_2016_long_070816-web/.

41. Braga, Weisburd, and Turchan, "Focused Deterrence Strategies and Crime Control."

42. Michael Fitzgerald, "Operation Ceasefire Is Paying Dividends," *The Record*, January 31, 2014, http://www.recordnet.com/article/20140131/A_NEWS 0803/401310319.

43. "Amsterdam Copies Cardiff's Approach to Reducing Violence," BBC News, December 11, 2012, http://www.bbc.co.uk/news/uk-wales-south-east-wales-20669062; and "Violence Research Group," Cardiff University School of Dentistry, accessed March 13, 2013, http://www.cardiff.ac.uk/violence-research-group.

44. "Prof Jonathan Shepherd at TEDxCardiff 2012," video, 19:33, posted by TEDxTalks, April 10, 2012, http://www.youtube.com/watch?v=RduvYOxSuSM.

45. UNODC and Gobierno de Coahuila, *Evaluación de Impacto Ley Para la Regulación de le Venta y Consumo de Alcohol en el Estado de Coahuila de Caragoza* (Mexico: Centro de Excelencia, 2017).

46. Ignacio Cano, Emiliano Rojido, and João Trajano Sento-Sé, *Mapping of Homicide Prevention Programs in Latin America and the Caribbean* (Rio de Janeiro: Laboratório de Análse da Violência, Universidade do Estado de Rio de Janeiro, 2016), 84–86, http://www.lav.uerj.br/docs/rel/2016/Relato%CC%81rio%20 Final%20Ingle%CC%82s.pdf.

47. Thomas Abt and Christopher Winship, *What Works in Reducing Community Violence: A Meta-Review and Field Study for the Northern Triangle* (Bethesda, MD: Democracy International, 2016), https://www.usaid.gov/sites/default/files/USAID-2016-What-Works-in-Reducing-Community-Violence-Final-Report.pdf.

48. Ibid.

49. City of Minneapolis Health Department, *Blueprint for Action to Prevent Youth Violence*, August 2013, http://www.minneapolismn.gov/www/groups/public/@health/documents/webcontent/wcms1p-114466.pdf.

50. Prevention Institute, "Prevention Institute Full Recommendations for Preventing Gun Violence," March 2018, https://www.preventioninstitute.org/publications/prevention-institute-full-recommendations-preventing-gun-violence.

51. Waller, *Smarter Crime Control*, 145.

52. Waller, *Smarter Crime Control*, 221.

53. "New York Crime Rates 1960-2016," Disaster Center, accessed June 13, 2018, http://www.disastercenter.com/crime/nycrime.htm.

54. Sheyla Delgado et al., "The Effects of Cure Violence in the South Bronx and East New York, Brooklyn," Research and Evaluation Center, John Jay College of Criminal Justice, published October 2, 2017, https://johnjayrec.nyc/2017/10/02/cvinsobronxeastny/.

55. "New Citywide Resources to Reduce Gun Violence," NYC Office to Prevent Gun Violence, accessed August 8, 2018, http://www1.nyc.gov/site/peacenyc/resources/community-resources.page.

CHAPTER 10

1. See chapter 7 and "Smart Spending on Citizen Security: Beyond Crime and Punishment," Inter-American Development Bank, accessed November 11, 2018, https://flagships.iadb.org/sites/default/files/dia/chapters/Chapter-7-Smart-Spending-on-Citizen-Security-Beyond-Crime-and-Punishment.pdf.

2. Washington State Institute for Public Policy, *Benefit-Cost Technical Documentation: May 2017* (Olympia, WA: Washington State Institute for Public Policy, 2017), particularly 45–81, http://www.wsipp.wa.gov/TechnicalDocumentation/WsippBenefitCostTechnicalDocumentation.pdf.

3. "Benefit–Cost Results," Washington State Institute for Public Policy, modified December 2017, http://www.wsipp.wa.gov/BenefitCost.

4. Rachel E. Morgan and Grace Kena, "Criminal Victimization, 2016," US Department of Justice, Bureau of Justice Statistics, December 2017, NCJ 251150, https://www.bjs.gov/content/pub/pdf/cv16.pdf.

5. Government Accountability Office, *Costs of Crime: Experts Report Challenges Estimating Costs and Suggest Improvements to Better Inform Policy Decisions* (Washington, DC: Government Accountability Office, 2017), https://www.gao.gov/assets/690/687353.pdf.

6. Washington State Institute for Public Policy, *Benefit-Cost Technical Documentation.*

7. Camilla Schippa, "This Is How Much Violence Costs Mexico's Economy," World Economic Forum, May 2016, https://www.weforum.org/agenda/2016/05/this-is-how-much-violence-costs-mexicos-economy/.

8. See this book's introduction and Jennifer Bronson, "Justice Expenditure and Employment Extracts 2015—Preliminary," US Department of Justice, Bu-

reau of Justice Statistics, June 29, 2018, NCJ 251780, https://www.bjs.gov/index. cfm?ty=pbdetail&iid=6310.

9. National Research Council, *The Growth of Incarceration in the United States: Exploring Causes and Consequences* (Washington, DC: The National Academies Press, 2014), 5–7.

10. "Together for Safer Canadian Municipalities," Canadian Municipal Network on Crime Prevention, accessed August 8, 2018, http://safercities.ca/home.

11. European Forum for Urban Security, *Methods and Tools for a Strategic Approach to Urban Security* (Paris: European Forum for Urban Security, 2016); and EUROsociAL Program, *Regional Model for a Comprehensive Violence and Crime Prevention Policy*, Collection Working Paper No. 33 (Madrid: EUROsociAL Program, 2015), 27, http://sia.eurosocial-ii.eu/files/docs/1461686840-DT_33-_Mod elo%20regional%20Prevencion%20Violencia%20(ENG).pdf.

12. José Luis Chicoma, Liliana Alvarado, and Dalia Toledo, *Descifrando el Gasto Público en Seguridad (Determining the Public Expenditure on Security)* (Mexico: Ethos, 2017), http://ethos.org.mx/wp-content/uploads/2017/07/SeguridadFnlDigi tal.compressed.pdf.

13. Irvin Waller, *Less Law, More Order: The Truth about Reducing Crime* (Westport, CT: Praeger, 2006), 114–15; and Irvin Waller and Veronica Martinez Solares, "Smarter Crime Control: Putting Prevention Knowledge into Practice," in *Crime Prevention: International Perspectives, Issues, and Trends*, ed. John A. Winterdyk (Boca Raton, FL: CRC Press, 2016), 447–75.

14. Giffords Law Center to Prevent Gun Violence, PICO National Network, and Community Justice Reform Coalition, *Investing in Intervention: The Critical Role of State-Level Support in Breaking the Cycle of Urban Gun Violence* (San Francisco: Giffords Law Center to Prevent Gun Violence, 2018), http://lawcenter. giffords.org/wp-content/uploads/2018/02/Investing-in-Intervention-02.14.18.pdf.

15. See chapter 2 in this book and Canadian Municipal Network on Crime Prevention and University of Ottawa, *Examples of Proven Crime Prevention Programs: Action Brief 2016.3* (Ottawa, ON: Canadian Municipal Network on Crime Prevention, 2017), http://safercities.ca/wp-content/uploads/2016/10/CMNCP_AB_3_FI NAL_sept12_DIGITAL.pdf.

16. Irvin Waller, *Smarter Crime Control: A Guide to a Safer Future for Citizens, Communities, and Politicians* (Lanham, MD: Rowman & Littlefield, 2014), 142–44; "Results: Proven Results in Reducing Violence," Cure Violence, accessed August 10, 2018, http://cureviolence.org/results/; and Sheyla A. Delgado et al., "The Effects of Cure Violence in the South Bronx and East New York, Brooklyn," Research and Evaluation Center, John Jay College of Criminal Justice, published October 2, 2017, https://johnjayrec.nyc/2017/10/02/cvinsobronxeastny/.

17. Waller, *Smarter Crime Control*, 118–19; and this book's chapter 4.

18. Ibid.

19. Tim Murphy, "Did This City Bring Down Its Murder Rate by Paying People Not to Kill?" *Mother Jones*, July/August 2014, https://www.motherjones.com/poli

tics/2014/06/richmond-california-murder-rate-gun-death/; and Martha Ross, "Let's Invest in Summer Jobs to Maximize Their Impact," *The Avenue* (Blog), February 23, 2018, https://www.brookings.edu/blog/the-avenue/2018/02/23/lets-invest-in-summer-jobs-programs-to-maximize-their-impact/.

20. Waller, *Smarter Crime Control*, 149–51; and J. Purtle et al., "Hospital-Based Violence Intervention Programs Save Lives and Money," *Journal of Trauma and Acute Care Surgery* 75, no. 2 (August 2013): 331–33, doi: 10.1097/TA.0b013e318294f518.

21. Waller, *Smarter Crime Control*, 42–48; and The National Academies of Sciences, Engineering, and Medicine, *Proactive Policing: Effects on Crime and Communities* (Washington, DC: The National Academies Press, 2018), https://doi.org/10.17226/24928.

22. Murphy, "Did This City Bring Down Its Murder Rate by Paying People Not to Kill?"; and Martha Ross, "Let's Invest in Summer Jobs to Maximize Their Impact."

23. Waller, *Smarter Crime Control*, 127.

24. "Crime Prevention through Sports," Doha Declaration, UNODC, accessed August 13, 2018, https://www.unodc.org/dohadeclaration/en/topics/crime-prevention-through-sports.html.

25. Colin Webster and Sarah Kingston, *Anti-Poverty Strategies for the UK: Poverty and Crime Review* (York, England: Joseph Rowntree Foundation, 2014), http://eprints.leedsbeckett.ac.uk/849/7/JRF%20Poverty%20and%20Crime%20Review%20June%202016.pdf; and William A. Pridemore, *Poverty Reduction and Social Protection as Sustainable Development Goals for Violence Prevention* (Albany, NY: School of Criminal Justice, University at Albany, State University of New York, 2015), http://www.who.int/violence_injury_prevention/violence/7th_milestones_meeting/Pridemore_Targets_1.3_and_10.2_poverty_and_social_protection.pdf.

26. Chicoma, Alvarado, and Toledo, *Descifrando el Gasto Público en Seguridad*.

27. Waller, *Smarter Crime Control*, 76–79.

28. "Benefit-Cost Results," Washington State Institute for Public Policy.

29. "Cost of Crime Calculator," RAND Corporation, Center on Quality Policing, accessed August 10, 2018, https://www.rand.org/jie/justice-policy/centers/quality-policing/cost-of-crime.html.

30. Kathryn E. McCollister, Michael T. French, and Hai Fang, "The Cost of Crime to Society: New Crime-Specific Estimates for Policy and Program Evaluation," *Drug and Alcohol Dependence* 108, no. 1-2 (April 2010): 98–109, https://www.drugandalcoholdependence.com/article/S0376-8716(09)00422-0/fulltext.

31. 718,000 out of 1,316,000 in state prisons. See Peter Wagner and Wendy Sawyer, "Mass Incarceration: The Whole Pie 2018," press release, *Prison Policy Initiative*, March 14, 2018, https://www.prisonpolicy.org/reports/pie2018.html.

32. "US Crime Rates 1960-2016," Disaster Center, accessed August 10, 2018, http://www.disastercenter.com/crime/uscrime.htm.

33. Samuel Perrault, "Criminal Victimization in Canada, 2014," *Government of Canada*, accessed August 10, 2018, https://www150.statcan.gc.ca/n1/pub/85-002-x/2015001/article/14241-eng.htm#a1.

34. "Together for Safer Canadian Municipalities," Canadian Municipal Network on Crime Prevention, accessed August 8, 2018, http://safercities.ca/home.

35. Laura Jaitman, ed., *The Costs of Crime and Violence: New Evidence and Insights in Latin America and the Caribbean* (Washington, DC: Inter-American Development Bank, 2017), https://publications.iadb.org/bitstream/handle/11319/8133/The-Costs-of-Crime-and-Violence-New-Evidence-and-Insights-in-Latin-America-and-the-Caribbean.pdf?sequence=7&isAllowed=y.

36. Irvin Waller and Jeffrey Bradley, "Waller and Bradley: A New Jail Is No Solution to Making the Public Safer," *Ottawa Citizen*, May 9, 2017, https://ottawacitizen.com/opinion/columnists/waller-and-bradley-a-new-jail-is-no-solution-to-making-the-public-safer.

37. "Crime in England and Wales: Year Ending March 2018," Statistical Bulletin, UK Office for National Statistics, modified July 19, 2018, https://www.ons.gov.uk/peoplepopulationandcommunity/crimeandjustice/bulletins/crimeinenglandandwales/yearendingmarch2018; and Jamie Grierson, "Warnings of 'Public Health Emergency' as Violent Crime Surges," *The Guardian*, July 19, 2018, https://www.theguardian.com/uk-news/2018/jul/19/knife-crime-up-16-per-cent-england-and-wales.

38. "Crime in England and Wales Statistical Bulletins," UK Office for National Statistics, accessed August 10, 2018, https://www.ons.gov.uk/peoplepopulationandcommunity/crimeandjustice/bulletins/crimeinenglandandwales/previousReleases; and "Rape Crisis England and Wales Headline Statistics," Rape Crisis England and Wales, accessed August 10, 2018, https://rapecrisis.org.uk/statistics.php.

39. Waller, *Rights for Victims of Crime*, 60–62.

40. Alan Travis, "One in Five Women Have Been Sexually Assaulted, Analysis Finds," *The Guardian*, February 8, 2018, https://www.theguardian.com/uk-news/2018/feb/08/sexual-assault-women-crime-survey-england-wales-ons-police-figures; "Rape Crisis England and Wales Headline Statistics," Rape Crisis England and Wales, accessed August 10, 2018, https://rapecrisis.org.uk/statistics.php.

41. "Crime in England and Wales Statistical Bulletins," UK Office for National Statistics, accessed August 10, 2018, https://www.ons.gov.uk/peoplepopulationandcommunity/crimeandjustice/bulletins/crimeinenglandandwales/previousReleases.

42. Matt Ford, *Trends in Criminal Justice Spending, Staffing, and Populations* (London: Centre for Crime and Justice Studies, 2017), https://www.crimeandjustice.org.uk/sites/crimeandjustice.org.uk/files/Trends%20in%20criminal%20justice%20spending%2C%20staffing%20and%20populations%2C%20Dec%202017.pdf.

43. Andrew Sparrow, "Prison Population Should Be Halved, Say Former Home Secretaries," *The Guardian*, December 22, 2016, https://www.theguardian.com/

society/2016/dec/22/prison-population-should-be-halved-say-former-home-secre
taries.

44. One estimate from the year 2000 pegged the total cost of crime at £60
billion. But crime, particularly nonviolent crime, has decreased since then, according to the British Crime Survey, by about 50 percent. See Sam Brand and
Richard Price, *Home Office Research Study 217: The Economic and Social Costs of
Crime* (London: UK Home Office, 2000), http://webarchive.nationalarchives.gov.
uk/20110218140137/http://rds.homeoffice.gov.uk/rds/pdfs/hors217.pdf.

45. Chicoma, Alvarado, and Toledo, *Descifrando el Gasto Público en Seguridad*,
graph 6.

46. National Institute of Statistics and Geography (INEGI), *National Survey
on the Dynamics of Household Relationships 2016* (Mexico: INEGI, 2017), http://
en.www.inegi.org.mx/proyectos/enchogares/especiales/endireh/2016/.

47. Chicoma, Alvarado, and Toledo, *Descifrando el Gasto Público en Seguridad*.

48. Ibid.

49. Ibid.

50. Arturo Cervantes Trejo, "The Cost of Crime and Violence for the Private
Sector in Mexico: The Importance of Their Involvement in Violence Prevention,"
Chemonics, Inc., white paper, developed for JPV-USAID, México, 2018. Available
from the author at cervantes@post.harvard.edu.

51. Christine Murray, "Mexico Manufacturing Surge Hides Low-Wage Drag on
Economy," *Reuters*, June 2, 2014, https://www.reuters.com/article/us-mexico-econ
omy-analysis-idUSKBN0ED20H20140602; and Irvin Waller, Veronica Martinez
Solares, and Oscar Aguilar, "Investing in Smart on Crime Would Save 10,000 Lives
and Generate Five Million Jobs: The Evidence-Based Case to Invest in Smart on
Violent Crime in Mexico," unpublished, 2018.

52. Taylor Goebel, "Cost of Crime in Latin America Accounts for 3.5% of
Region's GDP," *UPI*, March 3, 2017, https://www.upi.com/Cost-of-crime-in-Latin-
America-accounts-for-35-of-regions-GDP/8541488546177/; and "Cost of Crime
Calculator."

53. Schippa, "This Is How Much Violence Costs Mexico's Economy."

54. World Bank, *Development Report 2011: Conflict, Security, and Development* (Washington, DC: International Bank for Reconstruction and Develop-
ment/The World Bank, 2011), https://siteresources.worldbank.org/INTWDRS/
Resources/WDR2011_Full_Text.pdf.

CHAPTER 11

1. Irvin Waller, *Smarter Crime Control: A Guide to a Safer Future for Citizens,
Communities, and Politicians* (Lanham, MD: Rowman & Littlefield, 2014), 14–17.

2. US Department of Education, "Report: Increases in Spending on Corrections
Far Outpace Education," news release, July 7, 2016, https://www.ed.gov/news/
press-releases/report-increases-spending-corrections-far-outpace-education.

3. "Violence Cost Mexico 18% of Its GDP Last Year, Report Says," Fox News, April 4, 2017, http://www.foxnews.com/world/2017/04/04/violence-cost-mexico-18-its-gdp-last-year-report-says.html; Caroline Kuritzkes, "Increased Mexico Security Spending Not Delivering Security Gains: Report," *InSight Crime*, August 14, 2017, http://www.insightcrime.org/news-briefs/increased-mexico-security-spending-not-delivering-security-gains-report; and José Luis Chicoma, Liliana Alvarado, and Dalia Toledo, *Descifrando el Gasto Público en Seguridad (Determining the Public Expenditure on Security)* (México: Ethos, 2017), http://ethos.org.mx/wp-content/uploads/2017/07/SeguridadFnlDigital.compressed.pdf.

4. Chicoma, Alvarado, and Toledo, *Descifrando el Gasto Público en Seguridad*.

5. Government of Canada, "Police Resources in Canada, 2016," modified March 29, 2017, https://www150.statcan.gc.ca/n1/daily-quotidien/170329/dq170329c-eng.htm.

6. "Emergency Preparedness and Response," Federation of Canadian Municipalities, accessed November 10, 2018, https://fcm.ca/home/issues/emergency-preparedness-and-response.htm.

7. Council of Canadian Academies, *Policing Canada in the 21st Century: New Policing for New Challenges* (Ottawa, ON: Council of Canadian Academies, 2014), http://www.scienceadvice.ca/uploads/eng/assessments%20and%20publications%20and%20news%20releases/policing/policing_fullreporten.pdf.

8. Matt Ford, *Trends in Criminal Justice Spending, Staffing and Populations* (London: Centre for Crime and Justice Studies, 2017), https://www.crimeandjustice.org.uk/sites/crimeandjustice.org.uk/files/Trends%20in%20criminal%20justice%20spending%2C%20staffing%20and%20populations%2C%20Dec%202017.pdf.

9. Alan Travis, "Crime Rise Is Biggest in a Decade, ONS Figures Show," *The Guardian*, July 20, 2017, https://www.theguardian.com/uk-news/2017/jul/20/official-figures-show-biggest-rise-crime-in-a-decade.

10. Richard Garside et al., *UK Justice Policy Review*, vol. 6 (London: Centre for Crime and Justice Studies, 2017), 16, https://www.crimeandjustice.org.uk/sites/crimeandjustice.org.uk/files/CCJS%20UKJPR6%2C%2026%20June%202017.pdf.

11. Melissa Hamilton, "Is Crime Going Up or Down in England and Wales? What Crime Statistics Actually Tell Us," *The Conversation*, modified July 28, 2017, https://theconversation.com/is-crime-going-up-or-down-in-england-and-wales-what-crime-statistics-actually-tell-us-81532.

12. Jamie Grierson, "Warnings of 'Public Health Emergency' as Violent Crime Surges," *The Guardian*, July 19, 2018, https://www.theguardian.com/uk-news/2018/jul/19/knife-crime-up-16-per-cent-england-and-wales.

13. "Public Attitudes toward Crime and Criminal Justice-Related Topics," Sourcebook on Criminal Justice Statistics, University of Albany, School of Criminal Justice, accessed August 8, 2018, https://www.albany.edu/sourcebook/tost_2.html#2_j.

14. Sean Collins, "This Study Found That Major US Cities Spend Millions More on Policing than on Social Programs," *Blavity*, accessed August 8, 2018, https://blavity.com/center-popular-democracy-policing-budget-study.

15. Kate Hamaji et al., *Freedom to Thrive: Reimagining Safety & Security in Our Communities*, (Brooklyn: Center for Popular Democracy, 2017), http://populardemocracy.org/sites/default/files/Freedom%20To%20Thrive%2C%20Higher%20Res%20Version.pdf.

16. "World Prison Brief Data," Institute for Criminal Policy Research and Birkbeck, University of London, accessed August 8, 2018, http://www.prisonstudies.org/world-prison-brief-data; and UN Office on Drugs and Crime, *Global Study on Homicide 2013: Trends, Contexts, Data* (Vienna,: UN Office on Drugs and Crime, 2014), https://www.unodc.org/documents/gsh/pdfs/2014_GLOBAL_HOMICIDE_BOOK_web.pdf.

17. Rebecca Roberts, "Criminal Justice After Austerity: Are There Radical Possibilities?" *Independent*, July 4, 2017, https://www.independent.co.uk/news/long_reads/criminal-justice-austerity-a7814456.html.

18. National Research Council, *The Growth of Incarceration in the United States: Exploring Causes and Consequences* (Washington, DC: The National Academies Press, 2014), https://www.nap.edu/catalog/10419/fairness-and-effectiveness-in-policing-the-evidence.

19. President's Commission on Law Enforcement and Administration of Justice, *The Challenge of Crime in a Free Society: A Report by the President's Commission on Law Enforcement and Administration of Justice*, Government of the United States of America, February 1967, https://www.ncjrs.gov/pdffiles1/nij/42.pdf.

20. National Criminal Justice Commission, *The Real War on Crime: The Report of the National Criminal Justice Commission*, ed. Steven Donziger (New York: Harper, 1996).

21. "Interim Report," The Youth Violence Commission, July 2018, 4–5, http://yvcommission.com/wp-content/uploads/2018/07/Interim-Report-FINAL-version-2.pdf.

22. Giffords Law Center to Prevent Gun Violence, PICO National Network, and Community Justice Reform Coalition, *Investing in Intervention: The Critical Role of State-Level Support in Breaking the Cycle of Urban Gun Violence* (San Francisco: Giffords Law Center to Prevent Gun Violence, 2018), http://lawcenter.giffords.org/wp-content/uploads/2017/12/Investing-in-Intervention-12.18.17.pdf.

23. "Cuomo, Murphy, Malloy Among Governors Forming Group to Study Gun Violence, Offer Solutions," CBS New York, April 25, 2018, http://newyork.cbslocal.com/2018/04/25/governor-gun-violence-study/.

24. Mayors for Smart on Crime, accessed August 8, 2018, https://www.smarton-crime.us/mayors/.

25. "German Congress on Crime Prevention and Annual International Forum on Crime Prevention," Violence Prevention Alliance, accessed August 26, 2018, http://www.who.int/violenceprevention/participants/gcocp/en/.

26. Michelle Marinho and Dandara Tinoco, "A New Campaign Against Latin America's Epidemic of Homicide," *Open Society Foundations*, May 23, 2017, https://www.opensocietyfoundations.org/voices/new-campaign-against-latin-amer ica-s-epidemic-homicide.

27. Instinto de Vida website (in Spanish), accessed August 8, 2018, https://www. instintodevida.org/#block-4395.

CHAPTER 12

1. "Together for Safer Canadian Municipalities," Canadian Municipal Network on Crime Prevention, accessed August 8, 2018, http://safercities.ca/home.

2. Kathleen Harris, "Trudeau Says He's Looking Abroad for Ideas on Curbing Gun Violence," CBC News Canada, July 30, 2018, https://www.cbc.ca/news/poli tics/trudeau-gun-violence-funeral-1.4767165.

3. Barry Friedman, "We Spend $100 Billion on Policing. We Have No Idea What Works," *Washington Post*, March 10, 2017, https://www.washingtonpost.com/ posteverything/wp/2017/03/10/we-spend-100-billion-on-policing-we-have-no-idea-what-works/?utm_term=.00900c8c9e90.

4. "Interim Report," The Youth Violence Commission, July 2018, 4, http://yv commission.com/wp-content/uploads/2018/07/Interim-Report-FINAL-version-2. pdf.

5. "Interim Report," The Youth Violence Commission, July 2018, 4, http://yv commission.com/wp-content/uploads/2018/07/Interim-Report-FINAL-version-2. pdf.

6. "Interim Report," The Youth Violence Commission, July 2018, 5–10, http:// yvcommission.com/wp-content/uploads/2018/07/Interim-Report-FINALversion-2. pdf.

7. "Mayor Announces Urgent Review of Homicide and Serious Violence Cases," Mayor of London, accessed November 12, 2018, https://www.london.gov. uk/press-releases/mayoral/violence-reduction-unit-to-appoint-new-director.

8. John Carnochan, Twitter post, January 1, 2018, @JohnCarnochan.

9. A quote I ascribe to Lord Butler when he was Home Secretary in England in the 1960s.

10. Kathryn E. McCollister, Michael T. French, and Hai Fang, "The Cost of Crime to Society: New Crime-Specific Estimates for Policy and Program Evalua- tion," *Drug and Alcohol Dependence* 108, no. 1-2 (April 2010): 98–109, https://doi. org/10.1016/j.drugalcdep.2009.12.002.

11. Matt Gutman, Robert Zepeda, Jim Vojtech, Cameron Brock, and Roger Lee, "Goldman's Family Speaks Out 20 Years After 'Empty' Victory in O.J. Simpson Civil Suit," ABC News, accessed November 13, 2018, https://abcnews.go.com/US/ ron-goldmans-family-speaks-20-years-empty-victory/story?id=45233200.

12. Jean Casarez, "Goldman Attorney Ready for 'Round Two' of Trying to Collect from O.J. Simpson," CNN, accessed November 13, 2018, https://www.cnn.com/2017/10/01/us/oj-simpson-goldman-family/index.html.

13. Alex Johnson, "Fate of Sandy Hook Lawsuit Against Gun Maker Could Be Decided By a Slingshot," NBC News, accessed November 13, 2018, https://www.nbcnews.com/news/us-news/fate-sandy-hook-lawsuit-against-gun-maker-could-be-decided-n820776.

14. John Lobato and Jeffrey Theodore, "Federal Sovereign Immunity," Harvard Law School, Federal Budget Policy Seminar, Briefing Paper No. 21, modified May 14, 2006, unpublished, http://www.law.harvard.edu/faculty/hjackson/FedSovereign_21.pdf.

15. Patrick Sharkey, Gerard Torrats-Espinosa, and Delaram Takyara, "Community and the Crime Decline: The Causal Effect of Local Nonprofits on Violent Crime," *American Sociological Review* 82, no. 6 (October 2017): 1214–40, doi.org/10.1177/0003122417736289.

16. Shannon Watts, "American Women Are Leading the Way on Gun Sense," *Medium*, April 25, 2018, https://medium.com/@shannonwatts/american-women-are-leading-the-way-on-gun-sense-74060fd23672.

17. "Mayors Against Illegal Guns," Everytown for Gun Safety, accessed July 28, 2018, https://everytown.org/mayors/.

18. Irvin Waller, *Less Law, More Order: The Truth about Reducing Crime* (Westport: CT: Praeger, 2006), 114–15.

19. "Boston," National Network for Safe Communities at John Jay College of Criminal Justice, accessed July 28, 2018, https://nnscommunities.org/impact/city/boston.

20. Howard Spivak and Deborah Prothrow-Stith, "Murder Is No Accident: Guest Editorial: Violence Prevention Through Public Health and Youth Development," *Applied Developmental Science* 9, no. 1 (2005), 2–4.

21. Ibid.

PRINCIPAL SOURCES

Abt, Thomas, and Christopher Winship. *What Works in Reducing Community Violence: A Meta-Review and Field Study for the Northern Triangle.* Bethesda, MD: Democracy International, 2016. https://www.usaid.gov/sites/default/files/USAID-2016-What-Works-in-Reducing-Community-Violence-Final-Report.pdf.

Agenda to Build Black Futures. "Our Agenda: Solutions." Accessed May 21, 2018. http://agendatobuildblackfutures.org/our-agenda/solutions/#1.

Alberta Government. "Alberta Celebrates Five Years of Safe Communities with More Resources to Reduce Gang Activities." Accessed August 11, 2018. https://www.alberta.ca/release.cfm?xID=33229D26C40FD-ED6A-F3B2-A090B33AF9C841A9.

Alberta Government, Alberta's Crime Reduction and Safe Communities Task Force. *Keeping Communities Safe: Report and Recommendations.* Edmonton, AB: Government of Alberta, 2007. https://open.alberta.ca/dataset/4a051c27-945f-4cb3-bcf1-fff1f1930f14/resource/3d5f24f7-263c-4716-bdc4-de4f3819e9a1/download/keepingcommunitiessafe-v3-sm.pdf.

Aldinger, Carmen, Julio Nogera, Jerry Reed, Alexander Butchart, Nancy Cardia, Keith Cernak, and Peter Donnelly. *Why Invest in Violence Prevention?* Geneva and Newton: Violence Prevention Alliance and Education Development Center, 2011. http://www.who.int/violenceprevention/publications/why_invest_in_violence.pdf.

Alexander, Michelle. *The New Jim Crow: Mass Incarceration in the Age of Color Blindness.* New York: New Press, 2010.

Archibold, Randal C. "Violence Suffocated a Father's Poetry, But Not His Voice." *New York Times*, May 13, 2011. https://www.nytimes.com/2011/05/14/world/americas/14sicilia.html.

Asher, Jeff. "Murder Is Up Again in 2017, But Not as Much as Last Year." *Five ThirtyEight*, July 13, 2017. https://fivethirtyeight.com/features/murder-is-up-again-in-2017-but-not-as-much-as-last-year/.

Audit Commission. *Misspent Youth: Young People and Crime*. London: Audit Commission, 1996.

Austin, James, and Michael P. Jacobson. *How New York City Reduced Mass Incarceration: A Model for Change?* New York: New York University School of Law, 2013. https://www.brennancenter.org/sites/default/files/publications/How_NYC_Reduced_Mass_Incarceration.pdf.

BBC News. "Guns in the US: The Statistics Behind the Violence." January 5, 2016. http://www.bbc.com/news/world-us-canada-34996604.

Berger, Michele W. "Cleaning Up Vacant Lots Makes Neighborhoods Safer." *Penn Today*, March 8, 2018. https://penntoday.upenn.edu/index.php/news/cleaning-vacant-lots-makes-neighborhoods-safer.

Berman, Greg, and Julian Adler. "How New York City Reduced Crime and Incarceration." *City and State New York*, March 7, 2018. https://www.cityandstateny.com/articles/opinion/commentary/how-new-york-city-reduced-crime-and-incarceration.html.

Black Demographics. "African American Population by State." Accessed May 23, 2018. http://blackdemographics.com/population/black-state-population/.

Blades, Lincoln A. "Black Teens Have Been Fighting for Gun Reforms for Years." *Teen Vogue*, February 23, 2018. https://www.teenvogue.com/story/black-teens-have-been-fighting-for-gun-reform-for-years.

Blueprints for Healthy Youth Development website. Accessed May 25, 2018. http://www.blueprintsprograms.com/.

Braga, Anthony A., David M. Hureau, and Andrew V. Papachristos. "Deterring Gang-Involved Gun Violence: Measuring the Impact of Boston's Operation Ceasefire on Street Gang Behavior." *Journal of Quantitative Criminology* 30 (2014): 113–39.

Braga, Anthony A., David Weisburd, and Brandon Turchan. "Focused Deterrence Strategies and Crime Control: An Updated Systematic Review and Meta-Analysis of the Empirical Evidence." *Criminology and Public Policy* 17, no. 1 (2018): 205–50.

Braga, Anthony A., and David L. Weisburd. *Policing Problem Places: Crime Hot Spots and Effective Prevention*. New York: Oxford University Press, 2012.

Brassiolo, Pablo. "Domestic Violence and Divorce Law: When Divorce Threats Become Credible." Barcelona, Spain: Universitat Pompeu Fabra, 2011. http://conference.iza.org/conference_files/SUMS2012/brassiolo_p7630.pdf.

Bronson, Jennifer. "Justice Expenditure and Employment Extracts, 2015—Preliminary." US Department of Justice, Bureau of Justice Statistics. NCJ 251780, June 29, 2018. https://www.bjs.gov/index.cfm?ty=pbdetail&iid=6310.

Buchanan, Cate, ed. *Gun Violence, Disability, and Recovery*. Sydney: Surviving Gun Violence Project, 2014.

Burrows, Stephanie, Alexander Butchart, Nadia Butler, Zara Quigg, Mark A. Bellis, and Christopher Mikton. "New WHO Violence Prevention Information System: An Interactive Knowledge Platform of Scientific Findings on Violence." *Injury Prevention* 24, no. 2 (April 2018): 155–56. https://doi.org/10.1136/injuryprev-2017-042694.

Butchart, Alexander. *Ensuring Security and Fundamental Rights in Urban Settings.* Hannover: Deutscher Präventionstag, 2010. http://www.praeventionstag.de/nano.cms/vortraege/id/1298.

Campbell, Carla A., Robert A. Hahn, Randy Elder, Robert Brewer, Sajal Chattopadhyay, Jonathan Fielding, Timothy S. Naimi, Traci Toomey, Briana Lawrence, and Jennifer Cook Middleton. "The Effectiveness of Limiting Alcohol Outlet Density as a Means of Reducing Excessive Alcohol Consumption and Alcohol-Related Harms." *American Journal of Preventive Medicine* 37, no. 6 (December 2009): 556–69.

Campbell Collaboration website. Accessed May 25, 2018. https://campbellcollaboration.org/.

Canadian Municipal Network on Crime Prevention. "Action Briefs for Municipal Decision Makers." Accessed July 15, 2018. http://safercities.ca/evidence-on-crime-prevention/.

Cano, Ignacio. "Breaking Down the Silos between Latin America's Homicide Reduction Programs." *Open Society Foundations.* Published September 22, 2016. https://www.opensocietyfoundations.org/voices/breaking-down-silos-between-latin-america-s-homicide-reduction-programs.

Cano, Ignacio, Emiliano Rojido, and João Trajano Sento-Sé. *Mapping of Homicide Prevention Programs in Latin America and the Caribbean.* Rio de Janeiro: Laboratório de Análise da Violência, Universidade do Estado de Rio de Janeiro, 2016. http://www.lav.uerj.br/docs/rel/2016/Relatório%20Final%20Inglês.pdf.

Cawley, Marguerite. "Mexico Victims' Survey Highlights Under-reporting of Crime." *InSight Crime*, October 1, 2014. https://www.insightcrime.org/news/brief/mexico-victimization-survey-highlights-reporting-gap/.

CBS Chicago. "CPD Defends Budget Increase for 2018, to Hire More Officers and Implement Reforms." Published November 2, 2017. https://chicago.cbslocal.com/2017/11/02/police-department-budget-hearings/.

Ceccheti, Roberta. "End Violence: The Global Partnership to End Violence Against Children." Presentation, Global Partnership to End Violence Against Children Meeting, September 2016.

Center for Evidence-Based Crime Policy. "Review of the Research Evidence." Accessed May 22, 2018. http://cebcp.org/evidence-based-policing/what-works-in-policing/research-evidence-review/.

Centers for Disease Control and Prevention. "Adverse Childhood Experiences (ACEs)." Modified April 1, 2016. https://www.cdc.gov/violenceprevention/acestudy/.

——. "Intimate Partner Violence: Prevention Strategies." Modified August 22, 2017. https://www.cdc.gov/violenceprevention/intimatepartnerviolence/preven tion.html.

——. *National Intimate Partner and Sexual Violence Survey (NISVS): 2010 Summary Report.* Atlanta, GA: National Center for Injury Prevention and Control, 2011. https://www.cdc.gov/violenceprevention/pdf/NISVS_Report2010-a.pdf.

——. "Violence Prevention: Child Abuse and Neglect: Consequences." Modified April 5, 2016. https://www.cdc.gov/violenceprevention/childabuseandneglect/consequences.html.

Cerdá, Magdalena, Melissa Tracy, and Katherine M. Keyes. "Reducing Urban Violence: A Contrast of Public Health and Criminal Justice Approaches." *Epidemiology* 29, no. 1 (January 2018): 142–50.

Chalfin, Aaron, and Justin McCrary. "Criminal Deterrence: A Review of the Literature." *Journal of Economic Literature* 55, no. 1 (March 2017): 5–48. https://doi.org/10.1257/jel.20141147.

Chavez, Edna. *March for Our Lives (Full Speech).* Video, 7:48. Posted by Community Coalition, March 28, 2018. https://www.youtube.com/watch?v=BinNvKznltA.

Chiaramonte, Perry. "US Murders Concentrated in 5 Percent of Counties." *Fox News*, April 26, 2017. http://www.foxnews.com/us/2017/04/26/us-murders-con centrated-in-5-percent-counties.html.

Chicoma, José Luis, Liliana Alvarado, and Dalia Toledo. *Descifrando el gasto público en seguridad (Determining the Public Expenditure on Security).* México: Ethos, 2017. http://ethos.org.mx/wp-content/uploads/2017/07/SeguridadFnlDig ital.compressed.pdf.

City News. "Audette Shephard Marks 10th Anniversary of Son Justin's Murder." Published June 27, 2011. http://toronto.citynews.ca/2011/06/27/audette-sheph ard-marks-10th-anniversary-of-son-justins-murder/.

Clark, Patrick. "Preventing Future Crime with Cognitive Behavioral Therapy." *National Institute of Justice Journal* 265 (April 2010): 22–26.

Cloud, David, and Chelsea Davis. *Treatment Alternatives to Incarceration for People with Mental Health Needs in the Criminal Justice System: The Cost-Savings Implications.* New York: Vera Institute of Justice, 2013. https://www.vera.org/publications/treatment-alternatives-to-incarceration-for-people-with-mental-health-needs-in-the-criminal-justice-system-the-cost-savings-implications.

Cohen, Larry, and Mego Lien. "Collaboration Multiplier: A Tool to Strengthen Multi-Sector Efforts to Prevent Violence at the Regional Level." Presentation, Violence Prevention Alliance Annual Meeting, September 6, 2016.

Cohen, Mark A., and Alex R. Piquero. "New Evidence on the Monetary Value of Saving a High-Risk Youth." *Journal of Quantitative Methodology* 25, no. 1 (March 2009): 25–49. https://doi.org/10.1007/s10940-008-9057-3.

Coker, Ann L., Heather M. Bush, Patricia G. Cook-Craig, Sarah A. DeGue, Emily R. Clear, Candace J. Brancato, Bonnie S. Fisher, and Eileen A. Recktenwald. "RCT Testing Bystander Effectiveness to Reduce Violence." *American Journal of Preventive Medicine* 52, no. 5 (May 2017): 566–78.

College of Policing. "About Us." Accessed August 11, 2018. http://www.college.
police.uk/About/Pages/default.aspx.

College of Policing. "What Works for Crime Reduction: Crime Reduction Toolkit."
Accessed July 17, 2018. http://whatworks.college.police.uk/toolkit/Pages/Toolkit.
aspx.

Comité Interministériel de prévention de la délinquance et de la radicalisation.
National Crime Prevention Strategy. France: CIPDR, 2013.

Communities That Care. "Research and Results." Accessed May 21, 2018. https://
www.communitiesthatcare.net/research-results/.

Community Safety and Countering Crime Branch, Research Division. *Tyler's
Troubled Life.* Ottawa, ON: Public Safety Canada, 2016. https://www.public-
safety.gc.ca/cnt/rsrcs/pblctns/2016-r005/index-en.aspx.

Cormack, Lucy. "Domestic Violence Advocates Call for Awareness of Brain Injury
Among Survivors." *Sydney Morning Herald,* February 5, 2018. https://www.smh.
com.au/national/nsw/domestic-violence-advocates-call-for-awareness-of-brain-
injury-among-survivors-20180202-h0sdjk.html.

Council of Canadian Academies. *Policing Canada in the 21st Century: New
Policing for New Challenges.* (Ottawa, ON: Council of Canadian Academies,
2014). http://www.scienceadvice.ca/uploads/eng/assessments%20and%20publi
cations%20and%20news%20releases/policing/policing_fullreporten.pdf.

Cure Violence. "Results: Proven Results in Reducing Violence." Accessed August
10, 2018. http://cureviolence.org/results/.

Delgado, Sheyla A., Laila Alsabahi, Kevin Wolff, Nicole Alexander, Patricia Cobar,
and Jeffrey A. Butts. "The Effects of Cure Violence in the South Bronx and
East New York, Brooklyn." *Research and Evaluation Center, John Jay College of
Criminal Justice.* Published October 2, 2017. https://johnjayrec.nyc/2017/10/02/
cvinsobronxeastny/.

Del Real, Jose A. "The U.S. Has Fewer Crimes. Does That Mean It Needs Fewer
Police?" *New York Times,* January 7, 2018. https://www.nytimes.com/2018/01/07/
us/crime-police.html?smid=tw-share.

de Waard, Jaap. *What Works: A Systematic Overview of Recently Published Meta
Evaluations: Synthesis Studies Within the Knowledge Domains of Situational
Crime Prevention, Policing, and Criminal Justice Interventions 1997-2018.* The
Hague: Ministry of Justice and Security, Law Enforcement Department, Unit for
General Crime Policy, 2018. Update of the October 2017 version.

Dierkhising, Carly B., Susan J. Ko, Briana Woods-Jaeger, Ernestine C. Briggs,
Robert Lee, and Robert S. Pynoos. "Trauma Histories Among Justice-Involved
Youth: Findings from the National Child Traumatic Stress Network." *European
Journal of Psychotraumatology* 4, no. 1 (December 2013): 20274.

Doleac, Jennifer L. "New Evidence That Lead Exposure Increases Crime."
Brookings Institution, June 1, 2017. https://www.brookings.edu/blog/up-
front/2017/06/01/new-evidence-that-lead-exposure-increases-crime/.

Dopp, Alex R., Charles M. Borduin, David V. Wagner, and Aaron M. Sawyer. "The
Economic Impact of Multisystemic Therapy through Midlife: A Cost–Benefit

Analysis with Serious Juvenile Offenders and Their Siblings." *Journal of Consulting and Clinical Psychology* 82, no. 4 (August 2014): 694–705. https://doi.org/10.1037/a0036415.

"Do U.S. Gun Deaths Since 1968 Outnumber Deaths in All American Wars?" Snopes. Accessed June 25, 2018. https://www.snopes.com/fact-check/gun-deaths-wars/.

Drug Policy Alliance. *From Prohibition to Progress: A Status Report on Marijuana Legalization.* New York: Drug Policy Alliance, 2018. http://www.drugpolicy.org/sites/default/files/dpa_marijuana_legalization_report_feb14_2018_0.pdf.

Dupuy, Kendra, Scott Gates, Håvard M. Nygård, Ida Rudolfsen, Siri Aas Rustad, Håvard Strand, and Henrik Urdal. *Trends in Armed Conflict, 1946-2016.* Oslo: Peace Research Institute Oslo, 2017. http://www.css.ethz.ch/en/services/digital-library/articles/article.html/a7992888-34fc-44e6-8176-2fcb3aada995/pdf.

Eastern State Penitentiary. "The Big Graph." Accessed July 27, 2018. https://www.easternstate.org/explore/exhibits/big-graph?platform=hootsuite.

Easton, Mark. "London Killings: No Easy Answers to Gun and Knife Crime." *BBC*, Published April 5, 2018. http://www.bbc.com/news/uk-43655748.

Ellsberg, Mary, Diana J. Arango, Matthew Morton, Floriza Gennari, Sveinung Kiplesund, Manuel Contreras, and Charlotte Watts. "Prevention of Violence against Women and Girls: What Does the Evidence Say?" *The Lancet* 385, no. 9977 (April 18, 2015): 1555–66. https://doi.org/10.1016/S0140-6736(14)61703-7.

End Violence Against Children. "Take Action: Our 2016-2020 Strategy." Accessed May 21, 2018. http://end-violence.org/take-action/strategy.

England and Wales, Office for National Statistics. "Appendix Tables: Homicide in England and Wales." Accessed June 25, 2018. https://www.ons.gov.uk/peoplepopulationandcommunity/crimeandjustice/datasets/appendixtableshomicideinenglandandwales.

European Commission. "Judicial Cooperation." Accessed May 22, 2018. https://ec.europa.eu/info/law/cross-border-cases/judicial-cooperation_en.

European Commission Directive 2012/29/EU on establishing minimum standards on the rights, support and protection of victims of crime, L315/57.

European Forum for Urban Safety. *Methods and Tools for a Strategic Approach to Urban Security.* Paris: European Forum for Urban Safety, 2016.

European Forum for Urban Safety, Federation of Canadian Municipalities, and United States Conference of Mayors. *Agenda for Safer Cities: Final Declaration.* Montreal: European and North American Conference on Urban Safety and Crime Prevention, 1989.

———. *Final Declaration.* Paris: II International Conference on Urban Safety, Drugs and Crime Prevention, 1991.

EUROsociAL Program. *Regional Model for a Comprehensive Violence and Crime Prevention Policy.* Collection Working Paper No. 33. Madrid: EUROsociAL, 2015. http://sia.eurosocial-ii.eu/files/docs/1461686840-DT_33-_Modelo%20regional%20Prevencion%20Violencia%20(ENG).pdf.

Everytown for Gun Safety Action Fund. "New Gun Violence Prevention Group 'Everytown for Gun Safety' Unites Mayors, Moms, and Millions of Americans on New Paths to Victory: State Capitols, Corporate Responsibility, Voter Activation." April 16, 2014. https://everytown.org/prss/new-gun-violence-prevention-group-everytown-for-gun-safety-unites-mayors-moms-and-millions-of-americans-on-new-paths-to-victory-state-capitols-corporate-responsibility-voter-activation/.

Falk, Örjan, Märta Wallinius, Sebastian Lundström, Thomas Frisell, Henrik Anckarsäter, and Nóra Kerekes. "The 1% of the Population Accountable for 63% of All Violent Crime Convictions." *Social Psychiatry and Psychiatric Epidemiology* 49, no. 4 (April 2014): 559–71. https://doi.org/10.1007/s00127-013-0783-y.

Farrington, David P. "The Developmental Evidence Base: Psychosocial Research." In *Forensic Psychology*, edited by Graham J. Towl and David A. Crighton, 161–81. Chichester, UK: Wiley, 2010.

Farrington, David P., ed. *Integrated Developmental and Life-Course Theories of Offending.* Vol. 14, *Advances in Criminological Theory.* London: Routledge, 2017.

Farrington, David P., and Brandon C. Welsh. "Saving Children from a Life of Crime: The Benefits Greatly Outweigh the Costs!" *International Annals of Criminology* 52, no. 1-2 (2014): 67–92. https://doi.org/10.1017/S0003445200000362.

Federal Bureau of Investigation. "Table 3: Crime in the United States by State, 2016." Accessed August 28, 2018. https://ucr.fbi.gov/crime-in-the-u.s/2016/crime-in-the-u.s.-2016/tables/table-3.

Feucht, Thomas, and Tammy Holt. "Does Cognitive Behavioral Therapy Work in Criminal Justice? A New Analysis from CrimeSolutions.gov." *National Institute of Justice Journal* 277 (September 2016): 10–18.

Fleitas Ortiz de Rozas, Diego M., Germán Lodola, and Hernán Flom. *Delito y violencia en América Latina y el Caribe: Perfil de los países de la región.* Buenos Aires: Edición de la Asociación para Políticas Públicas, 2014.

Florence, Curtis, Jonathan Shepherd, Iain Brennan, and Thomas R. Simon. "An Economic Evaluation of Anonymized Information Sharing in a Partnership between Health Services, Police, and Local Government for Preventing Violence-Related Injury." *Injury Prevention* 20, no. 2 (April 2014): 108–14.

Follman, Mark, Gavin Aronsen, and Deanna Pan, "US Mass Shootings, 1982-2018: Data from Mother Jones Investigation." *Mother Jones*, May 18, 2018. https://www.motherjones.com/politics/2012/12/mass-shootings-mother-jones-full-data/.

Fontanot, Isabel Mejía. "Tackling Crime and Violence in Latin America with Cognitive Behavioral Therapy." *Poverty Action Lab.* Published December 14, 2017. https://www.povertyactionlab.org/blog/12-14-17/tackling-crime-and-violence-latin-america-cognitive-behavioral-therapy.

Ford, Matt. *Trends in Criminal Justice Spending, Staffing and Populations.* London: Centre for Crime and Justice Studies, 2017. https://www.crimeandjustice.org.uk/sites/crimeandjustice.org.uk/files/Trends%20in%20criminal%20justice%20spending%2C%20staffing%20and%20populations%2C%20Dec%202017.pdf.

Ford, Tiffany, and Wesley Epplin. "Does Chicago Really Need More Police Officers?" *Chicago Tribune*, October 6, 2017. http://www.chicagotribune.com/news/opinion/letters/ct-letters-chicago-police-budget-violence-20171005-story.html.

Fourth R, The. "Fourth R Research & Evaluation." Accessed August 3, 2018. https://youthrelationships.org/fourth-r-findings.

Fox, James Alan. "As the Next Mass Shooting Looms." *USA Today*, June 19, 2016. https://www.usatoday.com/story/opinion/2016/06/19/orlando-gun-control-mass-shootings-column/86033174/.

Fox News. "Violence Cost Mexico 18% of its GDP Last Year, Report Says." Published April 4, 2017. http://www.foxnews.com/world/2017/04/04/violence-cost-mexico-18-its-gdp-last-year-report-says.html.

Friedman, Barry, "We Spend $100 Billion on Policing. We Have No Idea What Works." *Washington Post*, March 10, 2017. https://www.washingtonpost.com/posteverything/wp/2017/03/10/we-spend-100-billion-on-policing-we-have-no-idea-what-works/?utm_term=.af76e93d89e4.

Gaetz, Stephen. *The Real Cost of Homelessness: Can We Save Money by Doing the Right Thing?* Toronto: Canadian Observatory on Homelessness, 2012. http://homelesshub.ca/sites/default/files/costofhomelessness_paper21092012.pdf.

Garside, Richard, Matt Ford, Helen Mills, and Rebecca Roberts. *UK Justice Policy Review*. Vol. 6, May 2015–June 2016. London: Centre for Crime and Justice Studies, 2017. https://www.crimeandjustice.org.uk/sites/crimeandjustice.org.uk/files/CCJS%20UKJPR6%2C%2026%20June%202017.pdf.

Giffords Law Center to Prevent Gun Violence. "Annual Gun Law Scorecard." Accessed May 22, 2018. http://lawcenter.giffords.org/scorecard/.

Giffords Law Center to Prevent Gun Violence, PICO National Network, and Community Justice Reform Coalition. *Investing in Intervention: The Critical Role of State-Level Support in Breaking the Cycle of Urban Gun Violence*. San Francisco: Giffords Law Center to Prevent Gun Violence, 2018. https://lawcenter.giffords.org/wp-content/uploads/2018/02/Investing-in-Intervention-02.14.18.pdf.

Gillis, Tory. "Success Stories Abundant, Money Is Not for Housing First in Regina." *CBC News*. Published March 1, 2017. http://www.cbc.ca/news/canada/saskatchewan/success-stories-abundant-money-is-not-for-housing-first-in-regina-1.4003797.

Gladwell, Malcom. "Million-Dollar Murray: Why Problems Like Homelessness May Be Easier to Solve than to Manage." *The New Yorker*, February 13, 2006. https://www.newyorker.com/magazine/2006/02/13/million-dollar-murray.

Global Commission on Drug Policy. *Advancing Drug Policy Reform: A New Approach to Decriminalization*. Geneva: Global Commission on Drug Policy, 2016. http://www.globalcommissionondrugs.org/wp-content/uploads/2016/11/GCDP-Report-2016-ENGLISH.pdf.

Global Partnership to End Violence Against Children website. Accessed May 22, 2018. http://www.end-violence.org/.

Gorman-Smith, Deborah, Andrea Kampfner, and Kimberly Bromann. "What Should Be Done in the Family to Prevent Gang Membership?" In *Changing Course: Preventing Gang Membership*, edited by Nancy M. Ritter, Thomas R. Simon, and Reshma R. Mahendra, 75–89. Washington, DC: US Department of Justice and US Department of Health and Human Resources, 2013.

Government Accountability Office. *Costs of Crime: Experts Report Challenges Estimating Costs and Suggest Improvements to Better Inform Policy Decisions.* Washington, DC: Government Accountability Office, 2017. https://www.gao.gov/assets/690/687353.pdf.

Grawert, Ames, and James Cullen. *Crime in 2017: Updated Analysis.* New York: Brennan Center for Justice and New York University School of Law, 2017. https://www.brennancenter.org/sites/default/files/analysis/Crime_in_2017_Updated_Analysis.pdf.

Gray, Benjamin J., Emma R. Barton, Alisha R. Davies, Sara J. Long, Janine Roderick, and Mark A. Bellis. "A Shared Data Approach More Accurately Represents the Rates and Patterns of Violence with Injury Assaults." *Journal of Epidemiology and Community Health* 71, no. 12 (October 2017): 1–7.

Griner, Allison. "The Better Way to Support Rape Victims: Put Their Needs First." *The Guardian*, March 13, 2018. https://www.theguardian.com/global/2018/mar/13/restorative-justice-putting-the-needs-of-victims-first?CMP=share_btn_tw.

Groenhuijsen, Marc. "The Draft UN Convention on Justice and Support for Victims of Crime, With Special Reference to Its Provisions on Restorative Justice." *International Annals of Criminology* 46, no. 1/2 (2008): 121–136. https://pure.uvt.nl/ws/files/1089104/draftun.PDF.

Groenhuijsen, Marc, and Rianne Letschert. *Compilation of International Victims' Rights Instruments.* Tilburg, Netherlands: Wolf Legal Publishers, 2012.

Hamaji, Kate, Kumar Rao, Marbre Stahly-Butts, Janaé Bonsu, Charlene Carruthers, Roselyn Berry, and Denzel McCampbell. *Freedom to Thrive: Reimagining Safety & Security in Our Communities.* Brooklyn: Centre for Popular Democracy, 2017. http://populardemocracy.org/sites/default/files/Freedom%20To%20Thrive%2C%20Higher%20Res%20Version.pdf.

Harocopos, Alex, Bennett Allen, Sarah Glowa-Kollisch, Homer Venters, Denise Paone, and Ross Macdonald. "The Rikers Island Hot Spotters: Exploring the Needs of the Most Frequently Incarcerated." *Journal of Health Care for the Poor and Underserved* 28, no. 4 (November 2017): 1436–51. https://doi.org/10.1353/hpu.2017.0125.

Heller, Sara B. "Summer Jobs Reduce Violence among Disadvantaged Youth." *Science* 346, no. 6214 (December 5, 2014): 1219–23. https://doi.org/10.1126/science.1257809.

Hernández de Frutos, Teodoro, and Esther Casares García. "The Drop in Crime Rates: A Multivariate Analysis of Long-Term Trends." *Sociology Mind* 8, no. 1 (January 2018): 25–45.

Hillis, Susan, James Mercy, Adaugo Amobi, and Howard Kress. "Global Prevalence of Past-Year Violence Against Children: A Systematic Review and Minimum Estimates." *Pediatrics* 137, no. 3 (March 2016): 2–13.

"Hispanic Population of the United States in 2016, By State (in 1,000)." Statista. Accessed May 23, 2018. https://www.statista.com/statistics/259850/hispanic-population-of-the-us-by-state/.

Hoelscher, Kristian, and Enzo Nussio. "Understanding Unlikely Successes in Urban Violence Reduction." *SSRN Electronic Journal* 53, no. 11 (June 2015): 2397–416.

Holloway, Katy R., and Trevor H. Bennett. "Drug Interventions." In *What Works in Crime Prevention and Rehabilitation*, edited by David Weisburd, David P. Farrington, and Charlotte Gill, 219–36. New York: Springer New York, 2016.

Homel, Peter, Sandra Nutley, Barry Webb, and Nick Tilley. *Investing to Deliver: Reviewing the Implementation of the UK Crime Reduction Programme*. London: Home Office Research and Statistics Directorate, 2004.

Hsiao, Celia, Deborah Fry, Catherine L. Ward, Gary Ganz, Tabitha Casey, Xiaodong Zheng, and Xiangming Fang. "Violence Against Children in South Africa: The Cost of Inaction to Society and the Economy." *BMJ Global Health* 3, no. 1 (January 2018): 1–7.

Institute for Criminal Policy Research. "World Prison Brief." Accessed July 27, 2018. http://www.prisonstudies.org/world-prison-brief-data.

Institute for Economics and Peace. *SDG 16 Progress Report: A Comprehensive Global Audit of Progress Available on SDG 16 Indicators*. Sydney: IEP, 2017. https://reliefweb.int/report/world/sdg16-progress-report-comprehensive-global-audit-progress-available-sdg16-indicators.

Instituto Nacional de Estadística y Geografía. *Encuesta Nacional sobre la Dinámica de las Relaciones en los Hogares (ENDIREH) 2016*. Aguascalientes: INEGI, 2017. http://www.beta.inegi.org.mx/proyectos/enchogares/especiales/endireh/2016/.

Inter-American Development Bank. "Smart Spending on Citizen Security: Beyond Crime and Punishment." Accessed November 11, 2018. https://flagships.iadb.org/sites/default/files/dia/chapters/Chapter-7-Smart-Spending-on-Citizen-Security-Beyond-Crime-and-Punishment.pdf.

International Centre for the Prevention of Crime. *Informe, Experiencias Exitosas en Prevención de la Criminalidad en América Latina: Una Perspectiva Territorial de las Políticas Públicas de Seguridad en América Latina*. Montreal: International Centre for the Prevention of Crime, 2015. http://www.crime-prevention-intl.org/uploads/media/Informe_Experiencias_exitosas_en_AL_2015_VF.pdf.

———. *National Prevention Strategies for Youth Violence: An International Comparative Study*. Montreal: International Centre for the Prevention of Crime, 2017. http://www.crime-prevention-intl.org/fileadmin/user_upload/Publications/2017/National_Prevention_Strategies_for_Youth_Violence_Final.pdf.

Jaitman, Laura, ed. *The Costs of Crime and Violence: New Evidence and Insights in Latin America and the Caribbean*. Washington: Inter-American Development Bank, 2017. https://publications.iadb.org/bitstream/handle/11319/8133/The-Costs-of-Crime-and-Violence-New-Evidence-and-Insights-in-Latin-America-and-the-Caribbean.pdf?sequence=7&isAllowed=y.

Jewkes, Rachel. "(How) Can We Reduce Violence Against Women by 50% over the Next 30 Years?" *PLOS Medicine* 11, no. 11 (November 25, 2014): e1001761.

Jones, Damon E., Mark Greenberg, and Max Crowley. "Early Social-Emotional Functioning and Public Health: The Relationship Between Kindergarten Social Competence and Future Wellness." *American Journal of Public Health* 105, no. 11 (November 2015): 2283–90. https://doi.org/10.2105/AJPH.2015.302630.

J-PAL Policy Bulletin. *Practicing Choices, Preventing Crime.* Cambridge: Abdul Latif Jameel Poverty Action Lab and Innovations for Policy Action, 2017.

Kaeble, Danielle and Mary Cowhig. "Correctional Populations in the United States, 2016." NCJ 251211. US Department of Justice, Bureau of Justice Statistics. April 2018. https://www.bjs.gov/content/pub/pdf/cpus16.pdf.

Kanno-Youngs, Zolan. "'Interrupters' Help Reduce Violence in New York City." *Wall Street Journal*, October 2, 2017. https://www.wsj.com/articles/interrupters-help-reduce-violence-in-new-york-city-1506916800.

Karasek, Sofie. "I'm a Campus Sexual Assault Activist. It's Time to Reimagine How We Punish Sex Crimes." *New York Times*, February 22, 2018. https://www.nytimes.com/2018/02/22/opinion/campus-sexual-assault-punitive-justive.html.

Karmen, Andrew. *New York Murder Mystery: The True Story behind the Crime Crash of the 1990s.* New York: New York University Press, 2000.

Kennedy, David. *Don't Shoot: One Man, a Street Fellowship, and the End of Violence in InnerCity America.* New York: Bloomsbury, 2011.

Khurshid, Samar. "Why Does Crime Keep Falling in New York City?" *Gotham Gazette*, January 8, 2018. http://www.gothamgazette.com/city/7410-why-does-crime-keep-falling-in-new-york-city.

Know Violence in Childhood. *Global Report 2017: Ending Violence in Childhood.* New Delhi: Know Violence in Childhood, 2017. http://globalreport.knowviolenceinchildhood.org/.

Krause, Kathleen H., Stephanie S. Miedema, Rebecca Woofter, and Kathryn M. Yount. "Feminist Research with Student Activists: Enhancing Campus Sexual Assault Research." *Family Relations* 66, no. 1 (February 2017): 211–23.

Krisch, Maria, Manuel Eisner, Christopher Mikton, and Alexander Butchart. *Global Strategies to Reduce Violence by 50% in 30 Years: Findings from the WHO and University of Cambridge Global Violence Reduction Conference 2014.* Cambridge: University of Cambridge Institute of Criminology Violence Research Centre, 2015. https://www.vrc.crim.cam.ac.uk/VRCconferences/conference/violencereductionreport.

Krug, Etienne G., Linda L. Dahlberg, James A. Mercy, Anthony B. Zwi, and Rafael Lozano. *World Report on Violence and Health.* Geneva: World Health Organization, 2002.

Kuritzkes, Caroline. "Increased Mexico Security Spending Not Delivering Security Gains: Report." *InSight Crime.* Published August 14, 2017. https://www. insightcrime.org/news/brief/increased-mexico-security-spending-not-delivering-security-gains-report/.

Lee, Bandy X., Finn Kjaerulf, Shannon Turner, Larry Cohen, Peter D. Donnelly, Robert Muggah, Rachel Davis, et al. "Transforming Our World: Implementing the 2030 Agenda Through Sustainable Development Goal Indicators." *Journal of Public Health Policy* 37, no. 1 (September 2016): 13–31. https://doi.org/10.1057/ s41271-016-0002-7.

Leonard, Lucie, Laura Dunbar, and Irvin Waller, "Effective Crime Prevention to Build Safer Cities and Communities." In *Ciudad y Seguridad,* edited by Andres Suarez and Franz Vanderschueren. Mexico City: Fondo Editorial del Estado de México and Universidad Alberto Hurtado, 2016.

Lind, Dara, and German Lopez. "Why Did Crime Plummet in the US?" *Vox,* published January 19, 2016. https://www.vox.com/cards/crime-rate-drop/crime-rate.

Lopez, German. "I've Covered Gun Violence for Years. The Solutions Aren't a Big Mystery." *Vox,* modified May 18, 2018. https://www.vox.com/policy-and-politics/2018/2/21/17028930/gun-violence-us-statistics-charts.

Lum, Cynthia, and Christopher S. Koper. *Evidence-Based Policing: Translating Research into Practice.* London: Oxford University Press, 2017.

Maguire, Mike. "The Crime Reduction Programme in England and Wales: Reflections on the Vision and the Reality." *Criminal Justice* 4, no. 3 (2004): 213–37.

Mallea, Paula. *Beyond Incarceration: Safety and True Criminal Justice.* Toronto: Dundurn, 2017.

Marinho, Michelle, and Dandara Tinoco. "A New Campaign Against Latin America's Epidemic of Homicide." *Open Society Foundations,* published May 23, 2017. https://www.opensocietyfoundations.org/voices/new-campaign-against-latin-america-s-epidemic-homicide.

McCollister, Kathryn E., Michael T. French, and Hai Fang. "The Cost of Crime to Society: New Crime-Specific Estimates for Policy and Program Evaluation." *Drug and Alcohol Dependence* 108, no. 1-2 (April 2010): 98–109. https://doi. org/10.1016/j.drugalcdep.2009.12.002.

McCrary, Justin. "Using Electoral Cycles in Police Hiring to Estimate the Effect of Police on Crime: Comment." *American Economic Review* 92, no. 4 (March 2002): 1236–43. http://www.jstor.org/stable/3083311.

McFee, Dale R., and Norman E. Taylor. *The Prince Albert Hub and the Emergence of Collaborative and Risk-Driven Community Safety.* Ottawa, ON: Canadian Police College, 2014.

McKean, Scott. "Community Well-Being and Safety of Toronto's Neighborhoods." Presentation, CMNCP Workshop on Increasing Canadian Investment in Crime Prevention in Municipalities, October 30, 2017.

Mexico. *Ley general para la prevención social de la violencia y de la delincuencia.* Accessed July 19, 2018. https://www.juridicas.unam.mx/legislacion/ordenamiento/ley-general-para-la-prevencion-social-de-la-violencia-y-la-delincuen-cia.

Mikton, Christopher R., Alexander Butchart, Linda L. Dahlberg, and Etienne G. Krug. "Global Status Report on Violence Prevention 2014." *American Journal of Preventive Medicine* 50, no. 5 (May 2016): 652–59.

Minh, Anita, Flora Matheson, Nihaya Daoud, Sarah Hamilton-Wright, Cheryl Pedersen, Heidi Borenstein, and Patricia O'Campo. "Linking Childhood and Adult Criminality: Using a Life Course Framework to Examine Childhood Abuse and Neglect, Substance Use, and Adult Partner Violence." *International Journal of Environmental Research and Public Health* 10, no. 11 (October 2013): 5470–89.

Ministry of Community Safety and Correctional Services. *Community Safety and Well-Being Planning Framework: A Shared Commitment in Ontario, Booklet 3.* Toronto: MCSCS, 2017.

Molnar, Beth E., Robert M. Goerge, Paola Gilsanz, Andrea Hill, S. V. Subramanian, John K. Holton, Dustin T. Duncan, Elizabeth D. Beatriz, and William R. Beardslee. "Neighborhood-Level Social Processes and Substantiated Cases of Child Maltreatment." *Child Abuse and Neglect* 51 (January 2016): 41–53.

Morgan, Rachel, and Grace Kena. "Criminal Victimization, 2016." US Department of Justice, Bureau of Justice Statistics, NCJ 251150, December 2017. https://www.bjs.gov/content/pub/pdf/cv16.pdf.

Muggah, Robert. "How to Protect Fast-Growing Cities from Failing." Video, 14:48. Filmed October 2014, TEDGlobal, Rio de Janeiro, BR. https://www.ted.com/talks/robert_muggah_how_to_protect_fast_growing_cities_from_failing.

Muggah, Robert, and Juan Carlos Garzón. "What It Will Take to Stem the Violence in Latin America." *Los Angeles Times*, August 22, 2017. http://www.latimes.com/opinion/op-ed/la-oe-muggah-latin-america-violence-20170822-story.html.

Muggah, Robert, and Nathalie Alvarado. "Latin America Could Cut Its Murder Rate by 50 Percent. Here's How." *Americas Quarterly*. Published October 4, 2016, http://www.americasquarterly.org/content/latin-america-could-cut-its-murder-rate-50-percent-heres-how.

Musu-Gillette, Lauren, Anlan Zhang, Ke Wang, Jizhi Zhang, Jana Kemp, Melissa Diliberti, and Barbara A. Oudekerk. *Indicators of School Crime and Safety: 2017.* Washington, DC: US Department of Education, Institute of Education Sciences, National Center for Education Statistics, Bureau of Justice Statistics, 2018. https://nces.ed.gov/pubs2018/2018036.pdf.

Mwale, Temi. *Ending Youth Violence Through Community Healing.* Video, 18:42. Filmed June 2017. TEDxHamburg, Hamburg, DE. http://www.tedxhamburg.de/ending-youth-violence-through-community-healing-temi-mwale.

Nagin, Daniel S. "Deterrence in the Twenty-First Century." *Crime and Justice* 42, no. 1 (2013): 199–263. https://doi.org/10.1086/670398.

National Academies of Sciences, Engineering, and Medicine. *Proactive Policing: Effects on Crime and Communities.* Washington, DC: The National Academies Press, 2018. https://doi.org/10.17226/24928.

National Association of VOCA Assistance Administrators website. Accessed May 22, 2018. http://www.navaa.org/.

National Crime Prevention Centre. *Building the Evidence Evaluation Summaries: Results from the Stop Now and Plan (SNAP) Program.* Ottawa: Public Safety Canada, 2013. https://www.publicsafety.gc.ca/cnt/rsrcs/pblctns/rslts-stp-nwpln/index-en.aspx#toc8.

National Network for Safe Communities at John Jay College website. Accessed July 28, 2018. https://nnscommunities.org.

National Research Council. *Fairness and Effectiveness in Policing: The Evidence.* Washington, DC: The National Academies Press, 2004. https://www.nap.edu/catalog/10419/fairness-and-effectiveness-in-policing-the-evidence.

———. *The Growth of Incarceration in the United States: Exploring Causes and Consequences.* Washington, DC: The National Academies Press, 2014. https://www.nap.edu/catalog/18613/the-growth-of-incarceration-in-the-united-states-exploring-causes.

Newham, Gareth. *A Decade of Crime Prevention in South Africa: From a National Strategy to a Local Challenge.* Research report written for the Centre for the Study of Violence and Reconciliation, 2005. http://csvr.org.za/docs/crime/decadeofcrime.pdf.

New York Times Editorial Board. "Jobs for the Young in Poor Neighborhoods." *New York Times*, March 14, 2016. https://www.nytimes.com/2016/03/14/opinion/jobs-for-the-young-in-poor-neighborhoods.html.

"Number of Murder Victims in the United States in 2016, By Weapon." Statista. Accessed May 23, 2018. https://www.statista.com/statistics/195325/murder-victims-in-the-us-by-weapon-used/.

"Number of Reported Murder and Nonnegligent Manslaughter Cases in the United States from 1990 to 2016." Statista. Accessed May 23, 2018. https://www.statista.com/statistics/191134/reported-murder-and-nonnegligent-manslaughter-cases-in-the-us-since-1990/.

Nuttall, Christopher P., dir., and Peter Goldblatt and Chris Lewis, eds. *Reducing Offending: An Assessment of Research Evidence on Ways of Dealing with Offending Behaviour.* London: Home Office Research and Statistics Directorate, 1998.

Obbie, Mark. "The Wonk's Guide to What Works, and What Doesn't, When Policing Violent Crime." *The Trace.* Published August 11, 2016. https://www.thetrace.org/2016/08/policing-tactics-what-works/.

Oesterle, Sabrina, Margaret R. Kuklinski, David J. Hawkins, Martie L. Skinner, Katarina Guttmannova, and Isaac C. Rhew. "Long-Term Effects of the Communities That Care Trial on Substance Use, Antisocial Behavior, and Violence Through Age 21 Years." *American Journal of Public Health* 108, no. 5 (May 2018): 659–65.

Ontario Office for Victims of Crime. "Audette Shephard." Accessed May 25, 2018. http://www.ovc.gov.on.ca/board-members/audette-shephard/.

Papachristos, Andrew V., and David S. Kirk. "Changing the Street Dynamic: Evaluating Chicago's Group Violence Reduction Strategy." *Criminology and Public Policy* 14, no. 3 (August 2015): 525–58.

Pathfinders for Peaceful, Just and Inclusive Societies. *The Roadmap for Peaceful, Just and Inclusive Societies: A Call to Action to Change Our World.* New York: Center on International Cooperation, 2017. https://cic.nyu.edu/sites/default/files/sdg16_roadmap_en_20sep17.pdf.

Pearl, Betsy, and Ed Chung. "Resisting 'Tough on Crime': Smarter Ways to Keep American Cities Safe." *Center for American Progress.* Published February 1, 2018. https://www.americanprogress.org/issues/criminal-justice/news/2018/02/01/445678/resisting-tough-crime-smarter-ways-keep-american-cities-safe/.

Peckham, Nicole. "Ontario Ministry of Community Safety and Corrections, Community Safety and Well-Being Planning: A Shared Commitment in Ontario." Presentation, Canadian Municipal Network for Crime Prevention Workshop on Increasing Canadian Investment in Crime Prevention in Municipalities, October 30, 2017.

Peterson, Cora, Sarah DeGue, Curtis Florence, and Colby N. Lokey. "Lifetime Economic Burden of Rape Among US Adults." *American Journal of Preventive Medicine* 52, no. 6 (June 2017): 691–701.

Piquero, Alex R., and Alfred Blumstein. "Does Incapacitation Reduce Crime?" *Journal of Quantitative Criminology* 23, no. 4 (October 2007): 267–85.

Prevention Institute. "Prevention Institute Summary of Recommendations to Prevent Gun Violence." Accessed May 23, 2018. http://www.preventioninstitute.org/publications/prevention-institute-summary-recommendations-prevent-gun-violence.

Prevention Institute and Center for the Study of Social Policy. *Cradle to Community: A Focus on Community Safety and Healthy Child Development.* New York: Prevention Institute and Center for the Study of Social Policy, 2017. https://www.preventioninstitute.org/sites/default/files/publications/PI_Cradle%20to%20Community_121317_0.pdf.

Programa EUROsociAL. *Modelo Regional de Política Integral para la Prevención de la Violencia y el Delito. Colección Documentos de Trabajo n°33.* Madrid: EUROsociAL, 2015. http://sia.eurosocial-ii.eu/files/docs/1452505585-SC110T1705EFU_MODELO_REGIONAL_EFUS(WEB).pdf.

Project Longevity. "Focused Deterrence: Group Gun Violence by the Numbers." Accessed May 24, 2018. http://www.project-longevity.org/copy-of-gun-violence-outcomes.

Prothrow-Stith, Deborah, and Howard R. Spivak. *Murder Is No Accident: Understanding and Preventing Youth Violence in America.* San Francisco: Jossey-Bass, 2004.

Public Safety Canada. "Crime Prevention Inventory." Accessed August 18, 2018. https://www.publicsafety.gc.ca/cnt/cntrng-crm/crm-prvntn/nvntr/index-en.aspx.

Public Safety Canada, Community Safety and Countering Crime Branch, Research Division. *Tyler's Troubled Life: The Story of One Young Man's Path Towards a Life of Crime.* Ottawa, ON: Public Safety Canada, 2016.

Purtle, Jonathan, Rochelle Dicker, Carnell Cooper, Theodore Corbin, Michael B. Greene, Anne Marks, Diana Creaser, Deric Topp, and Dawn Moreland. "Hospital-Based Violence Intervention Programs Save Lives and Money." *Journal of Trauma and Acute Care Surgery* 75, no. 2 (August 2013): 331–33. doi: 10.1097/TA.0b013e318294f518.

Rand Corporation. "Gun Violence." Accessed May 22, 2018. https://www.rand.org/topics/gun-violence.html.

Reaves, Brian A., and Matthew J. Hickman. *Police Departments in Large Cities, 1999-2000.* Washington, DC: Bureau of Justice Statistics, 2002. https://www.bjs.gov/content/pub/pdf/pdlc00.pdf.

Roeder, Oliver, Lauren-Brooke Eisen, and Julia Bowling. *What Caused the Crime Decline?* New York: Brennan Center for Justice, 2015. https://www.brennancenter.org/sites/default/files/analysis/What_Caused_The_Crime_Decline.pdf.

Roth, Alisa. *Insane: America's Criminal Treatment of Mental Illness.* New York: Basic Books, 2018.

Sanders, Matthew R., and Trevor G. Mazzucchelli. *The Power of Positive Parenting: Transforming the Lives of Children, Parents, and Communities Using the Triple P System.* New York: Oxford University Press, 2017.

Savoie, Josée. *Analysis of the Spatial Distribution of Crime in Canada: Summary of Major Trends.* Ottawa: Statistics Canada, 2008. http://www.statcan.gc.ca/pub/85-561-m/85-561-m2008015-eng.htm.

Sawatsky, Murray J., Rick Ruddell, and Nicholas A. Jones. "A Quantitative Study of Prince Albert's Crime/Risk Reduction Approach to Community Safety." *Journal of Community Safety and Well-Being* 2, no. 1 (March 2017): 3–12. https://journalcswb.ca/index.php/cswb/article/view/38/74.

Schweig, Sarah, Nazmia E. A. Comrie, and John Markovic. *Co-Producing Public Safety: Communities, Law Enforcement, and Public Health Researchers Work to Prevent Crime Together.* Washington, DC: Center for Court Innovation, 2016. https://www.courtinnovation.org/sites/default/files/documents/co_producing_public_Safety.pdf.

Senn, Charlene Y., Misha Eliasziw, Paula C. Barata, Wilfreda E. Thurston, Ian R. Newby-Clark, H. Lorraine Radtke, and Karen L. Hobden. "Efficacy of a Sexual Assault Resistance Program for University Women." *New England Journal of Medicine* 372, no. 24 (June 11, 2015): 2326–35.

Serrano, Rodrigo. *Mejorando la seguridad de los latinoamericanos a través de un gasto público más preventivo, focalizado e inteligente.* Private communication.

Sherman, Lawrence W. "Attacking Crime: Police and Crime Control." *Crime and Justice* 15 (January 1992): 159–230. https://doi.org/10.1086/449195.

———. "The Rise of Evidence-Based Policing: Targeting, Testing, and Tracking." *Crime and Justice* 42, no. 1 (2013): 377–451. https://doi.org/10.1086/670819.

Shoichet, Catherine E. "Mexican Poet Becomes Crusader for Peace after Son's Slaying." *CNN*. Modified May 5, 2011. http://www.cnn.com/2011/WORLD/americas/05/05/mexico.poet.activist/index.html?hpt=Sbin.

Shute, Jon. "Family Support as a Gang Reduction Measure." *Children and Society* 27, no. 1 (January 2013): 48–59.

Sierra-Arévalo, Michael, and Andrew V. Papachristos. *Focused Deterrence Strategy Reduces Group Member Involved Shootings in New Haven, CT*. New Haven: Yale University Institution for Social and Policy Studies, 2015. https://isps.yale.edu/research/publications/isps15-025.

Simon, Thomas R., Nancy M. Ritter, and Reshma R. Mahendra, eds. *Changing Course: Preventing Gang Membership*. Washington, DC: US Department of Justice and US Department of Health and Human Resources, 2013.

Smart on Crime. *America's Mayors Are Getting Smart on Crime*. Video, 1:51. Posted by "seeprogress," January 31, 2018. https://www.youtube.com/watch?v=55rW5a-6mlY&feature=youtu.be.

———. *It's Time to Get Smart on Crime*. Video, 2:05. Posted by "seeprogress," October 10, 2017. https://www.youtube.com/watch?v=DC8qD9D7tQI&feature=youtu.be.

Snider, Carolyn, Depeng Jiang, Sarvesh Logsetty, Trevor Strome, and Terry Klassen. "Wraparound Care for Youth Injured by Violence: Study Protocol for a Pilot Randomized Control Trial." *BMJ Open* 5, no. 5 (May 2015): 1–6. https://doi.org/10.1136/bmjopen-2015-008088.

South Africa. "Safety and Security White Paper, 1998." Accessed July 19, 2018. https://www.gov.za/documents/safety-and-security-white-paper#Section5.

———. "White Paper on Safety and Security, 2016, Civilian Secretariat on the Police." Accessed July 19, 2018.

Spooner, Kallee, David C. Pyrooz, Vincent J. Webb, and Kathleen A. Fox. "Recidivism Among Juveniles in a Multi-Component Gang Re-entry Program: Findings from a Program Evaluation in Harris County, Texas." *Journal of Experimental Criminology* 13, no. 2 (June 2017): 275–85.

Steven, David. *If Not Now, When? Ending Violence Against the World's Children*. New York: Center on International Cooperation, 2014. https://cic.nyu.edu/sites/default/files/violence_children_final.pdf.

———. "Peaceful, Just and Inclusive Societies: Delivering SDG16+." Presentation, Center on International Cooperation Meeting, 2016.

Stevens, Katharine B. "Pre-K Isn't Just Academic." *American Enterprise Institute*. Published July 27, 2017. http://www.aei.org/publication/pre-k-isnt-just-academic/.

Stewart, Claire. "Homicide in Scotland 2016-17 Figures." *Violence Reduction Unit*. Published October 10, 2017. http://www.actiononviolence.org.uk/news-and-blog/homicide-in-scotland-2016-17-figures?page=3.

Substance Abuse and Mental Health Services Administration. "Topics: Prevention of Substance Abuse and Mental Illness." Accessed May 25, 2018. https://www.samhsa.gov/prevention.

Taylor, Gregory. *A Focus on Family Violence in Canada.* Ottawa: Public Health Agency of Canada, 2016. http://healthycanadians.gc.ca/publications/depart ment-ministere/state-public-health-family-violence-2016-etat-sante-publique-violence-familiale/alt/pdf-eng.pdf.

Tiratelli, Matteo, Paul Quinton, and Ben Bradford. "Does Stop and Search Deter Crime? Evidence from Ten Years of London-Wide Data." *British Journal of Criminology* 58, no. 5 (August 2018): 1212–31. https://doi.org/10.1093/bjc/azx085.

Tobin, Mike. "Chicago Records 762 Homicides in 2016, Up 57% from Previous Year." *Fox News.* Modified July 5, 2017. http://www.foxnews.com/us/2017/01/01/1-chicagos-bloodiest-years-ends-with-762-homicides.html.

Toronto Police Service. *Action Plan: The Way Forward.* January 2017. http://www.tpsb.ca/items-of-interest/send/29-items-of-interest/546-action-plan-the-way-for ward-modernizing-community-safety-in-toronto.

"Total Number of Murders in the United States in 2016, By State." Statista. Accessed May 23, 2018. https://www.statista.com/statistics/195331/number-of-murders-in-the-us-by-state/.

Tough, Paul. "The Poverty Clinic: Can a Stressful Childhood Make You a Sick Adult?" *The New Yorker,* March 21, 2011. https://www.newyorker.com/maga zine/2011/03/21/the-poverty-clinic.

UN Children's Fund. *INSPIRE Indicator Guidance and Results Framework: Seven Strategies for Ending Violence Against Children.* Geneva: UN Children's Fund, 2018.

UN Commission on Crime Prevention and Criminal Justice. *UNODC Input for United Nations System-Wide Guidelines on Safer Cities.* Vienna: United Nations Office on Drugs and Crime, 2018.

———. *Outcome of the Expert Group Meeting on Restorative Justice in Criminal Matters.* Vienna: UN Economic and Social Council, 2018.

UN Economic and Social Council, 4th Year. Resolution 9, "Guidelines for the Prevention of Urban Crime." RES/1995/9, July 24, 1995. In *Resolutions and Decisions of the UN Department of Economic and Social Affairs 1995.* Vienna: United Nations, 1999.

UN Economic and Social Council, 27th Session. Draft Resolution 15, "Restorative Justice in Criminal Matters." E/CN.15/2018/L.5, May 14–18, 2018. In *Resolutions and Decisions of the UN Department of Economic and Social Affairs 2018.* Vienna: United Nations, 2018.

UN Economic and Social Council, 37th Session. Resolution 13, "Action to Promote Effective Crime Prevention." RES/2002/13, July, 24, 2002. In *Resolutions and Decisions of the UN Department of Economic and Social Affairs 2002.* Vienna: United Nations, 2002.

UN Executive Committee on Economic and Social Affairs. *2017 HLPF Thematic Review of SDG 5: Achieve Gender Equality and Empower All Women and Girls.* New York: United Nations, 2018. https://sustainabledevelopment.un.org/con tent/documents/14383SDG5format-revOD.pdf.

UN General Assembly, 40th Session. Resolution 34, "Declaration of Basic Principles of Justice for Victims of Crime and Abuse of Power." A/RES/40/34, November 29, 1985. In *Resolutions and Decisions of the UN General Assembly 1985.* New York: United Nations, 1985.

UN General Assembly, 70th Session. Resolution 1, "Transforming Our World: The 2030 Agenda for Sustainable Development." A/RES/70/1, October 21, 2015. In *Resolutions and Decisions of the UN General Assembly 2015.* New York: United Nations, 2015.

UN-Habitat. *Safer Cities Program: Special Issues Paper for Habitat III.* New York: United Nations, 2015. http://habitat3.org/wp-content/uploads/Habitat-III-Issue-Paper-3_Safer-Cities-2.0.pdf.

United Nations. "Why Should You Care About the Sustainable Development Goals?" Accessed May 22, 2018. https://www.un.org/sustainabledevelopment/blog/2015/09/why-should-you-care-about-the-sustainable-development-goals/.

University of Queensland, Australia. "Triple P Evidence Base." Accessed May 22, 2018. https://pfsc-evidence.psy.uq.edu.au/.

UN Office on Drugs and Crime. "Center of Excellence in Information on Government, Crime, Victimization and Justice." Accessed May 22, 2018. http://www.cdeunodc.inegi.org.mx/index.php/en-2/.

———. *Compendium of United Nations Standards and Norms in Crime Prevention and Criminal Justice.* Vienna: United Nations, 2006. https://www.unodc.org/pdf/criminal_justice/Compendium_UN_Standards_and_Norms_CP_and_CJ_English.pdf.

———. *Discussion Guide for the Fourteenth United Nations Congress on Crime Prevention and Criminal Justice.* Vienna: Commission on Crime Prevention and Criminal Justice, 2018.

———. *Global Study on Homicide, 2013.* Vienna: UNODC, 2014. https://www.unodc.org/documents/gsh/pdfs/2014_GLOBAL_HOMICIDE_BOOK_web.pdf.

———. *Guide for Policy Makers on the Implementation of the United Declaration of Basic Principles of Justice for Victims of Crime and Abuse of Power.* New York: UNODC, 1999.

———. *Handbook on the Crime Prevention Guidelines: Making Them Work.* Vienna: United Nations, 2010. https://www.unodc.org/pdf/criminal_justice/Handbook_on_Crime_Prevention_Guidelines_-_Making_them_work.pdf.

———. *United Nations Standards and Norms in Crime Prevention at Your Finger Tips.* Vienna: UNODC, 2006.

UN Sustainable Development Knowledge Platform. "Sustainable Development Goals." Accessed May 22, 2018. https://sustainabledevelopment.un.org/?menu=1300.

UN Women. *A Framework to Underpin Action to Prevent Violence Against Women.* New York: UN Women, 2015. https://www.ohchr.org/Documents/Issues/Women/WRGS/PreventionFrameworkNov2015.pdf.

US Department of Education. "Report: Increases in Spending on Corrections Far Outpace Education." Published July 7, 2016. https://www.ed.gov/news/press-releases/report-increases-spending-corrections-far-outpace-education.

US National Institute of Justice. CrimeSolutions.gov website. Accessed July 13, 2018. https://www.crimesolutions.gov/.

Van Dijk, Jan, Andromachi Tseloni, and Graham Farrell, eds. *The International Crime Drop: New Directions in Research.* London: Palgrave Macmillan, 2012.

Violence Prevention Alliance. *Cost of Care: The Burden of Violence-Related Injuries and Road Traffic Crashes to the Healthcare System of Jamaica.* Kingston: VPA, 2017. https://monagis.files.wordpress.com/2018/02/cost-of-care-final-report.pdf.

Vitale, Alex S. *The End of Policing.* London: Verso, 2017.

Waller, Irvin. *Less Law, More Order: The Truth about Reducing Crime.* Westport, CT: Praeger, 2006.

———. *Rights for Victims of Crime: Rebalancing Justice.* Lanham, MD: Rowman & Littlefield, 2011.

———. *Smarter Crime Control: A Guide to a Safer Future for Citizens, Communities, and Politicians.* Lanham, MD: Rowman & Littlefield, 2014.

Waller, Irvin, and Audrey Monette. "The Relevance of the UN Sustainable Development Goals to Crime Prevention in Canadian Municipalities." Action brief. Ottawa: Canadian Municipal Network on Crime Prevention and University of Ottawa, 2018. https://drive.google.com/file/d/1Mfd9ryqYvzUpCzQVrRCQ9CQWTkZPd5Nj/view.

Waller, Irvin, and Jeffrey Bradley. "Municipal Crime Prevention Offices: Importance, Role, Function, and Models." Action brief. Ottawa: Canadian Municipal Network on Crime Prevention and University of Ottawa, 2017. https://drive.google.com/file/d/1KT2oOsSq-n8piDgasFFkXNZ-YcDGAWla/view.

———. "What Is Effective Crime Prevention for Municipalities?" Action brief. Ottawa: Canadian Municipal Network on Crime Prevention and University of Ottawa, 2018. https://drive.google.com/file/d/16ONZyCiivNBPIEocywOnqTswcuLYrRnw/view.

Waller, Irvin, and Veronica Martinez Solares. "Smarter Crime Control: Putting Prevention Knowledge into Practice." In *Crime Prevention: International Perspectives, Issues, and Trends*, edited by John A. Winterdyk, 446–75. Boca Raton: CRC Press, 2016.

Washington State Institute for Public Policy and University of Washington Evidence-Based Practice Institute. *Updated Inventory of Evidence-Based, Research-Based, and Promising Practices: For Prevention and Intervention Services for Children and Juveniles in the Child Welfare, Juvenile Justice, and Mental Health Systems.* Modified November 14, 2017. http://www.wsipp.wa.gov/Publications?reportId=605.

Webster, Colin, and Sarah Kingston. *Anti-Poverty Strategies for the UK: Poverty and Crime Review.* York: Joseph Rowntree Foundation, 2015.

Weisburd, David, David P. Farrington, and Charlotte Gill, eds. *What Works in Crime Prevention and Rehabilitation: Lessons from Systematic Reviews.* Springer Series on Evidence-Based Crime Policy. New York: Springer, 2016.

Welsh, Brandon C., Michael Rocque, and Peter W. Greenwood. "Translating Research into Evidence-Based Practice in Juvenile Justice: Brand-Name Programs, Meta-Analysis, and Key Issues." *Journal of Experimental Criminology* 10, no. 2 (June 2014): 207–25. https://doi.org/10.1007/s11292-013-9182-3.

WHO Violence News (@WHOviolencenews). "New Video Uncovers the Link between Early Trauma and Lifelong Illness." Twitter, January 24, 2018, 10:24 p.m. https://twitter.com/WHOviolencenews/status/956412321403981825?t=1&cn=Z mxleGlibGVfcmVjc18y&refsrc=email&iid=76c3b6e677b64d43bd3170dedb8310 be&uid=240729428&nid=244+272699392.

Williams, Damien J., Dorothy B. Currie, Will Linden, and Peter D. Donnelly. "Addressing Gang-Related Violence in Glasgow: A Preliminary Pragmatic Quasi-Experimental Evaluation of the Community Initiative to Reduce Violence (CIRV)." *Aggression and Violent Behavior* 19, no. 6 (November 2014): 686–91. https://doi.org/10.1016/j.avb.2014.09.011.

Wolfe, David A., Claire Crooks, Peter Jaffe, Debbie Chiodo, Ray Hughes, Wendy Ellis, Larry Stitt, and Allan Donner. "A School-Based Program to Prevent Adolescent Dating Violence: A Cluster Randomized Trial." *Archives of Pediatrics and Adolescent Medicine* 163, no. 8 (August 2009): 692–99. https://doi.org/10.1001/archpediatrics.2009.69.

Wong, Jennifer, Jason Gravel, Martin Bouchard, Carlo Morselli, and Karine Descormiers. *Effectiveness of Street Gang Control Strategies: A Systematic Review and Meta-Analysis of Evaluation Studies.* Ottawa: Public Safety Canada, 2012. http://www.deslibris.ca/ID/232345.

World Bank. *World Development Report 2011: Conflict, Security, and Development.* Washington, DC: International Bank for Reconstruction and Development, 2011. https://siteresources.worldbank.org/INTWDRS/Resources/WDR2011_Full_Text.pdf.

World Federation of United Nations Association. "SDG 16+ Forum." Accessed May 25, 2018. http://www.wfuna.org/sixteenplusforum.

World Health Assembly. *Strengthening the Role of the Health System in Addressing Violence, in Particular Against Women and Girls, and Against Children.* Geneva: World Health Organization, 2014. http://apps.who.int/iris/handle/10665/162855.

World Health Organization. "Child Maltreatment." Infographic, 2017. http://www.who.int/violence_injury_prevention/violence/child/Child_maltreatment_infographic_EN.pdf?ua=1.

———. *Global Plan of Action to Strengthen the Role of the Health System Within a National Multisectoral Response to Address Interpersonal Violence, in Particular Against Women and Girls, and Against Children.* Geneva: World Health Organization, 2016. http://apps.who.int/iris/bitstream/handle/10665/252276/9789241511537-eng.pdf;jsessionid=AB507F304BFB10B3D1 C14B43D081AC05?sequence=1/.

———. *Global Status Report on Road Safety 2015.* Geneva: World Health Organization, 2015. http://www.who.int/violence_injury_prevention/road_safety_status/2015/en/.

———. *INSPIRE: Seven Strategies for Ending Violence Against Children.* Geneva: World Health Organization, 2016. http://apps.who.int/iris/bitstream/handle/10665/207717/9789241565356-eng.pdf;jsessionid=597E369ED7B4D6618C940507139FE704?sequence=1.

———. *Promoting Gender Equality to Prevent Violence Against Women.* Geneva: World Health Organization, 2009. http://apps.who.int/iris/bitstream/handle/10665/44098/9789241597883_eng.pdf?sequence=1&isAllowed=y.

———. *Violence Prevention Alliance Global Campaign for Violence Prevention: Plan of Action for 2012-2020.* Geneva: Violence Prevention Alliance, 2012. http://www.who.int/violence_injury_prevention/violence/global_campaign/gcvp_plan_of_action.pdf.

———. *Violence Prevention: The Evidence.* Geneva: World Health Organization, 2009. http://apps.who.int/iris/bitstream/handle/10665/77936/9789241500845_eng.pdf?sequence=1.

———. "Violence Prevention Information System (Violence Info)." Accessed July 28, 2018. http://apps.who.int/violence-info/.

———. *World Report on Violence and Health.* Geneva: World Health Organization, 2002.

World Health Organization, UN Office on Drugs and Crime, and UN Development Program. *Global Status Report on Violence Prevention 2014.* Geneva: World Health Organization, 2014. http://apps.who.int/iris/bitstream/10665/145086/1/9789241564793_eng.pdf?ua=1&ua=1.

Youth Guidance. "BAM—Becoming a Man." Accessed May 25, 2018. https://www.youth-guidance.org/bam/.

Youth Justice Board website. "Home." Accessed July 19, 2018. https://www.gov.uk/government/organisations/youth-justice-board-for-england-and-wales.

Youth Violence Commission. http://yvcommission.com/.

INDEX

Page references for figures are italicized

ABOUT THE AUTHOR

Irvin Waller is emeritus professor of criminology at the University of Ottawa. Over his long tenure, he has inspired generations to work for upstream prevention of crime. In addition to his teaching career, Waller also has traveled the world to over fifty countries over fifty years giving keynote speeches and consulting with governments, NGOs, and international agencies on using science and reason to end violent crime. Some of his many consultancies include the World Health Organization, Inter-American Development Bank, and the World Bank.

Among Waller's too-numerous-to-name international accolades are awards for his role in pioneering the United Nations' Victim Magna Carta, which has influenced the International Criminal Court and changed crime policy from Japan to Mexico. He also has received recognition from governments in Europe, North America, and Mexico for his contributions in shifting the world agenda to embrace prevention. A respected authority on victim support and rights, Waller has played key roles in establishing and leading the World Society of Victimology and the International Organization for Victim Assistance. In addition, he has been a member of numerous national and international commissions and task forces focused on safety and security around the world. Among them is South Africa's Task Force on Safety and Security during the Mandela administration. Waller also is the author of three other books including *Less Law, More Order; Rights for Victims of Crimes;* and *Smarter Crime Control.* Each of these shares in simple language the solid violence prevention science of effective solutions and best practices to support justice for victims. They are in multiple languages, including Chinese and Spanish.

A native of England with degrees from the University of Cambridge in economics and criminology, Waller now lives in Canada with his wife and partner, Susan Tanner.